PROBATION & PAROLE
Theory & Practice
2nd edition

HOWARD ABADINSKY
Saint Xavier College, Chicago

PRENTICE-HALL, INC., Englewood Cliffs, New Jersey 07632

Library of Congress Cataloging in Publication Data

Abadinsky, Howard, 1941-
    Probation and parole.

    Bibliography: p.
    Includes index.
    1. Probation—United States.   2. Parole—United
States.   I. Title.
HV9278.A2 1981   354.6′3′0973   81-10623
ISBN 0-13-715979-X   AACR2

Editorial/production supervision by *Linda Stewart*
Cover design by *Tony Ferraro Studio*
Manufacturing buyer: *Ed O'Dougherty*

Prentice-Hall Series in Criminal Justice

James D. Stinchcomb, Editor

Printed in the United States of America
10   9   8   7   6   5   4   3   2

Prentice-Hall International, Inc., *London*
Prentice-Hall of Australia Pty. Limited, *Sydney*
Prentice-Hall of Canada, Ltd., *Toronto*
Prentice-Hall of India Private Limited, *New Delhi*
Prentice-Hall of Japan, Inc., *Tokyo*
Prentice-Hall of Southeast Asia Pte. Ltd., *Singapore*
Whitehall Books Limited, *Wellington, New Zealand*

To the memory
of Leonard Berman
and Barbara Berman

Contents

PART II   PAROLE

PART III   TREATMENT AND SUPERVISION IN PROBATION AND PAROLE

PART IV   SPECIAL PROGRAMS AND RESEARCH

Preface

The first edition of this book began shortly after I received an adjunct appointment at St. John's University. I was a Senior Parole Officer for the New York State Division of Parole and this was my first formal teaching position. I attempted to locate a textbook on probation and parole and was faced with two alternatives: a well-written text by a former (deceased) Division of Parole executive, which was out-of-date, or a "reader" with articles that were often out-dated or on a graduate level. Instead, I selected a book on corrections and began to collect materials to supplement the text. The "supplement" became a manuscript and the first edition of this book.

Working on a text and designing a course at the same time turned out to be fortuitous. The "work-in-progress" was tested out in the classroom and the result was a text with a curriculum format. This "accidental" design has been retained in the second edition.

After fourteen years in parole, I accepted an academic appointment at Western Carolina University. Here, for the past three years, I have been teaching courses on probation and parole while working on a second edition. The result is this book which has been developed and refined as a teaching instrument for college educators.

I would like to acknowledge the assistance I received from the American Probation and Parole Association and the following individuals:

John R. Ackermann
(New York State Division of Probation)

Sidney I. Dwoskin
(Los Angeles County Probation Department)

James P. Foley
(Massachusetts Probation Department)

Gail D. Hughes
(Missouri Division of Probation and Parole)

Robert E. Keldgord
(Sacramento County Probation Department)

Malcolm MacDonald
(Texas Adult Probation Commission)

John J. Maceri
(New York State Division of Probation)

Randy J. Polisky
(Virginia Division of Probation and Parole)

J. P. Pratt, II
(South Carolina Probation, Parole and Pardon Board)

Raymond H. Wahl
(Utah Adult Probation and Parole)

Deborah Star
(California Department of Corrections)

Donald Atkinson
(Maryland Division of Parole and Probation)

Dr. James Boudouris
(Iowa Division of Adult Corrections)

Claude T. Mangrum
(San Bernardino County Probation Department)

Barbara Broderick
(New York State Division of Parole)

Barbara Martin Reid
(Traynor Halfway House, Columbus, Ohio)

Edith P. Fletcher
(Massachusetts Half-Way Houses, Incorporated)

Marion Goldberg
(New York State Division of Probation)

George H. Cox
(Georgia Board of Pardons and Paroles)

Martin S. Schugam
(Maryland Juvenile Services Administration)

James Hammond
(Washington State Board of Prison Terms and Paroles)

chapter 1

Probation
and Parole
in Criminal Justice

Probation and parole are linked to particular segments of the criminal justice sequence, and criminal justice is tied to the criminal law of a particular jurisdiction, state or country. Thus, the criminal law and its enforcement determines who will be subjected to probation and parole. This law differs from country to country and from one period of time to another. What is an outstanding accomplishment in a capitalist society can be a capital crime in a socialist one. What is a lawful enterprise one day (e.g., producing alcoholic beverages) is the crime of "bootlegging" on another. The criminal law reflects the need to protect the person, the property, and the norms of those who have the power to enact laws—the criminal law reflects power relations in society. Thus, the harmful activities of those with power are often not even defined as criminal (e.g., antitrust violations) but may instead constitute only a civil wrong. In 1980, thirty-seven manufacturers are accused of being part of an 18-year nationwide conspiracy to fix the prices of corrugated containers and sheets, a multibillion-dollar scheme that defrauded American consumers. Thirty-four manufacturers merely settled out of court, an option not available to most persons who become the clients of probation and parole agencies *(New York Times,* June 17, 1980: D1). When the criminal law is invoked, the results may also represent distinctions in power; for example, prosecution for burglary routinely invokes more significant penalties than those for business crime. Marshall Clinard and his associates note* (1979: xix):

*Clinard, Marshall, Peter C. Yeager, Jeanne Brissette, David Petrashek, and Elizabeth Harries 1979: *Illegal Corporate Behavior.* Washington, D.C.: U.S. Government Printing Office.

A single case of corporate law violation may involve millions and even billions of dollars of losses. The injuries caused by product defects or impure or dangerous drugs can involve thousands of persons in a single case. For example, in one case, the electrical price-fixing conspiracy of the 1960s, losses amounted to over $2 billion, a sum far greater than the total losses from the 3 million burglaries in any given year. At the same time, the average loss from a larceny-theft is $165 and from a burglary $422, and the persons who commit these offenses may receive sentences of as much as five to ten years, or even longer. For the crimes committed by the large corporations the sole punishment often consists of warnings, consent orders, or comparatively small fines.

Irwin Ross (1980) reports that since 1970, of the over 1000 major corporations in the United States, eleven percent have been involved in major delinquencies, e.g., anti-trust violations, bribery (not including crime they commit in foreign countries). Robert Lefcourt observes (1971: 22):

> The myth of "equality under law" would have us believe that everyone is subject to society's laws and those who violate laws are subject to prosecution. Yet in criminal courts across the country it can be easily observed that law enforcement affects most exclusively the working-man and the poor. . . . The other criminals, the extremely wealthy, the corporations, the landlords, and the middle-class white-collar workers are rarely prosecuted and almost never suffer the criminal court process as defendants.

WHAT IS A CRIME? WHO IS A CRIMINAL?

Quite simply, a *crime* is any violation of the criminal law, and a *criminal* is a person convicted of a crime. This raises an important question: Is a person who violates the criminal law a "criminal" if he/she is not apprehended and/or convicted? We need to consider that most reported crimes do not result in an arrest and conviction. Furthermore, studies indicate that most crimes are simply not reported to the police. Thus, has a probationer or parolee been rehabilitated, or has he/she become more successful at avoiding detection?

It is important for the study of probation and parole to consider who actually becomes identified as a criminal. A composite sketch of the "average" offender convicted of a crime would reveal that he (90 percent are male) is usually young, poor, and often from a minority group. As noted earlier, the law protects offenders from the middle and upper strata, while law enforcement discriminates against the poor. Abraham Blumberg notes that society cannot enforce every law and punish every lawbreaker (some laws are merely symbolic, e.g., adultery statutes) without causing mass paranoia, violent conflict, and savage repression (1971: 46). If not all laws are enforced and not all lawbreakers arrested, how is law enforcement decided? Jack Douglas states that the police arrest those who are most easily convicted: those least likely to be able to defend themselves adequately and who are the least likely to file a suit over such matters as false arrest or brutality—the poor (1971: 28). He concludes that such "organizational" factors reinforce the criminal law's bias against the poor.

Differential legal treatment of the poor has resulted in a profound sense of injustice and alienation. Whereas a Patty Hearst can afford F. Lee Bailey, poor defendants must settle for some form of "legal welfare." Since both the prosecutor and legal aid/public defender are paid by the state, the latter is often viewed by defendants as merely an extension of the former (Casper, 1972: 110–111):

> Put in abstract form, it might be stated as follows: any two or more persons receiving money from a common source must have common interests. In the context of defendant-public defender relations, it urges that since both the prosecutor and the public defender are employed by "the state," they *cannot* fight one another. He who pays the piper calls the tune in this world, and if the same source is paying the public defender and the prosecutor, the reasonable expectation is that they will work together.

There have been studies which indicate that the law is not enforced in the same manner in different areas of the same jurisdiction. In an urban ghetto, for example, the police may not view a crime against a minority person as particularly serious. The same crime against a white person, however, will bring a vigorous response, especially if the perpetrator was not white.

Offenders who have already been convicted of a crime become part of the official records of law enforcement agencies. This increases their susceptibility to arrest, a fact of life with which all probation and parole personnel must deal. Some offenders are given the opportunity to avoid being put through the criminal justice process. Later we will examine the use of programs that seek to "divert" offenders out of the criminal justice process and into some other method of being handled. Such programs can easily become another method for providing differential treatment whereby the middle class can avoid the stigma and severity of the criminal process, while the poor are made to face the full force and fury of criminal sanctions.

In response to the question of who is a criminal, there are some observers who see the offender as *victim:* of poverty, discrimination, and unequal and unjust laws and law enforcement. In any event, it is obvious that most persons on probation and parole come from an underclass.

RESPONDING TO CRIME

Early responses to deviant behavior ranged from the payment of fines to trial by combat, banishment, and death by torture. A primitive system of vengence, *lex talionis,* an eye for an eye, was passed down from generation to generation as each family, tribe, or society sought to preserve its own existence without recourse to a written code of laws. About 4000 years ago, Hammurabi, King of Babylonia, set down a written code of laws. Although in written form, his law continued the harsh tradition of *lex talionis* and a wide range of crimes carried the death penalty.

Later, the Hebrews adopted the concept of an eye for an eye, but under the law of the Old Testament this was interpreted to mean financial compensation for the victim of crime or negligence (there was no compensation for murder which carried the death penalty). A perpetrator who was unable to pay was placed in involuntary servitude, a precursor to the concept of probation. This servitude could not last more than six years, and masters had rehabilitative obligations and responsibilities to their servants.

The Romans derided the use of fines for criminal offenses and utilized the death penalty extensively in ways that have become etched in history. The fall of the Roman Empire resulted in there being very little "rule of law" throughout Europe. When law was gradually restored, fines and restitution became an important form of punishment as those in power sought to increase their wealth. Offenders who were unable to pay were often enslaved or subjected to mutilation or death. Trial by combat also flourished, in part because of the difficulty in proving criminal allegations. With the spread of Christianity, trial by combat was replaced with trial by ordeal, an appeal to devine power. A defendant who survived the ordeal, passing through fire, for example, was ruled innocent. Trial by ordeal was eventually replaced with trial by jury. Throughout the Middle Ages in Europe there was a continuation of the extensive use of public execution, often accompanied by torture, flaying, or the rack.

For many centuries there existed an extreme disparity in the manner in which punishment was meted out, with the rich and influential receiving little or no punishment for offenses that resulted in torture and death for the less fortunate. This was forcefully challenged in the eighteenth century with the advent of the *Classical School*.

CLASSICAL SCHOOL

The *Classical School* was a philosophy influenced by Jean Jacques Rousseau's concept of the social contract: a mythical state of affairs wherein each person agrees to a pact whose basic stipulation is that conditions of law are the same for all—all men are created equal (as in the language of the Declaration of Independence). "The social contract establishes among the citizens an equality of such character that each binds himself on the same terms as all the others, and is *thus* entitled to enjoy the same rights as all the others" (Rousseau, 1954: 45). Thus, Rousseau asserts: "One consents to die—if and when one becomes a murderer oneself—in order not to become a murderer's victim" (p. 48). In order to be safe from crime, we have all consented to punishment if we resort to crime. Punishment, however, is to be meted out without regard to station—all are equal and all shall suffer equally for equal offenses. The philosophy of Rousseau and the Classical School was revolutionary and, indeed, served to influence both the American and French Revolution—at a time of severe disparity in punishment, Rousseau demanded equality.

Throughout Europe of the eighteenth century there was a revolt against abuses in criminal justice, which often included being "examined" in secret with torture freely applied to gain "confessions." This revolt was given prominence by Cesare Bonesana, Marchese de Beccaria (1738–1794), usually referred to as Cesare Beccaria, whose *Essay on Crimes and Punishment** was published in 1764. Building on

---

*Republished by Bobbs-Merrill in 1963 with a translation by Henry Paolucci.

the work of Rousseau, Beccaria called for laws that were precise and matched to punishment intended to be applied equally to all classes of men. Thus, he argued, the law should stipulate a particular penalty for a specific crime and judges should mete out identical sentences for each occurrence of the same offense.

As a result of Beccaria's work there were great changes in the legal systems of Europe. The French Code of 1791, for example, left only the question of guilt to the judgment of the court. Punishment was in accord with the severity of the offense. The influence of the Classical School was spread by others: William Blackstone (1723–80), Jeremy Bentham (1748–1832), and Samuel Romilly (1757–1818). As a result of their work the English criminal law was coded by 1800.

Basic to Classical thought is the concept of "free will." Human beings are endowed with the ability to choose between right and wrong. However, they are also hedonistic—seeking pleasure and avoiding pain. Punishment, therefore, must be designed to deter antisocial, albeit pleasurable acts. Punishment is to be devoid of vengeance and instead utilitarian: limited to that which is necessary to deter a person (with free will) from criminal behavior. Since every person is rational, endowed with free will, punishment is not to be varied to suit the person or the circumstances of the offender. Ian Taylor and his colleagues sum up Classical thought as a theory of social control: "It delimits first, the manner in which the state should react to criminals, second, those deviations which permit individuals to be labeled as criminals, and third, the social basis of criminal law" (1973: 2–3). They note that Classical theory found important support among the rising middle class, whose interests it best protected. They point out, however, that Classical theory is unrealistic insofar as it can be operational only in a society where property and wealth are equally distributed—where everyone has an *equal* stake in the system (p. 6). For free will to be operable, each person in society must be equal with respect to choosing crime or doing otherwise. Of course, in the eighteenth century, as now, the ability to do "otherwise" was closely linked to one's social and economic situation.

An obvious shortcoming of Classical theory soon became apparent. It was unrealistic to ignore any and all mitigating circumstances. Even Beccaria believed that certain persons—the insane and incompetent—should be treated in a special manner. In attempting to apply the law without any consideration of circumstances, the court was faced with meting out identical punishment to first offenders and repeaters, to children and adults. Taylor and colleagues note: "It was impossible in practice to ignore the determinants of human action and to proceed as if punishment and incarceration could be easily measured on some kind of universal calculus" (1973: 7). It was against this background that what has been referred to as the Neo-Classical School arose.

NEOCLASSICAL SCHOOL

Vernon Fox notes that the *Neoclassical School* was characterized by (1976: 37):

1. Modification of the doctrine of free will, which could be affected by pathology, incompetence, or other conditions, as well as premeditation.

2. Acceptance of the validity of mitigating circumstances.
3. Modification of the doctrine of responsibility to provide mitigation of punishments with partial responsibility in such cases as insanity, age, and other conditions that would affect "knowledge and intent of man at the time of the crime."
4. Admission into court procedures of expert testimony on the question of degree of responsibility.

Taylor and his colleagues (1973: 9–10) state that the Neoclassical model is, with some modifications, the prevailing model for criminal justice in the western world.

POSITIVE SCHOOL

August Comte, (1798–1857), the "father" of positivism, advocated a "science of society." He argued that the methods and the logical form of the natural sciences are applicable to the social sciences (Giddens, 1976: 59). Within criminology (the scientific study of crime), positivism was given impetus by Cesare Lombroso (1835–1909), a Venetian physician, who published L'uomo delinquente (The Criminal Man) in 1876. The criminal, he proposed, was a "primitive," a throwback to earlier developmental stages through which non-criminal man had already passed. (The influence of Darwinism is obvious). Lombroso's research centered on physiological characteristics believed indicative of criminality, although his later work noted the importance of environmental factors in causing crime.* Lombroso's contribution to the study of crime is that it is to be carried out according to the principles of science (as opposed to those of law and philosophy).

Basic to the positive approach is a denial of the concept of "free will" (a philosophically-based legal concept—not scientific). Crime is not simply behavior that is freely chosen by rational men, but it is the behavior of persons having certain characteristics: biological, psychological, social. In place of "free will," positivists substituted a chain of inter-related causes and a deterministic basis for criminal acts: the criminal could not do "otherwise." Since criminal behavior is the result of conditions (e.g., psychological, sociological) over which the offender has no control, s/he is not culpable, and thus punishment is inappropriate. However, since s/he does represent a threat to society, s/he must be "treated," "corrected," "rehabilitated." In practice, the change of emphasis from punishment to "correction" did not result in a less severe response to criminal offenders. Some critics contend that rehabilitation has opened the door to a host of questionable schemes for dealing with offenders under the guise of "treatment" and "for their own good." The American Friends Service Committee notes: "Retribution and revenge necessarily imply punishment, but it does not necessarily follow that punishment is eliminated under rehabilitative regimes" (1971: 20).

The views of the Classical, Neoclassical, and Positive Schools are important because they transcend their own time and continue to be applicable to contemporary

*See Cesare Lombroso, Crime, Its Causes and Remedies. Montclair, N.J.: Patterson Smith, 1968. Originally published in 1911.

issues in criminal justice. The question remains: Do we judge the crime or the criminal? This is a central question in the continuing debate over sentencing—determinate versus indeterminate—that is discussed in Chapter 9. Probation and parole, it is often argued, emanate from a positivistic response to criminal behavior, a view that will be disputed later in this book.

This book is concerned with probation and parole as part of the criminal justice process. Let us locate these two services within criminal justice.

PROBATION AND PAROLE
IN CRIMINAL JUSTICE

What follows is a synoptic look at the criminal justice sequence highlighting probation and parole services:

1. The process is triggered by the commission of a crime—if the crime comes to the attention of the police. As noted earlier, most crimes do not.
2. The process will continue if an "alleged perpetrator" is arrested. As noted earlier, most crimes that are reported to the police do not result in an arrest.

Probation and Parole in the Criminal Justice System
(A General Schematic)

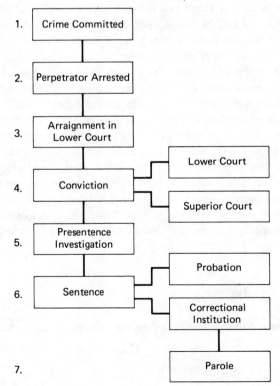

3. The alleged perpetrator is brought before a judicial officer (he/she may receive a summons instead in certain cases), charges are read, counsel arranged, and bail set. The arrestee is now a defendant.

4. If a judicial officer determines that there is evidence adequate for a *prima facie* case, it will be docketed for action in lower court in the case of a misdemeanor; felonies are heard in superior court. In the event of a conviction, more often a plea of guilty (as a result of "plea bargaining"), the probation officer usually becomes involved for the first time.

5. Following conviction, the probation officer prepares a presentence report which offers the judge a basis for informed sentencing (à la Positive theory or perhaps, Neoclassical).

6. If the sentencing judge imposes probation, the probation agency will provide for the supervision of the offender, now officially a criminal, in the community. If the offender is sentenced to imprisonment, he/she will be removed to a correctional institution. At some time, the criminal, now an inmate, will become eligible for parole release.

7. If the inmate is paroled, he/she will be supervised in the community by a parole officer.* In some states inmates released by a method other than parole will also be supervised by a parole officer.

It is important to understand the interdependence of various segments of criminal justice. This can be done by a brief look at the allocation of criminal justice resources. A disproportionate share of the criminal justice budget goes to that agency having the most public visibility, the police. Other parts of the process are starved for funds. Underfunding causes the court and prosecutor's office to concentrate on the number of dispositions in order to prevent a backlog of cases from becoming completely unmanageable. This, in turn, results in "bargain justice" that is often neither a bargain nor just. When a probation agency is understaffed, judges tend to send "marginal" cases to prison instead of using probation. Since prisons are underfunded and overcrowded, there is pressure on the parole board to accelerate the release of inmates, and the "revolving door" of criminal justice continues to spin.

While criminal justice agencies, from the police to parole, are interdependent, they do not, in toto, comprise a *system:* arranged so that they are connected to form a unity. A more accurate description would be a network or a "loosely coupled system" (Hagan, Hewitt & Alwin, 1979). Criminal justice is comprised of a series of subsystems, and instead of a "system" criminal justice in this book will be referred to as a "process."

ITEMS FOR STUDY

1. The definition of crime will be a determining factor in deciding who is subjected to probation and parole.

*The actual title may vary from state to state.

2. The enforcement of the criminal law will be a determining factor in deciding who is subjected to probation and parole.
3. The Classical response to crime requires a level of relative equality that is unrealistic.
4. The Positive response to crime, a denial of free will, can mean that criminals are not personally responsible for their acts.
5. Agencies of criminal justice are so interdependent that a misallocation of criminal justice resources results in dislocation, if not chaos.

PART I

Probation

chapter 2

The Court System

A *probation agency* provides three basic services to the courts:

1. Juvenile services
2. Presentence investigation
3. Supervision of offenders

The administration of these services may be under the auspices of the judiciary, or they may be administered by a separate agency. Before looking at these services and their administration, it is necessary to look first at the court systems, federal and state.

THE FEDERAL COURT SYSTEM*

At the entry level for criminal cases in the federal systems are *U.S. Magistrates,* appointed by district court judges for eight-year terms. The Magistrate (often called Commissioner) conducts preliminary proceedings and nonfelony trials held without a jury. The Magistrate is authorized to issue warrants and may assist district court judges to review habeas corpus petitions from prisoners.

*The information in this section is taken from Melvin Lewis, Warren Bundy, and James L. Hague, *An Introduction to the Courts and Judicial Process* (Englewood Cliffs, N.J.: Prentice-Hall, 1978), Chaps. 3, 4.

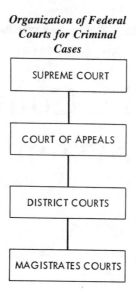

**Organization of Federal
Courts for Criminal
Cases**

```
┌─────────────────────────┐
│     SUPREME COURT       │
└─────────────────────────┘
             │
┌─────────────────────────┐
│    COURT OF APPEALS     │
└─────────────────────────┘
             │
┌─────────────────────────┐
│     DISTRICT COURTS     │
└─────────────────────────┘
             │
┌─────────────────────────┐
│   MAGISTRATES COURTS    │
└─────────────────────────┘
```

District Courts have general jurisdiction over cases involving the violation of federal laws. They actually have exclusive jurisdiction in only a relatively few types of criminal cases; most of their jurisdiction is shared with the state courts. For example, bank robbery is both a federal and a state crime. There are 94 district courts with 400 judges appointed by the President for life terms. No district cuts across a state line and no state has less than one district. The largest district is the Southern District of New York, with 27 judges operating from Foley Square in the Borough of Manhattan in New York City. The District Court holds trials and hears appeals from a Magistrate's Court.

The *U.S. Court of Appeals* (sometimes referred to as circuit courts) has 11 courts and 97 judges appointed by the President for life terms. The number of judges in each circuit varies from 3 to 15. Each of the 11 courts serves a circuit and each of the 50 states, the District of Columbia, and the territories is assigned to a particular circuit. Each circuit, except the District of Columbia, encompasses at least three states. The Court of Appeals sits in panels of at least three judges and hears cases appealed from the District Courts. This court has only appellate jurisdiction and does not act as a trial court.

(There are also specialized courts in the federal system, e.g., the Court of Claims, but only the Court of Military Appeals handles criminal matters).

The *U.S. Supreme Court,* the only court established by the Constitution, consists of nine judges appointed by the President for life terms. The great importance of this court is based on its power of ''judicial review'': authority to rule on the constitutionality of laws and acts of the other branches of government. The decisions of the Supreme Court have had a dramatic impact on criminal justice. The important decisions on probation and parole are discussed in subsequent chapters.

THE STATE COURT SYSTEMS

State court systems are organized on three basic levels of jurisdiction: limited, general, and appellate. Courts at each of these levels may be further classified by the type of cases that they are authorized to hear—criminal, civil, or a combination of both.

At the first level are courts of *limited jurisdiction*. These courts represent almost 80 percent of the total number of courts in the United States and are where the vast majority of legal actions, predominantly misdemeanor and traffic cases, begin and usually end. These courts have trial jurisdiction over nonfelony cases and may act on preliminary proceedings in felony cases. It is at this level of the judiciary that a great deal of criticism has been leveled, with some observers referring to it as "rough justice." At this level is the greatest amount of variation in patterns of organization within the court system in general. Two states have no courts of limited jurisdiction, a few have single statewide systems of limited courts, and the majority have several different types of limited courts covering the same geographic area. Thus, residents of a particular area may have to go to different courts to pay a traffic fine, be tried for a misdemeanor, or for juvenile proceedings.

*Organization of State
Courts for Criminal
Cases**

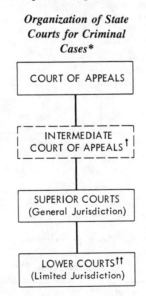

*Whereas there is only one federal system, each state has its own court structure. This diagram, although approximating all, does not necessarily reflect any single state court system.
†Some states have an intermediate court of appeals between the superior court and the court of last resort.
‡These would include county courts, magistrates courts, traffic courts, justices of the peace, and juvenile courts.

State Court System with Three Levels:
Idaho Court System, 1975

SUPREME COURT

5 Justices

Jurisdiction:
- Appeals from administrative agencies.
- Original jurisdiction in claims against state (advisory opinions).
- Appeals from interim orders and final judgments in District Court.

DISTRICT COURT (7)

24 Judges

Jurisdiction:
- Original jurisdiction in civil. Domestic relations.
- Original jurisdiction in criminal. Felonies, post-conviction review.
- Appeals from lower courts and state agencies and boards.

Appeals de novo.
Jury trials.

MAGISTRATES DIVISION OF DISTRICT COURT (7)

64 Judges

Jurisdiction:
- Civil actions over $5,000. Property rights, probate, small claims under $300.
- Misdemeanors, felony preliminaries.
- Juvenile.

Jury trials except in small claims.

↑ Indicates route of appeal.

At the next level are courts of *general jurisdiction,* also called superior or major trial courts. Most states are divided into judicial districts for the organization of general jurisdiction courts, with each circuit or district consisting of one or more counties. Other states have general jurisdiction courts organized along county lines, and some states have more than one type of general jurisdiction court—either two circuit-type systems or a mixture of circuit with a county-based system.

Courts of general jurisdiction are unlimited in the civil and/or criminal cases they

State Court System with Four Levels: North Carolina Court System, 1975

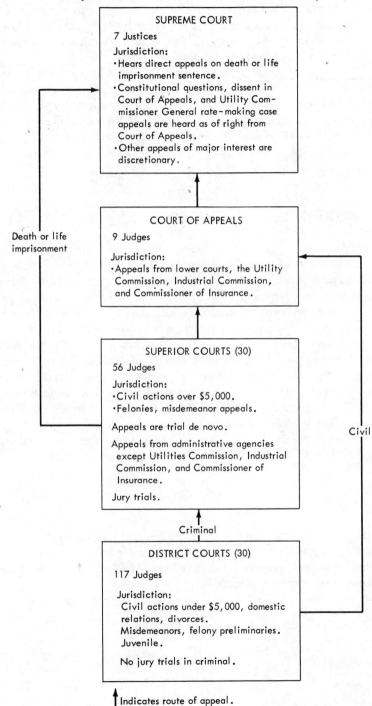

SUPREME COURT

7 Justices

Jurisdiction:
- Hears direct appeals on death or life imprisonment sentence.
- Constitutional questions, dissent in Court of Appeals, and Utility Commissioner General rate-making case appeals are heard as of right from Court of Appeals.
- Other appeals of major interest are discretionary.

Death or life imprisonment

COURT OF APPEALS

9 Judges

Jurisdiction:
- Appeals from lower courts, the Utility Commission, Industrial Commission, and Commissioner of Insurance.

SUPERIOR COURTS (30)

56 Judges

Jurisdiction:
- Civil actions over $5,000.
- Felonies, misdemeanor appeals.

Appeals are trial de novo.

Appeals from administrative agencies except Utilities Commission, Industrial Commission, and Commissioner of Insurance.

Jury trials.

Criminal

Civil

DISTRICT COURTS (30)

117 Judges

Jurisdiction:
Civil actions under $5,000, domestic relations, divorces.
Misdemeanors, felony preliminaries.
Juvenile.

No jury trials in criminal.

↑ Indicates route of appeal.

17

are authorized to hear. A majority of serious criminal cases are tried in these courts. In most states there is some overlapping of jurisdiction between courts at the general and limited levels, and often among courts at the same level. In addition to hearing original actions, three-fourths of the courts of general jurisdiction hear cases on appeal from the courts of limited jurisdiction.

Courts of *appellate jurisdiction* are at the top of the judicial organizational structure. They are further grouped into courts of last resort and intermediate appeals courts (in the 23 states where they have been established). Intermediate courts hear appeals from courts of original jurisdiction. Courts of last resort have jurisdiction over final appeals from either courts of original jurisdiction or intermediate appellate courts. They may also have other responsibilities: for example, administrative authority over some or all of the courts in the state.

JUVENILE COURTS

The juvenile court system differs from state to state and even within states. Jurisdiction over juveniles may be located in the court of general jurisdiction, in a separate juvenile court, or in various types of limited jurisdiction courts. It is possible that within one state juvenile jurisdiction may be located in two or more different types of courts. In five states the court of general jurisdiction handles juvenile matters except for a few counties where a separate juvenile court has been established or juvenile jurisdiction has been vested in a court of limited jurisdiction. In 15 states and the District of Columbia juvenile jurisdiction is exercised exclusively by the court of general jurisdiction. Where the court of general jurisdiction acts as the juvenile court, a separate division often handles juvenile proceedings. Eight states have established a statewide system of juvenile or family courts with exclusive jurisdiction over juvenile cases. In six states juvenile jurisdiction is exercised by a single court of limited jurisdiction, and in the remaining states, jurisdiction is shared among courts of general and limited jurisdiction, and separate juvenile courts.

ITEMS FOR STUDY

1. The federal court system is unitary, with four levels of jurisdiction. Most significant in criminal cases is the power to declare statutes or actions unconstitutional.
2. State court systems are organized on three basic levels of jurisdiction, although variations among them are plentiful.
3. Juvenile court systems vary from state to state and even within a state.

chapter 3

History
and Administration
of Probation

Although probation services have their origins in recent history, probation has historical antecedents that reach back into the twelfth century.

HISTORICAL ANTECEDENTS

In the twelfth century, *pardons* became an aspect of the king's authority to determine the punishment to be imposed for various offenses. The pardon included the power to commute or remit the prescribed penalty in individual cases and was often used to induce criminals to inform on their confederates or to join the military (Hurnard, 1969: vii, 1, 327).

Benefit of clergy dates back to the thirteenth century and originally exempted ecclesiastics from criminal liability under secular law (Hall, 1952: 110). Instead, clerical defendants were permitted to be tried in "court Christian," where they usually received lenient treatment (Hurnard, 1969: 375–78). There was a gradual extension of the benefit of clergy to increasing numbers of lay persons (Hall, 1952: 112), and until 1487 anyone who knew how to read might even commit murder without suffering serious punishment. Until 1547, such persons were merely subjected to having an M branded on their left thumb (Hall, 1952: 110n). In 1706, the literacy test was eliminated and benefit of clergy was extended to all persons, thus losing any real meaning. It was generally replaced by transportation, first to the American colonies and later to Australia (Hall, 1952: 117–18). In 1827, benefit of clergy was officially abolished in England, where it had been serving only to mitigate the death penalty for certain offenses (Hall, 1952: 139). The American colonies generally recognized the doctrine of benefit of clergy as a device for saving a defendant from capital punishment. It was later abolished (Friedman, 1973: 61–62) and after the Revolution was no longer part of American criminal justice.

Judicial reprieve was used in the English courts to serve as a temporary suspension of sentence to allow the defendant to appeal to the crown for a pardon. Although it was originally meant to be only a temporary postponement, it eventually developed into a judicial reprieve whereby sentences were often never actually imposed.

JOHN AUGUSTUS (1784–1859)

This pioneer of modern probation was born in Woburn, Massachusetts and became a successful shoemaker in Boston. In 1852, *A Report of The Labors of John Augustus* was published at the request of his friends, and in it Augustus wrote: "I was in court one morning . . . in which the man was charged with being a common drunkard. He told me that if he could be saved from the House of Correction, he never again would taste intoxicating liquors: I bailed him, by permission of the Court" (Augustus, 1972: 4–5). Thus began the work of the nation's first probation officer, a volunteer who worked without pay.

Augustus would appear in court and offer to bail a defendant. If the judge agreed, and they usually did, the defendant would become Augustus's charge. Augustus would assist the person in finding work or a residence; Augustus's own house was literally filled with people he had bailed. When the defendant returned to court, Augustus would report on his progress toward rehabilitation and recommend a disposition in the case. These recommendations were usually accepted.

His first experience with a drunkard led to an interest in helping others charged with the same offense. During the first year of his efforts he assisted 10 drunkards who, because of his work, received small fines instead of imprisonment. He later helped other types of offenders, young and old, men and women, and was able to report only 10 absconders out of 2000 cases.

The work of John Augustus received support from judges and newspapers, which reported on his efforts. However, prosecutors viewed him as an interloper who kept court calendars crowded by preventing cases from being disposed of quickly. Policemen and court clerks opposed his work because they received money for each case disposed of by a commitment to the House of Correction. Because of his voluntary work, Augustus neglected his business and eventually experienced financial ruin. He required the help of friends for his support.

His work was apparently very effective and the people he helped were able to remain free of alcohol and gainfully employed. Augustus thoroughly investigated each person he considered helping, taking account of "the previous character of the person, his age and the influences by which in the future he would likely be surrounded . . ." (1972: 34). Augustus kept a careful record of every case in which he intervened and was able to provide statistics on the persons he had helped.

ORIGINS OF MODERN PROBATION

The origins of modern probation in the United States following Augustus date back to the middle of the nineteenth century and the establishment of prisoners aid societies and childrens aid societies. The work of these groups had an important effect on the courts because many employed paid agents. These agents worked in the criminal courts primarily to rescue children, for whom there were no special courts. Although their work, like that of John Augustus, was unofficial, it was similar to probation in practice and results. The agents investigated and placed children in homes or with child-care institutions. Later, under the authority of new laws, they conducted investigations for the court and acted as guardians of neglected children and young offenders (Glueck, 1933: 226–27).

In 1869, Massachusetts provided for a visiting agent of the Board of Charities to investigate and be present when a child was being tried in court. The agent was also responsible for child placement. In 1873, a Michigan law authorized a county agent to investigate, place out, and visit delinquent children. For adult offenders, at that time anyone over 16, the suspended sentence, an extension of English common law, was used in many states. Some states authorized the fixing of conditions to the suspended sentence, and these were the forerunners of probation regulations (Glueck, 1933: 226–27).

Probation Begins in Massachusetts

In 1878, Massachusetts passed a law that authorized the Mayor of Boston to hire a probation officer who would be supervised by the superintendent of police. The Massachusetts courts had been using "bailing on probation," as noted in the work of John Augustus. A case would be adjourned before the imposition of sentence and the defendant would be released on bail. The person acting in the capacity of a probation officer would guarantee the return of the defendant to court at the end of the adjournment period. This became the period of supervision and the court had the power to extend it, discharge defendants, fine or imprison them. In most other states probation developed out of the suspended sentence and did not involve the fixing of bail.

Maryland, in 1894, authorized its courts to suspend sentence generally or for a specific time, and they could "make such orders to enforce such terms as to costs, recognizance for appearance, or matters relating to the residence or conduct of the convicts as may be deemed proper." The Baltimore courts also began using agents of the Prisoner's Aid Society and later appointed salaried probation officers. Missouri, in 1897, enacted a "bench parole law," which authorized the courts to suspend sentence under certain conditions. The courts also appointed officers, misnamed "parole officers," to carry out this probation work (Glueck, 1933: 227–28).

The 1878 Massachusetts law, the first of its kind, authorized a probation officer to investigate cases and recommend probation when appropriate (Glueck, 1933: 227–28). The second state to adopt a probation law was Vermont, 20 years later. The 20-year lapse between probation laws in Massachusetts and Vermont is probably the result of the poor communications of that period. In 1898, Vermont authorized the appointment of a probation officer by the courts in each county, each probation officer serving all the courts in a particular county. Another New England state, Rhode Island, soon followed with a probation law that was novel. It placed restrictions on who could be granted probation. These included persons convicted of treason, murder, robbery, arson, rape, and burglary. This violated one of the basic principles of modern corrections: judge the offender, not just the offense. The restrictive aspects of Rhode Island's probation law were copied by many other states. The Rhode Island probation law, which applied to children and adults, also introduced the concept of a state-administered probation system. The State Board of Charities and Correction appointed a state probation officer and deputies, "at least one of whom should be a woman" (Glueck, 1933: 229–31).

THE TURN OF THE CENTURY

The spread of probation was accelerated by the juvenile court movement (Task Force on Corrections, 1966: 27), which started in the Midwest and developed quite rapidly. In 1899, Minnesota enacted a law that authorized the appointment of county probation officers, but the granting of probation was limited to those under 18. Four years later this was changed to 21. In April 1899, Illinois enacted the historical Juvenile Court Act, which authorized the world's first juvenile court (Glueck, 1933: 231). The law also provided for the hiring of probation officers to investigate cases referred by the courts, but it made no provision for the probation officers to be paid.

However, charitable organizations and private philanthropists provided the funds to pay the probation officers. At the end of the first year Chicago had six probation officers who were supported by the Juvenile Court Committee of the Chicago Women's Club. In addition, in each police district a police officer spent part of his time out of uniform performing the duties of a probation officer. On July 1, 1899, Illinois' first juvenile court judge addressed the captains of Chicago's police districts: "You are so situated that you, even more than the justices, can get at the underlying facts in each particular case brought before you by the officers of your command. I shall want you to select some good reliable officers from each district for the work of investigating juvenile cases" (Schultz, 1973: 465).

In 1899, Colorado enacted a compulsory education law which enabled the development of a juvenile court using truant officers as probation officers (Glueck, 1933: 232). By 1925, probation was available for juveniles in every state. Availability of probation for adults followed, becoming fact in every state by 1956 (Task Force on Corrections, 1966: 27).

The first directory of probation officers in the United States, published in 1907, identified 795 probation officers working mainly in the juvenile courts. Like the first probation officer in Illinois, Mrs. Alzina Stevens (Schultz, 1973: 465), many were volunteers, and some who were paid worked only part time. By 1937, there were more than 3800 persons described as probation officers (Killinger and Cromwell, 1974: 171), and by 1965 there were 6336 probation officers for juveniles and 2940 probation officers supervising adult felons (Task Force on Corrections, 1966: 30).

ADMINISTRATION OF PROBATION

"Probation in the United States is administered by hundreds of independent agencies operating under a different law in each State and under widely varying philosophies, often within the same State"* (Task Force on Corrections, 1966: 28). Of the 1929 agencies offering adult probation services, 56 percent were on a state level and the rest were at the county or municipal level; of the 2126 agencies providing juvenile probation services, 57 percent were local and the rest were state agencies (U.S. Bureau of the Census, 1978: 2). Adult probation is the exclusive responsibility of state-level agencies in 26 states, whereas in 22 states, the state and local governments share responsibility for the administration of this function. In California, New Jersey, and the District of Columbia, adult probation is a local responsibility (U.S. Bureau of the Census, 1978: 103).

In 22 of the 26 states where adult probation is a state function, it is administered by the executive branch of government. In Colorado, Iowa, and South Dakota it is administered by both the state executive and judicial branches. In Hawaii the adult probation system is administered by the state judiciary (U.S. Bureau of the Census, 1978: 103).

Of the 22 states where adult probation is the responsibility of both state and local governments, the state system is administered by the executive branch in 19 states; in 18 of these 19 states the local system is part of the judicial branch; and in New York, the nineteenth state, both state and local systems are part of the executive branch. In the remaining three states, both the state and local adult probation systems are administered by the judiciary (U.S. Bureau of the Census, 1978: 103).

The administration of juvenile probation services is no less complicated (U.S. Bureau of the Census, 1978: 103–104). Take heart, the administration of parole services to be discussed later is relatively simple—one agency per state.

For purposes of clarity, probation systems can be separated into six categories:

1. *Juvenile*. Separate probation services for juveniles are administered on a county or local level, or on a statewide basis. In either case, the administration of juvenile

*Texas, for example, has 107 independent, autonomous, local district probation agencies handling adult cases.

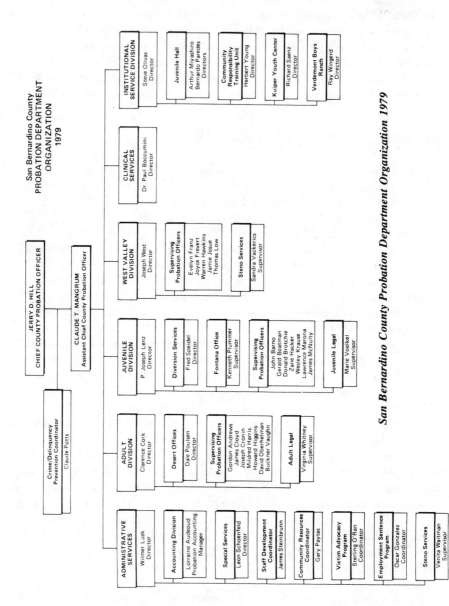

San Bernardino County
PROBATION DEPARTMENT
ORGANIZATION
1979

JERRY D. HILL
CHIEF COUNTY PROBATION OFFICER

CLAUDE T. MANGRUM
Assistant Chief County Probation Officer

Crime/Delinquency
Prevention Coordinator
Claude Potts

ADMINISTRATIVE SERVICES
Wilmer Lusk
Director

Accounting Division
Lorraine Audeoud
Probation Accounting
Manager

Special Services
Leon Schoenfeld
Director

Staff Development
Coordinator
James Steinbrunn

Community Resources
Coordinator
Gary Paytas

Victim Advocacy
Program
Sterling O'Ran
Coordinator

Employment Sentence
Program
Oscar Gonzalez
Coordinator

Steno Services
Venita Waitman
Supervisor

ADULT DIVISION
Clarence Cork
Director

Desert Offices
Dale Poulsen
Director

Supervising
Probation Officers
Gordon Andrews
James Cloyd
Joseph Cronin
Mildred Harris
Howard Higgins
David Oberhelman
Buckner Vaughn

Adult Legal
Virginia Whitney
Supervisor

JUVENILE DIVISION
P. Joseph Lenz
Director

Diversion Services
Fred Speidel
Director

Fontana Office
Kenneth Plummer
Supervisor

Supervising
Probation Officers
John Barno
Gerald Boatman
Donald Brotchie
Zane Hacker
Wesley Krause
Lawrence Marona
James McNulty

Juvenile Legal
Marie Voeikel
Supervisor

WEST VALLEY DIVISION
Joseph West
Director

Supervising
Probation Officers
Evelyn Franz
Joyce Frevert
Warren Hawkins
Jamie Josue
Thomas Low

Steno Services
Sandra Vackeres
Supervisor

CLINICAL SERVICES
Dr. Paul Boccumini
Director

INSTITUTIONAL SERVICE DIVISION
Steve Olivas
Director

Juvenile Hall
Arthur Miyashiro
Bernardo Paredes
Directors

Community
Responsibility
Training Unit
Herbert Young
Director

Kuiper Youth Center
Richard Saenz
Director

Verdemont Boys
Ranch
Ray Wingerd
Director

San Bernardino County Probation Department Organization 1979

24

probation is effectively separated from probation services that are provided for adults.

2. *Municipal*. Independent probation units are administered by the lower courts under state laws and guidelines.
3. *County*. Under laws and guidelines established by the state, a county operates its own probation agency; this system is similar to the municipal.
4. *State*. One agency administers a central probation system, which provides services throughout the state.
5. *State combined*. Probation and parole are administered on a statewide basis by one agency.
6. *Federal*. Probation is administered as an arm of the courts.

There are two major issues with respect to the administration of probation:

1. Should probation be part of the judicial or executive branch of government?
2. Should probation be administered by the state or by local government?

Kim Nelson and colleagues summarize the issues (1978: 91–92):

Those who support placement of probation in the judicial branch contend that:

1. Probation would be more responsive to the courts.
2. Relationship of probation staff to the courts creates an automatic feedback mechanism on the effectiveness of dispositions.
3. Courts will have greater awareness of resources needed.
4. Courts might allow their own staff more discretion than they would allow to members of an outside agency.
5. If probation were incorporated into a department of corrections, it might be assigned a lower priority than it would have as part of the court.

On the other hand, placement of probation in the judiciary has certain disadvantages:

1. Judges are not equipped to administer probation.
2. Services to probationers may receive lower priority than services to the courts.
3. Probation staff may be assigned duties unrelated to probation.
4. Courts are adjudicatory and regulative rather than service-oriented bodies.

Placement in the executive branch has these features to recommend it:

1. Allied human service agencies are located within the executive branch.
2. All other corrections subsystems are located in the executive branch.
3. More coordinated and effective program budgeting as well as increased ability to negotiate fully in the resource allocation process becomes possible.
4. A coordinated continuum of services to offenders and better utilization of probation manpower are facilitated.

When compared, these arguments tend to support placing probation in the executive branch. The potential for increased coordination in planning, better utilization of manpower and improved services to offenders cannot be dismissed.

A state-administered probation system has decided advantages over local administration. A total system planning approach to probation as a subsystem of corrections is needed. Such planning requires state leadership. Furthermore, implementation of planning strategies requires uniformity of standards, reporting, and evaluation as well as resource allocation.

ITEMS FOR STUDY

1. Modern probation can be traced to the activities of John Augustus and prisoners' and children's aid societies.
2. The use of probation was given impetus by the juvenile court movement.
3. Probation systems can be separated into six categories.
4. The major issues with respect to probation administration are: Should it be under the judicial or executive branch? Should it be under state or local government?

chapter 4

Juvenile Services

Before looking at the services provided by the juvenile court, it is important to understand the history and the philosophy of this court.

JUVENILE COURT

Following the Illinois Juvenile Court Act of 1899, there was a rapid proliferation of separate courts for juveniles (Schultz, 1973: 457), the result of efforts of the "child-saving movement" headed by feminist reformers of the late nineteenth century. The juvenile court was designed to remove children from the criminal process by creating programs for delinquent, dependent, and neglected young persons. The legal basis for such activity was *parens patriae,* whereby the state could intervene on behalf of persons in need of care, such as the mentally ill, the retarded, and children. Within this concept a child is not accused of a crime but, instead, is to be given guidance and assistance. Young persons charged with offenses, dependent and neglected children, and "status offenders" (e.g., truants) came under the broad jurisdiction of the juvenile court.

A book on the juvenile court originally published in 1927 presents an important insight into the prevailing concepts upon which the juvenile court was founded (Lou, 1972: 2):

> These principles upon which the juvenile court acts are radically different from those of the criminal courts. In place of judicial tribunals, restrained by antiquated procedure, saturated

in an atmosphere of hostility, trying cases for determining guilt and inflicting punishment according to inflexible rules of law, we have now juvenile courts, in which the relations of the child to his parents or other adults and to the state or society are defined and are adjusted summarily according to the scientific findings about the child and his environments. In place of magistrates, limited by the outgrown custom and compelled to walk in the paths fixed by the law of the realm, we have now socially-minded judges, who hear and adjust cases according not to rigid rules of law but to what the interests of society and the interests of the child or good conscience demand. In the place of juries, prosecutors, and lawyers, trained in the old conception of law and staging dramatically, but often amusingly, legal battles, as the necessary paraphernalia of a criminal court, we have now probation officers, physicians, psychologists, and psychiatrists, who search for the social, physiological, psychological, and mental backgrounds of the child in order to arrive at reasonable and just solutions of individual cases.

(We have in the foregoing statement a clear use of the philosophy of the Positive School—critics might say, the Positive School run amok.)

The differences between the philosophy of the juvenile court and adult criminal courts is reflected in the terminology used:

Adult criminal court	Juvenile court
Defendant	Respondent
Charges/indictment	Petition
Arraignment	Hearing
Prosecution/trial	Adjudication
Verdict	Finding
Sentence	Disposition

The terminology reflects, as does the underlying philosophy, a nonpunitive approach to dealing with troubled and troublesome youngsters. We often hear critics decry the lack of sufficient punishment inflicted in the juvenile court. Such comments indicate a complete misunderstanding of this court, which *should not* punish. To include punishment as a basis for the juvenile court is to undermine its reason for existence.

However, because of the noncriminal approach, the usual safeguards of due process that were applicable in criminal courts were absent in juvenile court proceedings. The right to counsel, to confront and cross-examine adverse witnesses, and to avoid self-incrimination were some of the basic rights denied to juveniles. Because the focus of the juvenile court was to provide "treatment," procedures were often vague, and the judge, with the assistance of the probation officer, was given broad powers over young persons. Anthony Platt concludes (1974: 4):

Granted the benign motives of the child savers, the programs they enthusiastically supported diminished the civil liberties and privacy of youth. Adolescents were treated as though they were naturally dependent, requiring constant and pervasive supervision. Although the child savers were rhetorically concerned with protecting children from the physical and moral dangers of an increasingly industrialized and urban society, their remedies seemed to aggravate the problem.

The increasing concern over the operation of the juvenile court was reflected in the *Gault* decision (to be discussed in more detail later). In 1967, the U.S. Supreme Court decided the case of Gerald Gault, a 15-year-old who had been committed to a state training school by an Arizona juvenile court judge. The court ruled that Gault had been denied due process and ordered procedural safeguards that guaranteed a minimum of due process in all juvenile courts.

STATUS OFFENDERS

In addition to having jurisdiction over children who have been arrested and charged with committing an offense, juvenile courts often have authority over *status offenders*. These are children who have not committed any offense for which an adult could be prosecuted. They are sometimes referred to as *persons in need of supervision* (PINS) or *children in need of supervision* (CHINS), and they may be habitual truants or "incorrigibles" who are "out of control of parental or lawful authority." Platt argues: "The child savers went beyond mere humanitarian reforms of existing institutions. They brought attention to—and, in doing so, invented—new categories of youthful behavior which had been hitherto unappreciated" (1974: 3–4). Juvenile court jurisdiction over status offenders is an issue of some controversy (see, e.g., Abadinsky, 1976, and Thomas, 1976). The National Council on Crime and Delinquency and the American Society of Criminology have called for the removal of status offenders from the jurisdiction of the juvenile court.

Those who support continued jurisdiction argue that status offenders are not essentially different from those youngsters committing delinquent acts—they are children in need of services, and without the intervention of the juvenile court these services would not be forthcoming. Opponents argue that juvenile court intervention does not help youngsters; the services are inadequate and intervention intensifies existing problems by stigmatizing children.* Some European countries provide nonjudicial assistance for such children. In Sweden, a child welfare council performs the function. It consists of five members, including a lawyer, a clergyman, and a teacher. The council has a professional staff that provides services to children and their families. Norway and Denmark have similar systems. Belgium has Committees for the Protection of Youth, which provide services to families unable to cope with the problems presented by their children. Scotland has Children's Panels for all non-serious juvenile offenders and other children in need of services.

In the United States most PINS petitions are filed by the children's parents, ostensibly because the youngsters are beyond their control. Quite often, the problem is in the home; the child is merely a symptom of a wider problem. Children often

*For a review of these issues and some research findings see Weis, et al., 1980.

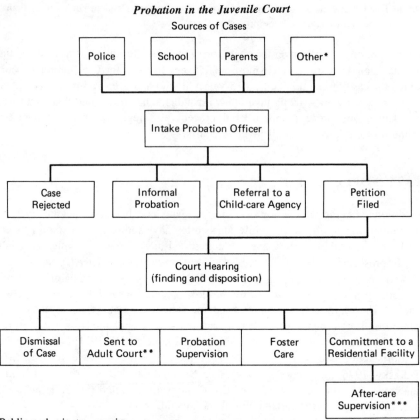

Probation in the Juvenile Court

Sources of Cases

*Public and private agencies.
**Juveniles who commit serious offenses may be sent to adult courts for trial.
***Supervision provided by the probation department or a juvenile after-care (parole) agency.

become status offenders by running away from pathological family situations, such as alcoholic or abusing parents. Girls are often subjected to juvenile court because of sexual activity that goes "unnoticed" when committed by boys.

Children who are found to be status offenders are usually warned or placed on probation in their initial encounter with the court. Probation status may include placement in foster care or a group home. However, if a youngster fails to cooperate with the treatment program, he/she can be returned to court for further disposition. This can lead to a training school placement. Probation supervision in juvenile (and often adult) court tends to be inadequate because of a shortage of staff. Children may be removed from their homes because there are not enough probation officers to provide supportive services—this can be quite costly to the child and the taxpayer.

There is an additional problem with respect to status offenders: the differential treatment of females (Female Offender Resource Center, 1978: 1):

Decision Points within the Juvenile Justice System

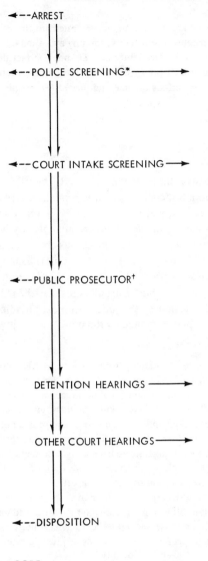

◄--ARREST

A patrol officer decides whether or not to make a formal arrest, but has no authority to detain.

◄--POLICE SCREENING*————►

A youth officer decides whether or not the youth should be referred to court and if so, whether or not the youth should be detained pending the initial court hearing.

◄--COURT INTAKE SCREENING——►

A court worker — and in some cases a prosecutor or judge — decides whether or not a petition should be filed and if so, whether or not the youth should be detained pending final disposition. Most status offense complaints are initiated here.

◄--PUBLIC PROSECUTOR†

A prosecuting attorney decides, after reviewing the court worker's decision, whether to file a petition. The prosecuting attorney, however, has no role in determining whether to detain the youth.

DETENTION HEARINGS————►

The judge, usually based on the recommendation of a case worker, decides whether to detain the youth.

OTHER COURT HEARINGS——►

The judge, after review of previous decisions, decides whether to continue detention of the youth based on new information presented by a defense attorney.

◄--DISPOSITION

The judge decides the kind of care or treatment the youth will receive.

CODE:

Prosecution with Detention

———► Prosecution without Detention

◄ — — Dismissal or Diversion

*This stage is omitted in some jurisdictions, particularly in small communities that cannot afford a special youth officer. It may be handled by a social service employee rather than by a police employee.

†The prosecutor has authority to override decisions to dismiss or to prosecute based on social reasons. The authority exists in only two states.

Source: Female Offender Resource Center, *Little Sisters and the Law*, (Washington, D.C.: U.S. Government Printing Office), 1978.

Nearly 75 percent of females under 18 who are arrested and incarcerated are charged with *status offenses* such as disobeying their parents, promiscuity, running away and other acts for which adults cannot be charged and boys infrequently are. Despite the fact that the *crimes* of which girls are accused are categorized as less serious and less harmful to society, they are often held in detention for longer periods of time and placed less frequently in community programs than boys.

JUVENILE COURT PROCEDURE

There is a lack of uniformity among juvenile (sometimes called "family") courts throughout the United States. In about half the states juvenile probation services are administered by the juvenile court; in others, welfare, corrections, or other agencies provide probation services. In many states youngsters who are juveniles by law may be tried in adult criminal court if they are accused of certain serious crimes (e.g., rape or murder). In such cases the decision to try the juvenile in adult court is usually made in response to a motion by the prosecutor's office. The legal age of a juvenile varies from state to state from 16 to 18*. The juvenile court is usually closed to the public; its records are confidential and are usually sealed by the judge. In most jurisdictions a juvenile is not routinely fingerprinted or photographed by the police, and a juvenile's name is usually not printed in the newspapers**.

- The general public is ordinarily excluded, by statute, from attendance at juvenile court hearings, with exceptions within the discretion of the court, by 33 of the 51 jurisdictions. Eleven of the jurisdictions do not specify the exclusion of public attendance, but empower the court to admit or exclude usually in accordance with statutory guidelines. Four jurisdictions ordinarily admit the public in juvenile court hearings and provide the judge the discretionary power to make exceptions. Three jurisdictions do not include provisions in the statutes regarding public attendance at juvenile court hearings. Some jurisdictions provide clauses which allow the media in closed juvenile hearings, and general public attendance in hearings, if the case involves a serious or repeat offense.
- Public inspection of juvenile records requires express permission of the court in 42 of the 51 jurisdictions. Five of the jurisdictions allow *legal* records to be public, and one State allows the legal record to be public in any case alleged to be a repeat offense. Another jurisdiction allows the news media to inspect the police records of juvenile offenders on the condition that there be no public disclosure of identity.
- The public disclosure of juvenile identities ordinarily requires court permission in 47 jurisdictions. The few exceptions to the restriction of public disclosure of juvenile identities include cases when the juvenile offender has been classified as repeat (two jurisdictions), serious (one jurisdiction), or repeat-serious (one jurisdiction). (Smith and Alexander, 1980: 57)

*Of the fifty states and the District of Columbia: in thirty-nine jurisdictions it is under 18; in eight jurisdictions it is under 17; in four jurisdictions it is under 16. (Smith and Alexander, 1980: xix)

**With regard to the confidentiality of information within the juvenile justice system:

Charles Smith and his colleagues (1979) found that there is also a lack of uniformity in the exercise of discretionary powers inherent in the juvenile court. They (1979: xii) found an absence of written policies which

is especially acute among probation, court and protective services intake officials who make many of the critical decisions about dependent, abused, incorrigible, or delinquent juveniles. What policy does exist does not appear to significantly influence the decisions officials make.

Smith and his colleagues (1980b) also found that when confronted with similar cases, decision-makers will often render different decisions.

INTAKE SERVICES

Cases are referred to the juvenile court by the police, parents, school officials, or other private and public agencies. The case is first reviewed by an intake officer, usually a member of the probation staff. He/she interviews the young person; the policeman or agency representative; the victim(s), if available; and the child's parents or guardians. The intake officer has a dual function: legal and social service. The first is to determine if the juvenile court has jurisdiction and usually requires that the child and parents be advised of the right to counsel and the right to remain silent during the intake conference (Rubin, 1980: 304). H. Ted Rubin notes that "defense attorney participation at a conference is rare, waivers of rights tend to be finessed, and the norm is for the parents to encourage the child to discuss his or her participation in the alleged offense with the intake officer" (p. 104). The social service function involves a determination of the child's situation: home, school, physical, and psychological. Based on the information obtained, the intake officer must decide if the case is appropriate for formal court processing, by filing a petition, or if it can be handled as an *unofficial case*. Eugene Czajkoski points out that this screening authority is similar to that exercised by the prosecutor's office in the adult criminal process—the prosecutor decides which cases are to be prosecuted while the intake officer decides which cases are to be adjudicated (1973: 10–11).

Rubin notes that during the 1970s the prosecutor has come to dominate the intake process in many jurisdictions (1980: 299). "The clear trend is toward the inclusion of the prosecutor in either first- or second-level screening functions or, at the least, toward agreements with intake officers that prosecution must be consulted regarding recommendations for informal disposition of certain more serious or repetitive offenders" (p. 310). This activity is, at least in part, the result of a 1975 U.S. Supreme Court decision (*Breed* v. *Jones,* 421 U.S. 519), which held that once a child is adjudicated in juvenile court, he/she cannot be transferred to criminal court for processing on the same charge—this would constitute "double jeopardy." Rubin does not see this trend as a negative development. Probation officers, he notes, lack legal training and often fail to follow legal procedures during intake: "This failure to conduct careful legal screening has often led to unrepresented youngsters' accepting terms of informal probation or later admitting to the offense before the judge without anyone's having scrutinized the legal sufficiency of the case" (p. 304).

Unofficial Cases

Roughly one-half of all cases reaching the juvenile court are adjusted at intake; that is, they are disposed of without the filing of a petition. When the intake worker believes that it is possible to assist the young person without formal action, it is an *unofficial case*. These are usually cases that are too trivial to warrant court action or where the worker believes that casework rather than legal action is needed.

If the child and his/her parents are agreeable to the informal processing, the young person can be placed under the supervision of a probation officer, usually for about 90 days. Although this may save the young person and parents from the trauma of court action, unofficial handling has its critics. Informal processing requires an explicit or tacit adminission of guilt. The substantial advantages that accrue from this admission (the avoidance of court action) also act as an incentive to confess. This casts doubt on the voluntariness and the truth of admissions of guilt.

The period of informal probation can be a crucial time in the life of a young person. If successful, the youngster may avoid further juvenile court processing; if unsuccessful, he/she will face the labyrinth that is the juvenile justice process. No one is more aware of this than the probation officer, who, using all the skills and resources at his/her command, attempts to assist the youngster and the youngster's parents through the crisis. Counseling, group therapy, tutoring, vocational guidance, psychiatric and psychological treatment, and recreational services, if they are available, will be put to use to help the young person. If informal efforts are unsuccessful, the probation officer can file a petition that will make the case an official one.

Official Cases

The decision to file a petition is usually based on one or more of the following:

1. The child or parents deny the allegations.
2. Unofficial handling does not seem appropriate in view of the seriousness of the case.
3. Informal probation has failed.

In some courts the same probation officer may handle the case from intake through termination; in others, probation officers or other staff persons are involved in different stages of the court process. Ted Rubin and Jack Smith maintain that it is desirable to utilize a nonprofessional to present a case to court. After adjudication, they argue, the case should then be referred to a probation officer for study prior to the dispositional hearing. They believe that such a system provides for better use of the probation officer's time by freeing him/her from what are often clerical-type duties, such as serving notice upon the parties and having the case placed on the court calender, relative to the filing of a petition. Rubin and Smith believe that this will help the probation officer, who is essentially the helping agent of the court, from being identified as a "prosecuting agent" (1971: 29).

Hearings

There are several types of hearings in the juvenile court. These hearings are less formal than in the adult criminal (and civil) court. Judges usually do not wear robes and they sit at a desk instead of the high bench that is characteristic of the adult courts. These hearings are usually closed to the general public.

A judge may hold a *detention hearing* to determine if the young person (the respondent) should be held in a juvenile detention facility pending further court action. If the judge determines, usually with the help of the probation agency, that the respondent's behavior makes him/her a danger to himself/herself or to the safety of others, or that the respondent will probably not return to court voluntarily, the youngster can be held in detention. Detention facilities for juveniles have generally been inadequate. In some jurisdictions they are merely separate sections in an adult jail. In New York City, where I worked in juvenile (family) court, the primary detention facility for juveniles, Spofford, was plagued with violence and other problems characteristic of adult correctional institutions.

The *adjudiction hearing* is to determine the validity of the allegations contained in the petition. If the allegations are sustained, the judge makes a finding of fact and orders a predisposition report. At the *dispositional hearing* the judge decides on a program of treatment based on the contents of the predisposition report.

PREDISPOSITION REPORT

The goal of the juvenile court is to provide services. In order to do so on the basis of the best available information, the judge orders a *predisposition investigation*. The probation officer who conducts the investigation will present his/her findings in a report that includes the sociocultural and psychodynamic factors that influenced the juvenile's behavior, providing a social history that is used by the judge to determine the disposition of the case. Since the judge's decision will often be influenced by the contents of the report, it must be factual and objective—a professional statement about the child's family, social, and educational history and any previous involvement with public or private agencies. It also indicates the physical and mental health of the child, as reported by a court psychiatrist and/or psychologist. The report will include the following:

1. A review of court records
2. A review of school records
3. A review of police records
4. Interviews with family members
5. Interviews with the respondent
6. Interviews with teachers and school officials
7. Interviews with employers or youth workers
8. Interviews with clergy when appropriate
9. Interviews with complainant or witnesses
10. Results of any psychological or psychiatric exams
11. A recommdnation, which should include the treatment alternatives available in the case

The probation officer must present his/her findings with supportive statements as to the actual situation found in the investigation. Other than a recommendation, suppositions or opinions are to be avoided. Sometimes, the recommendation of the probation officer is not included in the report but is transmitted orally to the judge. The completed report should enable the judge to make the best disposition available based on the individual merits of the case and the service needs of the young person. One problem encountered at the disposition stage is a paucity of available alternatives for helping the youngster. This can be exacerbated by an (inexperienced) probation officer who recommends treatment that is simply not available. Quite often, a youngster will be placed on probation because of a lack of viable alternatives.

SOCIAL INVESTIGATION
IN THE JUVENILE COURT*

The Juvenile Division of the Circuit Court
The City of St. Louis
Presiding Judge: Honorable Gary M. Gaertner

In the Interest of:
Timothy Wells

Date of Report:
June 17, 1976

Birthdate:
July 22, 1962 (verified)

Case No.: 50550

Juvenile Officer:
William Russell

Previous Police and/or Court History

5-26-75   Unauthorized Use of Fire Hydrant.   Worker Russell. Timothy Wells was taken into custody at 12:30 p.m. at 3124 Hoffman on 5-18-75 by

---

*From the Law Enforcement Assistance Administration.

Officer Purcell. The arrest occurred after the officer observed Timothy with a fire hydrant wrench in his hand, turning on the fire hydrant at 3124 Hoffman. The officer turned off the above hydrant and the one on the next corner east at Lake and 15th Avenues. Case serviced and closed on 7-29-75.

5-10-76 Trespassing and Peace Disturbance. Worker Russell. Timothy Wells was taken into custody at his home, 3201 Octavia, at 8:30 a.m., on 4-17-76 by Officers Moore and Keller. The arrest occurred following a complaint filed on 4-15-76 by Bruce Kelly, Assistant Principal at Hawthorne School. Mr. Kelly reported that an ex-student at Hawthorne, Timothy Wells, came into the school yard and created a disturbance. When asked to leave, Timothy used profanity and threatened Mr. Kelly with bodily harm. Insufficient evidence, warrant refused; case referred to probation department for informal adjustment. The worker closed the case of 5-27-76 by referring the family to the St. Louis Speech and Hearing Center.

5-24-76 Common Assault. Worker Russell. Timothy Wells was taken into custody at 3038 Douglass at 6:45 p.m., on 5-21-76 by Officers Flynn and Burger. The arrest occurred following a complaint by one John Bullen of 3827 Broadway (on official court supervision on a suspended commitment to MSTS). Bullen reported that he was struck on the head with a baseball bat by Timothy Wells during a fight with Timothy and his brothers, Earl and William, and a sister, Dolores.

Following an investigation, Timothy Wells, Earl Wells, and John Bullen were all conveyed to the Juvenile Court and booked for common assault. All warrants were refused for insufficient evidence, and the matter was referred to the probation department for an informal adjustment. The case was closed on 5-27-76 after enrolling Timothy (Earl and William) in the Work Restitution Program for four weeks and referring Timothy to the St. Louis Speech and Hearing Center. On the following day, the worker learned of the petition for the present offense.

Reason for Hearing

Timothy was referred to the Court on 5-20-76 by the St. Louis County Juvenile Court. On 5-10-76, Timothy allegedly attempted to steal three pairs of sunglasses from the Kresge's Store, 7800 Kingston Road in St. Louis, Missouri.

Timothy has remained in the home since the alleged offense on 5-10-76. He has since received one subsequent referral for common assault. He has also been present and worked well on three Saturday mornings of the Work Program for Probationers.

Collateral Contacts

Informants. The child's parents, Florence and Marvin Wells, were interviewed in their home on 6-5-76. Numerous other contacts have been made with them since two other children, Earl and William, were assigned to the supervision of this worker on 2-20-76. Both parents seem interested and have been cooperative with this court representative.

Contacts with Other Agencies

St. Louis Speech and Hearing Center. The Center was contacted by telephone on 6-8-76 to verify Timothy's appointment for a hearing evaluation. Timothy has such an appointment scheduled for 2:30 on 6-26-76. The Center is capable of providing diagnostic and treatment services for an apparent hearing and speech disorder.

Family History

Home. Timothy resides with both parents, four sisters, two brothers, and a nephew at 3201 Octavia. The residence is a one-story brick home which includes three bedrooms, living room, kitchen, and an ample basement which has been partially converted for additional living quarters for Timothy, Earl, and William. A home visit made on 6-5-76 revealed that the residence is nicely furnished and was neat and orderly. Mr. and Mrs. Wells are purchasing the residence and make monthly installment payments of $106.00. The family moved to their present location in 1966.

Father. Marvin Wells was born in St. Louis on 12-1-36. He was the youngest of eight children. Mr. Wells reports that he finished high school and two years of business college before beginning employment as a machinist at Weiss Welding Works. He was employed there between 1960 and 1971. With the promise of a higher salary, he worked for the Kramer Tool Co., from 1971 to 1974 but returned to his former employer. He currently works from 3:30 p.m. to midnight Monday through Friday and grosses approximately $900 per month.

Mother. Florence Wells was born in St. Louis on 2-21-38. She was the fourth of eight children. She reports that she has completed high school and began work about three years ago when her youngest child, Christine, started school. Mrs. Wells has been working as a nurse's aid at the Laurel Heights Nursing Home. She works from 6:30 a.m. to 3:00 p.m. Sunday through Friday and earns approximately $300 per month. Mrs. Wells has stated that she has been suffering from hypertension for the past sixteen years.

Parents' Attitude. Marvin and Florence Wells blame Timothy for the present offense. He has admitted that he tried to steal the sunglasses. His parents feel that they are capable of discipline supervision and care for Timothy but they also admit that he has problems in which they need assistance. They feel that Timothy is angry and depressed because of an apparent hearing handicap. They are willing to seek help with this problem.

Other Family Information

The other children are Andrea (BD: 9-2-57), Alicia (BD: 12-11-59), Dolores (BD: 1-14-60), Earl (BD: 8-15-62), William (BD: 12-1-65), and Christine (BD: 5-16-70). Dolores, Earl, and William are also known to the Court. Dolores received a referral on 9-6-75 for peace disturbance and loitering (a group demonstration at Westside High School), serviced and closed on 1-27-76. Dolores is a student at Westside High School, and has a pre-school-age son, Michael, who also lives with the family. Earl has three referrals and William has one referral. At a hearing held on 1-21-76, Earl and William were found to have a committed a common assault and were both placed on official court supervision on a suspended commitment to Missouri Hills. They have been cooperative in keeping weekly appointments with the worker and following my instructions. There seem to be no special problems between Timothy and his siblings. However Timothy is most argumentative with William.

Personal History

Early Development.   Timothy was a full-term baby born without complications. Mrs. Wells stated that Timothy was unusually prone to illness in his childhood. He seemed to catch everything. She went so far as to state that the family moved to their present home in 1966 because the family physician recommended gas heat for Timothy over the coal-burning furnace which they had in their last residence.

Health.   Timothy is a black male who is 5 feet 4 inches tall and weighs 150 pounds. He is of medium complexion with brown eyes and black hair. Mrs. Wells reports that Timothy gets sick when he becomes overly excited.

Timothy has an apparent hearing and speech disorder. The problem reportedly was initially diagnosed by the school doctor at Northridge School who stated that Timothy would be totally deaf in his left ear by age 17.

School.   No direct school contact can be made during the summer vacation. However, Mr. and Mrs. Wells stated that Timothy was suspended from Hawthorne School in 1975 for behavior problems. He began school at Northridge School in September 1975 and continued there until around January 1976. Mrs. Wells reported that Timothy enjoyed school there and did well because he liked his teacher, Sister Frances. However when Sister Frances left the school, Timothy's school problems resumed. Mrs. Wells stated that she then stopped sending Timothy to the school because they could no longer afford it. She attempted to enroll Timothy in the public schools but could not make the arrangements. Thus Timothy did not attend any school for the second semester of the past school year.

Employment.   None.

Leisure-Time Activities.   Timothy enjoys boxing, basketball, and football.

However, his parents won't permit him to participate because of health reasons. Timothy and his parents report that he has no close friends.

Religion.   Timothy is Baptist but is inactive in church.

General Personality.   When asked, Timothy said he didn't think about himself. He said he has no problems and gets along with people. However, he also said that he has no friends, nor does he need them.

Child's Attitude.   Timothy admits and accepts responsibility for his behavior. He stated that he doesn't know why he tried to steal the sunglasses. He said he had $3 in his pocket at the time.

Timothy has a very negative attitude. He appears sullen and angry and his verbal responses are generally short and gruff, especially if you must ask him to repeat himself. He also has a short temper.

Psychological or Psychiatric Evaluation

Timothy was given a psychological evaluation on 7-2-75 by the Rev. Raymond A. Hampe, Ph.D., Associate Director, Department of Special Education, Archdiocese of St. Louis. A battery of three tests was administered. Timothy was referred by Malcolm Bliss Mental Health Center for placement in special class due to behavior problems at school (Hawthorne).

Timothy was seen as functioning in the borderline to slow range of mental ability with probable higher potential which is unavailable due to emotional factors and major weakness in his grasp of language concepts. "Timothy is an immature, willful, anxious, sensitive boy who has strong achievement motivation and desires to be accepted. He does not see himself as being successful and accepted and therefore is greatly frustrated." Timothy projected hostility toward the examiner but cooperated. No obvious sensory or motor impairments were noted.

In summary, Timothy was seen as being anxious for success but expecting failure. Recommendations were for the parents to offer additional responsibilities and privileges marked by confidence in his ability to succeed. A special school placement was offered to eliminate the normal school's constant source of negative self-evaluation.

Summary and Evaluation

This is the matter of Timothy Wells, who will be 14 years old on 7-22-76. Timothy is before the court for stealing three pairs of sunglasses from the Kresge's Store in St. Louis, Missouri, on 5-10-76. He admits doing so but offers no explanation. Timothy has a total of four referrals to the court, three of which occurred in June of this year.

Timothy's home situation is satisfactory. The parents are responsible working people who are purchasing a home. They express interest in their children and have demonstrated cooperation with this worker in connection with Earl and William, who are currently under supervision. The parents acknowledge that Timothy is a "problem child" and Mrs. Wells brought Timothy to my attention even before he officially came to the attention of the court.

Timothy is seen as an angry and frustrated youth. He has a low tolerance for frustration and a short temper which displays it. Timothy is sensitive to failure and has come to expect it of himself. He professes no problems which require correction but seems incapable of following advice and instructions.

Timothy apparently has some form of hearing and speech disorder. Mrs. Wells feels that his hearing is poor and speculates that Timothy has learned to compensate somewhat by learning to read lips. His speech is characterized by brief, to-the-point statements which are rather unclear. Timothy is scheduled for a thorough hearing evaluation on 6-26-76.

Timothy is seen as an appropriate candidate for rehabilitation within the community. His three referrals in June 1976 seem to indicate that his need to act out has reached a peak level. Although angry and frustrated at the world around him, Timothy's referrals are not of a serious nature. He is therefore not regarded as a serious threat to persons or property although his unstable emotional characteristics might indicate some further form of striking back. However, a strong incentive can be offered to curb recidivism.

The plan for Timothy involves a thorough hearing and speech evaluation and follow-up on recommendations made for therapy. Timothy should also undergo psychiatric therapy, most realistically at the Child Guidance Center. Further, Timothy should be enrolled in a special school setting where teaching is individualized and tutorial in nature and where the program is stimulating and rewarding for appropriate behavior. Such programs are offered at Providence School and Project Door. No firm recommendation can be made in regard to a specific school, as the referral procedure is still under way. Furthermore, Timothy should have a regular weekly appointment with his Deputy Juvenile Officer for further counseling and to coordinate plans.

Alternative Plans

Placement in either a community group home or at Missouri Hills. Placement outside the home has been ruled out because Timothy's problems do not include poor parental supervision. Rather, his problem involves insecurity which can best be treated in his home.

Restitution

The Victim Assistance Program report states that there was no loss suffered by the Kresge's Store, as the three pair of sunglasses involved were recovered. Furthermore, Timothy has worked well the past three Saturdays in the Work Program for Probationers. He has one more Saturday left in the original enrollment from the informal adjustment, so it is felt that he has made ample service restitution to the community.

Plan

It is therefore recommended that Timothy Wells be committed to the Division of Children's Service for placement at Missouri Hills. Further that the commitment be held in abeyance and said minor remain in the home of his parents on Official Court Supervision and subject to the following special rules. That said minor cooperate in prescribed hearing and speech therapy. To cooperate in prescribed psychiatric therapy. To keep a weekly appointment with the Deputy Juvenile Officer through September 1976. And further that the Deputy Juvenile Officer investigate an appropriate school setting for said minor for the fall term of 1976.

Respectfully submitted,

_____

William Russell
Deputy Juvenile
Officer

Approved by:

_____

Susan Davidson
Acting Supervisor

DISPOSITION HEARING*

William Price and his mother sat uneasily before the Judge. The allegations of the amended petition had been sustained on the basis of a full admission. The Judge was looking through the probation officer's report for information on which to base his disposition. His eye was drawn to the psychologist's report attached to the court report. The courtroom was silent, all eyes on the Judge.

In the report William was described as "fairly handsome" and "athletically built." The Judge glanced up and looked directly at the boy. William turned his eyes away. The Judge decided that the boy might be called handsome despite

*From Lawrence E. Cohen, *New Directions in Processing of Juvenile Offenders: The Denver Model* (Washington, D.C.: U.S. Government Printing Office, 1975).

his "waterfall" haircut and a slight case of acne, but he was certainly not sufficiently robust to be dubbed "athletic."

The psychologist's report indicated that William might or might not be aggressive to girls in the future. "That's not much help," the Judge thought, "it could apply to most young men. Chances are the boy feels worse about the situation than the girl. At least he *looks* remorseful."

"William, do you realize you could have seriously injured that girl?"

"I didn't mean to hurt her. I thought it was what she wanted."

"That was a dangerous supposition, young man. I hope you realize by now that any use of violence in any circumstances can have the most serious consequences. Society doesn't regard such things lightly."

"Yes, sir."

"Besides the offense with the girl, you also ran away from the officer who was trying to arrest you."

"I'm sorry about that. I guess I lost my head."

"Are you in the habit of losing your head?"

"No, sir. I just wasn't thinking."

"William," the Judge said sternly, "I have serious doubts about allowing you to remain in the community. How do I know you won't lose your head again and really hurt someone the next time?"

"I promise, Judge. I won't do anything foolish again."

The Judge turned to Mrs. Price and said sympathetically, "I know it has been very difficult for you to raise William by yourself. It would be a pity for all that effort to go to waste."

Tears welled up in Mrs. Price's eyes. "Yes, your Honor. Please let William come home. I know he'll be good. And I've changed my job now so I can be with him more," she said in a trembling voice.

William's eyes were focused on his mother while she talked. The Judge noted that concern for her was mirrored in his face.

"How has Bill been doing since he came home from Juvenile Hall, Mrs. Price?"

"Just like always, Judge. He's a good boy."

"William," the Judge said, "what would you do with yourself if I allowed you to remain in your home?"

"Go to school."

"I see you are one year behind in your school grade. Do you plan to finish high school?"

"Yes, sir." William's face noticeably brightened.

"And then what do you plan to do?"

"I guess I'll go in the service."

The Judge looked at the probation officer. "Mr. Clarke, I'm going to follow your recommendation and make William a ward of the court and place him on probation. If he stays out of trouble during the next year, I want him brought back to court so we can terminate his case. By my calculation he could be off probation about nine or ten months before he graduates. This should be long enough so that his record will not hinder him from entering the service."

The Judge turned back to William. "I hope you've learned a lesson from this, Son. You stay out of trouble and you should have a good opportunity to make something of yourself. The burden is on you. Don't spoil your chances for a career and for a decent life for yourself and your mother."

"Thank you, Judge," Mrs. Price said. "William is a good boy. I don't think he'll make any more trouble for anyone."

She and her son left the room, the boy with his arm around her shoulders.

JUVENILE COURT JUDGES

Central to implementing the helping philosophy of the juvenile court is the juvenile court judge. Unfortunately, the requisites for the position are often unmet. In part, the reason is in the anomaly of the position. While most judicial posts require a knowledge of law and legal procedure, the juvenile court judge, in addition, needs a working knowledge of several other disciplines: sociology, psychology, and social work. Were persons with such backgrounds available, the relatively low prestige of the juvenile court would make their recruitment difficult, if not impossible.

In practice, those who do sit on a juvenile court bench quite often represent a significant departure from the "theory" of who *should* be presiding. A presidential commission reported that half had not received undergraduate degrees; another fifth had no college education at all; and another fifth were not members of the bar (President's Commission of Law Enforcement and Administration of Justice, 1972: 217). Although more recent studies reveal an improvement in education and experience levels, important problems persist. Juvenile court judges come to the court from the general practice of law and have little knowledge of the philosophy and practices of the juvenile court. In addition, even attorneys well versed in law usually have little knowledge of child welfare agencies and other community resources. Rubin and Smith point out that most have had no experience with children of lower-class groups, the most likely youngsters to be in juvenile court (1971: 19). Judges who are appointed to the juvenile court often view it as a temporary "training" period prior to appointment to a more prestigious court (Kobetz and Bosarge, 1973: 316).

In order to deal with some of these difficulties, some states have mandated training for juvenile court judges. The National Council of Juvenile Court Judges sponsors a national college located on the campus of the University of Nevada at Reno. The college trains juvenile court judges and holds periodic sessions throughout the year to help juvenile court judges (and other personnel) keep abreast of the laws and behavioral approaches related to the problems of delinquency, neglect, and child abuse. The standard two-week sessions offer a review of important court decisions related to juveniles, procedural matters such as intake, dispositional hearings, and adjudication, child neglect and abuse. Other topics include drug abuse, juvenile institutions and their alternatives, waiver of cases, transfer to adult courts, and evidence, in addition to behavioral science applications in the court. The college also offers other specialized programs at various locations throughout the country. Additional programs for training juvenile court judges and other juvenile court personnel have been developed by various state councils of juvenile court judges.

Some jurisdictions are also using *referees* or *masters,* persons trained to hold juvenile court hearings and who can recommend findings and dispositions to the judge. The *referee* or *master* must be trained in the behavioral sciences and be familiar with community resources, in addition to having a legal background. The use of such personnel, skilled and specialized, is another improvement toward the original ideals that caused the juvenile court to come into existence.

DISPOSITIONS

There is a wide array of juvenile court dispositions:

Reprimand with unsupervised probation
Probation with supervision
Foster care
Private school or residential treatment
Training school
Mental hospital
Group home
Community-based day treatment
Community-based secure facility

Juvenile offenders are sometimes released in the custody of their parents for placement in private boarding schools, military academies, sanitoria, and so on. This disposition is most often limited to offenders from at least middle-income status, and Dale Mann notes: "One obvious effect is to guarantee that public institutions for juvenile offenders serve an underclass population" (1976: 12).

Goals in Decisions

	(1) Dismiss	(2) Informal Adjustment	(3) Consent Decree	(4) Probation	(5) Commitment/ Placement
Exposure of youngster to system	Terminate contact as soon as possible	Need for brief contact by community agency or probation office	Adjudication not required to provide necessary services	Adjudication required to provide necessary services	Maximum contact needed to provide external controls
Mobilization of individual and family resources	Not indicated at present	Need for brief external assistance to family	Need for external assistance to family		Substitute for family required at present
Intervention in school adjustment	Not indicated at present	If required can be accomplished by minimum intervention	Need to provide intervention to the degree necessary		Need to provide specialized education and training
Distributive justice	Prior behavior demands dismissal (offense seen as accidental, minor incident)	Prior behavior demands informal adjustment	Prior behavior demand consent decree	Prior behavior demand probation	Need to arrest continuing delinquent behavior

		Minimum risk but intervention required	Potential risk requiring active intervention	Obvious risk requiring removal from community
Protection of community and/or self	Not indicated at present	Not indicated at present		
Intervention in emotional adjustment and control	Not indicated at present	Need to provide brief intervention to assist child and family in stabilizing emotional adjustment and control	Need to provide necessary intervention to assist child and family in stabilizing emotional adjustment and control	Need to provide specialized environment and/or services to improve emotional adjustment and control
Intervention in peer relationships	Not indicated at present	Not indicated at present	Need to modify, encourage, and/or control peer relationships	Need to remove or extricate from specific negative peer relationships

Source: W. Parsonage, H. Urban, and F. Vondracek, ''Implementing Recent Innovations in Juvenile Justice,'' *Juvenile Justice* (August 1975), pp. 37–38.

Considerations for Decisions

	(1) Dismiss	(2) Informal Adjustment	(3) Consent Decree	(4) Probation	(5) Commitment/ Placement
Delinquent behavior	First substantiated complaint	First substantiated complaint	Prior contact on minor offenses	Prior contact on serious offenses	Several prior contacts on serious offenses
Family structure	Observed family strength and support	Indications of need for improvement of family structure	Questionable family strength and support needing active intervention		Weak and/or harmful family relationships
School adjustment	Acceptable school report	Marginal school adjustment	Questionable or unfavorable school adjustment needing active intervention		Unacceptable school adjustment with little potential for improvement
Nature of offense	Minor	Minor	Prior minor offense or more serious first offense	Serious prior offense or offenses	Serious and chronic offender

Threat to self and/or family	No apparent threat	No apparent threat	Questionable threat	Obvious threat
Emotional adjustment and control	Apparently good	Perhaps adequate but indicative of needing positive assistance	Questionable or inadequate but with potential for effective intervention	Inadequate with no apparent potential improvement
Attitude toward current situation	Realistic responsible	Realistic but somewhat irresponsible	Perhaps realistic but somewhat irresponsible	Unrealistic and irresponsible
Peer-group relationship	Apparently positive	Questionable	Questionable	Unacceptable with no apparent potential for improvement
Client response	Accepting	Accepting	Perhaps reluctant but capable of utilizing court services	Inability to utilize court services

Source: W. Parsonage, H. Urban, and F. Vondracek, "Implementing Recent Innovations in Juvenile Justice," *Juvenile Justice* (August 1975), pp. 37–38.

Females often receive harsher treatment in juvenile court because of a lack of alternative programs for them. "Although a sentencing judge may be willing to consider a variety of dispositional alternatives, he or she is often faced with only one program possibility—the state training school or reformatory" (Female Offender Resource Center, 1978: 13). Additionally, a survey of training schools for girls revealed (p. 18):

> And once institutionalized, girls are afforded fewer services and program opportunities than boys. Boys, on the other hand, suffer from disadvantages which result from confinement in larger institutions which are filled to capacity.
>
> We can only speculate as to the reasons for these discrepancies. Some people working in the juvenile system justify the differences in programs and services available in girls' institutions by arguing that it is cost effective to spend the limited funds which do exist on boys who commit more serious crimes and who outnumber girls in the system by nearly four to one.

Next, we review some of the dispositional alternatives, starting with probation supervision.

Probation Supervision

Probation is used in about half of the adjudicated delinquent cases. Juveniles should be receiving dispositions of probation when they are not seriously delinquent or in obvious need of intensive services available only in an institutional setting. However, youngsters with severe behavior problems may be placed on probation, not because it is necessarily the most appropriate response, but because it is the only treatment available.

As a condition of probation, juveniles are usually required to obey their parents, attend school regularly, be home at an early hour in the evening, and avoid disreputable companions and places. The probation officer supervising the youngster works toward modifying some of the youngster's attitudes in order to help the child relate to society in a law-abiding, prosocial manner. At the root of antisocial behavior in many juveniles is a difficulty in relating to authority and authority figures. Parents, school officials, and others who have represented authority to the young person have caused him/her to develop a negative, even hostile, attitude toward all authority. This leads to rebellion at home and at school, or against society in general (Shireman, 1960: 268). The probation officer must help the young person revise his/her ideas about people in authority. The officer may do this by providing a role model as a healthy authority figure, or may help the young person develop healthy attitudes toward others who can provide a desirable role model. These persons may be teachers, athletic coaches, or perhaps a recreation leader in the community.

The probation officer must be able to accept the young person and be able to demonstrate an attitude of respect and concern. The officer must be honest and firm with the youngster, setting realistic limits for him/her—something the parents are often unable (or unwilling) to do. Misbehavior or antisocial activities cannot be accepted, but the client must be.

In the course of the helping process, the probation officer will involve the family and meet with the young person on a regular basis. The officer will work with school officials, sometimes acting as an advocate for the child in order to secure a public school placement. This was always a difficult task for me when I worked with juveniles. The youngster has often exhibited quite disruptive behavior at school, and officials are resistive to his/her return. If necessary, the officer will seek placement in a foster home for the client (and in some circumstances, adoption).

Institutional Care

There are a variety of programs and facilities to which a juvenile can be sent; some are part of his/her conditions of probation. Facilities range from day-care schools to full residential treatment in a training school. The BUILD program in Harvey, Illinois, and the Denver, Colorado, Project New Pride are examples of day-care programming.

The Build Program*

The BUILD program in Harvey, Illinois, was begun in 1972 by a small group of black teachers and counselors who had been informally discussing the need for such a program since the 1969 riots. Near Chicago, the Harvey suburban area has a large black population as well as a low-status white population of industrial workers. The area has one of the highest suburban crime rates in the State of Illinois. The project was started by this group who volunteered their time and used borrowed spaces for an evening tutoring and job coaching program for 8 youths. The effort has grown in three years to a marginally financed but well equipped and staffed vocational education and job readiness skills program that has served 250 youths.

BUILD is financed by two sources: (1) it is reimbursed for the tuition of some of the students by the Illinois Division of Vocational Rehabilitation, and (2) it receives some funding from private donations. BUILD is currently seeking reimbursement from a local Board of Education under special education provisions which will pay the tuition of students not able to adjust to the regular public school setting. At present, however, many students attend free of charge. The program's financial position has had two main effects. On the one hand, it has hampered BUILD's vocational training diversification, but on the other hand, it has insured careful attention to the choice of equipment and technical instruction. These choices were facilitated by the volunteer assistance of businessmen and groups of locally employed craftsmen and technicians.

The Population Served. Enrollment in the program averages slightly over 50 youths at the present time. The program has an overall capacity of 75 to 100 youths.

*This section is taken from Dale Mann, *Intervening with Convicted Serious Juvenile Offenders* (Washington, D.C.: U.S. Government Printing Office, 1976).

92 percent of the enrollees are black and 8 percent are white.
67 percent are male—average age, 15.
33 percent are female—average age, 16½.

Of those currently enrolled, 7 youths have been adjudicated for a serious offense involving a crime against a person. While the remaining 46 youths have been adjudicated only for property offenses, approximately 15 percent of them are known by the community to have been involved in offenses against persons for which they have not been either arrested or adjudicated.

Admission to date have largely been by chance—based on who walks in, or whom the courts happen to refer—rather than on a determinate intake policy. The Institute is prepared to accept more serious offenders should the courts send them. In general, students are admitted when it has been determined that they cannot reasonably be expected to function in the regular school program. Referrals come primarily from the juvenile court and the State Division of Vocational Rehabilitation. The intake procedures begun by the Social Service Department are actually the beginning of the program's "needs assessment" rather than an admissions determination. If a referred youth really wants to come and he/she is in trouble, he/she is in.

Needs Assessment.   The needs assessment includes (1) social work interviews with the youth and his/her family to obtain educational, health, and family history, and (2) vocational counseling interviews to assess the youths' vocational goals and interests, work attitudes, temperament and hobbies. Following the interviews, the vocational conselor and/or the psychologist usually administer one or more psychological tests to obtain a better idea of the youth's needs. Each youth in the program also has a complete optometric examination in BUILD's optometry testing laboratory, which will eventually be used to train technicians in that field.

Individualized Program.   As soon as the needs assessment process provides the staff with sufficient data, a specific program plan is discussed with the youth, focusing on both short- and intermediate-range goals. The juvenile must agree to a program before training begins. It should be noted that there are no curriculum "demands" or "requirements" regarding which courses must be taken. There are, however, requirements within courses. There are no time requirements; instead, each student is allowed to progress at his/her own rate.

In addition to vocational and remedial teachers, each youth is assigned a counselor/outreach worker who at least initially picks up students in the morning and takes them home. The area lacks public transportation and most of the enrolled youth have a relatively low self-expectation and self-starting capacity. This "escort" practice both encourages attendance and affords the counselor the opportunity to become a familiar figure in the area and to the family, making family outreach and counseling somewhat easier.

Educational Program.   The program day begins, interestingly enough, at 11:00 a.m. Staff members relate the relatively high average daily attendance rate of 82 percent to the fact that the starting time is consistent with the life-style of the youth who stay up late at night. The staff feels the important thing is to get the youth into the habit of learning and training himself. Once that is accomplished, the adjustment to a more conventional day is easier. Students who have been placed and retained on jobs seem to support this rationale.

The selection of vocational areas for inclusion in the program has been carefully done. The focus is on a few areas in which there are known manpower needs, and in which there is opportunity for career advancement or job diversification. U.S. Department of Labor Job Market Analysis was used initially to determine what vocational areas fit that requirement. One example is the project's elaborate program in the graphic arts. A $30 billion-a-year industry, graphic arts presents a wide range of skill categories—from basic printing production and machine maintenance skills to sales, estimating, and advertising layout. The graphic arts program is popular with the students, who relate to its career advantages. The two other major vocational training areas are office machinery operation and maintenance and a soon-to-be-opened machinists' training program. In each of these areas, equipment care and personal safety rules are stressed.

In addition to the specifically vocational aspects of the curriculum, tutoring and classwork are offered in reading and math to assist the students in preparing for the GED high school equivalency test and otherwise upgrading their skills in these subjects. Ultimately, about 50 percent of the enrollees get an equivalency diploma.

As the youths progress in technical skills training, a Job Readiness component is introduced. They are instructed in making job applications, in dress and job interviewing techniques, and in interpersonal relations on the job. Within time limits, some job finding is conducted by the staff. As funds and volunteers increase, this component will be increased. Consistent with the recommendations of most studies in the field, however, staff members do not usually attempt to intervene directly in the hiring procedure. The staff estimates that most youth should spend about two-and-one-half years in the program.

Staff. The BUILD staff consists of the following: executive director; assistant executive director; director of social service; assistant director of social service; psychologist; social worker; counselor/outreach workers (4); vocational evaluator; technical instructors (8); part-time clerical workers (13).

An important feature in staff functioning is flexibility in responding to the program youth and their families. The staff seems to be well acquainted with each student and sensitive to the interrelationships among the youths and between the youths and individual staff members. This flexibility and sensitivity is due at least in part to the small 1:5 ratio of full-time program staff to students.

The staff is predominantly black, reflecting the racial composition of the area and the student population. The role modeling and identification contribute to the effectiveness of the program.

An outstanding characteristic of the staff is their eagerness to allow visitors to wander about, talk privately to the students, and elicit their opinions about the program. (Many correctional programs are much more secretive.)

The following statements were typical of student comments about the staff and the program in general:

"Usually offenders are forced to do things—here people are *invited* and instructors don't deal from a superior level."

"They treat us like adults here."

"Every day you are told you can do anything if you put your mind to it."

"They don't have all kinds of attendance rules."

"They don't bug you about things—instead they keep telling you how good you can be."

The flexibility and sensitivity of the staff are apparent in their policies of managing student disruption. They are aware of the violent history and potential of many of the students, but rather than simply take strict disciplinary action, they try to offer special attention in times of stress. When something seems to be building up in a student, a staff counselor sees him every day until the problems are talked out or in some way alleviated. The staff noted that often this stress is associated with problems at home. The availability of supervised temporary emergency quarters (group homes) is an important alternative to returning to an unsatisfactory home environment. BUILD hopes to acquire some apartments or houses for this purpose.

There are about two fights per week among students. These are handled by separating the antagonists and giving them both individual attention until the crisis is "talked down." Were individual attention not the norm of the program, these attempts might be seen as reinforcing aggressive behavior among the youth. The staff is not particularly disturbed by student fighting or emotional outbreaks, and their ability to (1) tolerate the fact that it does and will happen and (2) intervene quickly and nonpunitively enables them to maintain control and minimize interruptions to the program. After the outbreaks occur and during the "talk down" phase, the staff members learn as much as they can about what family, interpersonal, or situational occurrences precipitated the outbreak, and move to help the student resolve the problem.

Costs.   BUILD Institute is a testimony to what can be done with extremely limited funds by careful fiscal management and the creative use of volunteers. After the initial equipment outlays, approximately $2,000 per student per year is sufficient to cover the ongoing operating expenses of the community-based vocational program for 50 to 100 juvenile offenders. This compares quite favorably with the average $10,000 per bed in a juvenile correction institution [Note: 1975 prices.]

Evaluation.   As might be expected because of fiscal and staff limitations and the absence of any interested program funding agency, a systematic follow-up has not occurred. The program administration hopes to interest some outside agent in performing an independent evaluation within the next year.

Employment.   Records to date, although somewhat incomplete, indicate that approximately 90 percent of the enrollees have found employment, and that about half of these have found employment related to their training.

Schooling.   About half earn a high school equivalency diploma.

Recidivism.   Reliable recidivism data are not yet available.

Unexplained Finding.   One unexplained finding is the fact that youths funded by the Division of Vocational Rehabilitation, who received a monthly allowance in addition to tuition, had a consistently lower attendance rate than the other students. This finding should be explored further. If the purpose of the living allowances was the reduction of financial stress to ensure attendance, it appears to be having the opposite effect.

At least two questions have been raised about job training programs. First, how useful are programs designed to provide skills training if a recession has already shut off access to jobs? When the national unemployment figures fluctuate around 10 percent (and go much higher for black, inner-city adolescents) job guarantees are unrealistic, and, if they are, how useful is vocational training?

The second issue is more specifically related to the area of the serious juvenile offender. It has been said of some diversion programs that they are rehabilitating Boy Scouts, especially when compared to the serious offender group. Many Job Corps staff members, for example, acknowledge that their services have little success with the "hard-core umemployed" and "hard-core delinquent." Serious crime, in fact, seems to have increased in periods of both economic expansion and recession. One explanation of this may be that those individuals involved in serious crime, including juveniles, exist outside of the American economy.

Project New Pride*

Project New Pride is a community-based program offering services to adjudicated juveniles, many of whom have lengthy records of prior arrests and convictions. Most of these youngsters are either black or Chicano. New Pride operates on the premise that individuals must confront their problems in their own environment—example, within the community. To do this the offender must be guided in adopting and maintaining a conventional life-style as an alternative to the delinquent life-style he has known.

New Pride provides this direction by addressing the youths' typically very low esteem for themselves and others. Four main areas of service are incorporated in one program to help the client confront his problems in an integrated manner: academic education, counseling, employment, and cultural education.

Youngsters are referred to New Pride through Denver's Juvenile Court Probation Placement Division. Ninety-five percent of the clients are male. Referrals meet the following criteria:

*This section is taken from Carol Holliday Blew, Daniel McGillis, and Gerald Bryant, *Project New Pride* (Washington, D.C.: U.S. Government Printing Office, 1977).

1. They are 14 to 17 years of age.
2. They have a recent arrest or conviction for burglary, robbery, or assault related to robbery.
3. They have two prior convictions (preferably robbery, burglary, or assault).
4. They reside in Denver County.

New Pride selects 20 of these referrals at four-month intervals.

The Services.   For the first three months, youngsters in the program receive intensive services. A nine-month follow-up period continues treatment geared to the youth's needs and interests. The follow-up may involve daily to weekly contact. And in some instances, clients have been served continuously since project inception.

The services provided include the following:

Education.   Based on test results, participants are assigned to classes in either the New Pride Alternative School (located at project headquarters) or the Learning Disabilities Center.

The *Alternative School* provides one-to-one tutoring with relatively little lecturing. Staff are strongly supportive of student efforts, encourage their strengths, and try especially to make academic work rewarding to students who have previously experienced repeated failures. Emphasis is on reintegrating students into the regular school system.

The staff of the *Learning Disabilities Center* work intensively with clients to correct their perceptual and cognitive disabilities. New Pride stresses the relationship between learning disabilities and juvenile delinquency. In the treatment approach, learning disability therapy and academic tutoring are equally important. Tests administered to project youth in the first two years of operations showed that 78 percent of the New Pride participants were found to have at least two learning disabilities. The Learning Disabilities Center has recently received a separate grant and will be able to serve an increased number of clients.

> Shortly after Margaret entered the program, New Pride staff realized that she had poor sight and needed glasses. Her counselor helped her get a prescription and worked with her constantly. This disability corrected, Margaret displayed a notable improvement in her studies.

Counseling.   The project attempts to match clients with counselors who can best respond to their role model needs and personalities. Treatment is planned to enhance the youth's self-image and to help him/her cope with his/her environment. Counselors involve themselves in all aspects of their clients' lives and maintain frequent contact with family, teachers, social workers, and any others close to the youth. In the nine-month follow-up period, counselors continue to maintain a minimum of weekly contacts with a youth and his/her family.

> The Denver Juvenile Court Probation Placement Division referred Willy to New Pride. His counselor devoted most of the individual counseling sessions with Willy to the subject of

alcoholism as a medical problem. He took Willy to an alcohol treatment center to talk to experts, and gave him literature on alcoholism. Once Willy accepted alcoholism as a medical problem, he began trying to overcome his alcohol problem.

Employment. Job preparation is a key part of the program. The employment component is designed to introduce clients to the working world and its expectations, and to provide employment experience along with much needed income. During their first month of project participation, youths attend a job skills workshop on such topics as filling out application forms and interviewing. The job placement specialist counsels each client individually to develop vocational interests and to provide realistic appraisals of career ambitions and requisite skills. Actual "on-the-job training" occurs in the second and third months of program participation.

Cultural Education. New Pride takes youngsters who have known little more than their immediate neighborhoods and exposes them to a range of experiences and activities in the Denver area. Extensive community contacts have created a rich variety of opportunities, including visits to a television station to watch the news hour being prepared, ski trips, an Outward Bound weekend, sports events, restaurant dinners, and many other educational and recreational events.

Traditionally, juvenile services have been highly specialized and fragmented. Coupled with this fragmentation was the inconsistency in the delivery of services, which consequently produced negative experiences for some youth. New Pride's approach is to integrate all services, providing comprehensive treatment to its clients, all of whom are "hard-core" delinquents—multiple offenders with a myriad of social adjustment problems. For example, a single youth may receive remedial treatment for a learning disability, take courses for high school credit, be placed in a part-time job, participate in family counseling, and experience cultural events at theaters and museums. The staff is familiar with the range of each client's activities and can reinforce gains in any one area. That is why New Pride is a concept rather than just a group of people each trying to answer one problem of a delinquent youth.

New Pride provides intensive services with limited caseloads afforded by a high staff-to-client ratio. The staff include 11 at the central location, 7 at the Learning Disabilities Center, and a psychologist, a sociologist, and an optometrist to perform specialized services on an as needed basis. In addition, a well-organized program draws a large, diverse group of volunteers from community organizations and local colleges and universities. Students receive credits for a semester's work at New Pride as counseling interns. Community volunteers may tutor clients, develop special activity programs such as a yoga course or mechanical shop, or provide administrative and clerical assistance.

In many instances New Pride youths are tutored by volunteers who are not of the same ethnic or racial group. The staff feel that bringing together inner-city, minority, delinquent youths, and volunteers from widely varied backgrounds is vital. This contact helps both groups learn to cope with differences and gives them the opportunity to develop more favorable attitudes toward each other.

Willy and his volunteer tutor have developed a very special relationship. That Willy is Chicano and his tutor is white is not what makes their relationship so special. His tutor is blind. In part to show how much he appreciates his help, and in part to impress him, Willy is learning how to read Braille.

Arrangements and relationships established with local court and probation officials have been integral to successful project operations. Furthermore, New Pride is involved with and derives support from numerous community and business organizations. With the support of both the legal and business communities, New Pride has succeeded in responding to the needs of the youths and of their communities.

Project Achievements.   How successful has New Pride been? In keeping with its wide range of services, New Pride set six primary goals: "reducing recidivism for both referral and nonreferral offenses; job placement; school reintegration; and remediating academic and learning disabilities. The project defined these goals in explicit forms that could be measured and conducted in a careful evaluation. The impact of the remaining project activities of counseling, cultural education, and volunteer services was not directly measured.

New Pride's record in achieving its primary goals is impressive: during a 12-month period in the community, 32 percent of a control group were arrested at least once for referral offenses,* compared to 27 percent of New Pride clients. A similar reduction occurred in the rearrest rates for misdemeanor and status offenses.

The program also had considerable success in job placement. Following vocational training by New Pride, 70 percent of all clients were placed in full- or part-time jobs. The rearrest rate for employed clients was approximately one-third the rate for unemployed clients. New Pride participants also appeared to develop more positive attitudes toward education, as evidenced by a return to school rate of over 40 percent.

When Margaret entered New Pride, she was unemployed and not seeking employment, and was spending her days sleeping and watching television. After eight months of involvement with the program, she is working and is interested in getting her high school diploma. She has had no further police complaints. Based on her positive behavior, her probation has been terminated.

The data on New Pride's efforts to improve academic performance and remedy learning disabilities are too preliminary to report definitive results; however, the findings to date suggest potential successes. As noted earlier, New Pride's pioneering work in learning disabilities will be expanded under a separate grant from the Denver Anti-Crime Council.

Verdemont Ranch for Boys†

Verdemont Ranch for Boys was established in 1950 by the San Bernardino County Probation Department. Located approximately ten miles north of downtown San

---

*Burglary, robbery, or assault related to robbery.

†Source: 1979 Annual Report of the San Bernardino County Probation Department.

Bernardino off Cajon Boulevard near Devore, the Ranch is nestled at the base of the Verdemont Hills in a picturesque setting. The pine trees lining the entrance road to the Ranch are reminders of the first promoting boys who planted them in a parting ceremony.

The Ranch provides a rural residential treatment for a maximum population of 60 boys ages 14 through 17. The main goal of the program is to resolve boys' problems to the extent that they and their families can reunite; and the boys can return to their home, school and community within six months with a reasonable chance of success. In an effort to achieve this goal, each boy is screened by a committee composed of the Ranch Director, a Clinical Psychologist, a Probation Officer for the Aftercare Unit and a Supervising Group Counselor to insure that the boy is being placed in the appropriate program to best meet his individual needs. Individual treatment plans outlining both short-term and long-term goals are developed by Group Counselors for each boy within 14 days. The primary treatment modality consists of conjoint group counseling sessions where a boy and his parents along with other boys and their parents meet weekly in a therapeutic setting under the direction of the Group Counselors. Improved communication between parents and boys, as well as shared experiences and methods of handling problems, are the goals of the conjoint groups.

A full-time Clinical Psychologist reviews treatment plans, performs psychological testing, consults with staff, coordinates the counseling program and counsels individual boys. A Child and Adolescent Psychologist is available as needed to conduct testing and counseling. Medical services are performed by a contracted physician who travels to the Ranch, examines and treats referred boys and prescribes medication as needed.

The Ranch is proud of its on-grounds school program provided by the four school teachers, a teacher's aide and principal of the Herbert S. Bailey School. The full-time school program is geared toward individual study and progress to allow each boy to achieve his maximum possible potential during the six months he is on the Ranch. An average advancement in grade level of two to three years per subject is achieved. Such achievement often serves as a catalyst for continued school success as the boys return to their community school.

The Herbert S. Bailey School sponsors the 4-H Programs of home and industrial skills (electrical and woodworking projects) and the animal showings at the San Bernardino County Fair, Los Angeles County Fair, Orange Show and the Great Western Livestock Show. The Ranch, located in a rural setting, is a natural location for the development of its rich soil for production of food to feed its purebred registered hogs, cattle and sheep. The sense of responsibility, pride of accomplishment and self-esteem developed by the raising, caring for and showing of the animals and projects make the 4-H Program an integral part of the treatment success of the Ranch. The degree of success is measured by the numerous trophies and ribbons earned by the boys.

Another highlight occurs twice each year through the school's participation with the Kiwanis Club to present the Decathlon Program. It is a delight to observe the boys put forth considerable physical effort to achieve athletic records in specific events.

The Decathlon Awards Banquet rewards the winners with exceptional trophies and ribbons furnished by the Kiwanis Club.

The Para-Chaplain Program where a Catholic priest provides movies and special activities is a continued blessing to the Ranch. Casa de San Bernardino has developed both a group and individual drug/alcohol counseling program for the boys and sends a counselor to the Ranch each week. Interest in the drug/alcohol counseling groups has remained high among the boys, and many have received certificates for completion of the program. Psychiatric Interns from San Bernardino Valley College and Patton State Hospital, while gaining internship experience at the Ranch, have provided hundreds of hours of counseling and support which have been of considerable benefit to the boys.

The Work Experience Program was initiated in an effort to allow the boys an opportunity to apply for a specific job on the Ranch and gain the experience of graded work performance. Each boy submits an application for the job he desires, is interviewed and officially hired by the adult supportive staff member in charge of that specific area. Work in the kitchen and clothing room, with the custodial and outside grounds crew and in other areas is rewarded by furlough hours home depending on the job demands and level of qualifications for that specific job. Each boy is encouraged to seek a variety of experiences, for with these success experiences the self-concept and image of the boy improves.

The Journeyman Program offers the boys unique work and skill development experiences. This year they were offered the opportunity to develop concrete block wall construction skills when a retaining wall was constructed.

Each boy successfully completing the program promotes from the Ranch to Aftercare. The promotion ceremony is the final component of the treatment program at the Ranch where the boy's caseload counselor talks to the boy in front of all the other boys and staff at the Ranch and highlights his strengths and weaknesses, progress made and areas where continued growth is needed. The promotion ceremony is a success-building experience where the boy is given a promotion certificate by the Ranch Director, awards and ribbons he earned at 4-H shows which he may take home and special accomplishment certificates from school teachers and support staff.

Promotion from the Ranch to Aftercare is viewed as the beginning of the boy's return to his family and community and a fresh opportunity to benefit from the gained insight and growth made while in the program. A promotion report is written by the boy's caseload counselor. This report highlights the boy's progress and future treatment needs to be implemented by the Aftercare Probation Officer. Aftercare is a continuation of the boy's treatment program started while the boy was at the Ranch. The Aftercare Probation Officers have continued to be an integral part of the treatment program and provided an excellent service.

The Homeward Bound Program

Somewhere between day care and residential treatment is the Homeward Bound Program of Massachusetts, which is a prototype for similar programs throughout the United States.

Homeward Bound* is an outdoor-adventure model of treatment patterned after a British program to train merchant seamen. In addition to physical conditioning and outdoor activity, it provides for structured and stressful situations geared to unify groups of youngsters toward a common goal. It allows the participants to achieve "hard-win success in establishing confidence and a more positive self-image."

The Massachusetts Department of Youth Services operates a Homeward Bound School in the Colorado Rockies. Their program includes backpacking, high-altitude camping, solo survival, and rock climbing. Its participants are adjudicated delinquents referred by the courts and accepted on a "space available basis" only. The program is in two phases and lasts six weeks. It is voluntary, and prior to coming to Homeward Bound, the program is carefully explained to each referred youngster. Every successful participant is released directly home, thus avoiding other types of institutional care.

The school has no locks, fences, or secure rooms. Following an initial orientation at the school, the 32 boys are divided into brigades of eight each. During the day they work on community service projects, take short hikes, run some obstacle courses, and do calisthenics as part of a conditioning program. A few hours are also spent with a counselor developing an aftercare plan. In the evening there are classes in ecology, survival, search and rescue, overnight expeditions, and ropes and knots. Most of the youngsters do not pay attention. However, they soon discover that they are unable to manage on their first overnight expedition; packs are not in order, some gear is left behind, and the wrong food is taken along. The youngsters' first experience with not paying attention is a cold, wet, and hungry night. In subsequent classes, the youngsters are quite attentive and responsive.

The second phase of the program entails a cross-country trot through swamps, woods, and rivers, beginning at 5 a.m. and lasting until darkness, that leaves the participants exhausted. Each participant is then immediately asked to sign an agreement to continue in the program. Because of peer pressure and the challenge, it is unusual for a boy not to sign up. From then on, his time is taken up learning the intricacies of survival, navigation and logistics, first aid, and so on. Overnight and then three-day expeditions are held, all leading to a 10-day course across the Appalachian Trail in several feet of snow. Slow youngsters are helped by their peers and group interaction is intensified. There is excitement and danger, and personal skill and cooperation take on new importance.

The final test is a three-day solo survival experience: no peers, instructors, or supervision. All of the youngster's learning and experience are put to the test on this trip—alone for three days and nights, far from comfort and civilization. On the final evening, each boy receives a certificate and an emblem indicating his successful completion of the program.

The program proves to its participants the point that workers often try to make to their clients: "You are far more capable than you think you are." The need for discipline and restraint, as well as perseverance, is the important lesson taught at HB.

---

*This discussion is taken from Herb C. Willman, Jr., and Ron Y. F. Chun, "Homeward Bound," *Federal Probation* (September 1973).

A study of the program revealed that only 20.8 percent of the participants recidivated, compared to 42.7 percent of a control group.

The Group Home

Residential treatment can be classified according to the degree of custodial care provided. On the lower end of this "scale" is the group home. The home may be privately operated under contract with the state (or other level of government), or it can be operated by the state. Generally, anywhere from 6 to 15 youngsters live in the home at any one time.

The New York State Division for Youth group home is relatively small, housing about 7 youngsters. A typical home has several bedrooms, a bath, living room, kitchen, dining area, and basement recreation area. The Division attempts to place homes in residential areas that are in proximity to public transportation, public schools, and recreation facilities. The interior of the home approximates that of a large single-family dwelling.

The residents range in age from 13 to 17 years. They must possess sufficient strengths and stability to be maintained in this type of facility. The program is designed to help youths who:

1. Are in unresolvable conflict with their parents, but are not seriously disturbed or psychotic.
2. Have inadequate homes and need to develop skills for independent living.
3. Need to deal with community social adjustment problems in a therapeutic family environment.
4. Need to deal with individual adjustment problems and to learn about themselves in relation to others.
5. Need to develop self-confidence through successful experiences.

Each resident has daily chores, such as doing dishes, making the bed, and mowing the lawn. The houseparents perform the surrogate parent role by preparation of meals, ensurance of a curvew, help with homework, and other tasks usually handled by parents in healthy families. The youngsters attend local schools on a full-time basis, or they have a schedule that incorportes both school and employment.

There are regular group counseling sessions conducted by trained social workers. The sessions are geared to help youths understand and overcome problems that have led to the placement, and to define goals consistent with their individual ability. There are also individual counseling programs for those residents who need to be helped to live independently and for those who need assistance in improving their family relationships. Day-to-day counseling and conflict resolution are handled by the houseparents.

The program is geared to gain as much community acceptance and participation as possible. The first part of this concept is the small number of residents in each home. However, there have been incidents involving group home residents, some of a serious nature. To overcome community resistance, Citizen's Advisory Committees have been formed from the group home areas. An attempt is made to stress the success of the program and the relatively few incidents compared to the number of youngsters helped.

Clifford Simonsen and Marshall Gordon report that one problem experienced by the group home is inappropriate referrals—sending youngsters who cannot benefit from the services of a group home (1979: 227). A more serious problem, however, is community acceptance of a group home. It is generally agreed by both professionals and lay persons that the group-home concept is an excellent one for many youngsters coming to the attention of the juvenile court. Unfortunately, this has not been translated into community acceptance in many areas. Group homes, not only for troubled youngsters, but also for retarded and other handicapped persons, have been vigorously and, all too often, successfully resisted by local residents. Although we may recognize the value, and accept the moral imperative, of helping the unfortunate, we say *"not in my neighborhood." (L'hypocrisie est un hommage que le vice rend à la vertu.)*

Highfields

Another prototype program is Highfields, in New Jersey. This residential institution was established in 1950 as a short-term, noncustodial treatment center in the former mansion of Charles Lindbergh. The residents, about 20, have been adjudicated as delinquents and placed on probation. They stay at Highfields for a maximum of four months. The institution has no guards or locked doors, and there is a deliberate absence of authoritarian leadership. Youngsters work or attend school during the day, and in the evening they meet in groups of 10 for a daily therapy session. Family and friends are encouraged to visit, and residents are given passes to visit nearby areas and sometimes to go home for a visit.

The treatment objective is to give delinquent boys an opportunity for self-rehabilitation by achieving a series of preliminary and prerequisite goals. There are few formal rules, since the purpose is to enable the youngster to develop a non-delinquent orientation through *guided group interaction* (GGI). (GGI is discussed later in a review of the program at the Green Oak Center.) Control is exercised through the development of healthy peer-centered informal therapeutic situations.

There have been a number of studies on the effectiveness of Highfields, and claims and counterclaims abound (see Weeks, 1958, and Stephenson and Scarpitti, 1967).

Residential Treatment Center

I use the term *residential treatment center* (RTC) to identify private institutions that provide residential care for youngsters with or without the intervention of the juvenile court. Generally, these institutions provide a wide variety of enriched services; they also receive a great deal of public funding. Despite the fact that they receive tax-levy money, the RTC retains the privilege of screening their residents—a luxury not afforded to public institutions.

A persistent problem for the juvenile court in providing alternative institutional care for youngsters is the ability of private treatment institutions to refuse to accept children who do not "fit in" with their program. Probation officers can be frustrated in their attempt to find suitable placement for certain youngsters because of this problem. The probation officer makes an evaluation based on professional judgment. This is transmitted to the judge in the form of a recommendation. However, in the final stage the private institution can decide that the youngster is "incompatible" with their program (read: "too delinquent"; the RTC accepts youngsters who are referred to in the field as "boy scouts"). The court is then faced with the alternative of probation or a training school.

Training School

The training school is a public institution that accepts all youngsters sent by the courts. Each training school is usually set up to handle particular categories of juveniles. They may be assigned on the basis of age, aggressiveness, or delinquent history. This is done to avoid mixing younger juveniles with older ones, adjudicated delinquents with status offenders, or more disturbed youngsters with those having less serious problems. The training school usually provides a degree of security not available in other types of juvenile institutions. Juveniles are committed to training schools based on the following considerations:

1. There is *finding of fact* that the child has committed an offense that would be punishable by imprisonment if committed by an adult.
2. The parents are unable to control their child or provide for his/her social, emotional, and educational needs.
3. There is no other child welfare service available that is sufficient.
4. The child needs the services available at the training school.

The establishment of the Massachusetts Lyman School for Boys in 1847 began an era of providing separate facilities for juvenile offenders. The training, or reform, schools were patterned after adult prisons. They were regimented, with large impersonal dormitories. They provided some basic medical and dental treatment, and limited education and vocational training. Over the years there has been an increased emphasis on vocational training, remedial education, and rehabilitation through the use of social workers, teachers, psychiatrists, psychologists, and recreation workers (Willman and Chun, 1973: 52–53).

One training school, *The Warwick School for Boys,* is located 55 miles from New York City. It is one of six training schools operated by the New York State Division for Youth. The school is a pleasant-looking institution with 700 acres of lawns and trees, and houses about 170 residents in several dormitories. There are also some individual rooms which are assigned on a "merit" basis. The school's annual budget is about $2½ million, and it has a staff of 180 persons. There is a ratio of better than one staff member dealing directly with every two residents.

The daily schedule calls for two hours of compulsory academic instruction and two hours of physical education, with additional services for those who require more help. Both individual and group counseling are provided. Vocational training in such areas as mechanical drawing, woodworking, electricity, painting, and kitchen work is available and optional.

The residents are all adjudicated delinquents who have committed offenses ranging from petty larceny to rape and murder, all before their sixteenth birthday. There are no walls or gates around the school, and security is maintained through the use of supervised activities. Nevertheless, counselors report that there is fear in the surrounding community because some residents have become involved in criminal acts while outside the school. Despite the extensive services offered, some residents complain of too much idle time and poor food.

The cost of training schools is quite high. In 1975, the cost at Warwick was estimated to be $15,000 per resident annually. [The cost of any institution that operates around the clock (e.g., hospitals, nursing homes, prisons) is exorbitant. Such institutions require several work shifts and continuous lighting and heating; and constant use increases maintenance costs.]

Green Oak Center: GGI for Serious Juvenile Offenders*

At least one institution-based program is utilizing Guided Group Interaction with serious juvenile offenders. This 100-bed residential facility is the Green Oak Center in Michigan, which was established in 1960 as a "junior prison" or "readjustment center" for Michigan's most serious juvenile offenders. A maximum security special treatment unit, it consists of a one-story structure with five separate housing wings, located in Whitmore Lake (near Ann Arbor), Michigan. Green Oak Center is organizationally a part of, although physically and functionally detached from, W. J. Maxey Boys Training School. The Center serves delinquent males between the ages of 12 and 19 who cannot, for a variety of reasons, be accommodated in other facilities and programs within the State of Michigan's Office of Children and Youth Services (OCYS).

The Population Served.   Only adjudicated delinquent males between the ages of 12 and 19 can be admitted to Green Oak Center. GOC residents have been found to be in need of a program offering maximum security, intensive treatment, special education, and a highly structured environment. They are regarded as multiply handicapped and are said to represent the highest concentration of socially and emotionally maladjusted and disturbed youth within the State's programs for delinquents. Approximately 12 percent (125) of Michigan's annual admissions of male youth to juvenile correctional institutions enter GOC. Diagnostic descriptions of residents range from neurotic disturbances and serve character disorders (sociopathy) to

*This section is taken from Dale Mann, *Intervening with Convicted Serious Juvenile Offenders* (Washington, D.C.: U.S. Government Printing Office, 1976).

psychoses. In general, GOC is regarded as *the* placement for severely disturbed offenders who require lengthy institutional care. GOC operates at maximum capacity (100), with an active waiting list.

GOC's population primarily consists of urban youth (Wayne County, or Detroit, is the largest single source of referrals), many of whom are black. The residents of GOC are commonly characterized by extremely low self-esteem, a highly unrealistic self-concept, a history of consistent and severe failure, and a resultant lack of motivation. Their relationships tend to be quite inadequate, dominated by extreme distress and a lack of concern for others. They are typically described as socially inadequate in almost every way.

Educationally, about 80 percent of GOC residents function three or more years below their age-appropriate grade placement. About one-fourth of them have been described as educationally nonfunctional, in that they are unable to obtain overall achievement scores normally expected for fourth-graders on a standardized test.

An informal examination of the residents' data cards indicated that about 80 percent of them have committed violent, assaultive offenses; many of these have histories of repetitive violence. The approximately 20 percent who do not have a history of violent offenses are often offenders who have been transferred due to institutional management problems and emotional/mental disturbance. GOC has virtually no control over the selection process—example, they get the kids no one else wants. While GGI is not new, its implementation with a correctional population like that at Green Oak is unusual. Typically, those identified as serious offenders would simply be confined in a maximum security facility with a heavy custodial orientation. Although Green Oak Center is a relatively secure juvenile facility, one gets the clear impression that the number-one priority at the Center is helping the residents behave more responsibly. (GOC's formal goals include the rehabilitation of serious juvenile offenders while segregating these offenders in a secure facility.) The program philosophy implies the belief that in the long run, society is best protected by helping the offender become more responsible so that he can return to society without posing a threat to the safety of others.

The Treatment Program.   Upon admission, each resident is assigned to one of the five wings of the Center. This also constitutes an assignment to a GGI group. Each residential wing has two such groups, directed by the wing counselor. There is little choice about assignment to GGI groups, since availability of space is a major problem and assignment to a wing dictates assignment to a group. The wing teams are headed by social workers and have considerable autonomy for decision making, within overall institutional guidelines. The director clearly favors a participatory decision-making model, and this is reflected in the decentralized power structure of the institution. His plans for the future include further diffusion of decision-making power to the wing teams and to the groups of residents.

GGI has been the principal treatment intervention employed since 1972. Group leaders adhere closely to the theoretical design of GGI. They are nonintrusive, intervening only to redirect the group. The sessions are conducted by the residents themselves. The intended net effect of the 10 GGI groups is to create an institutional milieu which is itself therapeutic. The principles of group dynamics are utilized to transform the peer culture into a prosocial system of values and norms, rather than the more traditional institutional social system that reinforces delinquent behavior and generates a status hierarchy based on antisocial or asocial behavior and values.

The small-group discussions at GOC involve up to 10 boys, sitting in a tight circle. One boy is chosen by his peers to "have the meeting" that day. The meetings typically last about an hour or 90 minutes and are held four or five times a week. They focus on the boy chosen that day; his peers attempt to help him examine his behavior and improve upon it. Much confrontation accompanies these sessions, and there is constant pressure by the participants to be honest. Since the entire group may lose certain privileges when one of its members commits a serious infraction, there is considerable pressure to learn as much as one can about one's peers so as to make more informed decisions about things such as home leave or off-grounds passes. If such a decision results in an AWOL, for example, then the entire group may have to suffer the consequences.

One characteristic which distinguishes Green Oak Center's GGI program from some others is that the groups at Green Oak, while permitted a fair amount of decision-making autonomy, are not allowed to decide—or even to recommend—any negative sanctions for a resident. This is a staff function. The director noted that the residents would tend to be too punitive in deciding on the appropriateness of certain sanctions. It is also noteworthy that GOC staff members are expected to avoid being too authoritarian (so as to permit the peer culture to work effectively as a treatment tool) but at the same time not avoid accepting personal responsibility for making those decisions which cannot be allocated to the groups.

Staffing. In addition to the director and the wing counselors, all of whom hold graduate degrees in psychology or social work, the staff includes group leaders on each of the five wings; three youth specialists on each wing; a core teacher for each unit; a vocational instructor on each of the teams; clinical services (one psychologist and several psychiatric counsultants); program support services (a support services manager, four boys' supervisors, and six youth workers); and special education support services (including a secretary, two remedial language lab instructors, a health/physical education and recreation coordinator, a general studies teacher, a driver education instructor, some teacher aides, a recreation instructor, and two half-time recreation aides); and supportive clerical staff for the administrative office.

Costs. The cost of operating the entire Maxey complex, which includes GOC, is approximately $41 per resident per day, or $15,008 per resident per annum [in 1975]. The director of GOC believes that the Center's cost is probably close to that figure, perhaps slightly lower. These costs include all expenses related to the offender's stay at GOC (with the minor exception of the cost of the assigned community worker—a technicality which amounts to about 92 cents per day for each resident).

Evaluation. A major caveat should be noted: The data on GOC are not available for certain kinds of variables, and in other instances the available data are for very short follow-up periods. This situation will be much improved when the new computerized system becomes fully operational. The system is beginning to provide useful longitudinal data on GOC residents.

Recidivism.   Based on 3-month and 12-month postrelease data, Green Oak seems to do a commendable job, especially considering the nature of its clientele. For arrest data (which are the best indicators here, since "contact" with law enforcement officials might be expected for a recently released GOC youth, who is likely to attract some surveillance), the 1974–1975 baseline figure for GOC was 35 percent. This compares with arrest rates of 25 percent, 14 percent, and 39 percent for the other units of Maxey Training School,

> Overall, boys sent to GOC achieved only slightly poorer outcomes than boys sent to other institutions. If the first, second, and third discharges were combined, 34 percent of the boys at GOC achieved good outcomes, vs. 37 percent of the boys placed at Lansing or Maxey.

This evaluation must be supplemented by the reminder that GOC was dealing with the most serious offenders. These rates and percentages are not for control groups; rather, these rates compare GOC residents with residents of other facilities without controlling for the more serious risks associated with GOC residents, who tend to have both longer and more serious involvement in delinquent behavior.

Job and School Involvement.   Baseline data on job/school outcomes for 1974–1975 (at 3 months postrelease) again show GOC releases doing relatively well. Combining the categories "job full time" and "school full time," 42 percent of GOC releases were involved on a full-time basis, compared with rates ranging from 18 to 47 percent for other institutions. In fact, when part-time involvement in job/school was added, GOC had the fourth best record of the 10 institutions compared.

Length of Stay.   The average length of stay for GOC residents ($n = 96$) in the 1974–1975 baseline survey was about 10 months. (None were released in less than 3 months, 40 percent were released in 4 to 7 months, 33 percent released in 8 to 11 months, and 27 percent remained longer than 11 months.) Comparable length-of-stay data for other institutional centers included: Intensive Treatment Program, 226 days; Arbor Heights Center, 799; Adrian Training School (girls), 393; Adrian Training School (boys), 334; combined youth camps, 163; and Maxey Training School, 305 to 317 days. Again, GOC's record appears impressive, especially considering the presumed need for lengthy treatment of more seriously disturbed juveniles and considering that GOC graduates do about as well as others in terms of recidivism.

JUVENILE INSTITUTIONAL REFORM IN MASSACHUSETTS

It is symbolic that the state to first establish a training school should be the first to shut such institutions. From 1965 to 1968 the Massachusetts Division of Youth Services (DYS) was the subject of investigations as a result of allegations of brutality at its institutions. In 1969, as part of a reform effort, Jerome Miller was appointed

DYS Commissioner. His efforts were highlighted by a series of humanizing changes at juvenile institutions: no more shaved heads, institutional clothing, or striking residents. Miller moved the DYS away from an approach that emphasized discipline and punishment, in favor of therapeutic programming. Finally, the most dramatic of his reforms: Dr. Miller began closing institutions and placing residents on parole, in community-based private institutions,* or foster care. As of 1980, only 101 youngsters were being maintained in secure facilities, while another 1700 were in placement in group homes, foster care, etc. (Ryan, 1980: 23).

Dr. Miller left Massachusetts for a position in Illinois in 1973. Although Massachusetts has not reversed Dr. Miller's reforms, neither have other states been quick to follow the Massachusetts example. The trend in juvenile justice has been in the direction of severity. The wide media coverage given to serious crimes committed by youngsters has caused legislatures to increase sanctions—not a role for the juvenile court—or to move more offenses out of the juvenile court and into the adult criminal court. This trend was experienced in New York, where training school maximum commitments were increased to five years for certain serious juvenile offenders, with the first 12 months having to be spent in a "secure facility." Juveniles as young as 13 charged with certain serious offenses can be processed in the adult criminal court.

Lindsay Hayes and Robert Johnson argue that many of the problems endemic to adult prisons (see Chapter 8) are present in modern training schools. Despite the rhetoric of "treatment," the overriding concern of institutional management is security—preventing escapes. Institutionalization of youngsters and meaningful treatment, they argue, do not mix (1980: 13): "With rare and evanescent exceptions, not even a dedicated staff, a low resident-staff ratio, and diversified programming are sufficient to offset the general anti-therapeutic effects of the penal institution."

AFTER CARE/PAROLE

Aftercare is the planned release of a juvenile from an institution to supportive services in the community. The juvenile may continue under probation supervision or in some jurisdictions be supervised by other aftercare (parole) workers. Aftercare services are often provided by the same agency that administers the juvenile institutions. For example, I worked for the New York State Department of Social Welfare, which used to operate the state training schools. I had the title "Youth Parole Worker" and was responsible for supervising juveniles released from the boys training schools.

The first responsibility of the aftercare worker is to plan for the release and placement of the young person. Placement plans include where the juvenile will live, whether he/she is to work or attend school, or both, and arrangements for any

---

*Paul Lerman notes that community-based alternatives to institutionalization may not represent actual improvements. He points to numerous instances of child abuse in such settings (1980: 295–96).

supportive services that may be available in the community. The young person may be returned to his/her own home, if this is desirable, or be placed in an alternative setting, such as a foster home, group home, or halfway house. The aftercare worker usually investigates placement alternatives and finalizes a program plan which is submitted to the training school officials responsible for release decision making.

The release plans are evaluated at the institution, together with the child's social history and record of adjustment while in the training school. The decision to send a child home is based on the conditions in the home, the attitude of the parents, and their concern for the child's welfare. If the home situation is considered unsatisfactory, the child may be placed with a relative, in a group home, or in foster care. When a young person is placed in a group home or foster care, the worker will spend time with the foster parents or the home staff as well as with the child, to help the adjustment to the new surroundings. The worker will also continue to work with the natural parents to help them accept placement outside their home and to assist them in preparing for the youngster's eventual return to his/her own home.

ITEMS FOR STUDY

1. The underlying basis for the juvenile court is *parens patriae*.
2. The juvenile court is a clear manifestation of the Positive School.
3. The intake officer in the juvenile court has many of the functions of a prosecutor, for which he/she may not be equipped.
4. There are two types of cases handled by the juvenile court (with respect to acting-out behavior): unofficial and official.
5. The predisposition report serves as the basis for assisting a youngster adjudicated in juvenile court.
6. The position of judge in the juvenile court is a difficult one often beyond the ability of those who hold the position.
7. There are a variety of dispositions available to the juvenile court, and they should be designed to fit the needs of the child. Often, however, this is not the case.

chapter 5

Presentence Investigation

The second basic service provided by a probation agency is the presentence investigation, which, when reduced to writing, becomes the presentence report. The presentence report is usually made after the conviction of a defendant in a criminal case, and it has five purposes:

1. The primary purpose is to help the court make an appropriate disposition of the case. The report should help in deciding for or against probation, in determining the conditions of probation, in deciding among available institutions, and in determining the appropriate length of sentence. The American Bar Association notes that "the primary purpose of the presentence report is to provide the sentencing court with succinct and precise information upon which to base a rational sentencing decision" (1970: 11).*

2. The presentence report serves as a basis for a plan of probation or parole supervision and treatment. The report indicates problem areas in the defendant's life, his/her capacity for using help, and the opportunities available in his/her environment and in the community. During the investigation the offender usually begins to relate to the probation department, learning how probation officers work and getting some understanding of the nature of the agency.

*The ABA's *Standards Relating to Probation* is printed in 18 volumes. Price is $3.25 for a single volume; bulk-order prices are $2.50 each for 10 to 24 of the same title, and $2.00 each for 25 or more of the same title. They may be ordered from ABA Circulation Dept., 1155 E. 60th Street, Chicago, Ill. 60637.

3. The presentence report assists prison personnel in their classification and treatment programs. Institutions depend heavily upon the report, particularly during the early part of the inmate's stay, when the institution is trying to understand and plan a program for the individual. The report can provide valuable material that will help in planning for the care, custody, and rehabilitation of the inmate. This includes everything from the type of custody required and the care of physical needs, to the planning of the various phases of the institutional program. Many institutions will have very little, if any, background or social information material other than that provided by the presentence report. This means that the report will have a marked effect on the way in which an inmate is approached and viewed by the institution since they will take the word of the probation officer over that of the inmate. The ideal report can give focus and initial direction to institution authorities for treatment and training as well as care and management.
4. The presentence report serves to furnish parole authorities with information pertinent to release planning and consideration for parole, and determination of any special conditions of parole.
5. The report serves as a source of information for research in corrections and criminal justice. Unfortunately, because of a lack of uniformity in form and content of the report, their usefulness is somewhat limited.

In the report the probation officer attempts "to focus light on the character and personality of the defendant, and to offer insight into his problems and needs, to help understand the world in which he lives, to learn about his relationships with people, and to discover salient factors that underlie his specific offense and conduct in general," and "to suggest alternatives in the rehabilitation process" (Division of Probation, 1974: 48). The report is not expected to show guilt or innocence, only to relate the facts that the probation officer has been able to gather during the course of the investigation.

THE INTERVIEW

In probation and parole, much of the necessary information is received directly from people. In the presentence report, most of the information is gained by interviewing. These interviews are conducted in all types of surroundings; from hot and noisy detention pens, where dozens of people may be awaiting arraignment, to the relative quiet of the probation office.

Obviously, a quiet, comfortable setting with a maximum of privacy is the best environment for an interview. A place that lacks privacy or has numerous distractions will adversely affect the productivity of the interview. Sometimes, interviews are conducted in the defendant's home. This provides an opportunity to observe the offender's home situation, and adds an additional and sometimes vital dimension to the report.

The interview is an anxiety-producing situation for the defendant. Previous experiences in similar situations, such as questioning by the police, may have been quite unpleasant. The probation officer (p.o.) tries to lower this anxiety by cordially introducing himself/herself and explaining the purpose of the interview and the presentence report. This is especially important for the defendant who is not familiar with the court process.

The p.o. may try to deal with matters of concern to the defendant. A married male defendant may be engaged in a discussion of how his wife and children can secure public assistance in the event that he is imprisoned. The p.o. might offer to write a letter of referral for the wife to take with her to the Department of Welfare. In some way, the officer must show genuine concern and interest in the defendant, at the same time being realistic enough to expect many answers and statements from the defendant that will be self-serving. Since the p.o.'s contact with the defendant is limited, the officer cannot expect to probe deeply into the defendant's personality.

Some defendants will be overtly hostile, while others will mask their hostility with "wisecrack" answers. The p.o. must control both temper and temperament. He/she is the professional and must never lose sight of that fact during the interview. In questioning, open-ended queries such as "What have you been doing?" should be avoided. Questions should be specific but require an explanation rather than a simple answer of "yes" or "no." The p.o. must avoid putting answers into the defendant's mouth with such questions as: "Did you quit that job because it was too hard?"

When the investigation is complete, the defendant should be reinterviewed in order to give him/her an opportunity to refute certain information, or clarify any aspects of the report which are in conflict.

REVIEW OF RECORDS AND REPORTS

The probation officer will be reviewing several records and reports in the course of his/her investigation. The first is the arrest record of the defendant. This record will take the form of an arrest sheet from the Federal Bureau of Investigation or another law enforcement agency, such as the state police. These forms usually contain numerous abbreviations that must be deciphered by the p.o. if the record is to be useful. The arrest sheet does not describe the offense; it contains only the official charge, for example, *Burglary 3rd*. There is no mention of the type of premises that were burgled and what was taken. In addition, the sheet often omits the disposition of the arrest. The officer may not be able to determine from the report what happened to the case. Therefore, it is necessary to check with the agency that made the arrest and the court that processed the case.

The nature of the defendant's prior record is extremely important. The law of many jurisdictions provides for a harsher sentence if the defendant has a prior felony conviction. In addition, the defendant's eligibility for probation and a variety of treatment programs, such as drug rehabilitation, may be affected by his/her prior record.

The p.o. will review the reports concerning the current offense, in addition to interviewing the arresting officer. He/she will look for information that was omitted during the trial, possibly including mitigating or aggravating circumstances, and perhaps giving a different perspective on the offense. The officer will review any previous presentence reports as well as reports of other correctional agencies that have had contact with the defendant. These might include training schools or residential treatment centers, and prison and parole agencies. The p.o. will also review the school records of the defendant.

If there are any psychiatric or psychological reports available, the p.o. will review and analyze them. To do this, the p.o. must understand the nomenclature used by psychiatrists and psychologists, and the meaning of any tests administered by the latter.

The p.o. should make a judgment as to whether a psychiatric and/or psychological referral should be made during the probation investigation. Indiscriminate referrals to mental health clinics or court psychiatrists are wasteful since crime and delinquency are not necessarily symptomatic of an internalized conflict. In those cases where symptoms of mental disorder are obvious, and in those situations where the offender may benefit from an exploration of his/her problems, a referral should be made. If no referral is made or there is a lack of psychiatric and psychological information, the p.o. should present his/her own observations concerning the defendant's intellectual capacity and personality. This will include such things as the offender's contact with reality and ability to express thoughts.

If the p.o. has received conflicting information about the defendant, and is unable to reconcile the discrepancies, this should be pointed out in the report and not left up to the reader to discover (or *not* discover).

Of crucial importance in any presentence report are the sections entitled *Evaluative Summary* and *Recommendation*. Nothing should appear in either of these sections that is not supported by the rest of the report. The summary contains the highlights of the total report, and should serve as a reminder to the reader of the information that has already been presented. The recommendation is a carefully thought out statement, based on the officer's best professional judgment. It contains the alternatives that are available in the case and reflects the individualized attention that each case received (Carter, 1966: 41).

Robert Carter notes that the probation officer is in a unique position with respect to making a recommendation to the judge. "The officer has had an opportunity to observe the defendant in the community, not only from a legal-judicial, investigative perspective, but also from the viewpoint of a general life-style" (p. 41). In order to present a meaningful recommendation, the p.o. must have knowledge of the resources and programs that are available. Unfortunately, a p.o. sometimes submits a recommendation for a treatment program that is not available either in the community or at a correctional institution.

One question that the p.o. must decide in the recommendation is whether or not to recommend probation. In many jurisdictions a conviction for certain crimes, or a previous felony conviction, precludes a sentence of probation. The p.o. must know the statutes of the applicable jurisdiction. The officer must also weigh the potential danger of the defendant to the community, must evaluate the defendant's rehabilitation potential and ability to conform to probation regulations, and must consider whether probation will be construed by the community as too lenient in view of the offense committed, or as "getting away with it" by the defendant.

Carter (1978: 15) recommends that the presentence report "be tailored to meet the needs of individual criminal justice systems and be relatively short." He quotes John Hogarth (p. 15):

> There is considerable research evidence suggesting that in human decision-making the capacity of individuals to use information effectively is limited to the use of not more than five or six items of information. In many cases, depending on the kind of information used, the purposes to which it is put, and the capacity of the individual concerned, the limit is much less. Despite this evidence there is a noticeable tendency for presentence reports to become longer. One of the most unfortunate myths in the folk-lore concerning sentencing, is the notion that the courts should know "all about the offender." Quite apart from whether much of the information is likedly to be reliable, valid or even relevant to the decision possibilities open to the court, the burden of a mass of data can only result in information-overload and the impairment of the efficiency in which relevant information is handled. This suggests that if probation officers wished to improve the effectiveness of their communications to magistrates they would be advised to shorten their reports.

REQUIRING A PRESENTENCE REPORT

In some states the law requires a presentence report for crimes punishable by more than one year of imprisonment; in others the judge retains the discretion to order the report. In Missouri, for example, every person convicted of a felony will have a presentence investigation unless s/he waives this right. In Utah, long-form presentence reports are prepared in all cases involving felonies or serious misdemeanors involving violence. Short-form reports are prepared for some lesser misdemeanors. The American Bar Association recommended that all "courts should be supplied with sufficient resources to call for a presentence investigation and written report in every criminal case, including misdemeanors" (1970: 4). The President's Commission recommended that "all courts should require presentence reports for all offenders, whether reports result from a full field investigation by probation officers or, in the case of minor offenders, from the use of short forms" (1972: 355). A report by the Comptroller General of the United States (1976) states that in 46 percent of the cases sampled (in four representative counties in the United States) presentence investigations had not been made. Additionally, of those reports that had been completed, the Comptroller General found many that were deficient in information and/or verification of information.

CRITICISM OF THE PRESENTENCE REPORT

Abraham Blumberg maintains that some judges do not read the presentence report, while others carefully select passages condemning the defendant to read aloud in the courtroom in order to justify their sentences (1970: 157). He argues that many judges discount the report because of the hearsay nature of the information (pp. 160–61). Willard Gaylin is concerned with the enormous dependence on the presentence report that tends to make the probation officer, rather than the judge, the sentencer (1974: 13–14). In some jurisdictions the probation officer is overburdened with presentence reports and does not have the time to do an adequate investigation and prepare a (potentially) useful report. In courts where the judge usually pays little or no attention to the contents of the report, the probation officer will not be inclined to pursue the necessary information and prepare well-written reports. Jonas Robitscher (1980: 35), an attorney as well as a psychiatrist, states that while psychiatric reports and evaluations often make the difference between probation, a short sentence, or a long sentence, "Many of these reports and evaluations contain dynamic formulations about the cause of behavior based on as little as twenty minutes spent with the subject of the report."

Rodney Kingsnorth and Louis Rizzo (1979) investigated the relationship between plea bargaining, the probation officer's sentencing recommendation, and the final disposition of the case in a large western county. In this county, after the defendant has accepted a "bargain" in exchange for a plea of guilty, the case is sent to the probation department for a presentence investigation and sentencing recommendation. They found a very high correlation (93 percent) between the recommendation and the sentence, which is in accord with other research on this issue. However, Robert Dawson (1969: xi) states that the probation officer may write into the presentence report the recommendation that he/she believes will be well received by the judge. Czajkoski (1973) suggests that the prosecutor often finds a way of communicating the plea bargain agreement to the probation department and the latter responds with a conforming recommendation or no recommendation at all.*

Kingsnorth and Rizzo point out that in the county they studied the minutes of the plea bargaining session, including the details of the negotiated agreement, are sent to the probation department prior to the submission of the presentence report. They conclude that "probation officer concurrence with previously negotiated sentence agreements is a consequence, not of case characteristics but of pressures emanating from the organizational structure of which the probation is a part, namely, the court system itself" (1979: 9).

These, and other studies, serve to remind us that the probation officer is simply one actor in a rather complex setting. How much influence he/she can exert may often depend on procedural or structural variables, or perhaps the probation officer's force of personality.

---

*Walter Dickey found that in Wisconsin: "The prosecutor is often influenced by the recommendation in the report and the information underlying it. Some prosecutors frequently adopt the report's recommendations as their own recommendation to the court or use it as a benchmark in deciding on their recommendation. Sometimes a pleas agreement will include the condition that the prosecutor will adopt the report's recommendation as his own" (1979: 30).

CONFIDENTIALITY
OF THE PRESENTENCE REPORT

There is some controversy over whether or not the contents of the presentence report should be disclosed to the defendant (or his/her attorney). In some jurisdictions law or custom allow the defendant access to the report; other states give the judge the option of disclosing the contents of the report; and in some states the report is confidential by statute.

The basic argument against disclosure is that sources of information must be protected or they will hesitate to provide information. Family members or employers may fear retribution from the defendant if they provide negative information. In addition, the police may be reluctant to provide confidential information if the defendant will be privy to it.

The basic argument in favor of disclosure is to enable the defendant to contest information that he/she considers unfair, and to be protected from the effects of unfounded information. Norm Larkins, a probation officer in Alberta, Canada, states: "Disclosure of information has led probation officers to develop techniques whereby the information obtained by them and presented in the report is more objective and accurate (with less reliance on hearsay information)." Before the initial interview with the defendant is conducted, "it is explained that a copy of the report will be made available to the offender or his legal counselor prior to sentencing. It is the duty of the offender to bring to the judge's attention any mistakes or omissions which he feels would be important in influencing the sentencing" (1972: 59).

Dickey reports on some of the types of inaccurate or misleading information he found in probation reports in Wisconsin (1979: 33–34):

(1) rumors and suspicions that are reported without any factual explanation; (2) incomplete explanations of events that leave a misleading impression; (3) factual errors relating, usually, to the criminal record of the offender.

Rumors and suspicions are often reported in presentence reports and identified as such. The report that the rumor exists may be accurate. What is objectionable is the fact that the subject of the rumor may cause the reader to give more weight to the rumor than it deserves, if any. If the rumor is without foundation, reference to it is particularly troubling.

It is difficult to assess the impact of rumors, though they sometimes seem to directly affect correctional decisions. For example, one sex offender's presentence report contained the statement that the offender "was rumored to have killed his mother." This was referred to in several parole decisions before it was investigated. Upon inquiry, it was determined to the satisfaction of the parole board that the offender had been confined in another state at the time of his mother's death and had no connection to it.

Some reports do not contain complete information and are therefore misleading. One inmate's report contained the statement that he "had been arrested for attempted first degree murder after a barfight. The charges were later dropped." Investigation showed that the reason the charges were dropped was that the inmate was actually the victim of an attack and not the aggressor. The other person involved was later charged with a crime for the attack.

The most frequently recurring factual problem with the reports is related to past offenses.

The so-called "FBI Rap Sheet" or "Yellow Sheet" is part of the report. It contains a confounding listing of past offenses that is frequently repetitious, i.e., it reports the same offense more than once. The repetitions are not so identified. Past charges do not always contain their disposition, so the reader is never sure how many offenses there actually were, which were dropped and why, what the facts underlying the charges and offenses are, and what the outcome was.

In the Maryland federal district the contents of the presentence report are customarily revealed to the defendant. However, the probation officer's recommendation and other confidential information (e.g., psychiatric reports) are withheld. The American Bar Association recommends that all information that adversely affects the defendant should be discussed with the defendant or his/her attorney. The President's Commission stated that "in the absence of impelling reasons for non-disclosure of specific information, the defendant and his counsel should be permitted to examine the entire presentence report" (1972: 356). The National Advisory Commission recommends that the presentence report be made available to the defense and the prosecution (1973: 188). The Commission rejects the argument that sources of information will "dry up"; the Commission states that "(1) those jurisdictions which have required disclosure have not experienced this phenomenon; and (2) more importantly, if the same evidence were given as testimony at trial, there would be no protection or confidentiality" (p. 189).

Dickey found a most distressing problem related to the issue of erroneous information (1979: 35):

> Even when an alleged error is challenged at sentencing and a contrary finding made, it does not necessarily follow that the report will be corrected. When a judge makes a finding of fact that is inconsistent with the presentence report, he usually states the finding in the record of the sentencing hearing. Without more, this leaves the report itself uncorrected. The sentencing transcript is not made a part of the report; it is not attached to it. The oral finding does not signal anyone to amend the report or any of the copies of it. Subsequent users of the report, correctional and parole authorities, rely on the uncorrected report. Rarely is the report amended to reflect additional information or findings of fact inconsistent with it at sentencing.

Dickey also points out that defendants are often quite dissatisfied with the role of their attorneys with respect to the presentence report (p. 36):

> Another source of the sense of injustice is the belief that lawyers do not provide the court with positive information about the offender to supplement the presentence report which, it is frequently asserted, is incomplete. Sophisticated defendants realize that even the most forceful statements, if they are general, are of little value to their case. They recognize the importance of presenting the court with alternatives to confinement (i.e., job or school plan, place to live) if probation is sought or a specific statement of plans after release if a short period of confinement is the goal. These defendants are usually dissatisfied because they feel the court is forced to rely on an incomplete report because their lawyer did not provide the additional information.

In an effort to respond to this type of situation, I set up a unit of undergraduate criminal justice students from Western Carolina University in the Office of the Buncombe County Public Defender, North Carolina. Given the title *presentence interns,* the students acted as advocates on behalf of clients being represented by the public defender. An essential part of their responsibilities was the preparation of a presentence report supportive of the defendant. These reports were presented to the sentencing judge and defended by the public defender in oral arguments before sentencing. One interesting aspect of this program is that it required *no* funding source: the students received college credit and the public defender contributed secretarial services. A more extensive (funded) version of this effort is the New York City Legal Aid Society Pre-Trial Diversion and Presentence Program (see Abadinsky, 1979: 147–50, 258–61).

The courts have rather consistently upheld the confidentiality of the presentence report. This has usually been based on the (presumed) neutrality/objectivity of the probation officer—he/she has no interest in punishment; by disposition and training the p.o. is a helping, not a proscutorial agent. Thus, in the case of *Williams* v. *New York,* the judge imposed a sentence of death based on information in the presentence report. The defendant had been convicted of murder, but the jury recommended life imprisonment. The presentence report revealed that Williams was a suspect in 30 burglaries. Although he had not been convicted of these crimes, the report indicated that he had confessed to some and had been identified as the perpetrator of some of the others. The judge had referred to parts of the report which indicated that the defendant was ''a menace to society.''

Williams appealed the death sentence, arguing that the sentencing procedure violated due process of law ''in that the sentence of.death was based upon information supplied by witnesses with whom the accused had not been confronted and as to whom he had no opportunity for cross examination or rebuttal.'' The U.S. Supreme Court rejected this argument, stating:

Under the practice of individualizing punishments, investigational techniques have been given an important role. Probation workers making reports of their investigations have not been trained to prosecute but to aid offenders. Their reports have been given high value by conscientious judges who want to sentence persons on the best available information rather than on guesswork and inadequate information. To deprive sentencing judges of this kind of information would undermine modern procedural policies that have been cautiously adopted throughout the nation after careful consideration and experimentation. We must recognize that most of the information now relied upon by judges to guide them in the intelligent imposition of sentences would be unavailable if information were restricted to that given in open court by witnesses subject to cross-examination. And the modern probation report draws on information concerning every aspect of a defendant's life. The types and extent of this information make totally impractical if not impossible open court testimony with cross-examination. Such a procedure could endlessly delay criminal administration in a re-trial of collateral issues.

That was in 1949. In 1977, the Supreme Court ruled on a similar case, involving the death sentence of a defendant convicted of murder in Florida. In this case the court vacated the death sentence and ordered further sentence proceedings because the judge relied in whole or in part on a presentence report not fully disclosed to the defense (Oelsner, 1977: 23). In 1978, a U.S. Appellate Court in New York held that the rights of the defendant in sentencing would not be violated by the government's presentation of "information supplied by an unidentified informant where there is good cause for not disclosing his identity and the information he furnishes is subject to corroboration by other means." This case involved several organized crime figures (Lubasch, 1978: 28).

LONG- AND SHORT-FORM PRESENTENCE REPORTS

There are two basic types of presentence reports, the long form and the short form. The long form is usually more exhaustive and time-consuming than the short form. Increasing presssures on probation agencies for more presentence reports have resulted in the short form gaining popularity. Following are examples of both forms, short form first.

PRESENTENCE REPORT*

United States District Court
Central District of New York

Name: John Jones

Address:
   1234 Astoria Blvd.
   New York City

Legal Residence:
   Same

Age: 33

Date of Birth: 2-8-40
   New York City

Sex: Male

Date: January 4, 1974

Docket No.: 74–103

Offense: Theft of Mail by Postal Employee (18 U.S.C. Sec. 1709) 2 cts.

Penalty: Ct. 2–5 years and/or $2,000 fine

Plea: Guilty on 12-16-73 to Ct. 2 Ct. 1 pending

Verdict:

---

*From Division of Probation, "The Selective Presentence Investigation Report," *Federal Probation,* 38 (December 1974), pp. 53–54.

Race: Caucasian

Citizenship: U.S. (birth)

Education: 10th grade

Marital Status: Married

Dependents: Three
(wife and 2 children)

Soc. Sec. No.: 112-03-9559

FBI No.: 256 1126

Custody: Released on own
recognizance. No time in
custody.

Asst. U.S. Attorney:
Samuel Hayman

Defense Counsel: Thomas Lincoln,
Federal Public Defender

Drug/Alcohol Involvement:
Attributes offense to
need for drinking money

Detainers or Charges Pending:
None

Codefendants (Disposition):
None

Disposition:

Date:

Sentencing Judge:

Offense: Official Version.   Official sources revealed that during the course of routine observations on December 4, 1973, within the Postal Office Center, Long Island, New York, postal inspectors observed the defendant paying particular attention to various packages. Since the defendant was seen to mishandle and tamper with several parcels, test parcels were prepared for his handling on December 5, 1973. The defendant was observed to mishandle one of the test parcels by tossing it to one side into a canvas tub. He then placed his jacket into the tube and leaned over the tub for a period of time. At this time the defendant left the area and went to the men's room. While he was gone the inspectors examined the mail tube and found that the test parcel had been rifled and that the contents, a watch, was missing.

The defendant returned to his work area and picked up his jacket. He then left the building. The defendant was stopped by the inspectors across the street from the post office. He was questioned about his activities and on his person he had the wristwatch from the test parcel. He was taken to the postal inspector's office, where he admitted the offense.

Defendant's Version of Offense.   The defendant admits that he rifled the package in question and took the watch. He states that he intended to sell the watch at a later date. He admits that he has been drinking too much lately and needed extra cash for "drinking money." He exhibits remorse and is concerned about the possibility of incarceration and the effect that it would have on his family.

Prior Record

Date	Offense	Place	Disposition
5-7-66 (age 26)	Possession of Policy Slips	Manhattan CR. CT. N.Y., N.Y.	$25.00 Fine 7-11-66
3-21-72 (age 32)	Intoxication	Manhattan CR. CT. N.Y., N.Y.	4-17-72 Nolle

Personal History.   The defendant was born in New York City on February 8, 1940, the oldest of three children. He attended the public school, completed the 10th grade, and left school to go to work. He was rated as an average student and was active in sports, especially basketball and baseball.

The defendant's father, John, died of a heart attack in 1968, at the age of 53 years. He had an elementary school education and worked as a construction laborer most of his life.

The defendant's mother, Mary Smith Jones, is 55 years of age and is employed as a seamstress. She had an elementary school education and married defendant's father when she was 20 years of age. Three sons were issue of the marriage. She presently resides in New York City, and is in good health.

Defendant's brother, Paul, age 32 years, completed 2½ years of high school. He is employed as a bus driver and resides with his wife and two children in New York City.

Defendant's brother, Lawrence, age 30 years, completed three semesters of college. He is employed as a New York City firefighter. He resides with his wife and one child in Dutch Point, Long Island.

The defendant after leaving high school worked as a delivery boy for a retail supermarket chain then served 2 years in the U.S. Army as an infantryman (ASN 123 456 78). He received an honorable discharge and attained the rank of corporal serving from 2-10-58 to 2-1-60. After service he held a number of jobs of the laboring type.

The defendant was employed as a truck driver for the City of New York when he married Ann Sweeny on 6-15-63. Two children were issue of this marriage, John, age 8, and Mary, age 6. The family has resided at the same address (which is a four-room apartment) since their marriage.

The defendant has been in good health all of his life but he admits he has been drinking to excess the past 18 months, which has resulted in some domestic strife. The wife stated that she loved her husband and will stand by him. She is amenable to a referral for family counseling.

Defendant has worked for the Postal Service since 12-1-65 and resigned on 12-5-73 as a result of the present arrest. His work ratings by his supervisors were always "excellent."

Evaluative Summary. The defendant is a 33-year-old male who entered a plea of guilty to mail theft. While an employee of the U.S. Postal Service he rifled and stole a watch from a test package. He admitted that he planned on selling the watch to finance his drinking, which has become a problem, resulting in domestic strife.

Defendant is a married man with two children with no prior serious record. He completed 10 years of school, had an honorable military record, and has a good work history. He expresses remorse for his present offense and is concerned over the loss of his job and the shame to his family.

Recommendation. It is respectfully recommended that the defendant be admitted to probation. If placed on probation the defendant expresses willingness to seek counseling for his domestic problems. He will require increased motivation if there is to be a significant change in his drinking pattern.

Respectfully submitted,

Donald M. Fredericks
U.S. Probation Officer

ADULT PRESENTENCE REPORT

Somerset County Probation Department
State of New Jersey

Name: Howard Peter Williams

Alias: None

Born: June 2, 1950

Sex: Male

Address:
  409 Franklin Boulevard
  Franklin Township, N.J.

Place of Birth:
  New Brunswick, N.J.

Original Charge(s):
  Armed Robbery; Assault with Intent to Rape

Indictment No.: 128-71-M

Final Charge(s): Armed Robbery N.J.S. 2:A 141-1 & 2A:151-5
  Plea Bargain: Second count of indictment dismissed.

Conviction: *Plea:* X   *Date:* Dec. 13, 1972

Sentence Date: Feb. 9, 1973

Assigned:
  X (Public Defender),
  Paul P. Morgan

Judge: Paul E. Martin

Retained:

Date of Arrest: May 12, 1972   *Custodial Status:* ROR: (date)

Bail: $500 (revoked 10/16/72);   *Codefendant(s):* Allan Murray,
150 days jail time   Y.C.I., Pending Sentencing

Disposition: On Robbery charge, 7–10 years State Prison, Trenton, and on charge of Being Armed, additional term 3–5 years State Prison, Trenton; consecutive to sentence imposed on charge Robbery. 150 days jail time credit.

Circumstances of Offense

Official Version.   On May 12, 1972 at 8:05 p.m., police responded to the report of an armed robber at Glenn's Discount Center, 1450 Hamilton St., Franklin Twp., N.J. The perpetrators were described as two males, one of whom was armed with a shotgun. They had threatened the woman manager with the weapon, and had gotten away with several cartons of cigarettes. The getaway vehicle was observed almost immediately, and a high-speed chase ensued, lasting 20 minutes. The suspect's vehicle ran through several road-blocks, but was eventually halted with assistance from the New Brunswick Pol. Dept. after a collision with a parked car. Three subjects, including the defendant, were taken into custody. A 12-gauge shotgun, five (5) buckshot shells, and eight (8) cartons of cigarettes were found in the car.

Defendant's Version.   Defendant related that he was approached by Allan, a codefendant, who told him he knew of a place they could rob, and that it would be "an easy touch." Allan also supplied the shotgun and getaway car. Defendant admitted to holding a shotgun on the manager while Allan went to the cash register.

Remarks of Complainant, Victims, Witnesses.   The Victim was interviewed, but stated that she was so shaken by the incident that she preferred not to make a statement for the record.

Comments.   Police reports indicate that after the defendant forced the victim into the bathroom at gunpoint, he demanded that she remove her clothing and lay on the floor. When she refused to comply, the defendant threatened her, and said "I'll blow your head off." Defendant then placed his hand on her genital area and when she pushed his hand away, defendant slapped her face. The victim escaped when the defendant's attention was diverted by Allan, a codefendant.

Offense History

Detainers: None

Juvenile: Yes ✳✳ No ___
(See Attached)
Adult: Yes ✳✳ No ___

Age of First Conviction: _____ 19 Years _____

Offense: _____ Disorderly Person (Trespassing) _____

Explain: Police investigating a reported breaking and entering, found the defendant near a tire company warehouse at 11:22 p.m. Defendant admitted to trespassing and was fined $50.00 plus $10.00 Costs.

Previous Probation, Institutionalization, Parole. Defendant's brief exposure to juvenile probationary supervision by this department ended with incarceration following two violations within 10 days of each other. Since then, defendant has been returned to the institution as a parole violator. He has been at Annandale and Bordentown, where his overall adjustment could be considered as fair at best. Defendant's conduct and attitude while on parole were poor. Since being placed on probation in Middlesex County on March 6, 1972, defendant has been convicted of Armed Robbery twice.

Evaluation of Past Record and Comments. Records indicate that defendant's rejection of any form of authority accounts for his juvenile record. Defendant has been using heroin for the past six years. This, together with his many previous and continuing problems, has seen him become involved in more aggressive acting out against society. Defendant has thus far failed to respond to probation or parole supervision, and did not avail himself of an opportunity to complete a drug rehabilitation program.

Residence

How Long Has Defendant Lived in the Present:

Town or City: _____ 22 Years _____
County: _____ 22 Years _____
State: _____ 22 Years _____

Comments: Except for periods of incarceration, defendant has resided at one of two addresses on Franklin Boulevard, Franklin Township, N.J. for all of his life.

Family History

Parental. Def. is the younger of 2 sons born of his parents' marriage. Defendant's father deserted the family in 1958, and his mother moved to Elizabeth, N.J., where she entered a paramour relationship which produced 3 children. Def. was raised by his maternal grandparents but has been on his own since his grandmother died in 1968. Def. expressed affection for his grandmother, but admitted that she was unable to give him the necessary supervision and guidance.

Marital. Def. married one Geraldine (née Wilson Williams) on Nov. 25, 1969 at Franklin Twp., N.J. Two children were born of this marriage, which ended in divorce on Feb. 18, 1972. Defendant's children are Caroline, age 2½; and Howard, Jr., age 16 months. Def. indicated that his marital breakup was the result of his continued use of heroin and involvement in criminal activities. Def. related that his wife has since moved from this area, and her present whereabouts are unknown. Efforts by this department to locate defendant's wife have been unsuccessful.

Community Involvement and Ties

Def. is a lifelong area resident, and has several relatives residing in Franklin Twp., N.J.

Military History

Branch of Service:
Length of Service:
Type of Discharge:
Military Discipline:
Service No.

Comments: Def. was classified 4-F on May 15, 1970 by Local Board No. 40, Somerville, N.J.

Educational Achievement

In school now: Yes _____ No. ___**___
If yes, name of school:
Grade:
If no, highest grade completed: __eighth__
Age left school: __17 years__
Reason for leaving:
Incarceration (See Juvenile Record).

Comments on Educational Background.   It appears that defendant received a social promotion to the ninth grade, as he had failed all but one of his previous courses. Records indicate that defendant was a chronic discipline problem, in that he constantly challenged school authorities, and projected an image of belligerence. Defendant was tested at Annandale in 1965 and found to have I.Q. of 88.

Physical Information

Height: __5'7"__   *Weight:* __150 lbs.__

Distinguishing marks and discussion of physical appearance:
Abdominal scar (appendectomy)
3" scar upper right arm (knife wound)

Health
   Physical:
      No problems: _____
      Previous or existing problems:
Defendant related that he has had a kidney infection since April 1972.
   Mental:
      No problems: See Below
      Previous or existing problems:

Comments.   Def. was examined at the N.J. State Diagnostic Center at Menlo
Park on July 8, 1965. Def. was a patient at the N.J. State Hospital, Vroom
Building, Trenton, N.J. from Jan. 3, 1973 to Jan. 25, 1973. Def. entered the
Discovery House drug program on March 6, 1972 and was ejected by the staff
on May 3, 1972 due to ". . . an unwillingness on his part to conform to house
regulations, despite numerous opportunities to correct his attitude."

History of Drug and/or Alcohol Usage.   Def. admitted to a six-year history of
heroin addiction. He related that his last habit was 15 "bags" per day. Def.
refused to comment on how he supported his habit. Def. stated that he drinks
alcoholic beverages in moderation.

Drug and/or Alcohol Relevance to Present Offense.   Considering defendant's
drug history, it appears that his motivation was to obtain money for drugs.

Employment

   Social Security No.:   163-24-6197

Present Employment: Unemployed
   Employer:
   Address:
   Nature of Work:
   Employment Started: _____
   Earnings: _____
   Employer Comments:

Comments on Past Employment

   If Unemployable, Explain: _____Presently incarcerated_____

   Means of Subsistence during Periods of Unemployment: _____
Lived with relatives and friends.

   Occupational Skills, Ambitions, and Interests: _____
Def. has no occupational skills or interests, and voiced no ambitions for the
future.

Comments on Employment History.   Def. has been unemployed since Sept.

1971. His longest period of employment was with Revlon, Inc., Edison Twp., N.J., where he worked from Aug. 1969 to March 1970, as a Porter. Defendant's other periods of employment were generally for less than one month.

Financial Status

Assets:	None
Liabilities:	None

Analysis

Assessment of Factors Contributing to Present Offense

It appears that the codefendant Allan assembled a "team" to execute the present offense. Allan supplied the car and shotgun, as well as suggesting the place for the armed robbery. Murray was chosen to drive the car, while the def. handled the shotgun and threatened the woman manager. All three participants were heroin users, and it would seem that their motivation was to obtain money for drugs.

Assessment of Defendant's Personality, Problems, and Potentials as Related to Adjustment

Defendant's involvement in the present offense is seen as the last in a series of offenses against society which have become more aggressive and violent with the passage of time. He is the product of a broken home, and was never afforded the supervision and discipline necessary in his formative years. Defendant's marriage ended in divorce as the result of his drug abuse and criminal activity. Def. was a problem in school, and has never developed work habits. His heroin addiction has compounded the preexisting problems. Def. has failed to "make it" on probation, parole, or in a drug rehabilitation program. He appears to be unready to deal with his problems at the present time.

Community Resources of Potential Assistance in This Case
Not relevant.

Signature of Officer:

_____

Prior Record

Juvenile

4/2/65	Franklin Twp., N.J.	Intoxicated (found unconscious while being carried by two companions)	6/18/65 Juv. & Dom. Rel. Ct. of Som. City. N.J. one day exam at N.J. Diagnostic Center.

Between 4/19/65 and 4/27/65	Franklin Twp., N.J.	Larceny of 4 motor vehicles (subject admitted to taking 7 different cars)	
5/24/65	New Brunswick, N.J.	Larceny of Motor Vehicle	
6/6/65	Franklin Twp., N.J.	Open Lewdness (entered girls' locker room in high school and exposed himself to a girl in the nude by holding his penis)	7/29/65 Juv. & Dom. Rel. Ct. of Somerset County. Indet. term at Annandale Reformatory on all four complaints. Service of said sentences to run concurrently with each other. Paroled on 10/21/65.
6/26/67	Franklin Twp., N.J.	Idly Roaming Streets at night	12/8/67 Juv. & Dom. Rel. Ct. of Som. Cty. one year probation.
1/18/68	Franklin Twp., N.J.	Violation of Probation (Idly Roaming Streets at night)	1/19/68 Juv. & Dom. Rel. Ct. of Som. County cont. on prob.; 8:00 p.m. curfew.
1/28/68	Franklin Twp., N.J.	Unlawful Possession of Narcotics (Heroin) Violation of Probation (Curfew Violation)	2/9/68 Juv. & Dom. Rel. Ct. of Som. Cty. Ind. term N.J. Reformatory, to be delivered to the Y.R.C.C. at Yardville on each complaint service of said sentences to run concurrently with each other. 2/20/68 Transferred to Bordentown Unit. Paroled 7/3/69. Returned as Parole Violator 3/26/70. Discharged 2/11/71.
7/15/69	New Brunswick, N.J.	Disorderly Person (Trespassing)	$50.00 Fine, $10.00 Costs.
8/4/69	Clark Twp., N.J.	1. Carrying Concealed Weapon 2. Disorderly Person (possession of Narcotic Paraphernalia)	1. 2/19/70 Indictment dismissed prior to trial. 2. 1/28/71 $15.00 Fine, $10.00 Costs.
2/25/70	Franklin Twp., N.J.	Disorderly Person (Use of Narcotics —Heroin, as amended from original charge of Possession of Heroin)	3/16/70 6 months Somerset County Jail suspended. 18 mos. probation.
3/10/71	New Brunswick, N.J.	1. Carrying Concealed Weapon 2. Assault and Battery upon a Police Officer	3/6/72 Middlesex Cty Court. Indictment dismissed as a result of Plea Bargaining

5/13/71	Franklin Twp., N.J.	Disorderly Person (Failure to Give a Good Account and Failure to Register as a Narcotics User)	5/17/71 10 days Somerset County Jail.
5/23/71	New Brunswick, N.J.	Breaking and Entering Petty Larceny	3/6/72 Middlesex Cty. Ct., Ind. term at the Y.C.I., to be del. to the Y.R.C.C. at Yard-ville, susp., 5 years probation. Concurrent.
11/1/71	New Brunswick, N.J.	Possession of Revolver in Motor Vehicle without Requisite Permit to Carry Same	
7/10/72	New Brunswick, N.J.	Armed Robbery	12/5/72 Middlesex County Court. Found Guilty after Trial. Awaiting sentencing.

PRESENTENCE DIAGNOSIS*

California criminal courts have the option of sending, prior to sentencing, an individual convicted of a felony to the Department of Corrections for the purpose of obtaining a diagnostic evaluation and a recommendation for an appropriate sentence.

Felons are referred for up to 90 days of study and observation, within which period a report is made back to the court recommending a disposition in the case.

In arriving at the recommendations for each case referred by the courts, the Reception Center staff (of the Department of Corrections) performs a complete workup, utilizing both interviews and testing. Information on the life history, experiences, attitudes, psychiatric problems, and so on, of the individual is compiled in the Cumulative Summary, which is returned to the court together with the statement recommending either sentencing to prison or supervision in the community. In either event, RC staff have followed the practice of specifying the reasons for their recommendations.

Alternatives recommended for dealing with cases at the community level have included straight probation and probation with jail. Originally, the county referring a case for a diagnostic observation was to reimburse the state for the service. In 1965, the statute was modified to eliminate this requirement. The immediate effect was a marked increase in the utilization of the program.

INVESTIGATION STANDARDS FOR THE PROBATION OFFICES OF THE DISTRICT COURT DEPARTMENT AND THE BOSTON MUNICIPAL COURT DEPARTMENT

The goal of these investigation standards is to provide for pertinent, effective and uniform investigation substance and procedures for the probation officers

*The information in this section is from the California Department of Corrections.

within the District Court Department and the Boston Municipal Court Department of the Trial Court.

Purpose of the Reports

Probation investigation reports are prepared:

> To assist the judge in making a determination in a matter, generally criminal, before the court.

> To assist the probation officer in assessing the needs of those offenders who are placed under probation officer supervision.

Types of Reports

There are three probation investigation reports to be used depending on the informational needs of both the court and the probation officer:

Pre-trial Intake Report	The pre-trial intake report provides the court with readily available information that may be used at any stage of the criminal proceeding. This report is mandatory and is usually prepared prior to the defendant's initial court appearance.
Presentence Investigation Report	The presentence investigation report provides the court with more extensive data to assist in making disposition. This report is prepared at the request of the judge and following the determination of guilt or sufficiency of facts.
Post-disposition Investigation Report	The post-disposition investigation report provides the probation officer with information necessary to complete a Risk/Need classification of probation clients. It is conducted in those cases in which a defendant is placed under the supervision of a probation officer and information sufficient to complete a Risk/Need assessment and action plan needs to be obtained.

Standards for Probation Reports

1. The probation officer shall explain the purpose of the pre-trial intake report and where indicated the pre-sentence investigation report and the post-

disposition investigation report. (S)he shall explain the officer's role in the investigation process.

2. A pre-trial intake report shall be prepared by the probation officer prior to trial or probable cause hearing for all defendants appearing before the court on criminal charges.

3. The pre-trial intake report shall include readily available information consisting of identifying data, the defendant's residence, family, marital and employment status, the criminal record, and, if there be question of indigency, current finances and financial resources. Problem areas (physical, emotional, substance abuse, etc.), volunteered by the defendant, family, or other sources shall be noted in the pre-trial intake report. The pre-trial intake report may satisfy, in most instances, the dispositional/sentencing need of the judge.

4. Where more extensive information is required by the judge after a determination of guilt or finding of sufficiency of facts, a presentence investigation report shall be prepared by the probation officer.

5. The presentence investigation report is to provide the court with more extensive data. The probation officer shall confer with the judge to define the areas of such additional information required, and to establish a continuance date which would allow a reasonable amount of time to prepare the report. Generally the report should be completed within a 2-week period.

6. When scheduling a dispositional hearing in which the judge desires the presence of the probation officer, who has completed the presentence investigation report, notice should be given to the chief probation officer to assure the presence of the appropriate probation personnel at the hearing and such personnel shall attend, whenever possible, the dispositional hearing.

7. In addition to the pre-trial intake report data and the areas of additional information required by the judge in order to dispose of the case, the presentence investigation report shall include a summary that is an interpretation of the factual data included in the report and the probation officer's recommendation.

8. In addition to the pre-trial investigation data and the areas of information requested by the judge, the presentence investigation report shall include: the district attorney's investigative report, where available; the defendant's version of the offense(s) if (s)he is willing to furnish it; an analysis of the defendant's criminal history; a summary with an interpretation of the factual data included in the report; and the probation officer's recommendation as to the suitability of probation.

9. If requested by the judge, the presentence investigation report shall include the probation officer's recommendation concerning any special conditions of probation, and, where applicable, the offender's suitability for alternative dispositions.

10. If, in the course of the presentence investigation, the probation officer

discovers a physical or mental condition which in the probation officer's opinion requires professional evaluation, (s)he should recommend to the court that the defendant be referred to an appropriate resource.

11. Upon completion, the presentence investigation report shall be subject to review by the assistant chief probation officer or the chief probation officer.

12. The presentence investigation report shall be available to the judge prior to the designated date of disposition. There shall be prior availability for inspection of the presentence investigation report by the prosecutor and counsel for the defendant, subject to the provisions of the Massachusetts Rules of Criminal Procedure.

13. If a defendant is placed under probation officer supervision, a post-disposition investigation report shall be completed within 30 days after disposition in those cases in which there is not information sufficient to complete the Risk/Need assessment and action plan.

Reliability of Investigative Information

Information that is likely to influence (1) the judge's disposition/sentencing, (2) the probation officer's recommendations to the court, and (3) the probation officer's Risk/Need classification of client should be highly reliable. Therefore in preparing such investigation material and to assure a greater degree of reliability, probation officers should take the following steps:

1. The probation officer should identify the sources of information in the report.

2. The probation officer should make personal contact with informants or sources of information, when practicable, who can substantiate information. The probation officer should clearly state in the report those instances in which information has not been substantiated.

3. The probation officer should obtain pertinent documentation such as letters, clinical reports, school reports, certified statements, etc., when practicable. The probation officer should indicate when information in the report is supported by such documentation.

4. Sources of information should be identified in most instances; however, this does not exclude from a report relevant information from unnamed sources or informants with whom the probation officer has had personal contact. If a probation officer includes such information in an investigative report (s)he shall clearly indicate in the report that the information was obtained from sources or informants not being identified in this report.

ITEMS FOR STUDY

1. The presentence report has five purposes.

2. Information for the report is secured through interviews and the reviewing of records and reports.

3. States vary with respect to laws requiring a presentence report.
4. There is disagreement over the degree to which the presentence report influences sentencing.
5. There is some controversy over whether or not to disclose the contents of the report to the defendant. However, misleading or erroneous information in a report can 'have serious consequences for a defendant.

chapter 6

Supervision
of
Probationers

The dynamics of probation (and parole) supervision is discussed at length in Part Three. In this chapter we look at the granting of probation, conditions of probation, length of supervision, and violation of probation.

GRANTING PROBATION

Most states have statutory restrictions on who may be granted probation in felony cases. Crimes such as murder, kidnapping, and rape often preclude a sentence of probation, as do second or third felony convictions. When probation is a statutory alternative, judges differ in their approach to granting it. Although the recommendation of the probation department would be of obvious importance, some judges also seek advice from the police and the prosecutor. The geographic area where the court is situated may also affect the granting of probation. When court calendars are crowded, as they are in most urban areas, plea bargaining is more likely to result in probation being granted. The judge's feelings toward the particular offense or the offender may also enter into the sentencing decision. The many factors that determine if a defendant is granted probation contribute to the continuing controversy over "differential punishment."

However, there are factors which, to a greater or lesser extent, are considered in all cases relative to the granting of probation: the age and rehabilitation potential of the defendant; the defendant's criminal record, including indications of professional criminality and crimes of violence; the defendant's relationship with his/her family; evidence of any deviant behavior, such as drug abuse or sex offenses; and the attitude of the community toward the particular offense and the particular offender. There are also other questions which may be considered in determining whether or not probation is granted. Does the defendant's attitude toward the offense indicate genuine remorse? Was probation promised to the defendant to induce him/her to plead guilty? Will being placed on probation enable the defendant to provide the victim with restitution? Will being placed on probation enable the defendant to provide support and care for his/her family?

The quality of service provided by a probation agency must also be considered by the trial judge. Unfortunately, in some jurisdictions probation is nothing more than a suspending of sentence, since little or no supervision is actually provided.

The American Bar Association (ABA) presents the advantages of probation rather than imprisonment (1970: 3–4):

1. The liberty of the individual is maximized by such a sentence; at the same time the authority of the law is vindicated and the public effectively protected from further violations of the law.
2. The rehabilitation of the offender is affirmatively promoted by continuing normal community contacts.
3. The negative and frequently stultifying effects of confinement are avoided, thus removing a factor that often complicates the reintegration of the offender into the community.
4. The financial costs of crime control to the public treasury are greatly reduced by reliance on probation as an important part of the correctional system.*
5. Probation minimizes the impact on innocent dependents of the offender.

The ABA sets three conditions for a sentence of imprisonment rather than probation (pp. 3–4):

1. When confinement is necessary to protect the public from further criminal activity by the defendant.
2. When the offender is in need of correctional treatment which can effectively be provided if he/she is confined.
3. When the seriousness of the offense would be unduly depreciated if a sentence of probation were imposed.

CONDITIONS OF PROBATION

Although the Task Force on Corrections observed that "differential treatment requires that the rules be tailored to the needs of the case and of the individual offender" (1966: 34), this suggestion is often not put into practice. Probation departments require a defendant to sign a standard form which usually contains a variety of regulations that may or may not reflect the client's individual needs. There are also

*Imprisonment costs from 10 to 13 times as much as probation, according to most estimates.

special conditions that can be imposed by the judge or the probation department, such as fines and restitution. When a fine or restitution is beyond the ability of a defendant to pay, it may severely handicap the supervision process.

Sutherland and Cressey caution that when conditions of probation are too restrictive, the probation officer is inclined to overlook their violation. This can result in the probation officer losing the respect of the probationer (1966: 488). The ABA recommends that the conditions of probation be spelled out by the court at the time of sentencing, and emphasizes that they should be appropriate for the offender (1970: 9). However, probation regulations in different probation agencies tend to be markedly similar. They exhort the probationer to live a law-abiding and productive life, to work, and to support his/her dependents. They require that the offender inform the probation officer of his/her residence and that permission be secured before leaving the jurisdiction of the court. Some require that the probationer obtain permission before getting married, applying for a motor vehicle license, or contracting any indebtedness.

The South Carolina Probation, Parole, and Pardon Board is charged with the responsibility of supervising those offenders who have received a sentence of probation.

The following are conditions for Probation:

1. Refrain from the Violation of any State, Federal or Municipal Laws.
2. Refrain from associating with any person who has a criminal record.
3. Refrain from the unlawful use of intoxicants and you will not frequent places where intoxicants are sold unlawfully.
4. Refrain from the unlawful use of Narcotic Drugs and you will not frequent places where drugs are sold, dispensed or used unlawfully.
5. Refrain from having in your possession firearms or other weapons.
6. Work diligently at a lawful occupation.
7. Remain within the State of South Carolina unless permitted to leave by your supervising Probation Agent.
8. Agree to waive extradition from any State of the United States.
9. Follow the advice and instructions of the Probation Agent.
10. Permit the Probation Agent to visit your home, place of employment or elsewhere at any time.
11. Report to the Probation Agent as directed.
12. Pay all fines as ordered by the Court. Promptly notify the probation officer of any change in address or employment.

TERMS AND CONDITIONS OF PROBATION*

Fifth Judicial District Department of Court Services

Probation: *Number:*

Division: *Sentence:*

*From the Law Enforcement Assistance Administration.

To Whom These Presents Bring:

I, _____, having been granted (proba-
tion) (deferred sentence) on the _____ day of _____, 19_____, by
the District Court, Polk County, Iowa for the offense of _____ for
which the Court allowed me supervision under the authority of the Department
of Court Services. If sentence was deferred, the Court further ordered that I be
returned to the above named Court for further disposition on the _____ day of
_____ 19_____.

I do hereby agree to abide by the following terms and conditions as set forth
by the Court and Department of Court Services:

1. I will secure and maintain lawful employment as approved by my Probation Officer and I agree to contact same, within twenty-four (24) hours, if I lose
such employment.

2. I will support my dependents and fulfill all my financial obligations to the
best of my ability.

3. I will obey all laws and conduct myself honestly and responsibly in my
associations with others.

4. I will reside in Polk County, State of Iowa unless otherwise granted
permission by my Probation Officer.

5. I shall secure from my Probation Officer written and/or oral permission
before:
a.   changing employment
b.   borrowing money, going into debt, or buying on credit
c.   opening or using a checking account
d.   traveling outside my county of residence
f.   purchasing or operating a motor vehicle which shall be adequately
     covered by liability insurance
g.   changing place of residence

6. I will contact my Probation Officer as frequently as he may direct, by
oral/or written report.

7. I will not own, possess, carry or use a firearm or weapon of any kind.

8. I agree:
a.   to (completely abstain from) (limit) the use of alcoholic beverages
b.   to completely abstain from use of narcotic drugs, stimulants, hal-
     lucinogenics, or marijuana, except those prescribed to me by a licensed
     physician
c.   that upon request of my Probation Officer, I will submit to Toxicology
     testing
d.   to contact my Probation Officer immediately if I have any contact with
     Law Enforcement authorities
e.   that any information I have under my control, I will make available to
     my Probation Officer

9. I expressly agree and consent that should I leave the State of Iowa and be arrested in another state, I do hereby waive extradition to the State of Iowa from any state in which I may be found, and also agree that I will not contest any efforts by any jurisdiction to return me to the State of Iowa.

10. Special conditions:

_____

_____

_____

11. I understand that I am under the Supervision of the Fifth Judicial District Department of Court Services, and that any violation of the above conditions may be cause for a Report of Violation to be submitted to the Court which could lead to revocation of my probation privileges.

I hereby certify that I have had read to me the above stipulations, and I agree to co-operate fully with this Agreement until discharge by the Court. I further certify that I have received a copy of the Probation Agreement.

Signed and witnessed this _____ day of _____, 19_____.

_____   _____

Intake Agent   Signature

_____

Supervising Agent

Restitution

A number of jurisdictions impose restitution as a condition of probation. Steven Chesney discusses some of the issues in restitution as a condition of probation in Minnesota*:

It is clear that the most important determinant of whether an otherwise eligible defendant was to be ordered to make restitution was his supposed "ability to pay." As evident from both interviews with judges and from the cases themselves, this criterion was generally operationalized by choosing offenders who were white, well educated, and from the working and middle classes. This contrasted markedly with what is known about the criminal justice system in general. Those caught up in the system are overwhelmingly the poor, the lower class, and members of minority groups. Clearly, a large group of offenders, in whom the courts had little faith that restitution would be completed, were not ordered to make restitution.

*The remainder of this section, including the "Plan of Restitution," is taken from Steven L. Chesney, "The Assessment of Restitution in the Minnesota Probation Services," in *Restitution in Criminal Justice,* edited by Joe Hudson (St. Paul, Minn.: Minnesota Department of Corrections, n.d.), pp. 168–69, edited.

Considered in terms of the successful completion of restitution only, the pre-selection of middle-class offenders was the best way to ensure that restitution ordered was restitution collected. Generally, the groups favored to receive restitution as a condition of probation were the same groups who later successfully completed restitution. The court thus did not put itself into the position of ordering something it could not enforce. However, in terms of the use of restitution as a rehabilitative tool and as a method of victim compensation, the real needs may not have been addressed. One might assume that the well-educated and middle-class individuals or large and impersonal business that provided the bulk of the sample of victims were the victims least in need of compensation. Perhaps, the relatively well-educated and well-employed group of offenders that was able to pay restitution was the group of offenders for whom restitution had the least meaning.

Restitution may be one way that members of the more affluent social classes avoid prison. The data presented in this report may support this contention; members of the higher classes were the ones ordered to make restitution. Since some judges in the interviewed sample expressed approval of restitution as an alternative to prison sentences, some offenders may have gone to prison because the court assumed they couldn't earn enough money. In contrast, about as many judges made it clear that restitution was only considered after the individual was determined to be suitable for probation. In these cases the poor and unemployed escaped the sentence of restitution to the economic disadvantage of those in the higher social classes. If the use of restitution is to be extended for its rehabilitative and compensatory benefits, we must think of new ways to enable the poor to make restitution.

One way to enable poorer offenders to make restitution might be the increased use of partial restitution, even in amounts comprising only token attempts to make the victim whole. The argument for this approach is clouded, however, by the fact that such restitution may be less meaningful to both victim and offender, as evidenced by rate of failure of such sentences. Another alternative is greater correctional support and services for poorer probationers. Many agents reported that restitution obligations caused them to devote more time to job counseling and placement than they might otherwise have spent. One urban jurisdiction, for example, has found it necessary to specialize probation officers—one officer handles most restitution cases. Many other agents have expressed the need for vocational training or job placement programs for probationers. One largely untried alternative is the use of "in-kind" restitution service provided by the offender to the victim or to the community. Despite the approval expressed by the few victims and offenders who have experienced its use, it has few admirers on the bench. The undesirability of victim–offender contact, problems in supervising and evaluating the work performed, and the question of liability when a probationer is injured "on the job" are other reasons given by judges for not exploring this route. The successful experience of the community service by offenders program in England contradicts these fears. It has been found that such a program benefits offenders and the public. [See Beha et al., 1977: 15–20].

Without additional investments and special programs in support of the poorer or unemployed offender it is difficult to perceive how the potential rehabilitive uses of restitution can be realized. While correctional officers place faith in the rehabilitative effects of restitution, it is seldom used in the ways theorists have advocated as most rehabilitative. The emphasis on the ''creative restitution'' and its voluntary and expiative aspects was almost totally absent from the cases sampled, as was the emphasis on person contact through the contractual process between victim and offender as advocated by the Minnesota Restitution Center.

While restitution can hardly be termed a successful victim-compensation scheme, there are certainly valid arguments for its continued and expanded use. It does compensate some victims, and it does benefit some offenders (at least by keeping them out of prison). It should be possible to extend the use of restitution to benefit and compensate even more. However, there is an even simpler reason for the need to promote the use of restitution. This was best phrased by several judges and probation officers as ''a matter of simple justice.'' Restitution appeals to most of us at a very basic and deep level. It relates to our most fundamental notions of fairness and justice. This may explain why most victims questioned—even some who didn't receive a cent—would prefer to have their compensation come from the offender rather than the government. This could have important implications for the continued support by the public of the criminal justice system. It could also explain why conservatives and liberals are so uncritically supportive of a technique that has such a weak factual relationship to its professed goals.

Restitution is not addressed to a rehabilitative or victim compensatory need; instead, it answers a moral need. It reflects the way we feel that people should treat other people. As such, the evaluations of the effects of restitution may need to show only that it is no worse than other rehabilitative alternatives and that it does compensate some victims. Any effects beyond these are serendipitous because the *primary* goal of restitution is the elimination of the contradictions between our systems of morality and our criminal justice system.

PLAN OF RESTITUTION

To: Judge, Fifth Judicial District of Iowa

From: Probation Officer, Fifth Judicial District Department of Court Services

Date: December 17, 1973

Sentence and Charge

The record shows that on the 25th day of July 1973, the defendant appeared in Polk County District Court in person and with his attorney and entered a plea of guilty to the crime of Assault with Intent to Inflict Great Bodily Injury as defined in Section 694.6 of the 1973 Code of Iowa. The Court accepted said plea of guilty and requested that the Department of Court Services make a presentence investigation.

The record shows that on the 24th day of August 1973, the defendant appeared in Court with his attorney, this being the date set for sentencing. It was the order of the Court that the defendant be imprisoned at the Men's Reformatory at Anamosa, Iowa, for a term not to exceed one (1) year. It was further ordered that the sentence be suspended and the defendant be granted probation for a period of one (1) year.

On the 1st day of November 1973, a supplemental order was issued by the Court amending the original order. The supplemental order stated that the defendant would be responsible for payment of restitution as a condition of his probation.

On the 30th day of November 1973, a hearing was held in Polk County District Court to determine if the defendant's constitutional rights had been violated by the issuance of the supplemental order requiring payment of restitution. At this time, the defendant's appeal was denied. The defendant was ordered to pay restitution as stated in the order of November 1, 1973, and in accordance with Senate File 26. A violation of this order would be considered a violation of the defendant's probation.

Present Situation

The defendant is presently residing with his wife. There are no children of this marriage or for which the defendant pays child support. The defendant is employed. He has been temporarily laid off since December 12, 1973; however, he feels reasonably sure that he will be back at work by February of 1974. He has applied for unemployment benefits in the meantime. The defendant's usual salary would be $300.00 per month take-home. The defendant's wife is presently working two (2) jobs. She is employed full time by the United Way, where her take-home pay is $308.94 per month. Her second part-time job is with Blue Cross–Blue Shield, and her take-home pay here is approximately $100.00 per month. A list of the defendant's monthly expenses, totaling $659.24, is as follows:

Expense	Amount	Total—If Known
Rent	$120.00	
Finance co.	30.00	$630.00
Tire co.	15.00	225.00
Department store	20.00	200.00
Groceries	140.00	
Lawyer	25.00	700.00
Doctor	10.00	
Car repair	40.00	139.00
Renter's insurance	10.24	
Car, truck insurance	15.00	

Water	7.00	
Lights and gas	25.00	
Fuel oil	40.00	
Telephone	20.00	
Gas (car and truck)	40.00	
Miscellaneous	40.00	
Parking	12.00	
Car payment	45.00	643.00
Dentist	5.00	150.00
Total	$659.24	
Defendant	$300.00	
Wife	308.94	
	100.00	
total	$708.94	
less payments	659.24	
total	$ 54.70	

This figure does not include the $250.00 per month the defendant is to pay toward restitution.

Plan of Restitution

A summary listing of the bills incurred by the victims of this offense is as follows:

Expense	Amount	Insurance Paid	Balance
Ambulance	$ 42	$ —	$ 42
Doctor	128	75	53
Doctor	10	10	—
Doctor	1235	427.50	797.50
Doctor	35	35	2
Doctor	50	50	—
Anesthestist	139.40	139.40	—
Doctor	170	20	150
House of Vision	69.70	—	69.70
Doctor	17	—	17
Doctor	20	—	20
Iowa Lutheran	16	16	—
Iowa Lutheran	30	30	—
Car damage	78.49	78.49	—
Pharmacy	27.13	—	27.13
Pharmacy	6	—	6
Iowa Lutheran	1835.65	1835.65	—
Total	$3909.37	$2717.04	$1184.33

Receipts and insurance forms verifying the victim's bills are in the possession of this Agent and can be made available to the Court upon request.

In determining a reasonable Plan of Restitution, there seemed to be two (2) alternatives to consider. The first is that the defendant obtain a loan for the full or partial amount of expense incurred by the victim, reimburse the victim, and make monthly payments to the loan company. However, after talking with several loan companies, it was apparent to this Agent that a loan could not be obtained at this time by the defendant. The second alternative and the Plan to be submitted to the Court is that the defendant make monthly payments to the victims through the office of the Department of Court Services. The amount to be paid monthly figured at $25.00 and to continue through August 1974, which is the date the defendant is due for discharge from probation. At that time, the defendant will have paid a total of $200.00 in restitution.

Victim's Response

This Agent has talked with the victim at some length regarding his feelings toward the Plan of Restitution which is being submitted to the Court. Although the total to be paid does not nearly compensate the victims for their total expenses, the victim has indicated that he is very pleased to receive the amount settled on, as he did not originally feel he would get any reimbursement. He has expressed that his faith in justice is somewhat restored and is appreciative of the effort made on the Court's part to see that some restitution is made.

The victims have been informed that this payment of restitution in no way denies them the right to pursue recovery of additional compensation through civil action after August 1974, when the defendant is discharged from probation, if they should so desire.

Conclusion

This Plan of Restitution has been difficult to figure, primarily because of the great difference in the amount of the victim's expenses and the defendant's inability to pay. It is the opinion of this Agent that the Plan is a realistic one which the defendant will be able to follow.*

LENGTH OF SUPERVISION

The length of probation terms vary from state to state. The American Bar Association recommends that the term should be two years for a misdemeanor conviction and five years for a felony. States often allow for the termination of probation supervision

*The American Probation and Parole Association has actively promoted the concept of victim assistance through the IVSTP Project (''Improving Victim Services Through Probation''). IVSTP has provided assistance to juvenile and adult probation agencies seeking to initiate or improve their services to victims and witnesses.

prior to the end of the term, allowing the judge some needed flexibility since it is difficult to determine, at the time of sentencing, how long the term should be. Some states authorize early termination of probation without actually having statutory guidelines as to when it is to be exercised; others have specific guidelines or procedures for termination. In juvenile cases most jurisdictions provide for early termination by the judge upon a recommendation from the probation officer. The decision to terminate sometimes does not have any direct relationship to the merits of the case, but is more a reflection of the need to keep caseloads down to a manageable size. This means that probationers may be discharged even though they are in need of further supervision.

PROBATION VIOLATION

When any of the conditions of probation have been violated, there exists a "technical violation." When a violation involves a new crime, it is a nontechnical or new arrest violation. The probation agency response to a violation is a matter of discretion, and this discretion has been subjected to criticism. Czajkoski maintains that technical violations are often ignored by probation agencies until it is believed that the probationer has committed a new crime. "Invoking the technical violation thus becomes the result of the probation officer making the adjudication that a crime has been committed. The probationer has a hearing on the technical violation, but is denied a trial on the suspected crime which triggered the technical violation" (1973: 11–13).

The revocation process originates with probation officers, who exercise what Czajkoski refers to as a "quasi-judicial role" in that they decide whether or not to seek revocation. The probation officer's attitude toward the probationer and the violation will influence whether or not revocation action is initiated. Probation officers usually confer with their superiors and, if a violation is considered serious enough, a notice of violation will be filed with the court. The case will then be placed on the court calendar, and the probationer will be given a copy of the alleged violations and directed to appear in court for a preliminary hearing.

Preliminary Hearing

The accompanying flowchart indicates the possibilities presented at each stage of the probation revocation process. At the preliminary hearing the probationer can deny the charges of probation violation or plead guilty to them. If the plea is guilty, the judge may deal with the case at once. If the probationer denies the charges, a revocation hearing is scheduled. The judge may remand the probationer to custody pending the hearing, or can release the probationer on bail or on his/her own recognizance. The probation department will subsequently prepare a full violation-of-probation report, detailing the charges and providing a summary of the probationer's adjustment to supervision. This report is presented to the judge prior to the revocation hearing.

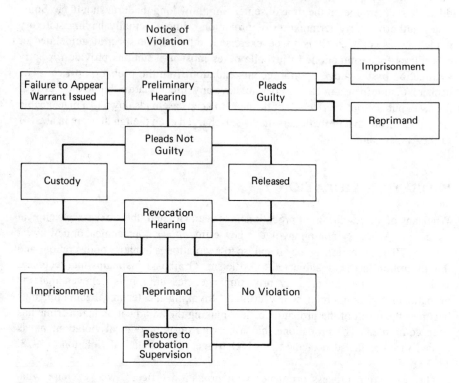

Revocation Hearing

At the revocation hearing the probationer will have an opportunity to testify and present witnesses. There may be an attorney present to represent him/her (according to the provisions outlined in the *Gagnon* and *Mempa* decisions in Chapter 7). A representative of the probation department will also be present. If the judge finds no violations, the probationer is restored to supervision. If the judge sustains any of the charges brought by the probation officer, the probationer can be reprimanded and restored to supervision, or the probation can be revoked and imprisonment ordered. In some probation cases the defendant is actually sentenced at the time of conviction, but the imposition of sentence is suspended in favor of probation. In other cases, the defendant is placed directly on probation without being sentenced. In the latter case, if the violation is sustained, the judge can revoke probation and sentence the probationer to a term of imprisonment. The sentence, however, must be in accordance with the penalty provided by law for the crime for which the probationer was originally convicted.

Probation violation procedures may vary slightly from jurisdiction to jurisdiction. Another item that varies is referred to as "street time."

LOUISIANA DEPARTMENT of CORRECTIONS

NOTICE OF PRELIMINARY HEARING

TO: _____

LSP NO.: _____   DATE: _____

DOCKET NO.: _____

SECTION I

RIGHTS OF THE PAROLEE/PROBATIONER

An alleged violator shall be afforded a preliminary hearing conducted by an independent hearing officer, to determine if there is probable cause to believe there has been a violation of the conditions of his parole/probation.

The alleged violator shall be given written notice as to the time and place of the preliminary hearing and the specific violation (s) he is alleged to have committed.

The alleged violator shall have the right to be represented by retained counsel, to speak in his own behalf, and/or bring documents or individuals who can give relevant information to the hearing officer.

The offender shall have the right to cross-examine adverse witnesses unless the hearing officer determines that this would subject them to risk or harm.

If an alleged parole/probation violator is indigent and unable to employ counsel, he has the right to request appointed counsel to represent him at the preliminary hearing. If such a request is made, the offender's eligibility for appointed counsel shall be made in compliance with the Supreme Court's Guidelines.

The preliminary hearing will be held as soon as possible after the arrest and detention of an alleged violator. The preliminary hearing is for the resolution of factual, not legal issues. Legal issues may, of coure, be dealt with in other forums.

Based on the information before him, the hearing officer should determine if there is probable cause to hold the offender for the final decision of the Parole Board/Court on a revocation. The hearing officer shall make a summary, or digest indicating the reasons for his decision and the evidence on which it was based.

The alleged violator shall be given a written copy of the hearing officer's decision and a summary of the proceedings.

If held more than sixty (60) days on a violation detainer, the alleged violator has a right to a revocation hearing before the board/court on his written request.

Street Time

A defendant is convicted of burglary and sentenced to three years' imprisonment. This sentence is suspended in lieu of probation. The probationer spends one year under supervision and then violates the conditions of his probation in an important respect. The judge revokes probation and orders the probationer to begin serving his three-year sentence. Question: Must the offender serve a maximum of three years in prison, or is the one-year of supervision ("street") time to be subtracted from the three-year sentence?

The answer to this question varies from state to state. Some states do not recognize time spent under supervision as time served against the sentence unless the full probationary or parole term is successfully completed. Some states provide street-time credit for probation violations not involving the commission of a new crime, and others leave it to the discretion of the judge.

Richard Hand and Richard Singer provide a review* of some of the legal issues involved:

> With the practices of the various jurisdictions so dramatically divided, it is appropriate to briefly examine the legal defenses and justifications which underlie the posture of those states which continue to deny credit and likewise to advance emerging constitutional theories which argue for credit.[1]
>
> The thrust of the constitutional argument for giving credit for time served to a revoked probationer or parolee is simply that if credit is not given, the prisoner, upon completion of sentence, will have served more time on parole (or probation) *and* in prison than that to which he was originally sentenced. Thus, in those jurisdictions which do not credit "street time" a prisoner might well serve without incident three-fourths or more of a parole term only to be revoked for a violation of condition of release and reincarcerated for the unserved portion of his sentence computed from the date of release from prison, undiminished by the months and perhaps years spent on parole.[2] This nonjudicial increase in sentence is accomplished without any of the constitutionally mandated due process protections which accompany conviction and sentence under

---

*Richard C. Hand and Richard G. Singer, *Sentencing Computation Laws* (Washington, D.C.: American Bar Association, 1974), Chapter 4; some notes deleted.

[1] See Note, A la Recherche du Temps Perdu: The Constitutionality of Denial of Credit on Revocation of Parole, 35 *U. Chi. L. Rev.* 762 (1968).

[2] *Gibbs* v. *Blackwell*, 354 F.2d 469 (5th Cir. 1965) represents the only case that might possibly be construed as a successful attack on the practice of denying "street time" credits. In Gibbs, supra, it appeared to the court that the petitioner had lost seven years parole time by virtue of technical violations of parole conditions. The court hinted that if such were the case application of the provision in question (18 U.S.C. Section 4205) might constitute cruel and unusual punishment.

normal circumstances. (Under modern standards, probation is increasingly deemed to be an independent sentence.)

McNeil v. *Director of Patuxent Institution,* 407 U.S. 245 (1972) established that a convicted person may not be held longer than the sentence imposed by the trial judge. There, a prisoner was sentenced to a term of five years (apparently *not* the maximum allowable), and complained that he had already spent six years at Maryland's Institution.[3] The Court found that the prisoner had indeed been confined in excess of his judicially imposed sentence despite the state's assertions that McNeil was being held for treatment. It is apparent from *McNeil,* and a substantial number of other cases as well, that *any* extra-judicial determinations which extend imprisonment beyond the term of the sentence set by the sentencing court violate due process of law.[4] In *Bates* v. *Rivers,* 323 F.2d 311 (D.C. Cir. 1963), Judge J. Skelly Wright in dissent found that the practice of denying credit to parole violators for time spent on parole was indistinguishable, in legal effect, from other non-judicial extensions of sentence.

> When the period fixed by judgment for the prisoner's release from custody and control has arrived, he may no longer be held under the original sentence—no matter whether he has or has not had parole granted or revoked. To keep him in confinement longer than called for by his sentence would be to deprive him of liberty without due process of law. The statute (18 U.S.C. Section 4205) should not be read to require an unconstitutional confinement. *Id.* at 315.

The practice of denying credit for "street time" also raises a number of equal protection issues. For example, a parolee who served several weeks on parole and who is then revoked has only those several weeks added to his custody. On the other hand, a parolee who observes his parole conditions for several years and is then violated for an identical offense, faces a term of custody that is substantially longer. Further, none would argue that a prisoner serving a sentence inside an institution may be held beyond his judicially imposed term, irrespective of his institutional record during the period of confinement. Yet the paroled person, by violating a condition of parole through actions which are

---

[3] McNeil was held under provision of Maryland's Defective Delinquent Statutes. Md. Ann. Code Art. 31B-5, et seq. (1975).

[4] *Jackson* v. *Indiana,* 406 U.S. 715 (1972) (confinement of prisoner for over three years pending a determination of competency to stand trial held illegal); *Baxstrom* v. *Herold,* 383 U.S. 107 (1966) (confinement of prisoners, upon completion of their prison sentences, to mental institutions absent adequate judicial approval or procedure held illegal); *North Carolina* v. *Pearce,* 395 U.S. 711, 718 (1969) (discussing unconstitutionality of increased sentences upon retrial, the Court said ". . . the constitutional violation is flagrantly apparent in a case involving the imposition of a maximum sentence after reconviction"); *Williams* v. *Illinois,* 399 U.S. 235 (1970) (confining indigent persons beyond the maximum statutory sentence for the offense simply because they are unable to pay fines which were imposed is illegal). Cf. *Rouse* v. *Cameron,* 373 F.2d 451 (D.C. Cir. 1966); *Short* v. *United States,* 344 F.2d 550 (D.C. Cir. 1965).

often noncriminal,[5] is subject to an increase in sentence simply because the form of custody at the time of the commission of the act was parole rather than imprisonment. Thus, the denial of "street time" credit results in vastly dissimilar treatment of convicted persons absent any compelling, or even legitimate, state purpose that would justify such differententiation.

Yet, these arguments notwithstanding, courts have consistently upheld the right of states to withhold "street-time" credits. Many have done so on the theory that denial of "street time" does not result in an extension of sentence since the releasee was not physically confined (not "in custody") and therefore, during this period of time, was not "serving" a sentence.[6] Most others, conceding that while probation and parole may involve custody, insist that it is not the type of custody which, in the "contemplation" of the sentencing court, satisfies a prison sentence.[7]

ITEMS FOR STUDY

1. States differ with respect to statutory restrictions on who may be granted probation. Intrastate variations and differences among judges also affect grants of probation.
2. A sentence of probation, as opposed to imprisonment, has certain advantages, although it is considered inappropriate in certain cases.
3. Although conditions of probation vary according to the jurisdiction, there are some provisions common to all.
4. Imposing restitution as a condition of probation has advantages and disadvantages.
5. The probation officer can be said to have a quasi-judicial role with respect to probation violation.

---

[5]See, e.g., Arluke, A Summary of Parole Rules, 15 *Crime and Delinquency* 267, 272–73 (1969); ABA Resource Center on Correctional Law and Legal Services, *Parole Conditions in the United States,* Table 1 and related text (1973).

[6]*Hedrick* v. *Steele,* 187 F.2d 261, 262 (8th Cir. 1951).

[7]*Dolan* v. *Swope,* 138 F.2d 301 (7th Cir. 1943); *Howard* v. *United States,* 274 F.2d 100 (8th Cir. 1960); *Yates* v. *Looney,* 250 F.2d 956 (10th Cir. 1958). For a discussion of the different problems which are raised in denials of "street time" credit upon revocation of probation, see Note, A la Recherche du Temps Perdu: The Constitutionality of Denial of Credit on Revocation of Parole, 35 *U. Chi. L. Rev.* 762, 773–775 (1968).

chapter 7

Legal Decisions Affecting Probation

Legal decisions that affect probation usually affect parole also, and vice versa. However, for purposes of study the significant legal decisions in probation and parole have been divided according to the primary thrust of the case.

THREE THEORIES OF PROBATION

Traditionally, an individual on probation has not been considered a free person, despite the fact that he/she is not incarcerated. The basis for imposing restrictions on a probationer's freedom is contained in three theories:

1. *Grace theory*. Probation is a conditional privilege, an act of mercy by the judge. If any condition of this privilege is violated, probation can be revoked.
2. *Contract theory*. The probationer signs a stipulation agreeing to certain terms in return for conditional freedom. As in any contractual situation, a breach of contract can result in penalties, in this case revocation of probation.
3. *Custody theory*. The probationer is in the legal custody of the court and is thus a quasi-prisoner with his/her constitutional rights being limited accordingly.

The legal decisions that are discussed in this chapter often challenge the foregoing theories (see Fisher, 1974: 23–29).

The legal decisions discussed here and in Chapter 12 should be viewed within their historical context. In 1966, the U.S. Supreme Court rendered the famous *Miranda* decision [*Miranda* v. *Arizona*, 384, U.S. 436, S. Ct. (1966)], which mandated that accused criminals be informed of certain rights (to remain silent, to have counsel). In 1967, in another Arizona case, the Supreme Court rendered the *Gault* decision, which gave certain rights to juveniles. In the same year came the *Mempa* decision, which gave probationers the right to have counsel in certain instances of probation violation. Five years later, the Court continued to show an "interest" in the rights of certain "status" persons (juveniles, probationers, welfare recipients, the mentally ill) when it handed down the *Morrissey* decision. The following year, 1973, the Court handed down the *Gagnon* decision.

Juvenile Court—*In Re Gault*, 387 U.S. 1, S. Ct. (1967)

The primary result of the *Gault* decision was to provide juveniles with procedural safeguards in the juvenile court. Since the juvenile court is a "treatment" court, in which the treatment professional is the probation officer, the decision had a significant impact on probation practice in that court.

Gerald Gault, age 15, was on probation in Arizona. On the basis of a verbal complaint that he had made an obscene phone call, he was arrested by the police. Gerald was held in the Children's Detention Home, which is run by the probation department. The probation officer filed a petition and a hearing was scheduled in juvenile court for the following day. No copy of the petition or the charges contained therein was given to Gerald or his parents. At the hearing Gerald's mother and two probation officers appeared before a juvenile court judge in the judge's chambers. No one was sworn and no transcript was made of the proceedings. Following this hearing, Gerald was held in detention for several more days and then released to his parents with a note from the probation officer stating that another hearing had been scheduled.

At the second hearing there was conflict over what transpired at the first hearing. For the second time the complainant was not present. The judge ruled that her presence was not necessary. At the conclusion of the hearing, Gerald was committed to the State Industrial School as a juvenile delinquent. Arizona law did not permit any appeal in juvenile cases. However, on a writ of *habeas corpus,* the case made its way up to the U.S. Supreme Court.

The Supreme Court ruled that Gerald had been denied due process of law. The Court ordered that in juvenile cases the respondent (equivalent to the defendant in adult cases) is entitled to:

1. Written notice of charges
2. Right to counsel
3. Right to confront and cross-examine witnesses
4. Privilege against self-incrimination

In 1966, in the case of *Kent* v. *United States* (383 U.S. 541), the Supreme Court had argued (footnotes deleted):

> While there can be no doubt of the original laudable purpose of juvenile courts, studies and critiques in recent years raise serious questions as to whether actual performance measures well enough against theoretical purpose to make tolerable the immunity of the process from the reach of constitutional guaranties applicable to adults. There is much evidence that some juvenile courts, including that of the District of Columbia, lack the personnel, facilities and techniques to perform adequately as representatives of the State in a *parens patriae* capacity, at least with respect to children charged with law violation. There is evidence, in fact, that there may be grounds for concern that the child receives the worst of both worlds: that he gets neither the protections accorded to adults nor the solicitous care and regenerative treatment postulated for children.

Subsequent to *Gault*, in 1970, the Supreme Court handed down a decision *In the Matter of Winship* (397 U.S. 358) which added the requirement of "proof beyond a reasonable doubt" when a juvenile is charged with an offense that would be a crime if committed by an adult.

Donald Horowitz has found that despite *Gault* and subsequent court decisions, counsel tends to appear infrequently in juvenile courts:

> this is largely attributable to the ability of those courts to resist reform of their procedures. When counsel does appear, he does not necessarily behave in an adversary fashion, if that is taken to mean challenging the factual allegations essential to a finding of delinquency. Dispositions without an adversary remains the norm because judges and lawyers tend to think that adversary tactics do not generally accord with the best interests of juveniles (1977: 202–203).

Probation Revocation—*Mempa* v. *Rhay*, 389 U.S. 128, 88 S. Ct. (1967)

Mempa was convicted of "joyriding" in a stolen car and placed on probation for two years. Four months later Mempa's probation was revoked on the ground that he had been involved in a burglary. A court hearing was held several weeks later during which the probation officer was the sole prosecution witness. The probationer was not represented by counsel, nor was he asked if he wished to have counsel appointed for him. Probation was revoked and a 10-year sentence imposed. Mempa appealed on the grounds that he was entitled to counsel at his revocation hearing. His petition was denied, and it worked its way up the appeals process to the U.S. Supreme Court.

The Supreme Court ruled that some rights could be lost if counsel were not present at a probation revocation hearing. It was noted that counsel can aid in "marshaling facts." The Court further stated that counsel is required "at every stage of a criminal proceeding where substantial rights of a criminal accused may be affected." Sentencing is a critical stage of the criminal procedure and since Mempa was sentenced at his revocation hearing, he was entitled to an attorney.

Probation Revocation—*Gagnon* v. *Scarpelli,*
411 U.S. 778, 93 S. Ct. (1973)

Scarpelli pleaded guilty to armed robbery in Wisconsin and was sentenced to 15 years imprisonment, but the sentence was suspended and he was placed on probation for seven years.

He was given permission to reside in Illinois under the Interstate Compact (discussed in Chapter 19). Shortly thereafter he was arrested with a codefendant while burglarizing a house in Illinois. Probation was revoked by Wisconsin without a hearing, and Scarpelli was incarcerated in a state reformatory to serve the original 15-year sentence.

Three years later, although already on parole from the reformatory, Scarpelli appealed on the basis that probation revocation without a hearing and counsel is a denial of due process. The case eventually reached the U.S. Supreme Court. The Court denied the need for counsel in this case because Scarpelli already had counsel when he was sentenced to 15 years, although at that time the imposition of sentence was suspended in favor of probation. However, the Court, citing guidelines established in *Morrissey* v. *Brewer* (see parole legal decisions in Chapter 13),held that the probationer is entitled to a notice of the alleged violations, a preliminary hearing to decide if there is sufficient cause to believe that probation was violated (in order to remand the probationer to custody), and a revocation hearing, which is "a somewhat more comprehensive hearing prior to the making of the final revocation decision."

The Court stated that at these hearings the probationer will have the opportunity to appear and present witnesses and evidence in his/her own behalf, and a conditional right to confront adverse witnesses. The Court determined that:

> Probation revocation, like parole revocation, is not a stage of a criminal prosecution, but does result in loss of liberty. Accordingly, we hold that a probationer, like a parolee, is entitled to a preliminary hearing and a final revocation hearing in the conditions specified in *Morrissey* v. *Brewer*.

The Court indicated that under certain circumstances relating to the peculiarities of a particular case, counsel must be provided for probationers and parolees at their preliminary and revocation hearings. The court set up the following criteria:

> Counsel should be provided in cases where, after being informed of his right to request counsel the probationer or parolee makes such a request based on a timely or colorable claim:
>
> 1. that he has not committed the alleged violation of the conditions upon which he is at liberty; or
> 2. that, even if the violation is a matter of public record or is uncontested, there are substantial reasons which justified or mitigated the violation and made revocation inappropriate and that the reasons are complex or otherwise difficult to develop or present.

The court went on to note:

> In passing on a request for the appoointment of counsel, the responsible agency also should consider, especially in doubtful cases, whether the probationer appears to be capable of speaking effectively for himself. In every case in which a request for counsel at a preliminary or final hearing is refused the grounds for refusal should be stated succinctly and for the record.

It should be noted that the U.S. Supreme Court, by setting up some sort of criteria for right of counsel, was attempting to stem the tide of litigation on this very point.

ITEMS FOR STUDY

1. There are three theories of probation that provide the basis for imposing restrictions on a probationer.
2. The most important decision to impact on the juvenile court was *In Re Gault*.
3. Probation revocation was effected by the *Gagnon* decision.

PART II

PAROLE

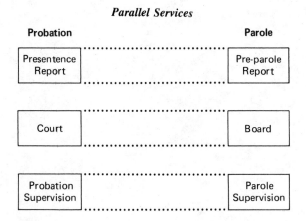

Parallel Services

Probation		Parole
Presentence Report		Pre-parole Report
Court		Board
Probation Supervision		Parole Supervision

chapter 8

Prisons
and Community-Based
Corrections

The degree of civilization in a society can be judged by entering its prisons.
Dostoyevsky

Who will we find upon entering America's prisons? Over 300,000 persons (including unsentenced prisoners); 97 percent are male; about half are black or Hispanic; more than 60 percent are under 30 years of age; most have not completed high school; and about 70 percent were employed just prior to their arrest, usually in blue-collar or service positions. Thus, in America's prisons are persons who are poorer, darker, younger, and less educated than the rest of the population. New York and California provide a profile of their prisoners:

If we were to generalize, we would say that today's offender is between the ages of 16 and 30; that he is likely to be unskilled, a school dropout and that he is inclined to be unrealistically optimistic about his future, despite these deficiencies.

He is more inclined to suspicion of others' motives than is the average, he tends to project blame for his failures on others, but his IQ is usually every bit as high as his counterpart on the street. His unhappy experiences with those in authority from childhood on have left him resentful of anything having the aura of authority; yet he respects, and responds to, directness. He prefers to "hear it like it is," but he is not above deviousness in his dealings with those who can be of use to him.

He has difficulty in forming close and lasting relationships with others and he is much more impressed with actions than with words. He may speak scornfully of the "square world" but chances are he would like to have full membership in it. He has the same need for love, security, and for happiness that we all have and he is prey to the same fears and worries that plague us all. He is capable of change if he can be motivated to desire it and to work for it.

If confined in a New York State correctional facility, he has a history of having had at least two, if not more, previous encounters with the law. He is one of a total of 14,000 offenders incarcerated throughout the State in a variety of facilities ranging from 2000-bed maximum security high-walled prisons to the 35-bed community-based urban treatment center. If a new arrival in a State prison, he can anticipate a stay of approximately 22 months (this is of course an average). If the offender is a woman, she is one in a total of fewer than 500 incarcerated adults. Male or female, there is a 70 percent chance that today's offender is black or Puerto Rican, and a 78 percent chance that he or she was reared in a large urban center where there was little touch with the so-called "good life" of American society.

As for the California inmate:

About 14 percent of all persons convicted of felonies are sent to state prison. Mainly, these are serious offenders. A large proportion have a prior history of violence.

While their crimes cover the entire range of felony misconduct, most of the men in state prison are sent there by the courts for these offenses—15.5 percent for homicide, 27.4 percent for robbery, 14.5 percent for burglary, 7.5 percent for assault, and 15.4 percent for drug crimes.

About 70 percent of the male inmates were either sent to prison for a crime of violence or have a prior history of violent behavior.

The median age of male inmates is 30.1 years, somewhat lower than in the past. The age median has been declining in recent years. About 24 percent of the male inmates are less than 25 years old.

Nearly half of the men in prison are native Californians. Three-fourths have lived in this state for at least 10 years. A total of 53 percent are minorities—18 percent Mexican, 33 percent black, and 2 percent other minorities.

The typical male inmate possesses average intelligence, and the median achievement level for newly received prisoners is just under eighth grade.

ORIGINS OF THE AMERICAN PRISON SYSTEM

A look at our English forebearers can help us understand the origins of the American prison system. The English system of laws and punishments of the sixteenth and seventeenth centuries impresses one with the extent to which the death penalty was used (often for seemingly minor offenses).* Little had changed since the Code of Hammurabi. The ("reform") movement away from execution in favor of incarceration is the result of the influence of the Classical School (Sellin, 1970: 19). In England, the efforts of John Howard (author of *The State of the Prisons*) influenced prison reform in the latter half of the eighteenth century, and his work was endorsed

---

*Jerome Hall reports: "Thus it is believed that Henry VIII executed 72,000 thieves and vagabonds during his reign" (1952: 116). Under George III as many as 220 offenses were punishable by death (p. 117).

and carried forward by the Quakers, both in England and America. Michael Ignatieff notes that Howard and the Quakers shared a common religious life-style that led them to favor imprisonment as a form of purgatory, "a forced withdrawal from the distractions of the senses into silent and solitary confrontation with the self." It was out of the solitude and silence that the convict "would begin to hear the inner voice of conscience and feel the transforming power of God's love" (1978: 58). The cornerstone of Quaker penitence was a penitentiary of silence and solitary, and discipline. Their first efforts in America resulted in the building of the Walnut Street Jail.

Walnut Street Jail

A chief characteristic of Colonial efforts at "correction" was that both poor* and criminals were treated the same (Walker, 1980: 15–16), often placed in wretched "houses of correction" and subjected to forced labor. In post-Revolutionary Philadelphia, the (Quaker) Philadelphia Society for Alleviating the Miseries of Public Prisons pressed the legislature to establish an institution that would provide solitary confinement in place of the use of prisoners "whose labor in chains in the city streets was causing so many riots and whose undisciplined confinement in crowded jails was a public scandal" (McKelvey, 1972: 6). The result was that in 1789 public labor was abolished and counties were authorized to send convicts sentenced to hard labor of more than one year to the Walnut Street Jail. In 1790, the construction of a separate cell house employing solitude was authorized (Sellin, 1970: 13–14).

At Walnut Street separate solitary cells were employed featuring a Bible, isolation, and hard work. In their cells inmates worked at a variety of handicrafts: shoemaking, tailoring, weaving, sawing wood, and so on. Convicts were blindfolded upon arrival and remained in their cells until released; they never saw another inmate. In this manner they were saved from the corrupting influence of their peers (Lewis, 1965: 2–3). While solitude may have driven some to madness, it was overcrowding that caused the demise of Walnut Street. Industry became unworkable in the congested circumstances, discipline lapsed, and riots occurred (McKelvey, 1972: 6–7). The original reports of success at Walnut Street, however, caused other states to change their laws and create similar institutions, such as Newgate in New York City.

Newgate

Thomas Eddy (1758–1827), a Tory who was briefly imprisoned during the Revolution, became interested in prisons through his own experience as a prisoner. Eddy was influenced by the Quaker prison in Pennsylvania and the Classical philosophers. In

---

*Paul Takagi states, however, that laws for the imprisonment of debtors "were not directed at the poor, but applied to wage laborers, the purpose of which was to create a constant supply of subservient workers. Falling in debt because of misfortune or because of the extortions of landlord and tradesman, the worker was summarily dispatched to the workhouse and remained there until the imprisoned worker agreed to pledge himself in servitude to the creditor" (1975: 19–20).

1796, he accomplished the building of New York's first penitentiary, located in Greenwich Village. It was named after the famous English penal institution, Newgate, and Eddy became its first agent. Consistent with the prevailing belief of prison reformers of that day, Eddy maintained that the goal of deterrence required inflicting pain on criminal offenders (Lewis, 1965: 4–6).

Although there was a great deal of similarity between the Walnut Street Jail and Newgate, the latter, unlike Walnut Street, was constructed for felons and did not have accommodations for vagrants, witnesses, and debtors. Eddy also discarded the idea that it was necessary to keep inmates in solitary all day. Instead, convicts slept in apartments measuring 12 feet by 18 feet and housing eight inmates.

Eddy encouraged religious worship, established a night school, and approved of provisions in the law that prohibited corporal punishment at Newgate. Despite improvements in treatment at the prison, Newgate experienced several riots. Eddy was eventually removed because of political considerations, and politics was to continue to have an unsettling effect on Newgate (Lewis, 1965: 30–37). McKelvey states that Eddy resigned in protest when the state turned the industries over to a private contractor in 1803 (1972: 7).

When difficulties increased at Newgate, a return to flogging was legislated in 1819. (Lewis, 1965: 46). In 1828, Newgate was abandoned in favor of a newly completed prison at Sing Sing (Department of Correctional Services, 1970: 9).

Pennsylvania after Walnut Street

The theories of the Philadelphia Society resulted in the building of Western State Penitentiary (opened in 1826) and Eastern State Penitentiary (opened in 1829). These institutions featured massive stone walls around a building that branched out from a central rotunda like the spokes of a wheel. The design prevented inmate contact, and prisoners remained in their cells except for one hour of exercise in a yard also designed to prevent inmate contact. The cost of constructing solitary institutions, however, was staggering and, outside of Pennsylvania, led to the development of the "Auburn System." McKelvey called it a practical compromise between separate confinement and congregate labor embodied in an architectural design that was to become the prototype for American prisons—the "factory system," using inmates as a source of cheap labor (1972: 8–13).

Auburn Prison

The next great milestone in American prison history is Auburn Prison, which became the world's most frequently copied prison. Designed by its first agent, William Brittin, it featured a center that was comprised of tiers of cell blocks surrounded by a vacant area, with a high wall around the entire institution. The cells measured 7 by 3½ feet and were 7 feet high.

As a result of an increase in prison discipline problems in New York, it was decided to divide Auburn's inmates into three classes. The most hardened inmates were placed in solitary; a less dangerous group spent part of the day in solitude and the rest of the time working in groups; and the "least guilty" worked together all day and were separated only at night. It was obvious that the Auburn officials had failed to learn from past experiences with solitary confinement. Inmates in the first group jumped off tiers, cut their veins, and smashed their heads against walls; over half of the deaths in the first year were among persons in solitary. As a result, solitary confinement was discontinued except as punishment for violations of prison rules (Lewis, 1965: 67–70).

With solitary confinement abandoned, a new system that would become world-famous was instituted at Auburn. Inmates left their cells each day and worked together in "congregate style." However, total silence was strictly enforced. (Prisoners were not even allowed to communicate with their families except through the prison chaplain.) Inmates had a common dining area and a common work area, and they ate and worked in complete silence. The Auburn system was an unrelenting routine of hard work, moderate meals, and solitary evenings in individual cells. Inmates were awakened early and marched to work before breakfast. They were marched back and forth from work to breakfast and lunch, and finally marched to dinner and from there back to their cells. They followed this routine six days a week. On Sundays, when there was no work, they were addressed by the prison chaplain, who stressed the American virtues of simple faith and hard work (New York State Special Commission on Attica, 1972: 8–9).

The administrators of Auburn believed that their most important task was the breaking of an inmate's spirit in order to drive him into a state of submission. There was some difference of opinion about what to do after the "breaking" process. One school of thought stressed deterrence as its goal and was determined to derive as much economic benefit as possible from inmate labor. (In fact, in the early days of its existence, Auburn actually made a profit.) Another school of thought held that rehabilitation was the ultimate goal and that, after breaking, inmates should be helped through education and religion so that they could return to society better persons (Lewis, 1965: 84).

Auburn, which became the prototype for other prisons in the United States, developed the infamous lockstep shuffle, and dressed its inmates in grotesque and ridiculous-looking black-and-white-striped uniforms. For a fee, free citizens could come to the prison and view the inmates, an act that was encouraged in order to further degrade its inhabitants. One of Auburn's most noted administrators, Elam Lynds, was proud of his record of ruling the prison with the lash.

Most American prisons patterned themselves after Auburn. The fortresslike buildings sprouted up throughout the country. They were bleak and silent factories with labor pools of broken people, stressing discipline and silence. Soon, the very punishment that prisons had been created to eliminate became widely used in the institutions themselves, and continued to be used into the twentieth century. By the end of the nineteenth century the concept of rehabilitation had virtually disappeared and prisons were viewed simply as places to keep criminals incarcerated. This was reflected even in the name of the warden's first assistant, the "principal keeper" (New York State Special Commission on Attica, 1972: 10–11).

The Auburn-style prisons built throughout the country were not without their critics. In 1870, a new generation of prison reformers organized the National Prison Association (NPA). They declared that rehabilitation, not punishment, was the primary goal of prisons. There were scattered efforts made to implement the principles of the NPA. One of the most famous was the founding of the Elmira Reformatory (New York State Special Commission on Attica, 1972: 12), which used the indeterminate sentence and parole, becoming a prototype for parole systems in the United States.

PAROLE

Three factors led to implementing parole release in the United States:

1. The decline of prison industries and thus prison-generated profits.
2. The expense of constructing Auburn-type (fortress) prisons.
3. Prison overcrowding and riots, and a corresponding need for prison discipline.

The use of convict labor often made prisons not only self-supporting but even profit-making ventures throughout the nineteenth and well into the twentieth century (Abadinsky, 1978). In addition to producing income, prison industries helped to maintain discipline and prevented the idleness that affects many modern prisons. There were three types of prison industry:

1. *Contract systems.* Inmate labor within the prison is sold to private interests, who provide the necessary machinery, tools, and raw materials. In some cases they also provided the supervisory staff.
2. *Lease system.* Inmates are leased out to private business interests for a fixed fee.
3. *State-use system.* Inmates produce goods for use or sale by state agencies.

In the latter part of the nineteenth century there were a series of scandals involving the use of inmate labor. During this period union labor and the National Anti-Contract Association, a manufacturers' group, attacked the use of convict labor, and various states began to pass restrictive laws. The use of convict labor, however, remained widespread until the Great Depression and the passage of the Hawes-Cooper Act (1929) and Ashurst-Sumners Act (1935). These federal statutes curtailed the interstate commerce in goods produced with convict labor. In the South, where convict labor was used extensively in agriculture and mining, the practice continued.

From 1870 to 1904 there was a significant rise in prison populations: 62 percent; from 1904 to 1935 it increased 140 percent (U.S. Attorney General, 1940: 27). During the late 1920s and early 1930s there was an outbreak of prison riots. To reduce prison populations and curtail rioting, new institutions would be required. However, the Auburn-style institution was proving quite expensive to build, as highlighted by the opening of Attica Prison in 1931, the most expensive prison ever built (New York State Special Commission on Attica, 1972: 13).

Intertwined with the realities of cost, overcrowding, and riots was the rhetoric of rehabilitation—parole release, it was argued, contributes to crime prevention by rewarding prisoners' reformative efforts. By 1935 there were more than 60,000 parolees in the United States (Prison Association of New York, 1936: 79–80), and by World War II reality or rhetoric had resulted in most states having parole laws. By 1942 only Virginia, Florida, and Mississippi were without any parole statutes (Barnes and Teeters, 1946: 821).

FROM PRISON TO "CORRECTIONAL INSTITUTION"

In 1944, the California prison system would undergo significant changes, changes that would influence the direction of penology for the rest of the country for three decades. As a result of scandalous situations he found in the prison system, Governor Earl Warren reorganized the California prison and parole system—"rehabilitation" became the key term, and the basis for rehabilitation was the indeterminate sentence. An inmate would "earn" his/her release by providing evidence of reformation. The indeterminate sentence would become the cornerstone of California corrections.

With reform came changes in terminology. Prisons became correctional institutions, guards became correction officers, and rehabilitation became "treatment." In 1954, the American Prison Association became the American Correctional Association. However, the reality of rehabilitation qua "treatment" did not match the rhetoric: 90 to 95 percent of prison expenditures continued to be for security and other non-rehabilitative functions.

The post-World War II era saw the "big house" replaced by correctional institutions. Many of the new wardens, now called superintendents, were university graduates steeped in sociological and psychological theory. The prison, now the correctional institution, became stratified between those whose primary responsibility was security, and the newer members of staff, the "treaters." These two groups were not only separated by the nature of their work, but by philosophy and education.

Into this environment of contradictions came thousands of new inmates—blacks and Hispanics. The rising black consciousness occurring outside the prison (e.g., Black Panthers) took on radical characteristics inside the prison. The Black Muslims emerged as a major separatist organization and confronted officials with demands based on religious freedom. Politicized inmates, black and white, confronted institutional officials with other demands, often coached in Marxist terminology. In the best tradition of the "big house," institutional officials responded with suppression. This led to legal action, with the courts imposing procedural, "due process" requirements on the prisons.* Add to this already volatile setting inmates who are younger and a great deal more violent than the older "big house" inmates, and the result is inevitable: riots—39 in 1969 and 70 in 1970 (Walker, 1980: 245). In 1971, the rebellion at the Attica Correctional Facility in New York was suppressed in the bloodiest one-day encounter between Americans since the Civil War:** state police and other law enforcement officers killed 43 persons, including 10 correctional employees. The aftermath of Attica was widespread criticism of correctional institutions, parole, and the indeterminate sentence. Although this criticism had been building for some time, Attica provided a flashpoint.

MODERN AMERICAN PRISONS

The American correctional institution, née prison, has some problems that are endemic and some that are relatively recent. Among the former is the location of most prisons—rural—as opposed to the place of residence of most inmates—urban. Most of the custodial staff in these institutions is drawn from more rural areas; they are white and politically conservative. Whereas the predominantly white inmates of the "big house" could relate to their keepers, the urban black and Hispanic finds no such comfort.

Another traditional aspect of the American prison is that it can function *only* with the assistance of the inmates—*rapprochement* between the keepers and the kept. Numerous studies of prison life note that the custodial staff is dependent on inmate leadership for the operation of an institution. In the "big house," *rapprochement* between white guards and white inmates kept the prison running, more or less smoothly and efficiently. In the correctional institution, however, *rapprochement* is difficult, strained, and at times disfunctional to orderly control. The correctional

---

*Until the 1960s the courts followed a "hands-off policy" which permitted prisons to operate free of judicial scrutiny. In the charged political atmosphere of the 1960s this began to change. In a series of decisions based on the Eighth Amendment's prohibition against cruel and unusual punishment, federal courts outlawed corporal punishment and restricted the use of solitary confinement. Litigation using Section 1983 of Title 42 of the United States Code, the "Civil Rights Act of 1871," also resulted in changes. Section 1983 was enacted during Reconstruction days to enable blacks who were deprived of civil rights to avoid the state courts. It provided a basis for prisoners to move directly into federal court. As a result, the courts ruled that prison officials cannot interfere with a prisoner's access to judicial relief, nor can a prisoner be punished for suing or criticizing prison officials in court. The United States Supreme Court ruled that if prison officials do not provide legal counsel, they must permit prisoners ("jail house lawyers") to help other prisoners with legal work (*Johnson* v. *Avery,* 393 U.S. 483, 1969). That Court ruled that prisons must also provide legal materials for inmates (*Younger* v. *Gilmore,* 404 U.S. 15, 1971). In *Wolff* v. *McDonnell* (418 U.S. 539, 1974) the Supreme Court ruled that minimal "due process" is required before inmates can be subjected to disciplinary action.

**If we exclude the Indian massacres of the late nineteenth century.

institution has a darker, younger, and more openly aggressive population. In the prison systems of several large states, inmates affiliated with street gangs having a variety of exotic names—Vice Lords, Blackstone Rangers, Aryan Brotherhood, Mexican Mafia—exercise a power and discipline that competes with correctional staff for control of the institution.

In the Illinois prison at Joliet, Stateville, guards were so fearful of the 2000 inmates that they maintained only perimeter control. New inmates were routinely gang raped, and the only thing the inmates were not permitted to do was escape. A new administration has restored order, but the calm is reportedly tense (Krajick, 1980b). The situation in the Rhode Island Correctional Institution became so difficult that formations of shotgun-wielding state troopers had to be brought in to keep the peace: "And the prisoners, who had taken over effective control of the prison in the vacuum created by the previous administration and won a landmark victory with a suit charging inhumane conditions, see themselves as being cheated out of the rewards of the successful suit and worse off than before" (Knight, 1978: 20). Michael Knight reports that since a federal court order directing sweeping changes "more than half of the 700 inmates spend from 18 to 23½ hours a day locked in those cubbyholes in a seething contest of wills between militant prisoners and a forceful new administration, as each group attempts to create its form of order out of years of violent, terror-filled chaos" (Ibid.). In 1978, prisoners at the state prison in Pontiac (Illinois) rioted, killing three guards and maiming two others (Krajick, 1980a: 16). In December 1979, eleven inmates escaped from the New Mexico State Penitentiary. On January 14, 1980, an outside expert called in to investigate the escape issued a report which declared that officials were "playing Russian roulette with the lives of inmates, staff and the public" (Serrill & Katel, 1980: 7). The prison had seven wardens in as many years, was overcrowded and understaffed with guards having no training. On February 2, 1980, a leaderless and uncontrolled riot broke out and fourteen guards were seized. The inmates went berserk and slew 33 fellow prisoners and destroyed the interior of the institution. Several guards were injured, but none were killed (Ibid.). At the time of the riot New Mexico correctional institutions were being sued by the American Civil Liberties Union for being in violation of humane, constitutional standards. Five months after the riot sweeping reforms were ordered by the Federal District Court. On October 15, 1980, the Florida State Prison at Starke was the scene of a riot during which one guard was stabbed to death and another scalded. The disorder broke out shortly after a memorial service for a guard who had been stabbed to death on October 12th. At the time, the prison was under a court order to transfer one-third of the inmate population to other facilities because of what a state court judge had called an "intolerable" level of violence. Four inmates had been stabbed to death since July. The court action came as a result of a suit filed by nine inmates who contended that the prison staff is unable to protect inmates (Associated Press, October 17, 1980).

As the examples above poignantly illustrate, the "state of our prisons" is often characterized by violence—against staff, against inmates. The danger to staff has caused some institutions to allow *de facto* control to be exercised by inmate groups whose methods of discipline are not restrained by constitutional guarantees or court orders.* To discuss rehabilitation under these circumstances. . . .

Dale Sechrest (1979), an official of the American Correctional Association (ACA), argues that

> much of the reform of prisons has been misdirected in the interests of rehabilitation programs based on the mental health model, while the real problem has been and continues to be in the very structure and operation of these institutions. In sum, how can a person placed in prison come to the point of developing a new life style if that person is placed in an environment in which the fear of bodily safety may be quite real, where food may be bad, where services, such as employment training and education, may not exist, and where basic health and safety minimums may not be met?

These conditions have led to a series of federal court decisions emanating from the implementation of the Civil Rights Law of 1871. These decisions have resulted in court orders directing changes in order to bring prisons into compliance with federal statutes and constitutional guarantees against "cruel and unusual" punishment. In the case of Alabama, a federal judge removed state control over the prisons and appointed a master to carry out the mandate of the court. By 1980 there were at least 20 states whose prisons were operating under court order (Herbers, 1980: 1).

In order to help "correct" corrections, the American Correctional Association has developed a Correctional Standards Program. The immediate goal is to encourage officials to seek accreditation for their prisons by adhering to minimum standards established by the ACA with respect to safety and sanitation, education, vocational training, and counseling. As a result of the riot at the State Penitentiary, New Mexico officials have agreed to implement the ACA standards.

PRISONS AS "TOTAL INSTITUTIONS"

Many of the problems that exist in prison are characteristic of a "total institution," which Erving Goffman defines as "a place of residence and work where a large number of like-situated individuals, cut off from the wider society for an appreciable period of time, together lead an enclosed, formally administered round of life" (1961: xiii). Total institutions include mental hospitals, convents, monasteries,

---

*A notable exception to this trend is the Texas Department of Corrections, whose 20,000 prisoners work in agriculture or prison industries that run like a clock: "There is little trouble, little strife. There is also little attempt at innovation, little talk of rehabilitation or reintegration of offenders" (Krajick, 1978a: 5). The Texas prison system is also described as the nation's most litigated system, with hundreds of cases alleging civil rights violations. These litigants include the U.S. Department of Justice, which alleges "inadequacy of medical services, inadequate protection of inmates from brutality by guards and inmate supervisors, unconstitutionally restricted access to the courts and denial of due process in disciplinary proceedings" (Krajick, 1978a: 10).

boarding schools, and military posts, as well as prisons. They have a tendency to "mold" persons into compliant and often shapeless forms in order to maintain discipline and a sound working order, or for other less utilitarian reasons. Prisons, and other total institutions, provide a dreary uniformity—clothing, sleeping quarters, food, and so on. Depersonalization and dehumanization pervade these instututions.

Total institutions encompass much of an inmate's life, and they leave him/her little room for self-assertion and individual decision making. Thus, when he/she leaves the institution he/she is often ill-prepared for life on the outside. Cut off from the real world, offenders often feel lost upon release. When the trauma of release is more than a parolee is able to tolerate, he/she may wish to return ''home'' to prison. A parole officer has to deal with many difficult situations; one of the most difficult, however, is when a client requests to be placed back in prison because he/she is unable to "make it on the street."

Goffman notes, however, that the impact of total institutions is usually of limited duration; after release, both the negative and positive experiences are soon left behind with no lasting effect. (This raises questions about the theory of *individual deterrence*.)

Norval Morris and Gordon Hawkins caution that it is unwise to dismiss prisons as complete failures. They note that the frequently cited statistic that about two-thirds of those who leave prison come back for new crime is a *legend:* "Most prison populations include about two-thirds who have been in prison before. It is easy but wrong to conclude that prisons therefore have a 60-to-70 percent failure rate" (in Frank, 1974: 106). Most studies indicate, to the contrary, that about two-thirds of those released from prison do not return. C. E. Reasons and R. L. Kaplan point out that prisons are continuously receiving their own failures who populate and repopulate the prison and who become disproportionately represented in prison populations (1975: 365).

COMMUNITY-BASED CORRECTIONS

In 1967, the President's Commission stated (1972: 398):

> Institutions tend to isolate offenders from society, both physically and psychologically, cutting them off from schools, jobs, families, and other supportive influences and increasing the probability that the label of criminal will be indelibly impressed upon them. The goal of reintegration is likely to be furthered much more readily by working with offenders in the community than by incarceration.

The Commission added that the cost of incarceration also made community-based corrections attractive. Although this was nothing more than a plea for increased probation and parole services, it is often viewed as the basis for a new approach to offenders under the rubric "community-based corrections." Vernon Fox states (1977: 11):

The Federal Rehabilitation Act of 1965 was significant in bringing community-based corrections into the governmental organization. To improve the rehabilitation procedures and to hold down the number of inmates in prisons and correctional institutions, Congress formally sanctioned the use of residential community centers or halfway houses preceding parole, the granting of brief leaves or furloughs in emergencies or the preparation for release, and work release programs for private employment or vocational training in the community in this Act of 1965.

In the intervening years, community-based corrections has often included an array of nonprison efforts: probation, parole, diversion, halfway houses, foster care, group homes, work release, and so on. It became a code word for "progressive corrections," and it was *de rigueur* for authors writing texts on probation and parole during the 1970s to include "community-based corrections," sometimes in the title of their work. Andrew Rutherford and Osman Bengur note (1976: 4, references deleted):

> The term "community-based" has produced considerable confusion. Claims, for example, have been made that some training schools are community-based by virtue of their location in a "community." The most thorough conceptual work that has been done on defining community-based focuses upon the nature of linkages between programs and the community. Programs, according to this definition can be differentiated on the basis of the *"extent and quality* of relationships between program staff, clients, and the community in which the program is located. . . . ." In this manner, community-based programs are viewed as being along a continuum ranging from the least to the most community-based. "Generally, as the frequency, quality, and duration of community relationships increase the program becomes more community-based."

Community-based corrections grew out of an amalgam of issues:

1. Growing concern over prison conditions.
2. The increasing cost of incarceration.
3. A belief in the efficacy of rehabilitative programs.

Several important factors led to the demise of the community-based corrections concept in many areas. The first was opposition from those communities into which offenders were to be placed. Community-based corrections did not necessarily mean being based in the offender's community. The second was the inability of rehabilitative efforts to impact on recidivism. Although early reports made claims of success, more rigorous analysis proved disappointing. A third factor was cost, especially for programs that had to be developed from start. This was often done with the aid of federal funding; when that waned, so did many programs. John Blackmore, writing in 1978, stated (p. 47):

> The American movement in favor of community corrections is now a decade old. It has reached its peak in many jurisdictions and is now in decline, amid criticism that in most states the community effort amounted to little more than an expansion of probation and the

operation of a few federally funded halfway houses and other programs that had no impact on the traditional corrections system.

David Greenberg questioned some of the basic assumptions of community-based corrections (1975: 4):

These program failures raise questions about the reasoning advanced in support of commu-nity corrections. One might ask why, if the community is so therapeutic, the offender got into trouble there in the first place? Indeed, an offender's home community, where he is already known as a delinquent or criminal, might pose more obstacles to the abandonment of criminal activity than some new residential location.

Greenberg points out that the advantages of community corrections were overstated. He notes that criminal activity can be a rational response to the absence of lawful opportunity, as a result of high levels of unemployment, for example. Furthermore (p. 5):

If it is true that lack of contact with good schools and adequate housing contribute to criminality and there are no good schools or adequate housing in the community, how can a community corrections center remedy this? It is in no position to improve the schools or bring apartments into conformity with housing codes.

Perhaps the greatest flaw of community corrections is that the rhetoric did not match the reality. Sol Chaneles comments (1980: 196):

When "Community Corrections" began to mean using condemned, flea-bag hotels con-verted into mini, urban prisons, prisoners were no closer to the mainstream of community life than when they were incarcerated in the remote boondocks, and community residents in the neighborhoods of these mini urban prisons were no more involved in the process of reintegration and rehabilitation than they were without them.

Community-based corrections programs that are relevant to probation and parole practice are reviewed in Part Four.

ITEMS FOR STUDY

1. Inmates in America's prisons represent an underclass population.
2. American prisons have their origins in the efforts of Quaker reformers of the eighteenth century, from whence we derive the term "penitentiary."
3. The "Auburn-type" fortress prison, utilizing convict labor, set the trend for American prisons into the twentieth century.
4. Three factors led to implementing parole release in the United States.
5. The postwar era saw penology being influenced by changes in the California prison system.

6. These changes were accompanied by a change in the prison population, which led to the prison riots of the late 1960s and 1970s.

7. The community-based corrections of the 1970s was flawed by assumptions that were unsound and a rhetoric that was unrealistic.

chapter 9

Parole History and the Indeterminate Sentence

PAROLE HISTORY*

Parole did not develop from any specific source or experiment, but is an outgrowth of a number of independent measures, including the conditional pardon, apprenticeship by indenture, the transportation of criminals to America and Australia, the English and Irish experiences with the system of Ticket of Leave, and the work of American prison reformers during the nineteenth century.

Conditional Pardons and Transportation to America

The transportation of criminals to the American Colonies began early in the seventeenth century. In the beginning no specific conditions were imposed upon those receiving these pardons. However, after a number of those pardoned had evaded transportation or had returned to England prior to the expiration of their term, it was found necessary to impose certain restrictions upon the individuals to whom these pardons were granted. It was about 1655 that the form of pardons was amended to include specific conditions and provide for the nullification of the pardon if the recipient failed to abide by the conditions imposed.

*This section is reprinted and edited from the *Parole Officer's Manual,* New York State Division of Parole, 1953.

Transportation to America

During the early days of transportation, the government paid a fee to each contractor for each prisoner transported. Subsequently, this was changed and the contractor was given "property in service" of the prisoner until the expiration of the full term. Once prisoners were delivered to the contractor, the government took no further interest in their welfare or behavior unless they violated the conditions of the pardon by returning to England prior to the expiration of their sentences.

Upon arrival of the pardoned felons in the Colonies, their services were sold to the highest bidder. The contractor then transferred the "property in service" agreement to the new master and the felon was no longer referred to as a criminal but became an indentured servant. This indenture bears a similarity to the procedure now followed by parole boards in this country. Like the indentured servant, a prisoner conditionally released on parole agrees in writing to accept certain conditions included on the release form that is signed by the members of the parole board and the prisoner. Even some of the conditions imposed today on conditionally released prisoners are similar to those included on the indenture agreement.

The termination of the Revolutionary War ended transportation to America, and England then sent her convicts to Australia until 1867.

England's Experience with Ticket of Leave

The English Penal Servitude Act of 1853, governing prisoners convicted in England and Ireland, substituted imprisonment for transportation. By this act, prisoners who received sentences of 14 years or less were committed to prison, but the judge was granted permissive power to order the transportation of individuals who had received terms of more than 14 years. This law also specified the length of time prisoners were required to serve before becoming eligible for conditional release on Ticket of Leave.

The Irish System of Ticket of Leave

Sir Walter Crofton became head of the Irish prison system in 1854, one year after the enactment of the Servitude Act. The Irish convict system under Crofton's administration became famous for its three stages of penal servitude, with the final stage being conditional release on Ticket of Leave. Ticket of Leave men residing in rural districts were supervised by the police, but those residing in Dublin were supervised by a civilian employee who had the title Inspector of Released Prisoners. He worked cooperatively with the police, but it was his responsibility to secure employment for Ticket of Leave men. He required them to report at stated intervals, visited their homes every two weeks, and verified their employment.

In England and Ireland after 1864, Prisoners Aid Societies were established, with the government contributing a share of funds equal to the sum raised by the Societies for their work. These Societies employed agents, who devoted their full time to the supervision of released prisoners.

Developments in the United States

By 1865, the Crofton System had been widely publicized in America. Supporters of Crofton's System, however, did not believe that the adoption of the Ticket of Leave would ever be accepted in the United States. Their attitude was apparently based on the conception that it would be un-American to place any individual under the supervision of the police, and they did not believe that any other form of supervision would be effective. A letter written by Crofton in 1874, in reply to an inquiry sent to him by the Secretary of the New York Prison Association, stressed that the police of Ireland were permitted to delegate competent individuals in the community to act as custodians for Ticket of Leave men, and he suggested a similar system for the United States.

Elmira*

The first convention of the American Prison Association met in Cincinnati on October 12, 1870, attended by American leaders in prison reform. A paper dealing with the indeterminate sentence and the possibilities of parole was presented by a noted Michigan penologist, Zebulon R. Brockway.

The year before the Cincinnati Convention, New York State had authorized the building of a reformatory at Elmira, New York. It was opened in 1876 and its first Superintendent was this same Zebulon R. Brockway.

The principle upon which the Elmira system was founded was that criminals can be reformed; that reformation is the right of the convict and the duty of the State; that prison authorities should have the right to lengthen or shorten the duration of his imprisonment and not allow him to be returned to society until he is rehabilitated.

This rehabilitation was to be accomplished by cultivating the inmate's self-respect and enabling him through industry and good conduct to raise himself to a position of progressively less restraint and eventual freedom.

The population was made up of the young offender between the ages of 16 and 30. The building contained cells, much as in the Auburn system, but the emphasis was on military organization and drill, vocational training, and academic education. The rule of silence enforced in the penitentiaries and the attendant brutal punishment was abolished.

The mark system of grading was established. Inmates were divided into three grades. At admission, each inmate was placed in the second grade. After six months of good conduct, he could be promoted to the first grade. Misbehavior sentenced him to third grade, where a month of good conduct was necessary to return to second grade and the cycle began again. Six months of good conduct in first grade could entitle him to a conditional release. Here for the first time in the United States, a parole system was actually put into practice as prisoners, on release, were continued under the jurisdiction of the prison for an additional six months.

*This section is taken from New York State Department of Corrections, *Corrections in New York State* (Albany, N.Y., n.d. [1970]).

One of the conditions of his parole was that he must report on the first day of every month to his guardian and provide an account of his situation and conduct. The guardian's report was then transmitted to the superintendent of Elmira. Parolees were required to report for a minimum period of six months. It was the belief that a longer period under supervision would be discouraging to the average parolee.

No thought was given to the training of prisoners toward their future adjustment in the community, and both prison administrators and inmates soon accepted the idea that reformed or unreformed, allowance of time for good behavior was automatic and release at the earliest possible date was a right rather than a privilege. After release, supervision was either nonexistent or totally inadequate.

THE INDETERMINATE SENTENCE

Although parole existed without the indeterminate sentence,* some form of indeterminacy is obviously necessary for parole. This indeterminacy, which has been the standard for sentencing in every state, has been subjected to increasingly severe criticism beginning with the publication of *Struggle for Justice* in 1971. The authors of this work, the American Friends Service Committee, noted that the indeterminate sentence and parole rest on a view of crime as an individual pathology that can best be dealt with by "treating" individual criminals. This view, often referred to as the "medical model of crime,"** tends to downgrade or ignore environmental factors such as poverty, discrimination, and unemployment (1971: 40–41). The Committee argued that our present level of knowledge does not offer a scientific basis for "treatment," even if the "medical model" were valid. Thus, offenders are made to stay in prison by parole boards until they are "treated" and "cured," although we offer no scientific basis for "treatment" and we cannot predict who will recidivate.

This argument had only limited acceptance and no practical success until 1974. In that year, Robert Martinson published "What Works?" (1974), a synopsis of his findings and those of his colleagues Douglas Lipton and Judith Wilks (the complete

---

*Inmates with determinate sentences were often eligible for parole after serving a portion of their sentence.

**"The medical model proposes that conditions have discoverable causes and scientific cures, that experts should exercise authority in the application of the cures, and the nonexperts, the rest of the population, should submit to the authority of these experts" (Robitscher, 1980: 38). Jonas Robitscher points out (1980: 44):

> This new approach to criminal behavior stressed deviance as pathology. The criminal was to be seen not as "bad" but as "mad," and he was to be given the benefit of the medical approach to madness. He should be helped to understand his unconscious motivation and to go through a process of psychoanalytic change. From today's viewpoint, we may feel not that the emphasis on dynamics was necessarily wrong, but that the belief that this new knowledge would answer the problem of crime was wrong.

work was published the following year; see Lipton et al., 1975). They surveyed 231 studies of correctional rehabilitative programs up until 1967, and Martinson concluded: *"With few and isolated exceptions, the rehabilitative efforts that have been reported so far have had no appreciable effect on recidivision"* (1974: 25). Actually, Martinson's summary is more critical than is the larger work. However, the report lent credence to the arguments of the American Friends Service Committee and their proposal to return to a classical approach to crime and criminals: "All persons found guilty of the same criminal act under the same circumstances are [to be] dealt with uniformly" (1971: 148).

Soon afterward, several new works critical of the indeterminate sentence and parole appeared. David Fogel presented the *justice model* (1975: 192):

> It is evident that correctional administrators have for too long operated with practical immunity in the backwashes of administrative law. They have been unmindful that the process of justice more strictly observed by the visible police and courts in relation to rights due the accused before and through adjudication must not stop when the convicted person is sentenced. The justice perspective demands accountability from all processors, even the "pure of heart."

Instead of the often hidden discretion exercised by parole boards, Fogel recommended, "(1) a return to flat time sentences with procedural rules in law governing sentence selection; (2) the elimination of both parole boards and parole agencies as we have known them" (1975: 204). Forthermore, whatever "treatment" is offered in prison is to be voluntary and shall in no way affect the release date of an inmate.

Andrew von Hirsch offered the concept of *just deserts* (1976), according to which the punishment is to be commensurate with the seriousness of the crime, once again the classical approach: "A specific penalty level must apply in all instances of law-breaking which involve a given degree of harmfulness and culpability" (von Hirsch and Hanrahan, 1978: 4). Indeterminacy and parole are to be replaced with a specific penalty for a specific offense.

In 1976, the Twentieth Century Fund Task Force on Criminal Sentencing offered a version of sentencing that can best be characterized as Neoclassical, the *presumptive sentencing system:* each subcategory of crime would have a presumptive sentence "that should generally be imposed on typical first offenders who have committed the crime in the typical fashion" (1976: 20, italics deleted). For succeeding convictions or other aggravating circumstances the judge could increase the presumptive sentence by a specific percentage. Mitigating circumstances could, similarly, reduce the sentence.

In sum, the basic thrust of the criticisms and proposals, be it the *justice model, just deserts,* or *presumptive sentencing,* was to limit judicial discretion and abolish the parole board and its discretionary release procedures. The focus was on inequity, disparate sentencing, and parole practices—a system that, it was argued, gives offenders a view of criminal justice as inherently unfair.

Support for the abolition of indeterminate sentencing and parole release existed in the law enforcement community and among more conservative elements in society. They traditionally viewed rehabiliation as "coddling" criminals, while parole was seen as a way to undermine deterrence and permit dangerous persons back into society.

Here was an issue on which both the "left" and the "right" could agree—but for quite different reasons. In the end, David Greenberg and Drew Humphries argue, the "right" coopted the issue of sentencing reform and parole and implemented changes that they see as increasing the length of time served by most offenders, now without the possibility of parole release (1980). In any event, by 1980 eight states had already adopted some form of determinate sentencing (Arizona, California, Colorado, Florida, Illinois, Indiana, Maine, North Carolina).

William Wilbanks and Nicolette Parisi argue that the change from indeterminate to determinate sentencing is more apparent than real (1979: 2):

> First, the sentencing process is neither indeterminate nor determinate. Rather, the distinction between the two labels is that they are at different points on a continuum. The difference is *quantitative,* not *qualitative.* A more accurate description of a sentencing structure refers to the degree or extent to which discretion or certainty is present. A better understanding of the sentencing process would be facilitated by looking at the various aspects of sentencing as *more or less determinate* or *having more or less discretion.*

It is this issue of discretion that presents the most obvious deficiency in the proposals discussed above. Although they all propose to deal with discretion exercised by judges and parole boards, they fail to deal with prosecutorial discretion. This discretion is exercised privately; it is not subject to official review; and prosecutorial discretion affects sentencing more often and more significantly than does judicial discretion. While a judge acting under some form of determinate sentencing scheme must apply a certain sentence for a particular crime, it is the prosecutor who determines *the particular crime.* In return for cooperation (i.e., a plea of guilty) the prosecutor can reduce the seriousness of an offense, and hence the sentence. The reverse is also true.* Thus, an offender who has been arrested for burglary, a felony, for example, can receive a five-year sentence. The prosecutor, for a host of reasons he/she need not disclose, can reduce the offense to criminal trespass, a misdemeanor, with a maximum sentence of one year. Determinate sentencing schemes merely shift discretion away from judges and parole boards and toward the prosecution end of criminal justice.**

*This was highlighted in a North Carolina case in which the defendant was charged with kidnapping and armed robbery. In exchange for a plea of guilty, the prosecutor offered to reduce the charges to armed robbery for which the sentence is 10 to 25 years. The defendant refused, and after a trial received a sentence of 21 to 60 years (Billy Pritchard, "Guilty Plea Would Have Cut Sentence," *The Asheville Citizen,* October 24, 1979: 21).

**Hagan, Bernstein and Albonetti (1980: 819) point out that the widespread expectation that sentencing reform and the abolition of parole will eliminate disparities denies the importance of the prosecutor in producing differential sentences.

Furthermore, the abolition of parole boards, a practical accomplishment of most determinate sentencing schemes, ignores the role of the board in reducing sentence disparity. Since the parole board reviews the sentences of all state prisoners, it can act as a review panel mediating disparate sentences for similar criminal behavior.

A second issue with respect to parole has been given scant attention. There is a presumption (e.g., American Friends Service Committee, 1971) that parole is based on a "medical model" or some humanitarian effort gone astray. However, the history of prisons and parole in the United States underscores the fact that parole release has traditionally been used as a vehicle for maintaining prison discipline and reducing prison overcrowding. Those who see parole as based on a rehabilitative model have bought the rhetoric but not the reality.

Let us look at a hypothetical example of the parole board as sentencing review panel.

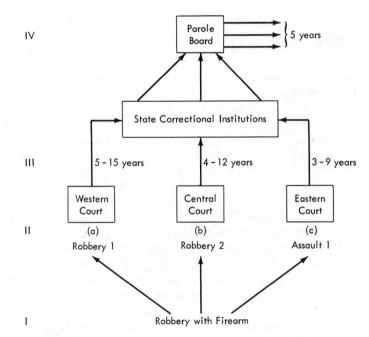

I   Three offenders, (a) (b) (c), each enter stores in different counties within the same state. They each brandish loaded revolvers and rob several hundred dollars.

II   Defendant (a) is processed in Western Court. Attempts at plea bargaining fail, he stands trial and is convicted of First Degree Robbery.
     Defendant (b) is processed in Central Court. He is allowed to plead guilty to Second Degree Robbery.
     Defendant (c) is processed in Eastern Court. He is allowed to plead guilty to First Degree Assault.

III Defendant (a) is sentenced to a minimum of 5 years and a maximum of 15 years in state prison.

Defendant (b) is sentenced to a minimum of 4 years and a maximum of 12 years in state prison.

Defendant (c) is sentenced to a minimum of 3 years and a maximum of 9 years in state prison.

IV   The parole board, recognizing that the three defendants have committed the same criminal acts and despite variations in the legal category of conviction (Robbery 1, Robbery 2, Assault 1), requires that each serve 5 years before being paroled.

Under a determinate sentencing scheme devoid of a parole board, the sentences for this hypothetical example would be:

defendant (a) would serve 8 years;
defendant (b) would serve 6 years;
defendant (c) would serve 4 years.

STRUCTURING DISCRETION

Disparate sentences imposed for similar offenses have produced a great deal of criticism. In its 1967 report, the President's Commission quoted Robert J. Jackson when he was U.S. Attorney General (1972: 357):

It is obviously repugnant to one's sense of justice that the judgment meted out to an offender should depend in large part on a purely fortuitous circumstance; namely, the personality of the particular judge before whom the case happens to come for disposition.

Another Attorney General, Edward H. Levi, commented that "if the imposition of punishment appears to be fickle—a matter of chance—or if it appears to be unequal with respect to socioeconomic groups, offenders who do suffer punishment for crimes may be left with an emotional scar that itself makes reunification very difficult." The Attorney General went on to say: "Today there is an accidental quality to the imposition of punishment" (speech before the Governor's Conference on Employment and the Prevention of Crime, Milwaukee, February 2, 1976). The National Advisory Commission has noted that "an offender who believes he has been sentenced unfairly in relation to other offenders will not be receptive to reformative efforts on his behalf" (1973: 178).

In order to respond to this disparity, the President's Commission recommended sentencing councils and appellate review (1972: 357–58):

The sentencing council consists of several judges of a multijudge court who meet periodically to discuss sentences to be imposed in pending cases. Sentencing councils are in use on a regular basis in at least three U.S. district courts. Foremost among their advantages is the opportunity they give for discussion of sentencing attitudes. From such a discussion a consensus on sentencing standards may emerge. The council provides occasion also for full consideration of available sentencing alternatives. The ultimate responsibility for determining sentence rests with the judge to whom the case is assigned, although the discussion and need to state reasons for a sentence tend to restrain the imposition of unreasonably severe or lenient sentences.

Appellate review would encourage the development of uniform and considered sentencing policies within a jurisdiction. It leads both the trial court and the appellate court to give sustained and explicit consideration to the justification for particular sentences. It provides a workable means of correcting unjust and ill-considered sentences, particularly those in which the punishment imposed is grossly inappropriate. While there is room for difference of opinion as to whether the appellate court should have authority to increase as well as decrease sentences appealed by the defendant, the Commission favors such authority. A committee of the American Bar Association special project has proposed detailed standards for appellate review procedures.

Carl Imlay and Elsie Reid state that "one of the expected advantages of this review is to contribute to an offender's rehabilitation by enhancing his belief that the system is fair and not subject to the unchecked caprice of one official" (1975: 15). They note that appellate review of sentencing can affect probation: the appellate court may find that the sentencing record is incomplete; the probation department would have to provide further information including an update on certain information already submitted. Imlay and Reid point out that the trend toward uniformity in sentencing, a more classical approach, is "in derogation of the notion of individualized sentencing" (p. 16). Indeed, sentence disparity is defended by referring to the positivist approach of making the sentence fit the offender and not merely having it reflect the crime. Thus, disparity may not be pejorative, but may merely be justifiable variation.

In an effort to deal with the foregoing issues, Leslie Wilkins and his colleagues (Wilkins et al., 1978) developed sentencing guidelines which, interestingly, are based on experience with setting up release guidelines for the U.S. Board of Parole (see Gottfredson et al., 1974). The researchers examined the variables actually considered by judges in rendering a sentencing decision (using a stepwise multiple regression to determine the amount that each variable contributed to the outcome). They state how the guidelines are to be used (Gottfredson et al., 1978: 29):

We envision that the judge will use the guideline items as a sort of benchmark, or check, against which to measure the sentence the judge tentatively plans to impose. If that sentence is within the range provided for by the guidelines, the judge need not provide particularized reasons for imposing the particular sanction, but will probably feel more comfortable in handing down that sentence. The guidelines themselves (i.e., the information base which makes up the guidelines) provide the reason for the sentence. The guidelines do not suggest an exact sentence but offer a small range so that the judge may distinguish between offenses and/or offenders which are grouped into somewhat broad categories. For example, the guidelines may consider only the offender's total number of prior felony convictions, but, by providing a range, the guidelines permit the judge to more heavily weigh a past robbery conviction than one for petit larceny without having to go outside the guidelines.

If, however, the judge wishes to impose a sentence outside the guidelines—which we estimate will normally happen about 10 to 20 percent of the time—either above or below, then the judge of course has the absolute freedom to do so. Nevertheless, we are suggesting that written reasons be given for such a departure. This much we believe is due the defendant, society, and the judge's colleagues. It is imperative that the reasons not simply be an expression of something already contained in the guidelines, or some phrase made meaningless through rote repetition (which we believe would occur frequently were written reasons required for *all* sentences), but that they instead by a thoughtful and "reasoned" justification for why the guidelines are inappropriate for the case at hand. A judge may still refer to an item in the guidelines, but rather than merely state the obvious—that the particular item was considered—the judge should explain why a different weighting was given the item.

Since the information contained in the presentence report is the basis for weighing the guideline variables, the role of the probation officer is of obvious importance. (As with determinate sentencing, however, sentencing guidelines do not respond to the issue of prosecutorial discretion.)

Parole board guidelines are discussed in Chapter 10.

ITEMS FOR STUDY

1. Parole release has its origins in the conditional pardon, transportation to America, the Ticket of Leave, and the Elmira Reformatory, with its indeterminate imprisonment structure.
2. The most pressing issue affecting parole is the controversy over the indeterminate sentence.
3. In response to criticism of disparate sentencing, various remedies have been proposed for structuring judicial, but not prosecutorial, discretion.

chapter 10

Administration
of
Parole

The administration of parole is less complex than that of probation because parole services are administered centrally on a statewide basis. There are two basic models for administering parole services. In one model, parole is placed under the administration of an independent parole board. In the other model, parole is placed within a larger department that also administers correctional institutions.

The Task Force on Corrections summarized the arguments for placing parole under an independent parole board (1966: 71):

1. The board is in the best position to promote parole and to generate public support and acceptance. Since the board is often held accountable for parole failures, it should be responsible for supervising parolees.
2. The parole board in direct control of administering parole services can more effectively evaluate and adjust the system.
3. Supervision by the parole board and its officers properly divorces the parolees from the correctional institution.
4. An independent parole board in charge of its own services is in the best position to present its own budget request to the legislature.

Critics in opposition to this model contend that it is wont to be insensitive to correctional programs in the institution, and that this insensitivity can result in the wrong persons being paroled (O'Leary and Nuffield, 1973: 380).

The Task Force on Corrections also summarized the arguments for including both parole and institutions in a single department of correction (1966: 71):

1. The correctional process is a continuum. All staff, institution and parole, should be under a single administration rather than being divided, with resultant competition for public funds and friction in policies.
2. A consolidated correctional department has the advantage of consistent administration, including staff selection and supervision.
3. Parole boards are ineffective in performing administrative functions. Their major focus should be on case decisions, not on day-to-day field operations.
4. ‘The growing number of programs partway between institutions and parole, such as work release, can best be handled by a single centralized administration.

Critics of this model maintain that institutional operating considerations rather than the offender's or the community's needs too often determine parole decisions. Overcrowding, a desire to get rid of "troublemakers," or the need to enforce relatively petty rules, may be the basis for parole decision making (O'Leary and Nuffield, 1973: 380).

The Task Force on Corrections believes that if the management of a state prison system is stagnant and the parole board is active and effective, parole services should be independent. However, if the opposite is true, or if both are equal with respect to effectiveness, then parole services should be combined within the department of correction (1966: 71).

CONDITIONAL RELEASE AND PAROLE

There are several ways for an offender to be released from a correctional institution. Few receive pardons and most do not remain in prison until the expiration of the sentences. Conditional release and parole are the two processes by which most inmates are released.

Conditional (Mandatory) Release

Conditional release means that an inmate is released at the expiration of his/her sentence, less time earned for good behavior (referred to as "good time"). In New York an inmate can earn good time at the rate of 10 days for each 30 days of time served. If serving a nine-year sentence, an inmate can be conditionally released at the end of six years. Good time can be lost for infractions of institutional rules. In some states, such as New York and Missouri, inmates who are conditionally released are subject to the same conditions as parolees and are placed under the supervision of a parole officer.

Parole

In practice, the parole board and not the sentencing judge determines how long an offender will serve in a correctional institution. Under the indeterminate sentencing procedure, a judge sets the maximum term (and perhaps a minimum term, depending

The Independent Model
Organization Chart of the New York State Division of Parole

Executive Clemency Unit*

OFFICE OF THE CHAIRMAN

Board of Parole

Counsel's Office

Executive Director

Finance Administrative Service Unit

Manpower Management Unit

Research Evaluation, Planning Unit

Institutional Services Unit

Field Services Unit

Bureau of Special Services

*Reports directly to Governor's Counsel.

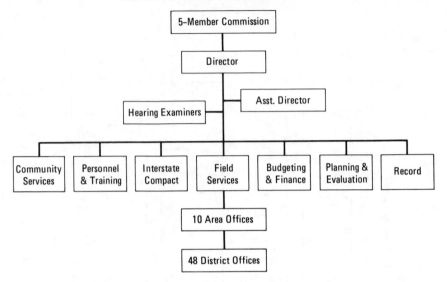

The Independent Model:
Florida Parole and Probation Commission*

*Note that this agency provides probation and parole services.

on state law), but the parole board determines how long an offender actually serves. The basis for the indeterminate sentencing procedure is rehabilitation, and the parole board is considered to be in the best position to evaluate an offender's progress toward this goal.

Parole Boards

Parole boards, the vehicle for operationalizing the indeterminate sentence, have come under increasing criticism. Several states have adopted some form of determinate sentencing and have abolished their parole (release) boards. In its place inmates are provided with time off for good behavior, usually on a day-for-day basis. That is, for each day of discipline-free behavior, the inmate receives a day off his/her sentence. A 10-year sentence, therefore, assuming good behavior, is actually five years of incarceration.

Parole board membership varies from 3 to 12, with the average being 5. With few exceptions, they serve full time and their appointment is the responsibility of the governor. Parole boards have been criticized because members may lack any relevant background or education. In only a few states are there any specific professional qualifications for board members. William Parker states that "the only real qualification may be the political responsiveness and reliability of the board members to the appointing power" (1975: 30). The role of politics and patronage in the appointment of parole board members is quite similar to their role in the selection of judges.

Typically, from one to three members briefly interview an inmate who is eligible

The Consolidated Model:
Ohio Department of Rehabilitation and Correction—Table of Organization

GOVERNOR

DIRECTOR
- Legal Services
- Public Information
- Institutional Liaison

DEPUTY DIRECTOR

ADMINISTRATIVE SERVICES
- Personnel
- Staff Development (Ohio Correction Academy)
- Labor Relations
- Equal Employment Opportunity
- Minority Recruitment
- LEAA Federal Grants Program

DIVISION OF CLASSIFICATION AND RESEARCH
- Program Evaluation
- Program Development
- Evaluation Services
- Research Coordination
- Bureau of Classification and Reception
- Reception Center Procedures
- Institutional Classification and Screening Procedures
- Institutional Release Procedures

DIVISION OF ADMINISTRATIVE AND FISCAL OPERATIONS
- Payroll and Fiscal Administration
- Operating and Engineering Services
- Ohio Penal Industries
- Capital Improvements
- Safety and Sanitation
- Internal Auditing

DIVISION OF PAROLE AND COMMUNITY SERVICES
- Adult Parole Authority
- Parole Board
- Parole Supervision
- Community Services
- Probation Development
- Administration and Research

DIVISION OF INSTITUTIONAL SERVICES

Correctional Institutions
- Chillicothe Correctional Institute
- Lebanon Correctional Institution
- London Correctional Institution
- Marion Correctional Institution
- Ohio Reformatory for Women
- Ohio State Reformatory
- Southern Ohio Correctional Facility

Institutional Services
- Educational
- Psychological
- Religious
- Security
- Social
- Volunteer
- Medical (Correctional Medical Center)
- Food Service

147

for parole. In a few states this aspect of the parole release process is handled by hearing examiners, who report back to the board with a recommendation. Some states do not conduct any hearing; decisions are made on the basis of written reports. David Stanley states that the parole hearing is of dubious value. It is a traumatic experience for the inmate, and board members are subjected to the rigors of holding hearings far away from home, with hours spent in travel and in prisons. Stanley reports hearings "are of little use in finding out whether the inmate is likely to succeed on parole" (1976: 42). He argues that a strong case can be made for abolishing hearings (p. 43):

> In cases where the information in the file and the board's own precedents plainly show that parole must surely be granted or denied, the hearing is a charade. In cases where the outcome is not so obvious it is a proceeding in which the inmate is at a great disadvantage and in which he has reason to say anything that will help his chances for parole. The atmosphere at such a hearing is full of tension and latent hostility. Under these circumstances the hearing is an ineffective way to elicit information, evaluate character traits, and give advice, all of which parole boards try to do.

One way to deal with some of these issues is to permit the inmate to have representation at the hearing. The National Advisory Commission believes that representation helps promote a feeling of fairness, and can enable an inmate to communicate better and thus participate more fully in the hearing. The Commission states that "representation can also contribute to opening the correctional system, particularly the parole process, to public scrutiny" (1973: 403). The Commission suggests that "lawyers are only one possible kind of representative; citizen volunteers also could serve as offender representatives." The Commission makes note of the fact that representation at parole hearings may be considered "annoying to parole officials." (There is fear that the hearing may take on the form of an adversary proceeding.) However, the Commission states that "these inconveniences seem a small price for the prospective gains."

In 1972, the U.S. Board of Parole initiated a pilot project that allowed inmates to have representatives at parole release hearings. These representatives included institutional staff, parents, peer-group members, family, friends, and employers. Later in the program inmates were also able to be represented by attorneys. A study of the project indicated that adults with representatives were paroled an average of six weeks earlier than inmates without representatives (Beck, 1975: 114–117).

Stanley also notes (1976: 43):

> Given the present parole system, hearings are necessary as an expression of our national tradition and culture. A man has his day in court before he is convicted and sentenced. In all sorts of situations we feel outraged if a person is not even confronted with the evidence before something adverse is done to him. In the hearing the prisoner is at least given a chance to state his case, correct erroneous statements, and impress the board with his determination (real or alleged) to reform.

In 1979, the U.S. Supreme Court, in a 5 to 4 decision, ruled in a Nebraska case *(Greenholtz* v. *Inmates,* 78-201) that the Constitution does not require that an inmate be given the opportunity to participate in parole board hearings or be informed of the reasons for denial of parole.

As in probation, there are restrictions on granting parole for certain offenses in different states. Some states prohibit parole for repeat offenders, while others deny parole opportunity for those convicted of kidnapping, escape from prison, assault on a correction officer, incest, and first-degree murder. The percentage of inmates released by parole also varies from state to state, and often with the degree of prison overcrowding. The amount of time that an inmate is required to serve before he/she is eligible for parole depends on the statutes in each state, and there are wide variations in minimum and maximum terms for the same crime in different states. These mimimums can be set by law, by the sentencing judge, or by the parole board. In some states an inmate is eligible for parole after completing a minimum sentence; in some states "good time" is deducted from the minimum. In others, an inmate is eligible for parole after serving one-third of the maximum sentence. Some states set eligibility according to the number of convictions for prior felonies. There are almost as many variations as there are parole boards.

A Parole Hearing

The following is an actual hearing that was held in New York, and the inmate being interviewed was granted parole (names have been changed).

EXAMINATION BY NELSON HARRIS, MEMBER OF THE BOARD OF PAROLE

Re: Smith, Louis, No. 092340136

Q. Louis Smith?

A. Yes.

Q. Smith, I am wondering if you got a chance on parole, what do you think would happen? Do you think the time is right?

A. I would go and pick up my life where I left it before.

Q. Do you think there was anything about the way you were living when you came in that needs changing?

A. A little could be altered so I am quite sure I would change them around now.

Q. Can you pinpoint, tell us some of the areas where you think you will change?

A. There is quite a few areas I can see where I am making mistakes. I am making a mistake coming here, that is one right there.

Q. Anything that you could do to stay out of places like this would definitely be something that would be of good intentions.

A. Yes.

Q. Do you have any plans? How are you going to try and go about making it when you get out of here?

A. First of all, I am starting back to work, which I am doing now and take it on from there.

Q. Staying in the big city area?

A. Yes.

Q. Can you cope with it?

A. I don't understand.

Q. Can you cope with the city, the bigness and all that?

A. Yes, I can.

Q. What is this job that you have?

A. It's the closest thing that they can give me to the job I have in the joint, that was all I have.

Q. Anybody that can get a foothold in that field really has something going for him and can make good money.

A. Yes.

Q. What can you do? How are your skills? What is the most you ever earned from it?

A. Well, the most I earned, brought in in one week was close to $500.

Q. You made that kind of money?

A. Yes.

Q. You noticed I have not referred to the crime?

A. Yes.

Q. You probably talked about it time and again.

A. Not very much, but some.

Q. This is thoroughly reported here. You did not have anything in your past like it and from what I read, it was certainly something you did not intend.

A. You are right, it wasn't intended. It was done through an accident. Mostly I was drinking and that is one problem I think I can handle now.

Q. Do you think you need anything outside yourself with reference to any drinking you did before?

A. I wasn't a regular drinker, I just drank sometimes. Now one thing I learned that if I get a problem, stay away from a bottle, that's what I learned.

Q. As a result of this, you also know that even though you don't drink all the time, it can still be a problem?

A. I found that out.

Q. Okay, your recommendations here are reasonably good and folks that have worked with you say they believe that there is no reason why you can't make it.

A. I hope I can.

Q. In the event you get the opportunity—

A. I hope I can make it.

Q. You feel that way?

A. Yes.

Q. Maybe there is something that you want to call to our attention?

A. No.

Q. Thanks for coming in. We will make a decision and let you know what it is.

Decision Making

Sol Rubin, former chief legal counsel of the National Council on Crime and Delinquency (NCCD), states that "parole boards exercise some functions that are exactly the same as judicial sentencing—for example, fixing minimum and maximum terms" (1974: 131). What criteria does a parole board use when it sets minimum and maximum terms, or when it is considering the parole release of an inmate? New York reports the following (New York Secretary of State, *Board of Parole,* chap. 12, pt. 1910: 15):

1. The inmate's previous criminal record; the nature and circumstances of the crime and his present attitude toward it; his attitude toward the police officer who arrested him, toward the district attorney who prosecuted him, toward the judge who sentenced him, and toward the complainant.
2. His conduct in the institution, his responses to efforts made to improve his mental and moral condition, together with his academic, vocational, and industrial records; his character, capacity, mentality, physical and mental condition, habits, attitudes; the kind of work he is best fitted to perform and at which he is most likely to succeed when he leaves the institution.
3. The environment to which he plans to return.
4. The kind of employment, educational, or other specified program secured for him.

The Florida Parole and Probation Commission, while including much the same type of criteria as New York, also lists "the capability of the Commission's field staff to provide adequate parole supervision once the person is paroled" (1974: 16).

Parker notes that many parole boards do not have written criteria for parole selection, or have statutes that are very broadly written and merely state that the inmate should "have a lawful occupation" or "not be a threat to himself or the community" (1975: 33). The American Law Institute in its *Model Penal Code* recommends to parole boards four primary reasons for denying an inmate parole (Gottfredson et al., 1975: 36):

1. There is a substantial risk that he will not conform to the conditions of parole.
2. His release at that time would depreciate the seriousness of his crime or promote disrespect for law.
3. His release would have a substantially adverse effect on institution discipline.
4. His continued correctional treatment, medical care, or vocational or other training in the institution would substantially enhance his capacity to lead a law-abiding life when released at a later date.

Parole boards usually consider the crime, the length of time served, the inmate's age, prior criminal history, use of drugs or alcohol, and institutional record. Some parole boards may request a recommendation from the prosecutor. All will certainly consider opposition to an inmate's parole from the police and the news media. A poll of parole board members revealed that their major consideration was whether or not they believed the inmate was likely to commit a serious crime if paroled (Gottfredson et al., 1975: 36).

In order to make these decisions, in addition to interviewing the inmate, the board members review the presentence report and institutional reports relative to the inmate's adjustment. Daniel Glaser recommends that the boards also make use of "prediction tables," compilations of statistics on the postrelease behavior of different types of offenders. Glaser believes that these tables will provide the basis for case prognostication (1969: 207).

Parole Board Guidelines

As criticism of parole and parole boards began to mount, the U.S. Board of Parole engaged a group of researchers to develop a model for improved parole decision making. The researchers, headed by Donald Gottfredson and Leslie Wilkins, derived a set of variables that they saw as fairly representative of those used by board members in making decisions—the most salient being seriousness of the offense and parole prognosis. The researchers also conducted a two-year study of 2500 federal parolees and uncovered a variety of success factors, which they reduced to nine variables and later reduced to seven. The combined variables "offense seriousness" and "parole prognosis" were presented in tabular form to derive a "salient factor score" that is used to determine length of actual imprisonment. Maurice Sigler, then

(1975) Chairman of the United States Board of Parole, discusses how the guidelines are utilized:

First, the examiner panel gives each case a salient factor score, ranging from zero to 11, with the higher the score, the better the prospects for successful completion of parole. The case gets points, or loses them, on the basis of such factors as prior convictions, prior commitments, education, employment history, marital status, etc. All of the factors were determined on the basis of research to have some predictability for success on parole.

The case is then given an offense severity rating—low, low moderate, moderate, high, very high, and greatest. This rating does not depend simply on the subjective judgment of the examiners. They are provided with a chart that lists offense categories under each severity rating.

Then, with the salient factor score, and the offense severity rating in hand, the examiners consult a second chart which indicates the amount of time an offender with a given background and salient factor score should serve for an offense of a given severity, assuming reasonably good institutional performance. For example, an offender with a salient factor score of 11 and an offense severity rating of low might be expected to serve 6 to 10 months before going out on parole. Or an offender with a salient factor score of 3 and a severity rating of very high may be expected to serve 55 to 65 months. For an offender with a severity rating of greatest, the most serious or heinous offenses, there is no maximum range stipulated.

For most offenders, the mix of salient factor score and offense severity rating involves a certain amount of risk in parole, and the system is intended to bring about a reasonable degree of fairness by insuring that they serve about the same amount of time as others in their situation.

But, for those cases where in the clinical judgment of the examiners the inmate has a much better prospect of success on parole than his score and rating suggest, the examiners can shorten the amount of time to be served below those specified by the guidelines. Or where the prospect of success on parole is much worse than that suggested by the score and rating, the examiners can extend the amount of time to be served beyond that specified.

THE FEDERAL PAROLE GUIDELINES*

Offense Severity (Some Crimes Eliminated or Summarized)	Salient Factor Score (Parole Prognosis)			
	Very Good	Good	Fair	Poor
Low: possession of a small amount of marijuana; simple theft under $1000.	6–10 months	8–12 months	10–14 months	12–18 months
Low/Moderate: income tax evasion less than $10,000; immigration law violations; embezzlement, fraud, forgery under $1000	8–12 months	12–16 months	16–20 months	20–28 months

*From Kevin Krajick, "Parole: Discretion Is Out, Guidelines Are In," *Corrections Magazine* 4 (December 1978).

Moderate: bribery; posession of 50 lb. or less of marijuana, with intent to sell; illegal firearms; income tax evasion $10,000 to $50,000; nonviolent property offenses $1000 to $19,999; auto theft, not for resale	12–16 months	16–20 months	20–24 months	24–32 months
High: counterfeiting; marijuana possession with intent to sell, 50 to 1999 lb.; auto theft, for resale; nonviolent property offenses, $20,000 to $100,000	16–20 months	20–26 months	26–34 months	34–44 months
Very High: robbery; breaking and entering bank or post office; extortion; marijuana possession with intent to sell, over 2000 lb.; hard drugs possession with intent to sell, not more than $100,000; nonviolent property offenses over $100,000 but not exceeding $500,000	26–36 months	36–48 months	48–60 months	60–72 months
Greatest I: explosive detonation; multiple robbery; aggravated felony (weapon fired—no serious injury); hard drugs, over $100,000; forcible rape	40–55 months	55–70 months	70–85 months	85–110 months
Greatest II: aircraft hijacking; espionage; kidnapping; homicide	Greater than above. No specific ranges because of limited number and extreme variation in cases.			

These guidelines have been adopted, sometimes in modified form, by many state parole boards. They go well beyond the *rehabilitative/medical model* on which the indeterminate sentence rests. Indeed, satisfactory progress in those institutional programs that are "rehabilitative" may not even affect the parole decision. Kevin Krajick points out that good institutional behavior is *expected,* not rewarded, although poor behavior can be punished with additional time (1978b: 49). The institutional adjustment of an offender has never been an accurate guide for predicting postinstitutional behavior; there is some evidence that certain offenders (e.g., substance abusers, professional criminals) most often perform well in prison and tend to be recidivists.

It is "just deserts" that is the primary focus of most (if not all) parole board guidelines; what amount of time does the offender *deserve.* In making this type of decision the board is not constrained by the legal category of the crime; members can deal with the actual circumstances of the offense. Since plea bargaining, by which most offenders are convicted, usually results in a lowered charge, the parole board can, in effect, abrogate plea bargains. This raises the issue of utilizing unproven charges in making parole decisions. For example, Robert Michaels was arrested and charged with kidnapping, robbery, and assault. In return for a plea of guilty, the charge of kidnapping and assault were dropped. However, when Michaels appears for parole consideration, both unproven allegations, kidnapping and assault, are considered by the board in deciding against parole and in favor of lengthy incarceration.

In effect, the use of guidelines focusing on "just deserts" is a form of deferred sentencing. Some critics state that there is no justification for deferring sentence (actually incarceration time) and that it creates problems by adding to the offender's uncertainty. Others argue, however, that the parole board is relatively free of the "heat" that certain crimes and criminals generate. The board is not under the same pressure as a judge who must sentence in open court under the gaze of the community and the news media. These observers stress that the parole board, using guidelines, is better equipped to make a rational decision commensurate with "just deserts."

A sample of parole board guidelines and policy follows.

PAROLE BOARD GUIDELINES*

(Do not use for inmates with sentences over 30 years.)

Prior Criminal Record

Guideline Rating: *Board Member Rating:*

For a rating outside the guidelines, please indicate the reasons:

Institutional Discipline

  Guideline Rating: *Board Member Rating:*

For a rating outside the guidelines, please indicate the reasons:

In completing this form, please use Board Member ratings for prior criminal record and institutional discipline.

	Yes	No
A. Has the inmate		
1. Failed on work release during the last year?	___	___
2. Escaped during the last year?	___	___
3. Violated probation or parole during the last 2 years?	___	___
4. Received an unfavorable psychiatric or psychological report during the last 6 months?	___	___

If any answers were Yes, deny parole. If all answers were No, continue to B.

---

*From Donald M. Gottfredson, Leslie T. Wilkins, Peter B. Hoffman, and Susan M. Singer, *The Utilization of Experience in Parole Decision-Making* (Washington, D.C.: U.S. Government Printing Office, 1974).

B. Does the inmate have *poor* institutional discipline? ____ ____
    If Yes, deny parole. If No, continue to C.

C. Does the inmate have *good* institutional discipline combined with a MINOR or NO prior criminal record? ____ ____
    If No, continue to D.

D. Does the inmate have a *serious* prior criminal record? ____ ____
    If Yes, continue to E. If No, skip to F.

E. (Only for inmates with a *serious* prior criminal record) Is the inmate at his first hearing? ____ ____
    If Yes, deny parole. If No, continue to F.

F. Do the following *unfavorable* factors apply to the inmate? ____ ____
    Please check all factors Yes or No.

	Yes	No
1. Factors relating to the inmate's prior criminal record:		
a. Habitual offender	____	____
b. Serious juvenile record	____	____
c. Short time between offenses	____	____
d. Professional criminal	____	____
2. Factors relating to the present offense:		
a. Bizarre nature of the offense	____	____
b. Lack of provocation	____	____
c. Relatively high degree of sophistication shown in the crime	____	____
3. Factors relating to conduct in the institution:		
a. Pattern of assaultive behavior	____	____
b. Rebellious, hostile	____	____
4. Factors relating to the inmate personally:		
a. No remorse, does not understand nature of the offense	____	____
b. Antisocial attitude	____	____
c. Alcohol or drug habit so serious as to raise questions as to the probability of his succeeding on parole	____	____
d. Incapable of coping with situations realistically	____	____

If any checks were Yes, continue to G. If all checks were No, parole.

G. Do the following *favorable* factors apply to the inmate?
    Please check all factors Yes or No.

	Yes	No

1. Factors relating to the present offense:
   a. Self-defense __ __
   b. Defense of helpless person __ __
   c. Acting under provocation __ __
   d. Diminished responsibility because of retardation
      or intoxication __ __
   e. Minor role in the offense __ __
2. Factors relating to conduct in the institution:
   a. Good adjustment __ __
   b. Good response to prison programs __ __
   c. Recent good conduct __ __
   d. Unusually helpful to authorities __ __
3. Factors relating to the inmate's condition (disabled,
   aged, terminally ill, debilitated) __ __
4. Likely to max out and needs supervision __ __
5. Factors relating to the postrelease situation:
   a. Probation to follow __ __
   b. Specialized program to follow __ __

If any checks were Yes, parole. If all checks were No,
deny parole.

Decision:
  Parole: *Deny parole:*

For a decision outside the guidelines, please indicate the reasons:

Inmate was paroled/denied parole because

Date: *Board Member:*

Policy Statement Concerning the Parole Decision

The Parole Board uses the following seven major criteria in determining whether to grant or deny parole:

1. *Seriousness of the offense.* It is the policy of the Board to take into consideration the nature and circumstances of the offense to determine whether the inmate has served sufficient time for the purposes of retribution and general deterrence. In assessing the seriousness of the offense, the Board will be guided by the official version of the offense and the length of the sentence imposed.

The Board will also consider a number of mitigating and aggravating factors, including the inmate's motivation for committing the offense, his/her role in the offense, the amount of loss and/or injury to the victim, and the degree of sophistication evidenced in the offense. The Board is particularly concerned with offenses which involved a weapon and/or physical injury or possible injury to the victim. The Board is also concerned with crimes of a repetitive nature, such as a series of burglaries, or drug sales which reflect extensive involvement in crime-oriented activities. In general, it is not Board policy to deny parole *solely* on the basis of the nature and circumstances of the offense; there are, however, certain instances where denial on this basis alone is required.

2. *Prior criminal record.* The evaluation of the prior criminal record plays a significant role in the decision-making process. In evaluating the inmate along this dimension, the Board will consider both the inmate's prior adult and juvenile records in order to determine the degree of his/her past involvement in crime-oriented activities. The Board is primarily concerned with the number and seriousness of the inmate's *convictions*. In most instances, the length and seriousness of the arrest record will not be used in determining the prior record rating; however, when there is evidence that the inmate has had numerous arrests, this factor will be used to increase the seriousness of the prior criminal record rating.

Since the evaluation of this factor is weighted heavily in the decision-making process, the Board has developed the following guidelines for evaluating the seriousness of the prior criminal record. These ratings are based primarily on a weighting of fines and the length of prior sentences to incarceration. It is important to note that these ratings do not include the *present* offense and that commitment to a training school will be considered as equivalent to a one-year sentence.

Prior criminal record is defined as follows:

No record: no previous convictions.

Minor record:
1. Fines and court costs only; or
2. Maximum active sentences* totaling no more than 18 months; or
3. Maximum active sentences* totaling no more than six months, if the inmate has fines and court costs in addition to active sentences on his record.

Moderate record:
1. Maximum active sentences* totaling more than 18 months, but no more than six years; or
2. Maximum active sentences* totaling more than six months, but no more than five years, if the inmate has fines and court costs in addition to active sentences on his record.

*An active sentence is a sentence on which the inmate served prison or jail time.

Serious record:
  1. Maximum active sentences* totaling more than six years; or
  2. Maximum active sentences* totaling more than five years, if the inmate has fines and court costs in addition to active sentences on his record.

The Board reserves the right to go outside these guidelines to take into consideration mitigating factors, or aggravating factors such as probations, suspended sentences, arrests, and the seriousness or frequency of the offenses.

In most instances, parole will be denied to inmates at first parole eligibility who have a prior criminal record rating of "serious."

  3. *Community supervision.* The Board places considerable emphasis on the inmate's adjustment to previous periods of probation and/or parole supervision. Recent failure on community supervision is interpreted as a sign that the prospective parolee is not ready to comply with parole conditions. It is therefore the policy of the Board to deny parole to inmates who have violated probation or parole within the last *two* years.

  4. *Institutional discipline.* The Board believes that one of its responsibilities is to maintain order in correctional facilities by denying parole to inmates who have failed to comply with institutional rules. Since this factor plays an important role in the decision-making process, the Board has defined three disciplinary classifications which incorporate the six categories of infractions in use by the Department of Corrections. It should be noted that these classifications are based on infractions committed *within the last year.*

Institutional discipline classifications are as follows:

Good discipline:
  1. No infractions during the last six months.
  2. No more than one infraction during the last year.
  3. No infractions in Category I.

Adequate discipline:
  1. No more than one infraction during the last six months.
  2. No more than three infractions during the last year.
  3. No more than one infraction in either Category I or II during the last year.

Poor discipline:
  1. Two or more infractions during the last six months.
  2. Four or more infractions during the last year.
  3. Two or more infractions classified as Category I or II.

The board members may go outside these guidelines to take into consideration mitigating factors, or aggravating factors such as escapes, crimes committed in prison, and infractions over a year old.

  5. *Escape.* It is Board policy to deny parole to an inmate who has either escaped *within the last year,* or who has been on escape and who has been returned to the institution within the last year.

  6. *Program participation.* The Board will consider information pertaining

*Ibid.

to the degree of the parole candidate's participation in and response to the educational, vocational, rehabilitative, and other programs available in the correctional facility. The Board is particularly concerned with the subject's performance on work release. It is Board policy to deny parole to inmates who have failed on work release *in the last year.* Failure in this program is interpreted as a sign that the parole candidate is unlikely to comply with parole conditions.

7. *Factors related to personal history of the subject.* In evaluating the parole candidate on this dimension, the Board will consider information pertaining to the inmate's civilian work record, level of education, occupational skills and family ties. In addition, the Board will consider whether the subject has a history of drug or alcohol abuse which may seriously decrease the likelihood that he/she will succeed on parole. Although the Board does not routinely request a psychological report on all candidates, there are certain cases where such a report is deemed appropriate. In most instances, parole will be denied to an inmate who has received an unfavorable psychiatric or psychological evaluation *within the last six months.*

Although the Board considers each case on its individual merits, there are several policies which determine the ways in which the parole criteria are applied in the decision-making process. It is the policy of the Board to *deny* parole to candidates who have conformed to any one of the following categories:

1. Failed on work release during the last year;
2. Escaped or returned from escape within the last year;
3. Violated probation or parole during the last *two* years;
4. Received an unfavorable psychiatric or psychological report within the last *six* months;
5. A "poor" institutional discipline rating; *or*
6. A "serious" prior record rating *and* who are at their first parole eligibility.

It is the policy of the Board to grant parole to inmates who have conformed to all of the following categories:

1. Served sufficient time for the purposes of retribution and general deterrence;
2. A "no" or "minor" prior record rating; *and*
3. A "good" institutional discipline rating.

In the case of marginal parole candidates—that is, inmates whose cases are not decided within the above-mentioned guidelines—the Board will also consider several favorable and unfavorable factors about the case:

Unfavorable factors:
1. Factors relating to the inmate's prior criminal record:
   a. Habitual offender
   b. Serious juvenile record

    c. Short time between offenses
    d. Professional criminal
2. Factors relating to the present offense:
    a. Bizarre nature of the offense
    b. Lack of provocation
    c. Relatively high degree of sophistication shown in the crime
3. Factors relating to conduct in the institution:
    a. Pattern of assaultive behavior
    b. Rebellious, hostile
4. Factors relating to the inmate personally:
    a. No remorse, does not understand nature of offense
    b. Antisocial attitude
    c. Alcohol or drug habit so serious as to raise questions as to probability of his succeeding on parole
    d. Incapable of coping with situations realistically

Favorable factors:
1. Factors relating to the present offense:
    a. Self-defense
    b. Defense of helpless person
    c. Acting under provocation
    d. Diminished responsibility because of retardation or intoxication
    e. Minor role in the offense
2. Factors relating to conduct in the institution:
    a. Good adjustment
    b. Good response to prison programs
    c. Recent good conduct
    d. Unusually helpful to authorities
3. Factors relating to the inmate's condition:
    a. Physically disabled
    b. Extremely aged
    c. Terminally ill
    d. Debilitated; further incarceration will serve no useful purpose
4. Likely to max out and needs supervision
5. Factors relating to the postrelease situation:
    a. Probation to follow
    b. Specialized program to follow

It is the policy of the Board to grant parole when none of the above unfavorable factors are evident in the case. In cases where one or more unfavorable factors are present, it is Board policy to grant parole only if there are one or more outstanding factors which can serve to counterbalance the unfavorable factors.

The following burglary case demonstrates how guidelines are applied to actual cases seen by the Board.

A CASE ILLUSTRATION*

In January of 1978, John McDougall was arrested for burglary at the apartment of Mrs. T.A. Green and was subsequently convicted of Burglary II in a jury trial in March of 1978. At the trial, Mrs. Green testified that on the night of January 11, 1978 she awoke around 11:00 P.M. to find McDougall searching through dresser drawers in her bedroom. She demanded that he leave. He approached the bed threatening, "shut up or you'll be sorry." She further stated that McDougall demanded to know where she kept her money. When she failed to answer, he struck her on the face and demanded that she get out of bed and get money for him. Mrs. Green protested that she could not do this as she was bedridden. At this point a neighbor, who nightly checked on Mrs. Green's welfare, knocked on the front door. McDougall fled through the back door. The neighbor called the police. McDougall was picked up shortly thereafter in an alley behind Mrs. Green's residence.

The offense apparently involved little planning. Mrs. Green was not injured.

Base Time and Severity of Crime

The possible number of months of prison term under the Boards minimum term guidelines are listed on the left. The months of prison term for the behavioral factors of McDougall's burglary are listed on the right.

Minimum Term Guidelines[1]
Conviction Information Form
Property—Part I

Possible months		McDougall's months
3	BASE TIME (FOR ANY PROPERTY OFFENSE)	3 months
9	ADDED BASE TIME FOR BURGLARY	9 months
6	VICTIM WAS VULNERABLE	6 months
6 to 24 .	DEGREE OF PLANNING	0
0 to 15 .	OBJECTIVE OF PLANNING	0
6	RESIDENTIAL PROPERTY CRIME	6 months
6	VANDALISM	0
6	HIGH SPEED CHASE	0
6	DAMAGE TO VEHICLE (OTHER THAN OWN) ...	0

---

*Source: Washington State Board of Prison Terms and Paroles.
[1]Effective July 1, 1979 these guidelines are subject to change at periodic reviews by the Board.

PROPERTY - PART II
TO BE COMPLETED WHEN VICTIM IS THREATENED/INJURED

12	VICTIM THREATENED/ASSAULTED	12 months
12	VICTIM PHYSICALLY/MENTALLY HANDICAPPED	12 months
12 to 30 .	VICTIM VULNERABLE BY AGE	0
9 to 24 .	METHOD OF VIOLENCE	9 months
6 to 24 .	INJURY TO VICTIM	0
3 to 24 .	MORE THAN ONE VICTIM INVOLVED	0
12	KIDNAPPING	0
9 to 24 .	NON-CONSENSUAL SEXUAL ABUSE	0
9 to 24 .	ADDITIONAL INCIDENT OF NON-CONSENSUAL SEXUAL ABUSE	0

ACT SEVERITY TIME   57 months

Public Safety Score Factors

John McDougall has never been committed to a juvenile institution, but he has two prior felony convictions as an adult. While he was not a hard drug user, he did have a history of marijuana use. During the two years prior to the current admission he had been living with friends and had not worked during this period. McDougall's score for the pre-admission items on the Public Safety Score is 6.5. He can earn an additional 4.5 points during his incarceration.

In this instance, let's assume that McDougall earned three additional points while in prison. He received two points because he committed no infractions. He earned one point for successful completion of work release. He did not have a verified job upon release.*

McDougall's total public safety score is 9.5.

A score of 9.5 for property offenders translates to:

1) A 52.4% chance of having no parole violations during the 18 month period after release;
2) A 16.9% chance of having a technical or misdemeanor violation during the 18 month period after release; and
3) A 30.7% chance of having a felony violation during the 18 month period after release.

With this score, he is eligible for a seven-month reduction** in addition to earned "good time" credits. Based upon his score and the chances of parole violations associated with his score, McDougall is eligible for a reduction of

---

*The last item on the Public Safety Score form is a combination of employment plans for release and involvement in a work or training release program.

**The formula for translating individual scores to possible reductions is complicated. Those who are interested in this can contact the Washington Board of Prison Terms and Paroles and request a copy of the guidelines.

16% (seven months) in his minimum term in addition to earned "good time" credits.

Prior Record

The Board is concerned about the repetition of criminal behavior and believes that the offender should be held responsible for the degree to which current behavior is a continuation of past behavior. Each prior conviction therefore, adds time to the minimum term.

John McDougall had two prior felony convictions from California. He was convicted of auto theft in August 1973 and burglary in January 1974. He served 18 months in a California correctional facility for these offenses.

For property offenders, each prior property offense adds six months to the minimum term. Offenses against persons add more. In this case, McDougall has two prior property offenses. These would add 12 months to the guideline minimum term.

NUMBER OF MONTHS ADDED FOR EACH PRIOR RECORD ENTRY
BY ADMISSION FELONY CLASS [1]

PRIOR RECORD CLASS	ADMISSION FELONY CLASS							
	MURDER	SEX OFFENSE	ROBBERY	ASSAULT	MAN-SLAUGHTER	PROPERTY OFFENSE [2]	DRUG OFFENSE	OTHER [3]
MURDER	96	48	48	48	48	18	24	18
SEX OFFENSE	24	24	12	12	12	6	6	6
ROBBERY	24	12	24	12	12	6	6	6
ASSAULT	24	12	12	24	12	6	6	6
MANSLAUGHTER	48	12	12	12	36	12	12	12
PROPERTY OFFENSE	6	6	6	6	6	6	6	6
DRUG OFFENSE	6	6	6	6	6	6	6	6
OTHER	6	6	6	6	6	6	6	6

[1] Note: Each column represents the felony class of the current admission. Each figure in a column is the number of months added for each entry within the prior record classes.

[2] Property offenses include felony classes Burglary, Check/Credit Card Abuse, Possession of Stolen Property, Theft, Auto Theft.

[3] Other offenses include felony classes Felon in Possession of a Firearm, Escape and all other types of criminal acts not included in the previous felony classes.

Recommended Minimum Term

No set of guidelines can be sufficiently detailed to account for every individual circumstance. In order to accommodate these subtle variations, a range of about 12½% has been created around each guideline term.

In the case of McDougall, the guideline range would be 60 to 78 months. The Board would set a term within this range unless extenuating circumstances are present.

```
ACT SEVERITY . . . . . . . . . . . . . . . . . . . . . . . . . . . 57 MONTHS
PRIOR RECORD . . . . . . . . . . . . . . . . . . . . . . . +12 MONTHS
GUIDELINE MINIMUM TERM . . . . . . . . . . . . . 69 MONTHS
```

Public Safety Score

PROPERTY OFFENDER (MALE)

PRE-ADMISSION ITEMS

SCORE		McDougall
	JUVENILE RECORD	
0	...COMMITTED TO JUVENILE INSTITUTION	0
1.5	...NEVER COMMITTED TO JUVENILE INSTITUTION	1.5
	HISTORY OF DRUG ABUSE	
0	...USE OF OPIATES	0
1.0	...USE OF SUBSTANCES OTHER THAN OPIATES, MARIJUANA OR HASHISH	0
2.0	...USE OF MARIJUANA OR HASHISH	2.0
3.0	...NEVER USED DRUGS	0
	ADULT CRIMINAL RECORD	
0	...FIVE OR MORE FELONY CONVICTIONS	0
0.5	...FOUR FELONY CONVICTIONS	0
1.0	...THREE FELONY CONVICTIONS	1.0
1.5	...TWO FELONY CONVICTIONS	0
2.0	...ONE FELONY CONVICTION	0
	EMPLOYMENT RECORD--TWO YEARS PRIOR TO ADMISSION	
0	...NEVER EMPLOYED	0
1.5	...UNEMPLOYED FOR ENTIRE TWO YEARS PRIOR TO ADMISSION	1.5
3.0	...UNEMPLOYED FOR MORE THAN SIX MONTHS DURING THE TWO YEARS PRIOR TO ADMISSION	0
4.5	...NOT EMPLOYED FOR MORE THAN SIX MONTHS DURING THE TWO YEARS PRIOR TO ADMISSION	0
	PERSONAL SUPPORT - LIVING ARRANGEMENT PRIOR TO ADMISSION	
0	...LIVING ALONE	0
0.5	...LIVING WITH SIBLINGS OR FRIENDS (INCLUDING COHABITATION).	0.5
1.0	...LIVING WITH PARENTS, PARENTS AND SIBLINGS, OR OTHER RELATIVES	0
1.5	...LIVING WITH SPOUSE AND/OR CHILDREN	0

SCORE ON PRE-ADMISSION ITEMS   6.5

CURRENT INCARCERATION ITEMS

	INSTITUTIONAL CONDUCT	
0	...ONE OR MORE "SERIOUS" INFRACTIONS	0
1.0	...ONE OR MORE "GENERAL" INFRACTIONS	0
2.0	...NO INFRACTIONS	2.0
	RELEASE EMPLOYMENT/WORK-TRAINING RELEASE PROGRAM INVOLVEMENT	
0	...EMPLOYMENT NOT VERIFIED, UNSUCCESSFUL TERMINATION FROM PROGRAM	0
0.5	...EMPLOYMENT NOT VERIFIED, DID NOT PARTICIPATE IN PROGRAM	0
1.0	...EMPLOYMENT NOT VERIFIED, SUCCESSFUL TERMINATION FROM PROGRAM	1.0
1.5	...VERIFIED EMPLOYMENT, UNSUCCESSFUL TERMINATION FROM PROGRAM	0
2.0	...VERIFIED EMPLOYMENT, DID NOT PARTICIPATE IN PROGRAM	0
2.5	...VERIFIED EMPLOYMENT, SUCCESSFUL TERMINATION OF PROGRAM	0

SCORE ON INSTITUTION ITEMS   3.0

TOTAL SCORE   9.5

Reconsideration Guidelines

The Board set a minimum term of 69 months for John McDougall.

The laws of the State of Washington provide that for good institutional behavior, McDougall will be eligible to earn a reduction of one-third of his minimum term. These are referred to as "good time" credits. He must be recommended for this reduction by the institution superintendent and have it approved by the Parole Board.

In addition to the "good time" reduction, the Board will consider an additional reduction of the minimum term. McDougall's public safety score indicates that he has better than a 50% likelihood of no violations on parole. He is, therefore, eligible for a reduction at his parole review hearing after having served all but one month of his projected length of confinement.

McDougall's Projected Length of Incarceration Based on Guidelines

McDougall's minimum length of confinement can be computed as soon as his minimum term is set:

Minimum Term	69 Months
Possible "Good Time" Credits	−23 Months
Sub-Total	= 46 Months
Possible Public Safety Score reduction	− 7 Months
Projected length of confinement	= 39 Months

If McDougall earns all of his possible "good time" credits and the Board grants the seven-month public safety factor reduction, his projected length of confinement for this offense is 39 months.

Hearing Examiners

Several jurisdictions utilize examiners to hold parole hearings. In these jurisdictions the parole board usually acts upon a report and recommendation from the examiner. The federal board uses eight examiners who handle about 75 percent of the parole interviews, with the remainder handled by board members. The examiner holds a hearing at the institution and dictates a summary that is sent to the board with a recommendation. The board then votes on whether to grant parole. The Florida Parole and Probation Commission also uses hearing examiners. Inmates are interviewed on an annual basis, after which a report of the examiner's findings and recommendation is submitted to the Commission for parole consideration (1974: 16–17).

Another hearing examiner model appears above. In this model the hearing officer makes a decision on whether or not to grant parole. As noted on the extreme right of the diagram, if the inmate is dissatisfied with the decision of the hearing officer, he/she can appeal to the full board of parole. It should be noted that the inmate is not interviewed by the parole board in this, or any other, hearing examiner model.

Hearing examiners are usually utilized to reduce the workload of the parole board. Since hearing examiners tend to be selected on the bais of professional competence, their use portends an improvement in the parole process.

Hearing Examiner Model

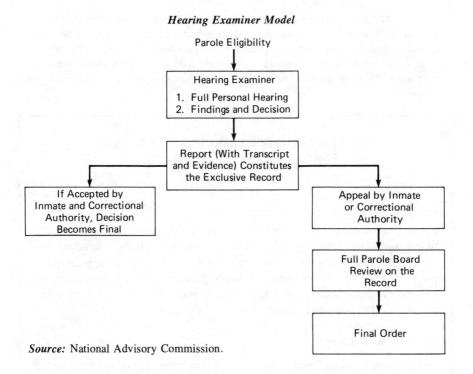

Parole Eligibility

Hearing Examiner
1. Full Personal Hearing
2. Findings and Decision

Report (With Transcript and Evidence) Constitutes the Exclusive Record

If Accepted by Inmate and Correctional Authority, Decision Becomes Final

Appeal by Inmate or Correctional Authority

Full Parole Board Review on the Record

Final Order

Source: National Advisory Commission.

Written Reasons for Parole Denial

In some jurisdictions, should parole be denied, an inmate is not provided with the reasons. This lack of information has been criticized by many in the legal and correctional field as being unfair and arbitrary. The following is a sample of a statement presented to an inmate by a state parole board whose policy is to provide written reasons whenever parole is denied:

After consideration of the circumstances of your present offense, and in the absence of any statement by the sentencing court tending to indicate the contrary, the Board has concluded that there are certain punitive and deterrent aspects to your sentence. In the absence of any special or equitable circumstances or any affirmative evidence that you can avoid criminal behavior and since your minimum sentence has not yet expired, the Board feels that the punitive and deterrent aspects of your sentence have not been fulfilled and that, therefore your release would not be compatible with the community welfare.

After consideration of all records relevant to your confinement, treatment and efforts towards self-improvement while in the State Prison system, the Board is unable to conclude that there is reasonable probability that you will return to society without violation of law.

After consideration of all relevant records and your hearing, the Board notes that you still minimize your delinquent behavior and indicate the shooting of the victim was accidental although you entered a plea of guilty. Professional staff reports still persuade the Board that you are lacking in insight into your delinquent activities, and that your judgment is impaired. It is further indicated that you are still a potential assaultive risk. The Board notes that your work record in the institution continues to be good. The Board is unable to conclude that there are sufficient affirmative indications to persuade the Board that you would be able to control your assaultive behavior and delinquent activities in the community. Parole is therefore denied, and you will be reheard as scheduled in this Notice of Decision.

STATE BOARD OF PARDONS AND PAROLES
PAROLE DECISION GUIDELINES
NOTICE OF ACTION

NAME & NO. _____   DATE _____

Parole Decision Guidelines help the Board make a prompt, consistent, soundly based, and explainable parole decision on an inmate serving a sentence less than twenty-one years. Guidelines help the Board decide on a presumptive parole release date for an inmate or decide that the inmate will complete his sentence without parole. For a specific and stated reason the Board, when making its decision, may depart from the Guidelines.

Crime Severity Level

An inmate's Crime Severity Level is selected from the table of offenses on the back of this sheet. The Board's Legal Investigation account of what occurred in the offense, not necessarily the name of the offense, determines the Severity Level. If an inmate's offense is not listed, the Severity Level of the most similar listed offense is chosen.

Parole Success Factors

The Board has thoroughly researched its parolee records and identified the factors most often linked with successful parolees. These statistical studies have shown that the following weighted factors have definite value in predicting success on parole. An inmate's Parole Success Likelihood Score is found by adding the points which apply to him.

A. AGE AT FIRST COMMITMENT   ____
   (26 or over   = 5)
   (22 –25   = 3)
   (18 –21   = 2)
   (17 or less   = 0)

B. PRIOR CONVICTIONS (JUVE-   ____
   NILE AND ADULT)
   (none   = 3)
   (1   = 2)
   (2 – 3   = 1)
   (4 or more   = 0)

C. PRIOR INCARCERATIONS   ____
   SINCE AGE 17
   (none   = 2)
   (1   = 1)
   (2 or more   = 0)

D. PAROLE AND PROBATION   ____
   REVOCATIONS
   (No revocations   = 4)
   (Probation only   = 2)
   (Parole only   = 1)
   (Both   = 0)

E. NO HISTORY OF HEROIN OR   —
OPIATE DRUG USE = 1
OTHERWISE   = 0

MONTHS PRECEDING CUR-
RENT OFFENSE   = 1
OTHERWISE   = 0

F. COMMITMENT OFFENSE   —
DID NOT INVOLVE BUR-
GLARY OR FORGERY   = 2
OTHERWISE   = 0

H. HAD WRAT SCORE OF 8 OR   —
HIGHER AT TIME OF DIAG-
NOSTIC TESTING   = 2
OTHERWISE   = 0

G. FULLY EMPLOYED DURING 6   —

Parole Success Likelihood Score =

Months-to-Serve Chart

The Board believes that the less serious an inmate's offense, the less time he should serve, and that the more likely he would succeed on parole, the less time he should serve. The following chart embodies these principles of justice and protection of society. Read across from an inmate's Crime Severity Level and down from his Parole Success Likelihood Score to find the indicated number of months to serve.

You may appeal this decision within the next 30 days, confining your appeal to the Crime Severity Level and Parole Success Likelihood Score. An attorney is not required. Detail your appeal reasons in a letter, or on the Inmate Appeal Form, to Appeals Officer, State Board of Pardons and Paroles, 800 Peachtree Street, N. E., Atlanta, Georgia 30308.

Parole Success Score

	Severity	Excellent 20–13	Good 12–11	Average 10–9	Fair 8–6	Poor 5–0
Crime	I	9	12	18	30	42
Severity	II	12	18	21	33	48
Level	III	18	24	30	36	54
	IV	24	30	36	42	60
	V	30	36	42	48	66
	VI	48	60	60	72	84
	VII	84	90	90	96	108

Parole Eligibility Month   _____

Crime Severity Level   _____

Parole Success Likelihood Score   _____

Months to Serve from Chart   _____

Chart Release Month   _____

Days Added for Disciplinary Report(s)   _____

Presumptive Parole Month   _____

Check One:

( ) The Board has tentatively decided to parole you during the above Presumptive Parole Month or Parole Eligibility Month, whichever is later.

Your release could be changed due to Disciplinary Reports not yet considered or due to delay in setting up a satisfactory parole program.

( ) Because your Presumptive Parole Month is later than your tentative discharge date, you should expect to be discharged from your sentence without parole.

( ) The Board has decided to depart from the Guidelines and take the following action:

FOR THE BOARD:

James T. Morris, Chairman
State Board of Pardons & Paroles

PAROLE DECISION GUIDELINES

Make a Better Parole System*

Parole Board Creates Decision-Making Guidelines For the Purpose of

Protecting Society
Basing Decisions on Sound, Pertinent Facts
Arriving at Consistent Decisions
Dispelling the Mystery from Parole
Making More Prompt Decisions

What Does Justice Demand?

Justice Demands that punishment should be tailored to fit both the offense and the offender.   This means, for example, that the leader of a five-county burglary ring who has a prior conviction record should serve considerably more time in prison than a 17-year-old first-offender burglar.

Justice demands that similar offenders serving for similar offenses should be punished similarly.   This means that wide disparities in sentence lengths ordered by different judges or stemming from plea bargains negotiated by different district attorneys or caused by different levels of ability among defense attorneys should be corrected.

Justice demands that the handling of offenders should be a flexible process throughout the punishment phase.   This means that after a person goes to

*Georgia State Board of Pardons and Paroles. Published November 1979

prison, it should not be too late to modify his punishment. New evidence may prove him innocent. Mitigating facts may indicate an excessive sentence. A terminal illness may justify letting him go home to die.

Parole Decision Guidelines Establish Justice

Parole Decision Guidelines help the State Board of Pardons and Paroles make a prompt, consistent, soundly based, and explainable parole decision on an inmate serving a sentence less than life imprisonment. Guidelines help the Board decide on a Presumptive Parole Release Month for the inmate or decide that he will complete his sentence without parole.

Crime Severity Plus Offender's Past Are Weighed.   The Board identifies an inmate's Crime Severity Level from a table of offenses ranked in groups from lowest to highest severity. The higher the severity, the longer the inmate will be required to serve. Then the Board calculates the inmate's Parole Success Likelihood Score simply by adding weighted factors with proven predictive value from the inmate's criminal and social history. A history of things such as prior imprisonment, parole or probation revocation, heroin use, and jobless-ness would increase the risk of paroling the inmate and cause him to be confined longer.

Board Is Guided to Same Decision on Similar Cases.   After identifying an inmate's Crime Severity Level and totaling his Parole Success Likelihood Score, the Board inserts these two facts into a Time-to-Serve Chart, which indicates the length of time the inmate should serve before release. To this may be added more time for Disciplinary Reports the inmate has received in prison.

The resulting Presumptive Parole Release Month, if approved by the Board, is announced to the inmate as the date he can expect to be paroled if he receives no future serious Disciplinary Reports. Often the Presumptive Parole Release Month is later than the inmate's sentence completion date, in which case the inmate is notified that he must complete his sentence without parole. Occasion-ally, the Board, when making its decision, may depart from the Guidelines, but it must give its specific written reason to the inmate.

The Time-to-Serve Chart virtually guarantees that inmates serving for simi-lar offenses with similar histories will be treated the same.

Centralized Viewpoint and Authority Promote Equity.   It would be difficult to over-estimate the importance of the Parole Board's investigative and decision-making authority being centralized and independent. The Board's unique central position enables it to compare a case with thousands of others Statewide, and its Constitutional authority allows it to reduce sentencing disparity. Excessive harshness is more readily reduced, but excessive leniency in the form of a too-light confinement sentence may be corrected partially by parole denial.

Any substitute prisoner-release mechanism triggered by numerous officials scattered in courthouses or prisons would be destined to be inequitable and not in the best interests of the citizens' safety or taxpayers' pocketbooks.

How Can Society Be Protected?

Protection Through Incapacitation.   An inmate whose prior conviction record, social history, and prison behavior indicate he will likely return to crime should be held in prison longer for society's protection.

Protection Through Deterrence.   The term of confinement should be long enough to "teach the inmate a lesson"—make him fear future imprisonment and thus deter him from future criminal behavior. Confinement should also be long enough to "make an example of the inmate"—show potential criminals in the inmate's neighborhood, town, and state that punishment can be substantial and thus deter them from committing crimes of their own.

Protection Through Rehabilitation.   Prison and parole don't necessarily rehabilitate. Rehabilitation, if it occurs, comes from within the offender. However, a person newly released from prison who wants to "go straight" can be helped to avoid temptations and pitfalls by a skilled individual who counsels and watches him.

Parole Decision Guidelines Promote Protection

Guidelines Keep Career Criminals in Prison Longer.   Citizens generally agree on the importance of keeping career criminals off the streets longer. This is helped toward accomplishment by Parole Decision Guidelines. Inmates with prior convictions, probation revocations, and parole revocations typically end up with such low Parole Success Likelihood Scores that they must complete their maximum sentences without parole.

Guidelines Preserve Imprisonment's Deterrent Value.   Deterrence was certainly in the minds of Parole Board Members when, developing the Guidelines, they ranked offenses from lowest to highest severity and mandated longer prison service for greater Crime Severity Levels. To do otherwise would have been to depreciate the seriousness of the offenses and risk curtailing the deterrent effect of imprisonment.

An example of the Board's deterrence philosophy in action is the fact that very few lifers who are confined for murder or rape are granted parole upon completing the minimum time set by law. The Board believes that more time than seven years is generally required to accomplish the punishment and deterrent purposes of a life sentence. (Lifers are not handled under Guidelines.)

Board Bolsters Parolee's Own Rehabilitative Efforts.   When an inmate is judged under Parole Decision Guidelines and released from prison, that does not end the Board's responsibility. The parolee must obey a set of Board-imposed conditions, violation of which may result in his return to prison. A parole officer makes surprise visits to the parolee's home and place of employment, as well as requires him to report regularly to the local parole office.

In addition to his surveillance role, the parole officer is a counselor who may help the parolee with family, budget, and job-placement problems or refer him to an appropriate agency for help.

All of the above do not guarantee that a person will succeed on parole. However, these things encourage efforts associated with rehabilitation and make backsliding unpleasant to the parolee. As a result, during Fiscal Year 1979, ninety percent of Georgia parolees completed their parole periods successfully, saving Georgia taxpayers the cost of keeping them in prison that additional time.

Parole supervision works. This is the message from the Uniform Parole Reports Program of the National Council on Crime and Delinquency. Parole revocation rates nationwide have consistently been well below the recidivism rates for persons discharged straight from prison. In Georgia the parolee success rate regularly exceeds the national average.

What Are Other Benefits of Guidelines?   The value of Parole Decision Guidelines in making release actions more consistent and soundly based has been discussed. There are other benefits:

Explainability—Under Guidelines a Notice of Action is sent to the inmate who has been considered for parole. It leads him step by step to show him how and why the Board arrived at its decision. If he thinks an error has been made, he may appeal. The same openness prevails when outside persons inquire about a parole decision. Gone is the mystery which once enveloped the decision-making process.

More Prompt Decisions—A person given a non-life felony sentence on or after January 1, 1980, has his case investigated and considered by the Board and receives notice of the decision within six to nine months after he enters the prison system. Virtually gone is the possibility of a decision being delayed past parole eligibility because of a late investigation.

Less Inmate Anxiety—Under Guidelines, routine yearly parole considerations are eliminated along with the resulting yearly crushing of hope in denied inmates. Most inmates learn the Board's intention early and only once.

No More Con Games—Once and for all the Guidelines strip away the false idea that to make parole an inmate simply must take on the appearance of a "model inmate." As a result, applicants for the prisons' educational and vocational courses and other good-sounding activities should have motives other than trying to con the Parole Board.

What Guidelines Will Not Do.   The Parole Board is not empowered to add more time to an inmate's sentence. If a person receives an excessively lenient sentence for a serious offense, the Guidelines guide the Board to deny parole to him, but they can do no more.

A non-life inmate *denied parole* will serve his sentence and will be discharged by the Department of Offender Rehabilitation under the Earned Time Program. The Parole Board has no control over this system.

The Board makes no claim that Guidelines will reduce crime, although Guidelines do help assure that career criminals will complete their sentences without parole.

Parole Decision Guidelines will not create better parents who will inculcate moral values in their children. Neither will they keep negligent parents from allowing their children to become criminals by the time they reach puberty—children who will later engulf the State prisons.

How Did Parole Decision Guidelines Come About?   Implementation of Parole Decision Guidelines in October 1979 was preceded by a two-year period of research and development. Case files on successful and unsuccessful Georgia parolees were studied to identify attributes significantly linked with success and failure. Using recognized statistical procedures, the research team isolated Parole Success Factors with proven predictive value in selecting candidates for parole who would not be a danger to society.

Board Members themselves monitored the research and participated especially in selecting Crime Severity Levels for the various offenses.

The Success Factors and Severity Levels were put together in a Time-to-Serve Chart which indicates how long inmates should serve. It should be stressed that these indicated confinement times were designed to match what the Board had been requiring in recent years. The big difference is that the Guidelines mandate consistency and introduce empirically based risk assessment.

By adopting Guidelines, the Georgia Board joined 16 other states which have implemented or are in process of implementing guides for structuring parole discretion.

Are Mandatory Sentences the Way to Go?   Some people have theorized that a specific mandatory sentence for each crime should be put into law and that a judge should be forced to pronounce it with little or no discretion to modify it. Proponents usually say that the mandatory sentence would be the *average* sentence for the crime given by the courts now. In effect, this compromise between the longest and the shortest sentences would force judges to give longer sentences to first offenders and shorter sentences to career criminals than are given at present.

Mandatory sentencing violates a basic element of justice in which judicial discretion allows a sentence to be tailored to fit the offender as well as the offense. Conceivably, if a calculating criminal considered the mandatory sentence for his planned crime light enough to risk getting caught, it would reduce the deterrent effect on him. If a jury felt a mandatory sentence was too severe in a particular case, it might fail to convict. Uncertainty has advantages.

Another drawback is the likely impact mandatory sentences would have on plea bargaining, which presently elicits guilty pleas from the vast majority of Georgia's criminal defendants. With nothing to bargain about, the resulting increase in jury trials—even a slight increase—would swamp the courts.

In practice—human ingenuity being what it is—the bargaining would continue, but it would be about the charge. A defendant's attorney, offering to trade a guilty plea, would bargain Rape down to Battery, would bargain Murder down to Manslaughter. The charade would go on and on.

Actually, bargaining about the charge is already with us. Since 1976 Georgia has had a mandatory minimum confinement sentence of five years for Armed Robbery. However, the Parole Board's Legal Investigations reveal repeated instances of Armed Robbery being plea-bargained down to Robbery or Robbery by Intimidation, thereby avoiding the five-year minimum. This points up yet another flaw in the mandatory sentencing idea: discretion would be removed from the judge and concentrated totally in the hands of the district attorney and his assistants.

What is the Parole Board's Role and Authority?   The State Board of Pardons and Paroles is composed of five members appointed by the Governor for seven-year terms subject to confirmation by the State Senate. Each year the Board elects one of its members to serve as chairman.

The Board was established in 1943 by an amendment to the Georgia Constitution. Its existence assures that the executive branch of government, in addition to the legislative and judicial, has a discretionary role in criminal justice. Thus in Georgia's justice system the Board provides a vital part of the checks and balances of tripartite government as established in the State Constitution and as mirroring the genius of the Constitution of the United States.

The Board has constitutional authority to grant paroles, pardons, and reprieves, to commute and remit sentences, and to restore civil and political rights. It has authority and staff to investigate cases and to supervise persons granted conditional clemency.

How Does the Board Get its Information?   Before the Board considers an inmate for parole, it conducts investigations, detailed reports of which become a part of the Board's case file, which is separate from files maintained by the Department of Offender Rehabilitation.

First, a parole officer studies arrest and court records and may talk with arresting officers, court officials, victims, and witnesses so he can write a *Legal Investigation* report on the details of the inmate's current offense and a summary of any prior offenses in the same county.

Next, a parole officer interviews the inmate and completes a *Personal History Statement* questionnaire. The inmate is asked, among other things, where he has resided, attended school, and worked; who his family members are and where they live; whom he has chosen as references; where he plans to live and work; and what his own account is of his crime.

Finally, a parole officer conducts a *Social Investigation,* which includes interviews with persons mentioned in the Personal History Statement as well as others. The written report presents a revealing picture of the inmate's life from birth to current imprisonment and may also indicate the degree of his truthfulness.

Before any inmate is paroled, the Board reviews a *Parole Review Summary* from the Department of Offender Rehabilitation. This discusses the inmate's behavior, attitude, physical status, mental and emotional condition, participation in activities, and performance in work and training.

The Board may, at its discretion, request detailed psychological and/or psychiatric opinions before considering a case.

Other documents in the case file usually include a Federal Bureau of Investigation record of arrests and convictions, Classification and Admission Summary (on the inmate's condition when he entered prison), Disciplinary Reports, all letters received, and summaries of information from headquarters' visitors.

ITEMS FOR STUDY

1. There are two basic models for administering parole, each with its own advantages and disadvantages.
2. Conditional (or mandatory) release is distinguished from parole release, although inmates released by either method may be under community (parole) supervision.
3. Parole boards have been criticized because their members are often inadequate to the task.
4. The parole hearing has been denounced as a ''necessary charade.''
5. In an effort to counter criticism of parole board discretion, many boards are using ''guidelines'' based on the concept of ''just deserts.''

chapter 11

Parole Services: Institutional and Field

INSTITUTIONAL SERVICES

Parole services are usually divided into institutional services and field services. The basic responsibility of the institutional parole staff is to prepare reports on inmates for the parole board. They also help inmates secure furloughs, work-release or halfway house programs, and they may assist with personal problems ranging from matters relating to a spouse and children to questions of a technical or legal nature.

Under ideal conditions, when an offender is first received at the institution he/she is interviewed by the parole staff. The results of the interview, psychiatric and psychological tests, and the information in the presentence report are then used to plan an institutional program for the inmate. The parole staff periodically updates the material with additional information. They discuss tentative release plans with inmates, and request the field staff to visit and interview family members and prospective employers. When an inmate is ready to meet the parole board, they provide a report on the inmate that includes an evaluation of changes made since he/she was first interviewed at the prison. The report may also contain a recommendation, if this is requested by the board.

Unfortunately, ideal conditions do not usually exist in the parole system. Because of a lack of trained staff most parole boards receive institutional reports that are "thrown together" from the presentence report right before the hearing (Parker, 1975: 32).

Institutional parole staff may also hold group meetings with new inmates to orient them about parole. These group sessions are then followed up with individual interviews. There are also pre-parole group sessions at which the parole staff attempts to lower anxiety about meeting the board. When an inmate has been granted parole, or is eligible for conditional release, he/she will meet with a parole staff member for a final discussion of the release program and the rules of parole, prior to leaving the prison.

Institutional parole staff, in some jurisdictions, are responsible for notifying local law enforcement agencies of the impending release of certain offenders.* They also determine the probable disposition of any warrants that have been lodged against an inmate. When appropriate, they will arrange for an out-of-state program under the Interstate Compact.

In some states, nonparole institutional staff perform the same, or similar, functions as institutional parole officers. For example, New York and California utilize correctional counselors in their institutions. The counselors in both of these states do not have any direct parole responsibilities. California describes the correctional counselor position as follows (California Personnel Board Announcement, March 26, 1975):

In a correctional institution, a Correctional Counselor's major responsibility is the study of the individual prisoner for purposes of understanding his needs and outlining a program for his rehabilitation. Following initial classification and assignment of the inmate to a rehabilitation program, the Counselor continues individual counseling and participates in the group counseling, study, and therapy programs aimed at preparing the inmate for eventual return to the community.

FIELD SERVICES

The second basic service of a parole agency is the field service. Field service staff usually operate out of district offices located throughout the state. They conduct field investigations requested by the institutional parole staff relative to release programs, and they supervise parolees. The Massachusetts Parole Board Service Office, for example, is administered by and established within the Parole Board. The central office is located in Boston and administers seven regional offices that serve the 14 counties in the State. The Service Office is responsible for supervising adult parolees released from county and state correctional institutions.

*Some states require that when an offender is released, the police in the area where he/she is to reside, or where the crime occurred, must be notified. In some instances the parolee must register with the local enforcement agency. Some states require notification or registration for all sex offenders, while some, such as New York, require it for second (or more) felony offenders.

ADULT PAROLE AUTHORITY
STATE OF OHIO*

427 Cleveland Avenue
Columbus, Ohio 43215

FU: 10/27/75

Nature of Report: Parole Plan Acceptance   *Date:* October 12, 1975

                                                  Crime and Sentence: Forgery

Parolee: John Smith   1-20

Number:

Office Address:
  100 Main St.,
  Cleveland, Ohio

Employed by:

From: Cuyahoga County   *Admitted:* 10/20/73

                                                  Paroled: 10/20/75

Reference is made to the Parole Plan Investigation Request of 10/3/75. This investigation has been completed.

Placement approved to: Mrs. John Smith (Mary)—Wife
                           100 Main Street
                           Cleveland (Cuyahoga County), Ohio

No one will call for parolee at the time of release

or

(Name of relative/friend) will call for parolee on date of release.

   On 10/6/75 this officer interviewed subject's wife at home. Mrs. Smith lives in a three-bedroom apartment on the poverty-ridden side of town. The home is neat and clean, however, and roomy enough to accommodate subject.
   Mrs. Smith and her two children (Matthew—6 and Mark—7) subsist on an ADC grant of $162 per month. Because of this meager income, the family is

*From Carol Holliday Blew, Kenneth Carlson, and Paul Chernoff, *Only Ex-offenders Need Apply: The Ohio Parole Officer Aide Program* (Washington, D.C.: U.S. Government Printing Office, 1976).

poorly clothed and housed. The children, however, are well fed and properly cared for.

Mrs. Smith seems very fond of her husband and is anxious to have him home. She hopes he will improve the family economically and that he will stabilize the children, who have been hard to manage lately. She prays that subject's drinking problem is at an end.

Tearfully, Mrs. Smith described the hardships she endured as a result of her husband's drinking. Unpaid bills, evictions, and lack of necessities were commonplace. Were it not for her church, relatives, and the relief dole, the family could not have survived. Despite his faults, Mrs. Smith claims subject can be responsible. Sober, he is trustworthy and reliable. Sometimes he would work steadily for three months or so before reverting to alcohol. These were the only really happy days for the family. During this interview, Mrs. Smith was quite attentive. She talked freely about her husband's confinement and the problems it presented. She also asked penetrating questions about parole and its obligation. This writer then reviewed the rules, after which she emphatically promised full cooperation.

On 10/12/75 we contacted John Jones of the Acme Tool Company. Mr. Jones owns a shop employing 35 people. He produced a letter from the inmate soliciting employment.

Mr. Jones is very civic-minded and has employed parolees before. He finds them satisfactory except for absenteeism. He also is interested in the Alcoholics Anonymous program and hopes to persuade Smith to participate eventually.

Mr. Jones is sorely in need of help and is willing to hire subject sight unseen, in spite of inexperience. Subject will work as a drill press operator at $2.75 per hour. He can begin work on 10/24/75. Advancement is dependent only on his ability.

Upon release, subject will have every opportunity. His wife is devoted to him and is willing to start anew. He will have an understanding and sympathetic employer; and, as far as we can determine, there is no community feeling against him. The only concern evidently is subject's history of excessive drinking.

From the foregoing, it is obvious that this subject's parole plan is satisfactory. This officer recommends, therefore, that this case be accepted for supervision.

Approved: *Respectfully submitted,*

_____   _____
Supervisor, Unit No. 10   Parole Officer

CONDITIONS OF PAROLE

Every conditionally released or paroled prisoner is required to sign an agreement to abide by certain regulations. This aspect of parole has its origins in the Ticket of Leave, and modern conditions of parole resemble Ticket of Leave regulations. Parole conditions are markedly similar throughout most jurisdictions, and are also very similar to probation regulations.

Sixty percent of the jurisdictions either prohibit or require permission to associate with or correspond with "undesirables," usually defined as persons with criminal records; 79 percent require periodic reports; 87 percent require permission for or notification of any change in employment or residence; and 72 percent require an initial arrival report within a certain period after release from prison (Parker 1975: 36).

The Attica Report noted that parole regulations are often petty and demeaning "or of such broad sweep that they lend themselves to arbitrary and selective enforcement by parole officers" (New York State Special Commission on Attica, 1972: xix). The Task Force on Corrections states that "the strictness with which parole rules are enforced varies greatly from jurisdiction to jurisdiction, depending in part on the training of the parole officer, but chiefly on the formal and informal policies of the parole system." The Task Force also points out that when rules are extremely detailed, they are often overlooked by the parole officer. The Task Force states that when the conditions of parole are very broad, parole officers and parolees seem to understand that certain rules will operate even though they are not explicitly set out in the parole rules (1966: 69).

The National Advisory Commission on Criminal Justice Standards and Goals (1973) recommends that parole rules be kept to an absolute minimum, with parole boards tailoring them to fit each individual parolee. Under their recommended system, parole officers would be given temporary authority to impose new conditions or amend old ones in accordance with the needs of the case, subject to the approval of the board of parole.

Conditions of parole can generally be grouped into two main categories: (1) those that tend toward reform and urge the parolee toward a noncriminal and productive life, and (2) those that can be used by parole officers to control the parolee's actions. The parole regulations of Florida and New York will provide samples of these categories.

CONDITIONS OF PAROLE

State of Florida

1. Promptly upon being released on parole, I will proceed to _____, Florida, where I will reside. Immediately upon my arrival, I

---

will report by mail, telephone, or personal visit to the Parole and Probation Supervisor under whose supervision I am to be paroled.

2. I will not change my residence or employment or leave the county of my residence without first procuring the consent of the Florida Parole and Probation Commission, which consent shall be obtained through my Parole and Probation Supervisor.

3. I will, before the fifth day of each month, until my final release, make a full and truthful report to my Parole and Probation Supervisor on the form provided for that purpose.

4. I will not use intoxicants of any kind to excess; nor possess any narcotics, marijuana, or drugs obtained illegally; nor visit places where intoxicants or drugs are unlawfully sold, dispensed, or used.

5. I will not visit gambling places or associate with persons of harmful character or bad reputation.

6. I will in all respects conduct myself honorably; work diligently at a lawful occupation; support my dependents, if any, to the best of my ability; and live within my income.

7. I will not own or carry with me any weapons without first securing the consent of my Parole and Probation Supervisor.

8. I will live and remain at liberty without violating the law.

9. If I should leave the State of Florida, whether with or without permission of my Parole and Probation Supervisor, I agree to return to Florida upon being directed to do so by the Florida Parole and Probation Commission and I do waive all extradition rights, process, and proceedings.

10. I will promptly and truthfully answer all inquiries directed to me by the Commission or by my Parole and Probation Supervisor and I will comply with all instructions he may give me.

11. If at any time it becomes necessary to communicate with my Parole and Probation Supervisor for any purpose and he is not accessible, I will direct my communication to the Commission, at Tallahassee, Florida.

12. I understand that I am to remain on parole until released therefrom by the Commission.

13. I agree not to own or to operate a motor vehicle or to secure a license to operate a motor vehicle without first procuring the consent of the Florida Parole and Probation Commission, which consent shall by obtained through my Parole and Probation Supervisor.

14. I agree, during the term of my parole, that upon being instructed by my parole supervisor, I will submit to a physical examination to determine whether or not any type of drug or narcotic is in my system.

I have been informed that Florida Statutes provide: *Anyone on probation or parole shall be required to contribute ten dollars ($10) per month toward the cost of his supervision and rehabilitation beginning 60 days from the date he is free to seek employment.*

RULES OF PAROLE

New York State Division of Parole

1. I will proceed directly to the area to which I have been released and, within twenty-four hours of my release, make my arrival report to that Office of the Division of Parole unless other instructions are designated on my release agreement.

2. I will make office and/or written reports as directed.

3. I will not leave the State of New York or any other State to which I am released or transferred, or any area defined in writing by my Parole Officer without permission.

4. I will permit my Parole Officer to visit me at my residence and/or place of employment and I will permit the search and inspection of my person, residence and property. I will discuss any proposed changes in my residence, employment or program status with my Parole Officer. I understand that I have an immediate and continuing duty to notify my Parole Officer of any changes in my residence, employment or program status when circumstances beyond my control make prior discussion impossible.

5. I will reply promptly, fully and truthfully to any inquiry of or communication by my Parole Officer or other representative of the Division of Parole.

6. I will notify my Parole Officer immediately any time I am in contact with or arrested by any law enforcement agency. I understand that I have a continuing duty to notify my Parole Officer of such contact or arrest.

7. I will not be in the company of or fraternize with any person I know to have a criminal record or whom I know to have been adjudicated a Youthful Offender except for accidental encounters in public places, work, school or in any other instance with the permission of my Parole Officer.

9. I will not own, possess, or purchase any shotgun, rifle, or firearm of any type without the written permission of my Parole Officer. In addition, I will not own, possess, or purchase any dangerous instrument or deadly weapon as defined in the Penal Law.

10. In the event that I leave the jurisdiction of the State of New York, I hereby waive my right to resist extradition to the State of New York from any state in the Union and from any territory or country outside the United States. This waiver shall be in full force and effect until I am discharged from Parole or Conditional Release. I fully understand that I have the right under the Constitution of the United States and under law to contest an effort to extradite me from another state and return me to New York, and I freely and knowingly waive this right as a condition of my Parole or Conditional Release.

11. I will not use or possess any drug paraphernalia or use or possess any controlled substance without proper medical authorization.

12. Special Conditions.

13. I will fully comply with the instructions of my Parole Officer and obey such special additional written conditions as he/she, a Member of the Board of Parole or an authorized representative of the Division of Parole, may impose.

LENGTH OF SUPERVISION

The length of time an offender must spend on parole is governed by the length of the sentence and the laws of the state where convicted. However, parole usually lasts more than two years, with individual states averaging from one to seven years. In New York a parolee is eligible for an unconditional discharge from parole after he/she has had an exemplary adjustment under supervision for at least three years. The South Carolina Probation, Parole, and Pardons Board follows a policy of giving consideration to the removal from parole, by the exercising of the pardon power, those parolees who have completed successfully at least 5 years under parole supervision. Other states permit an offender to be discharged from parole after a shorter period of supervision, as long as there have not been any indications of new criminality.

VIOLATION OF PAROLE

Parole violation procedures are in a state of flux as the result of court challenges. They may also vary from jurisdiction to jurisdiction. Accordingly, the procedures discussed in this section are general in nature and simplified for purposes of study. The accompanying flowchart presents an overview of the system and indicates the possibilities available at each stage of the process.

Probation violation remains part of the judicial (court) process, while parole violation is an agency administrative function divorced from the courts. The parole violation process begins with a request from the parole officer for a warrant based on alleged violations of parole. The warrant stage varies from agency to agency. Some states are rather conservative about issuing parole violation warrants, and this stage can be a time-consuming procedure. However, in New York a parole violation warrant can be issued by a senior parole officer immediately.

After a warrant is issued, it can be enforced by a parole officer, warrant officer, or other law enforcement personnel. If the parolee is already in custody (as the result of a new arrest), the warrant will be filed against him as a detainer. If the parolee is not in custody, an attempt will be made to enforce the warrant by arresting him.

Preliminary Hearing

After the parolee is in custody, he is given a list of the charges of parole violation alleged against him. He is entitled to a preliminary hearing at this stage. (If he waives this right, he will be held in custody pending a revocation hearing.) At the preliminary

Parole Violation Flowchart

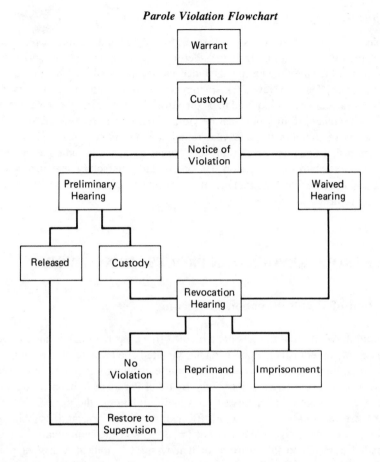

hearing the parolee will have an opportunity to challenge the alleged violations and to confront adverse witnesses, including his parole officer. The hearing officer who presides at the preliminary hearing may be another parole officer or other employee of the agency. The hearing officer determines if there are reasonable grounds to believe that the parolee has violated one or more of the conditions of parole, referred to as "probable cause." If probable cause is found, the parolee will be held in custody pending a revocation hearing. If probable cause is not found, the parolee will be restored to supervision.

Revocation Hearing

A revocation hearing is similar to a preliminary hearing except that it is more comprehensive. The purpose of the revocation hearing is to determine if the violation of parole is serious enough to revoke parole and return the parolee to prison. If parole is not revoked, the parolee is restored to supervision.

Delinquent Time

If parole is revoked, the question arises as to just how much time the parolee must serve in prison. This can vary from jurisdiction to jurisdiction. In New York a parolee receives credit for the time he spends under parole supervision ("street time") prior to his violation. Thus, in New York, an inmate who is paroled after serving two years of a four-year sentence is required to be on parole for two years, the remainder of his four-year sentence. If after one year he violates parole and is returned to prison, he will only have to serve the one year remaining on his sentence. However, in a jurisdiction that does not give credit for "street time," this same parolee will be required to serve two years in prison. The one year of satisfactory time on parole is not credited against his four-year sentence in the event of a parole violation that results in his being returned to prison.

THE PAROLE REVOCATION PROCESS IN NEW YORK*

Initiation of Parole Violation Proceedings

Executive Law provides that, where a parole officer has reasonable cause to believe that a person under his/her supervision has violated one or more of the conditions of parole in an important respect or has lapsed into criminal ways or company, he/she must report such facts to a member of the Board of Parole or someone designated by the Board of Parole. Under present rules and regulations, the parole officer must report these facts to a senior parole officer and obtain a warrant for retaking and temporary detention. After the warrant is issued and the individual is either apprehended pursuant to that warrant or that warrant is lodged at his/her place of detention, a notice of violation is given to the alleged parole violator within no more than three days after the execution of the warrant. This notice of violation is designated as Form 9011. It contains not only a short statement of charges but also informs the alleged parole violator of his/her rights under the Constitution and statutes, including therein his/her opportunity to obtain counsel and to a timely hearing. The form will soon contain a pre-printed request for the assignment of counsel as a convenience to the alleged violator. He/she is asked at the time of the presentation of his/her Form 9011 whether or not he/she wishes a preliminary hearing. If he/she waives a preliminary hearing, probable cause is deemed to have been found. However, if he/she requests a preliminary hearing, a date for such hearing is given to him/her which will be no more than 15 days after the execution of the warrant.

*Source: *New York State Parole: The Parole Revocation Process,* 1978–1979. A publication of the New York State Division of Parole. Edited.

186

Preliminary Violation Hearing

The Executive Law requires a preliminary hearing within 15 days after execution. It provides that the hearing officer not have any prior supervisory involvement with the alleged parole violator. In the greater majority of cases, preliminary hearings are conducted by persons designated as preliminary hearing officers. This is a separate title within the Division of Parole. The preliminary hearing officers are specially trained in the conduct of hearings, and are under the direct supervision of the Counsel to the Division of Parole. They are not under the supervision of any member of Field or Institutional Parole Services. Where a preliminary hearing officer is not available to conduct a hearing, the Board designates senior parole officers as persons who may conduct such hearings. These persons are selected outside of the area or bureau which was responsible for the supervision of the alleged parole violator.

The hearing is conducted pursuant to the rules of evidence as they apply in administrative hearings. Hearsay, though admissible, is never used alone in order to determine probable cause, except in those instances in which there is good and sufficient reason to do so, i.e., cases arising under the Uniform Act for Out-of-State Parole Supervision.

Although neither the statute nor case law so require, if an alleged parole violator wishes to be represented by counsel at his/her preliminary hearing the Division of Parole's policy is to permit such representation.

The alleged parole violator at a preliminary hearing is afforded the opportunity to confront his/her accuser, cross-examine the witnesses presented by the parole officer and to offer evidence on his/her own behalf. Once probable cause of violation of parole has been found with regard to one or more of the charges, the preliminary hearing officer will take no further evidence regarding any other charges which may have been brought against the alleged violator.

The Executive Law requires that all preliminary hearings be conducted locally. The Division of Parole conducts all preliminary hearings at local institutions, which requires that our preliminary hearing officers and others designated by the Board of Parole travel to local facilities throughout the State of New York. These hearings are conducted with a hearing reporter present, who immediately thereafter transcribes the record; and such record is available to the alleged parole violator at any time he/she so requests.

If probable cause is found, at the conclusion of the preliminary hearing, the preliminary hearing officer will send to the violator and/or his/her attorney a written statement of his/her finding of fact. If no probable cause is found, the alleged parole violator will be released from custody, and returned to parole supervision.

The Declaration of Delinquency

If probable cause is found at the preliminary hearing, the parole officer must thereafter prepare and forward to his/her senior parole officer a violation of parole report. This violation of parole report contains not only the specific charges being brought against the alleged parole violator, but a statement of all the facts upon which these violations are based, and also the names and addresses of all witnesses who will be called to prove those allegations (except where the disclosure of names and addresses of witnesses may create a danger to their safety). After a review of the violation of parole report, the senior parole officer will then send the violation of parole report, along with his/her analysis and recommendaton to a member of the Board of Parole for review. The Board member, after reviewing the above-referenced documents, may either cancel delinquency or declare the alleged parole violator delinquent. This normally occurs within 30 days of the finding of probable cause or the waiver of a preliminary hearing.

Final Revocation Hearing

Once a Board member has declared an alleged parole violator delinquent, the Division of Parole will then provide a final revocation hearing within no more than 90 days after the probable cause determination. Written notice of that hearing, along with a copy of the violation of parole report and any other available documents which will be presented before a presiding officer at the final revocation hearing, are sent to the alleged parole violator and/or his/her attorney no later than 14 days prior to the actual hearing.

The Executive Law provides for local revocation hearings where the alleged parole violator so requests. The Board on its own motion may designate a case for a local hearing. Most final revocation hearings take place at an institution ''reasonably near the place of the alleged violation or arrest.'' This is done in order to insure that, in all cases, witnesses for both sides will be available with as little inconvenience as possible and also to insure that counsel of his/her choosing will be available to the alleged parole violator.

The Executive Law provides that a final revocation hearing will be conducted by either a Board member or a hearing officer designated by the Board in accordance with the rules of the Board. The Executive Law authorizes the Chairman to appoint hearing officers to conduct such hearings. At present, there are five hearing officers statewide, four of whom conduct hearings on a regular basis in the New York City area. A hearing officer must have at least four years of experience as a practicing attorney admitted in the State of New York. Hearing officers are under the direct supervision of the Counsel for the Division of Parole. They are in no way supervised by any member of Field or Institutional Parole Services of the Division.

Hearing officers are empowered to conduct final revocation hearings by the taking of evidence, under oath. In all cases, the parole violator is informed of his/her right of confrontation, his/her right to cross-examine witnesses, and his/her right to present evidence on his/her behalf. The violator is also informed of his/her right to counsel and to have counsel appointed for him/her if he/she cannot afford to retain an attorney. Counsel for the indigent alleged parole violator will be appointed pursuant to the County Law Section of the Executive Law. Although there is no provision in law, and the alleged violator has the primary responsibility to obtain counsel, the Division of Parole does notify those agencies which provide legal aid to indigents of requests for counsel. Notices are sent to these agencies on a regular basis so that they are informed by the Division that counsel has been requested.

At the hearing, the charges are read to the alleged violator and he/she is asked to enter a plea of guilty, not guilty, guilty with an explanation or stand mute. He/she is then given an opportunity to hear the evidence and to cross-examine each witness. Witnesses, if any, will also be called on his/her behalf. All testimony taken is under oath.

All testimony is on the record, which is transcribed by a hearing reporter within two weeks after the hearing. The rules of evidence apply as in all administrative hearings. The hearing officers are well-versed in those rules of evidence and adhere to them at all times. If the hearing officer, after hearing all the evidence, is not satisfied that there is a preponderance of evidence to support a violation of parole in an important respect, he/she must dismiss the violation, cancel delinquency and restore the parolee or conditional releasee to supervision. If, however, he/she is satisfied that there is a violation of parole in an important respect, he/she must then report in writing to a member of the Board his/her finding of fact and recommendation. The Decision Notice contains detailed analysis of the finding of fact and recommendations of the hearing officer. A Board member reviews the recommendations, and either affirms or modifies the recommendation in writing. Although the Executive Law does not so require, where a Board member modifies the hearing officer's recommendation, reasons for that modification are also included in the Board signed Decision Notice. Copies of the Notice are sent to the alleged parole violator and his/her attorney.

Unlike prison release to parole which occurs when a panel of Board members appears at an institution, the affirmation or modification of a hearing officer decision is made by one commissioner, acting alone, and it is made without confrontation between the inmate and the commissioner. That is, the Board member will review the findings of fact and the recommendation, along with the verbatim transcript resulting from a full due process hearing in order to determine whether or not he/she should affirm or modify the recommendation of the hearing officer.

Appellate Process

If the person found to be in violation of parole so desires, he/she may utilize, as a matter of right, the administrative appellate process as set forth in Section 259-i (4) of the Executive Law by filing a notice of appeal with the Appeals Unit of the New York State Division of Parole at 1450 Western Avenue, Albany, New York 12203, within 30 days after the final decision is received. He/she then has four months in which to file a letter or brief perfecting the appeal, unless an extension is granted for good cause before the final date to perfect the appeal. If he/she so desires, a transcript of the entire proceeding being appealed will be provided to him/her. Upon a showing of indigency, a transcript may be provided without cost. He/she may present all

Parole Revocation Process of the New York State Division of Parole

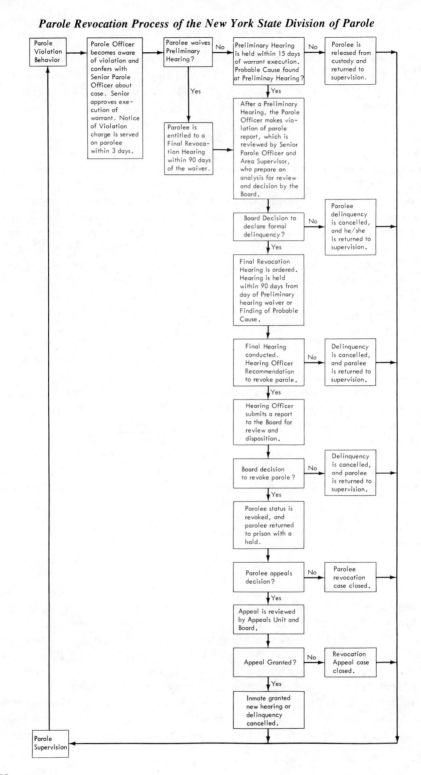

190

arguments he/she feels necessary in order to sustain his/her position. Three members of the Board of Parole, none of whom have had any prior dealings with this case, render a decision. Counsel, pursuant to Article 18-b of the County Law, is provided for the appellant if he/she so requests (259-i (4) of the Executive Law).

CLEMENCY

All states and the federal government have provisions for clemency. In 31 states and the federal government the chief executive holds the final clemency power, and in most of these states the parole board or a clemency board appointed by the governor

STATE OF NEW YORK–DEPARTMENT OF CORRECTIONAL SERVICES

№ 50299

SAMPLE COPY

WARRANT FOR RETAKING AND DETAINING A PAROLED
OR CONDITIONALLY RELEASED INMATE

TO ANY PAROLE OFFICER, PEACE OFFICER OR ANY OFFICER authorized to serve criminal process and to the superintendent or other person in charge of any jail, penitentiary, lockup or other place of detention in this State:

Having reasonable cause to believe that _____ **John Doe** _____
(Name)

Sing Sing Prison 6, *a parolee or conditionally released person under the supervision of the New*
(Number)

York State Board of Parole has violated his parole or Conditional release agreement, or has lapsed, or is probably about to lapse, into criminal ways or company, now, therefore, pursuant to the provisions of the Correction Law and the Rules and Regulations of the Board of Parole, I hereby order that said parolee or conditional releasee be retaken and placed in detention to await the action of the Board of Parole and for so doing, this shall be your sufficient warrant.

NEW YORK STATE BOARD OF PAROLE

Per **John Smith**
John Smith

Dated at _____ New York, N. Y. **12/23** _____ 19 **76**

FORM 9011 (REV. 12/77)

STATE OF NEW YORK

EXECUTIVE DEPARTMENT—DIVISION OF PAROLE

NOTICE OF VIOLATION

TO: _____ INST. # _____

NYSID # _____

You are charged with the following violations of the conditions of your release:

A Preliminary Hearing on these charges has been scheduled to take place at_____

on _____ at _____ M.

NOTICE TO RELEASEE

You have the right to a preliminary hearing. The purpose of this hearing is to determine whether there is probable cause to believe that you have violated a condition of your release in an important respect.

You have the right to appear at that hearing with counsel or to request the assistance of counsel at that hearing, and to speak on your own behalf.

You have the right to present witnesses who can give relevant testimony and introduce letters and documents. If you intend to produce witnesses, it is your responsibility to inform the Superintendent or person in charge of the facility where the hearing is to be held regarding the names of such witnesses in order that arrangements may be made for their admittance to the institution for purposes of the hearing. Such witness should have proper identification with them on the scheduled visit.

Subject to the duty of the preliminary hearing officer to refuse attendance for good cause, you have the right at that hearing to confront and cross-examine adverse witnesses who may be compelled to attend the hearing unless you have been convicted of a new crime while under your present release supervision.

You may waive or request the adjournment of this preliminary hearing. A waiver of this hearing is only equivalent to a finding that there is probable cause to believe that you have violated the conditions of your parole in an important respect. A waiver or a finding of probable cause will result in a review of your case by a Member of the Board of Parole who will determine whether to reinstate you to parole supervision or to order a final violation hearing.

I have read/been read the above charge(s) of the violation(s) of the conditions of my release and the notice to releasee, and I understand both.

☐ I do wish to have a preliminary hearing.

☐ I do NOT wish to have a preliminary hearing.

_____   _____
Date   Signature of Releasee

_____   _____
Location   Signature of Witness

investigates clemency applications at the request of the governor (Krajick, 1979: 48). Clemency consists of the reprieve, the commutation, and the pardon.

Reprieve

A reprieve, as we noted earlier, is the temporary suspension of the execution of sentence. Its use today is extremely limited, and usually concerns cases in which capital punishment has been ordered. In such cases a governor or the President can grant a reprieve—a stay of execution—to provide more time for legal action or other deliberations.

Commutation

A commutation is a modification of sentence to the benefit of an offender. Commutation has been used when an inmate provided assistance to the prison staff, sometimes during prison riots. It may also be granted to inmates with a severe illness, such as cancer. The laws governing commutation differ from state to state. In New York an inmate sentenced to more than one year who has served at least one-half of the minimum period of imprisonment, and who is not otherwise eligible for release or parole, may have his/her sentence commuted by the governor.

Pardon*

Historical Development

Following the American Revolution, it was necessary to find a new basis for the pardoning power to replace the English theory that it resided in the King as the fountainhead of justice and mercy. This new basis was found in the theory that the power to pardon was a sovereign power, inherent in the State, but not necessarily inherent in the executive or in any other given branch of the government. Rather, since the people were the ultimate sovereign, the power resided in them, and they could provide for its exercise through any agency of government they deemed proper.

And while historically the executive would seem the most natural agency in whom to entrust this power, the attitude of the American people after the Revolution was not such as to lead to this conclusion. The struggle with the mother country had left them suspicious of the executive. This was natural enough, for the royal governor was not usually sympathetic to the colonists. The champion of the people was usually the lower house of the legislature. It is, therefore, not surprising that the early constitutions which replaced the colonial charters tended to place restrictions upon the

*Information not explicitly cited is from U.S. Attorney General, *Attorney General's Survey of Release Procedures: Pardon* (Washington, D.C.: U.S. Government Printing Office, 1939), pp. 88–90, references deleted.

Governor's power in many respects, including the power to pardon. Only five states left this power in the governor alone. Six, including the newly admitted State of Vermont, provided that the governor could pardon only with consent of the executive council. Georgia deprived the governor of the pardoning power entirely, giving him only power to reprieve until the meeting of the assembly, which then could make such disposition of the matter as it saw fit. Connecticut and Rhode Island continued to function under their colonial charters, by which the pardoning power was exercised by the general assembly.

By the time the federal Constitution was written, however, opinion had begun to swing back toward placing greater power in the hands of the governor. The framers of the Constitution gave the pardoning power to the President without any limitations as to its exercise or any supervision by any other official or agency. The executive councils that several states had set up as a means of preventing too much power from being vested in one person began to lose favor about the same time, and a number of states began abolishing them, giving the sole power to the governor.

Toward the end of the nineteenth century there was an overwhelming movement to give the governor some assistance in this task by providing an advisory pardon officer or pardon board. Some states set up pardon boards not merely to advise the governor, but actually to exercise pardoning power, although the governor was everywhere a member, if not the controlling member, of the board.

The pardon has been used historically in the United States as a form of "parole." In the middle of the nineteenth century pardons accounted for over 40 percent of the releases from American prisons (Hibbert, 1968: 453). In Ohio, for example, whenever the state prison exceeded a certain number of inmates, the governor granted pardons in order to make room for new prisoners. As late as 1938, "parole" was simply a conditional pardon in many states (U.S. Attorney General, 1939: 296, 298). As the intermediate sentence came into use, the pardon boards, developed to advise the governor with respect to release, began to act independently, developing into parole boards. Despite the widespread use of parole, however, the power to pardon has continued.

The basis for a pardon may vary in different states, but it is not used extensively anywhere. In New York the only basis for a pardon is new evidence indicating that the person did not commit the offense of which he/she was accused and convicted. In Florida a pardon is a declaration of record that a person is relieved from the legal consequences of a particular conviction. As in New York, a pardon will be granted only to a person who proves his/her innocence of the crime for which convicted. Florida also has a *First Offender Pardon* which carries no implication of innocence and may be granted to an actual first offender. It restores civil and political rights and removes legal disabilities resulting from the conviction. The *Ten-Year Pardon* operates the same way, and may be granted to offenders who have had no convictions for 10 years after completing his/her sentence. In Georgia* a pardon is a declaration

*Georgia Board of Pardons and Paroles.

of record by the Board that a person is relieved from the legal consequences of a particular conviction. It restores civil and political rights and removes all legal disabilities resulting from the conviction.

Basis for Granting Pardon: Georgia

A pardon may be granted in two instances:

(1) A pardon may be granted to a person who proves his innocence of the crime for which he was convicted under Georgia law. Newly available evidence proving the person's complete justification or non-guilt may be the basis for granting a pardon. Application may be submitted in any written form any time after conviction.
(2) A pardon which does not imply innocence may be granted to an applicant convicted under Georgia law who has completed his full sentence obligation, including serving any probated sentence and paying any fine, and who has thereafter completed five years without any criminal involvement. The five-year waiting period after sentence completion may be waived if the waiting period is shown to be detrimental to the applicant's livelihood by delaying his qualifying for employment in his chosen profession. Application must be made by the ex-offender on a form available from the Board on request.

No pardon is automatic; the Board judges the merits of each individual case.

The Georgia Constitution states that persons who are convicted of Armed Robbery (committed on or after January 1, 1977) cannot be pardoned or paroled before serving at least five years, and states that persons whose death sentences are commuted by the Board to life imprisonment (on or after January 1, 1977) cannot be pardoned or paroled before serving 25 years.

Given the cyclical nature of prison/parole history, we can anticipate the use of conditional pardon in those states that have discontinued the indeterminate sentence and parole release. (One is even tempted to predict the "rediscovery" of parole, perhaps under a different title.)

ITEMS FOR STUDY

1. The institutional parole staff develop and organize information on eligible inmates for the parole board.
2. Parole field staff will provide information on the inmate's community situation or release plan.
3. Conditions of parole are similar, sometimes identical, to those used in probation.

4. Parole violation procedures can be contrasted/compared to those in probation, one being judicial, the other administrative.
5. Every state (and the federal government) has provisions for granting "clemency."
6. The use of "conditional pardons" can be expected in those states where the indeterminate sentence and parole release have been discontinued.

chapter 12

Legal Decisions Affecting Parole

As noted in Part One, legal decisions that affect probation also affect parole. Thus, the decision rendered in *Gagnon* v. *Scarpelli,* relating to probation, used precedents established in the *Morrissey* v. *Brewer* decision, which relates to parole. The three theories of parole are also similar, if not identical, to the three theories of probation.

THREE THEORIES OF PAROLE

Traditionally, an individual on parole has not been considered a free person, despite the fact that he/she has been released from imprisonment. The basis for imposing restrictions on a parolee's freedom is contained in three theories:

1. *Grace Theory*. Parole is a conditional privilege, a gift from the board of parole. If any of the conditions of this privilege are violated, parole can be revoked.
2. *Contract Theory*. Every parolee is required to agree to certain terms and conditions in return for his/her conditional freedom. A violation of the conditions is a breech of contract which can result in a revocation of parole.
3. *Custody Theory*. The parolee is in the legal custody of the prison or parole authorities, and as a result of this quasi-prisoner status, his/her constitutional rights are automatically limited and abridged.

The legal decisions discussed in this chapter often challenge one or more of the foregoing theories (see Fisher, 1974: 23–29).

The Parole Hearing—*Menechino* v. *Oswald,*
U.S. Ct. of Appeals, Second Circuit, 1970

Menechino was serving a 20 years to life sentence in New York for murder in the second degree. He was paroled in 1963 and returned to prison as a parole violator 16 months later. He subsequently appeared before the board of parole and admitted consorting with individuals having criminal records and giving misleading information to his parole officer.

Two years later Menechino appeared before the board for a release hearing and parole was denied. He brought a court action claiming that his rights were violated by the absence of legal counsel at both his revocation and parole release hearings. The case reached the U.S. Court of Appeals, which rendered a decision in 1970. The Court held that:

1. Parole proceeding is nonadversary in nature, since both parties, the board and the inmate, have the same concern, rehabilitation.
2. Parole release hearings are not fact-finding determinations since the board makes a determination based upon numerous tangible and intangible factors.
3. The inmate has no "present private interest" to be protected since he is already imprisoned, and this "interest" is required before due process is applicable.

The Court further stated that "it is questionable whether a board of parole is even required to hold a hearing on the question of whether a prisoner should be released on parole." Relative to the question of parole revocation, the court advised that a minimum of procedural due process should be provided since at this stage of the parole process a parolee has a present private interest in the possible loss of his conditional freedom.

Although Menechino's case before the federal court was initiated with regard to parole release, it set forth important legal arguments relative to parole revocation. The opinions of the three judges who heard the case clearly indicate that if he had initiated an action concerning his parole revocation, he would have won his case on a 2-to-1 basis. This fact was duly noted by the New York State Court of Appeals in the case of *Menechino* v. *Warden* discussed below.

The Parole Hearing—*Greenholtz* v. *Inmates of Nebraska Penal and*
Correctional Complex, 78-201

In 1979, the Supreme Court reversed a Court of Appeals decision in a class action brought by inmates of the Nebraska Penal and Correctional Complex. The inmates claimed that they had been unconstitutionally denied parole release by the Board of Parole.

At least once a year initial hearings must be held in Nebraska (according to state law) for every inmate, regardless of parole eligibility. At the initial hearing, the Board examines the inmate's total record and provides an informal hearing during which the inmate can present statements and documents in support of a claim for release.

If the Board determines from the record and hearing that the inmate is a likely candidate for release, a final hearing is scheduled. This is a somewhat unusual procedure, peculiar, perhaps, to the State of Nebraska. The Board then notifies the inmate of the month in which the final hearing will be held. At the final hearing, the inmate may present evidence, call witnesses, and be represented by private counsel of his choice. It is not a traditional adversary hearing since the inmate is not permitted to hear adverse testimony or to cross-examine witnesses who present such evidence. If parole is denied, the Board furnishes a written statement of the reasons for the denial within 30 days.

In upholding the procedure used by the Board of Parole, Chief Justice Burger, speaking for the Court, stated:

> When the Board defers parole after the initial review hearing, it does so because examination of the inmate's file and the personal interview satisfied it that the inmate is not yet ready for conditional release. The parole determination therefore must include consideration of what the entire record shows up to the time of the sentence, including the gravity of the offense in the particular case. The behavior record of an inmate during confinement is critical in the sense that it reflects the degree to which the inmate is prepared to adjust to parole release. At the Board's initial interviewing hearing, the inmate is permitted to appear before the Board and present letters and statements on his own behalf. He is thereby provided with an effective opportunity to insure, first, that the records before the Board are in fact the records relating to his case; and second, to present any special considerations demonstrating why he is an appropriate candidate for parole. Since the decision is one that must be made largely on the basis of an inmate's files, this procedure adequately safeguards against serious risks of error and thus satisfies due process.
>
> Next, we find nothing in the due process concepts as they have thus far evolved that requires the Parole Board to specify the particular "evidence" in the inmate's file or at his interview on which it rests the discretionary determination that an inmate is not ready for conditional release. The Board communicates the reason for its denial as a guide to the inmate for his future behavior. To require the parole authority to provide a summary of the evidence would tend to convert the process into an adversary proceeding and to equate the Board's parole release determination with a guilt determination. . . . the parole release decision is, . . . , essentially an experienced prediction based on a host of variables. The Board's decision is much like a sentencing judge's choice—provided by many states—to grant or deny probation following a judgment of guilt, a choice never thought to require more than what Nebraska now provides for the parole release determination.

Parole Revocation—*Menechino* v. *Warden,*
New York State Court of Appeals, January 12, 1971

Until recent times parole agencies operated without any interference from the judiciary. However, this all changed when the New York Court of Appeals handed down the *Menechino* decision, which granted parolees, for the first time, the right to counsel and the right to call their own witnesses at parole revocation hearings. Although the decision applied only to New York, it indicated the direction in which the courts would rule in future decisions.

This 4-to-3 decision caused the release of Joseph Menechino and required that an attorney be present at a parole revocation hearing. It also permitted a parolee to call upon witnesses who would speak in his behalf. The New York Court recognized that it was entering into an uncharted area of parole revocation. The issue they were called upon to resolve was stated succinctly at the very beginning of the majority opinion: "whether parolees are constitutionally entitled, under the Federal and State Constitutions, to the assistance of counsel in parole revocation hearings." *Menechino* cited other legal decisions, such as *Mempa* v. *Rhay* and *In Re Gault*. While probationers, juveniles, and welfare recipients had already obtained limited due process protections at hearings that might cause the loss of freedom or financial distress, these protections had not yet been granted to parolees.

Parole Revocation—*Morrissey* v. *Brewer*, 408 U.S. 471, 92 S. Ct. (1972)

This case marked the beginning of the U.S. Supreme Court's involvement with parole revocation procedures. Up until June 1972, the Supreme Court had not ruled in this area. The issue before the Court in this case was whether the due process clause of the Fourteenth Amendment required that a state afford an individual some opportunity to be heard prior to revoking parole.

Morrissey was convicted of the false drawing of checks in 1967 in Iowa. After pleading guilty, he was sentenced to seven years in prison. He was paroled from the Iowa State Penitentiary in June 1968. Seven months later, at the direction of his parole officer, he was arrested in his hometown as a parole violator and held in a local jail. One week later, after review of the parole officer's written report, the Iowa Board of Parole revoked Morrissey's parole, and he was returned to prison. Morrissey received no hearing prior to the revocation of his parole.

Morrissey violated the conditions of his parole by buying a car under an assumed name and operating it without the permission of his parole officer. He also gave false information to the police and insurance company concerning his address after a minor traffic accident. Besides these violations, Morrissey also obtained credit under an assumed name and failed to report his residence to his parole officer. According to the parole officer's report, Morrissey could not explain any of these technical violations of parole regulations adequately.

Also considered in the *Morrissey* case was the petition of Booher, a convicted forger who had been returned to prison in Iowa by the Board of Parole without any hearing. Booher had admitted the technical violations of parole charges to his parole officer when taken into custody.

The Supreme Court considered all arguments that sought to keep the judiciary out of parole matters, and it rejected the "privilege" concept of parole as no longer viable. The court pointed out that parole is an established variation of imprisonment of convicted criminals.

The Court noted that parole revocation does not occur in just a few isolated cases—it has been estimated that 35 to 40 percent of all parolees are subjected to revocation and return to prison. The Court went on to state that with the numbers involved, protection of parolees' rights was necessary. The court did note, however, limitations on a parolee's rights:

> We begin with the proposition that the revocation of parole is not part of a criminal prosecution and thus the full panoply of rights due to the defendant in such a proceeding does not apply to parole revocation. Supervision is not directly by the court but by an administrative agency which is sometimes an arm of the court and sometimes of the executive. Revocation deprives an individual not of absolute liberty to which every citizen is entitled but only the conditional liberty properly dependent on observance of special parole restrictions.

The Court noted that the traditional arguments against judicial intervention were no longer viable:

> It is hardly useful any longer to try to deal with this problem in terms of whether the parolee's liberty is a "right" or a "privilege." By whatever name the liberty is valuable and must be seen within the protection of the Fourteenth Amendment. Its termination calls for some orderly process however informal.

Also found in the decision is the New York State Court of Appeals response to the problem in the *Menechino* case. The U.S. Supreme Court held as follows:

> Society thus has an interest in not having parole revoked because of erroneous information or because of an erroneous evaluation of the need to revoke parole, given the breach of parole conditions. See Parole ex rel *Menechino* v. *Warden*.

The Supreme Court in *Morrissey* v. *Brewer* considered parole revocation as a two-stage process: (1) arrest of the parolee and preliminary hearing, and (2) the revocation hearing. Because there was usually a significant time lapse between the arrest and revocation hearing, the Supreme Court established the preliminary hearing for all parole violators. The Court set up the preliminary hearing in this fashion:

> Such an inquiry should be seen in the nature of a preliminary hearing to determine whether there is probable cause or reasonable grounds to believe that the arrested parolee had committed acts which would constitute a violation of parole condition.

The court specified that the hearing officer at this preliminary hearing be someone who is not involved in the case, that the parolee be given notice of the hearing, and that its purpose be to determine whether there is probable cause to believe that the parolee has violated a condition of his/her parole. On the request of the parolee, persons who have given adverse information on which parole violation is based are to be made available for questioning in the parolee's presence. Based upon this information presented before the hearing officer, there should be a determination if there is reason to warrant the parolee's continued detention. The court stated that "no interest would be served by formalism in this process; informality will not lessen the utility of this inquiry in redressing the risk of error."

In reference to the revocation hearing, the Court stated:

> The parolee must have an opportunity to be heard and to show if he can that he did not violate the conditions or if he did, that circumstances in mitigation suggest the violation does not warrant revocation. The revocation hearing must be tendered within a reasonable time after the parolee is taken into custody. A lapse of two months as the state suggests occurs in some cases would not appear to be unreasonable.

The Court also suggested minimum requirements of due process for the revocation hearing:

> Our task is limited to deciding the minimum requirements of due process. They include (a) written notice of the claimed violation of parole; (b) disclosure to the parolee of evidence against him; (c) opportunity to be heard in person and to present witnesses and documentary evidence; (d) the right to confront and cross-examine adverse witnesses (unless the hearing officer specifically finds good cause for not allowing confrontation); (e) a "neutral and detached" hearing body such as a traditional parole board, members of which need not be judicial officers or lawyers; and (f) a written statement by the fact finders as to the evidence relied on and reasons for revoking parole.

The U.S. Supreme Court left open the question of counsel when it stated: "We do not reach or decide the question whether the parolee is entitled to the assistance of retained or to appointed counsel if he is indigent."

For further discussion of the right to be represented by counsel, refer back to the *Gagnon* decision, Chapter 7.

Parole Board Liability—*Martinez* v. *State of California*, U.S. Supreme Court, January 15, 1980

In a unanimous decision, the Supreme Court affirmed the constitutionality of statutory provisions that provide parole officials with immunity from tort claims. In this instance, Thomas, a parolee, murdered Mary Martinez five months after his release from prison. The deceased girl's parents argued that in releasing Thomas parole authorities subjected Mary Martinez to deprivation of her life without due process of law.

Justice Stevens, who delivered the opinion of the court, stated:

> Like the California courts, we cannot accept the contention that this statute deprived Thomas' (a paroled offender) victim of her life without due process of law because it

condoned a parole decision that led indirectly to her death. The statute neither authorized nor immunized the deliberate killing of any human being. This statute merely provides a defense to potential state tort law liability. At most, the availability of such a defense may have encouraged members of the parole board to take somewhat greater risks of recidivism in exercising their authority to release prisoners than they otherwise might. But the basic risk that repeat offenses may occur is always present in any parole system.

Justice Stevens pointed out that in this decision "We need not and do not decide that a parole officer could never be deemed to 'deprive' someone of life by action taken in connection with the release of a prisoner on parole."

ITEMS FOR STUDY

1. The three theories that form the basis for imposing restrictions on parolees are almost identical to those in probation.
2. The *Morrissey* decision established minimum standards of "due process" for parolees.

PART III

TREATMENT AND SUPERVISION IN PROBATION AND PAROLE

chapter 13

Classification

Systems for classifying criminals (or typologies*) have been devised by such notables as Cesare Lombroso, Enrico Ferri, and Raffaele Garofalo, who, like their more contemporary colleagues, often disagreed with each other's systems (Schafer, 1969: 140, 142). Stephen Schafer suggests that the "legion" of systems can be arranged as follows (p. 142).

Legal. Criminals are placed into existing statutory categories.
Multiple-cause. Criminals are grouped according to biological and social factors.
Sociological. Criminals are classified according to societal factors.
Psychological. Criminals are divided along psychiatric lines.
Constitutional. Criminals are classified according to biopsychological functions.
Normative. Criminals are placed according to their proclivity for committing certain crimes.
Life-trend. Criminals are referred to according to their overall life-styles.

In corrections, classification is a process for determining the needs and requirements of offenders and thereby assigning them to programs according to their needs and existing resources (National Advisory Commission, 1973: 197). The classification schemes used in corrections are ostensibly for treatment purposes, but the National Advisory Commission notes that "even a cursory analysis of these schemes

*There is a technical difference between *classification* and *typology*. A typology is a form of categorization, whereas classification implies some form of action (e.g., treatment).

and the ways in which they are used reveals that they would more properly be called classification systems for management purposes'' (p. 197). In this respect, probation and parole agencies often use classification to determine the level of surveillance that should be employed in each case (p. 202).

The Commission reflects on its being "one of the ironies of progress that just as the development of 'treatment-relevant typologies' at last appears likely, there is growing disenchantment with the entire concept of the treatment model'' (p. 197).

Classification procedures are usually carried out through one of four organizational arrangements (pp. 205–16):

1. Classification within an existing institution
2. Classification committees
3. Reception–diagnosis centers
4. Community classification teams

The first system, when used within a state prison, usually involves a reception unit whose primary responsibility is to act as a diagnostic section. The professional personnel assigned to the unit make diagnostic studies and treatment recommendations. Treatment is based on a careful study of offenders by competent staff. This type of system suffers from several shortcomings. Reception unit reports are submitted to administrative authorities, and the concern of the latter may be with such problems as security rather than with treatment. As a result, recommendations may not be followed. Often, the diagnosis is not linked directly to any operationally available programs. With the current stress on research in criminal justice, this type of system has the additional handicap of usually not having a research component.

The classification committee is an arrangement whereby a professional committee studies case records and collectively makes judgments as to the disposition of inmates in the institution. In addition to making a diagnostic evaluation, the committee has the direct responsibility for converting inmate information into recommendations for inmate programs. The committee determines inmate security ratings, assigns individuals to educational and vocational training programs, and decides where they will work in the institution. In practice, the workload and the demands on time result in very little effective programming. Interviews with inmates tend to be brief and "ritualized." The staff on the committee usually have other pressing institutional responsibilities. In the end, the decisions of the committee tend to be based on administrative and not treatment needs.

The reception–diagnostic center is a manifestation of the late 1940s and early 1950s and the development of reception centers. Under this system, all offenders are sent to a central receiving institution for study, classification, and recommendations for training and treatment programs. A primary function of the reception center is to determine to which institution an offender is to be sent. The reception center system has several drawbacks. It places the major responsibility for collecting diagnostic information on one facility, thereby requiring a high degree of specialization. In addition, inmates tend to be held too long, and there is a great deal of anonymity. The

National Advisory Commission considers the system obsolete, especially with the current emphasis on developing and programming correctional efforts at the community level.

A more recent development in correctional classification is the community classification team. This model can include probation and parole officers who are responsible for collecting the social history, and local practitioners who provide the necessary medical and psychiatric information. Institutional personnel, on a state and local basis, in cooperation with the other members of the team, review the records and match the offender's needs to the appropriate programs available.

RECEPTION CENTERS IN CALIFORNIA AND GEORGIA

In California, an extensive evaluation is provided each person received at a Reception Center. Staff members compile a complete personal history on each inmate, incorporating information from many sources including law enforcement agencies, courts, other correctional programs, military authorities, probation offices, family members, friends, and employers.

Selected combinations of personality, educational achievement and intelligence tests, together with personal interviews and observations provide clues to past and present behavior patterns, problem areas, and treatment needs. This mass of information is put together in the form of a case summary which serves as a basis for institutional assignment, treatment plans, custody status, and parole programming.

Following the initial reception-diagnostic process, individuals are assigned to institutions judged best suited to their treatment, training, and security needs after review and approval by central office classification staff representatives.

In Georgia, there are two diagnostic and classification systems. All offenders 19 years old and under are initially sent to the Georgia Industrial Institute in Alto, Georgia. Offenders 20 years old and older are sent to the Georgia Diagnostic and Classification Center in Jackson, Georgia.

The diagnostic process begins the day an inmate arrives from sentencing. He/she is fingerprinted, photographed, and assigned to a cell according to age, crime and previous record.

The inmate is then examined by a medical doctor and a dentist. Any problems are treated immediately or referred to the institution where the inmate is to be assigned.

The next step is an interview conducted on a one-to-one basis with a member of the evaluation team. A complete social history is obtained and letters are sent out to verify information.

The inmate is then given a series of tests. These include personality, intelligence, and achievement tests, together with manual dexterity tests.

After four or five weeks of gathering psychometrics and background materials from the family and the FBI, the inmate is scheduled for a final interview and evaluation. During the final interview, the inmate's desires are made known and are evaluated in light of test scores and replies from past schools and jobs. Plans for correctional education, vocational training, work assignments, treatment programs, and institutional assignments are discussed.

The Classification Committee reviews each case for recommendations. The case is then sent to the assignment officer, who then assigns the inmate to the correctional institution that best meets his/her individual needs.

David Abrahamsen, a psychiatrist, notes that "classification is always forced on nature, and hence is artificial, which is one reason why people disagree on classification" (1969: 93). Abrahamsen divides his offender types into classes: (a) *momentary offenders* and (b) *chronic offenders*. Within class (a) he lists three categories (pp. 93–126):

1. *Situational offender*. This person may commit a crime because an overwhelming opportunity arises, or because of a compelling situation, such as a strong feeling of injustice or a need for self-defense, or in the course of a temporary mental condition, such as a reactive depression. While a transgression is being perpetrated, the offender's impulse to act antisocially is overpowering, but as soon as this impelling force vanishes, his ego rejects the crime.
2. *Accidental offender*. A person who unexpectedly runs into difficulties with the law through mistake or chance. For example, careless driving.
3. *Associational offender*. This person is influenced by his own criminalistic tendencies, however weak, and also by his surroundings when certain situations arise, especially with respect to others who may exert influence on him.

Within class (b), Abrahamsen lists five categories:

1. *Offenders with organic or functional disorders*. The personality structure of this group is impaired by some destructive agent, toxic, degenerative, or infectious, or by some functional agent which damages the personality ego. In this category are psychotics, mental defectives, epileptics, and all those individuals whom the law does not regard as criminally responsible.
2. *Chronic situational, accidental, and associational offenders*. This type is an acute version of the types in class (a).
3. *Compulsory–obsessional neurotic types*. This group consists of offenders such as kleptomaniacs, pyromaniacs, and child molesters.
4. *Neurotic sociopaths*. This type includes persons with faulty superego development who act out their aggressions in an antisocial manner.
5. *Environmental sociopaths*. These people are brought up in a criminal environment that adversely affects the superego, resulting in acts directed against society. Their only regret is getting caught and punished.

The Kennedy Youth Center, as described by Roy Gerard (in Hippchen, 1975: 94–103), uses a classification system that matches staff to residents, and treatment is based on the classification. This differs from most correctional institutions, where classification is usually based on security, not treatment, needs.

First, each resident is diagnosed on the basis of staff observations, a questionnaire completed by the youth, and an evaluation of his presentence report data.

Second, the youth is placed in one of four classification categories:

BC-1: Inadequate—immature delinquency
BC-2: Neurotic—disturbed delinquency
BC-3: Unsocialized—psychopathic delinquency
BC-4: Socialized—subcultural delinquency

Third, residents are matched to staff according to their classification and the particular attributes of the worker, including his/her interests and abilities to work with a particular type of youth.

Fourth, the type of treatment that would be beneficial for each category is built into and tied to the classification process. For example, youths in BC-1 tend to be dependent, and show a general lack of interest in things. They have a low frustration tolerance, and they require structure and support. For this category, rewards are given for mature behavior, for example, self-control, while punishments are avoided. Group and individual counseling are directive in their approach, and there are opportunities that are made available whereby the youngster can do something for others, and thus gain the "reward" of warm approval.

Another system for classifying probationers and parolees was developed by the Oklahoma Department of Corrections, based on an in-depth examination of 170 randomly selected offenders. As the result of probing their past criminal history, reasons for crime involvement, familial, peer and work parameters, and attitudes toward the future, the researchers decided on four typologies (Law Enforcement Assistance Administration, 1973: 31–40):

1. *Early offender:* any subject involved in a single criminal act for which he was adjudicated prior to his 21st birthday.
2. *Late offender:* any subject involved in a single criminal act for which he was adjudicated after his 21st birthday.
3. *Intermittent offender:* any subject who had been involved in a series of criminal acts, for which he had been adjudicated with at least a one (1) year interim period between adjudications.
4. *Persistent offender:* any subject who had been involved in a series of criminal acts, for which he had been adjudicated with no lapse of noncriminal involvement.

Early Offender.   This group, though average in intelligence, was more intelligent than the intermittent and persistent offenders. They were also more independent-minded, unconventional, hostile, rebellious, and headstrong than the other two groups. They are bohemian in outlook, imaginative, careless of practical matters, and somewhat frustrated and overwrought as compared to late offenders. The mean age of this category was 18.80 years of age, the youngest of the four groups, and 95 percent of these offenders were single in marital status. Two noteworthy findings were the greater use of marijuana and their indifference to their family. This alienation from the family, bohemian outlook on life, use of drugs, and detachment with practical matters reflects on the social disintegration and atomization of the present younger group of offenders. Efforts to reintegrate them in the family and in the community were indicated. Group therapy with some family involvement could be helpful. Their prognosis was good as these offenders had not developed the self-image of a criminal as yet.

Late Offender.   Their first criminal involvement was reported late in life at the age of 28.07 years, and their present age was 30.94 years. This group was comprised of 28.8 percent females and 34 percent Negroid members. Maritally, this group had more married persons (53.8 percent) and a large number of divorces (25 percent). They perceived their relationship with their parents as unsatisfactory. Psychologically, this group was the most normal of all the groups. This group was the least criminal in its attitudes and tendencies and was expected to do very well with minimal supervision.

Intermittent Offender.   These offenders committed offences intermittently and were the oldest of the four groups with a mean age of 30.11 yearars and with their onset of criminality of age 16.68 years. These offenders were artless and sentimental on the one hand and apprehensive, worrying, depressive, moody and brooding on the other hand. They had weaker superego strengths and were apt to disregard rules. When they were not employed, they felt greatly bothered, fearful, and worried. Showing neurotic tendencies, they needed psychiatric help. The appeared to have an equal chance of success or failure under probation or parole. Using Merton's typology, these offenders tended to make ritualistic adaptation. There was a good time lapse (4 to 5 years) between offenses, and it appeared that their offenses were periodic and episodic. They were law-abiding in most instances and only occasionally disregarded laws.

Persistent Offender.   These offenders moved in and out of prison. They were involved in burglary, auto theft, juvenile offenses, and probation or parole revocation. They were easily upset, low in frustration tolerance, forceful, highly anti-social, deficient in superego strength with few obligations, suspicious, mistrusting, unconcerned about other people, wrapped up in inner urgencies, dissatisfied, and maladjusted. All these characteristics put together indicate a psychopathic or sociopathic personality. They, however, did show some apprehension which does not fit in with the psychopathic characteristic. A majority of them (57 percent) perceived themselves as criminal. This self-concept and the psychopathic tendencies render them difficult cases for treatment and rehabilitation. They need intensive supervision, and every type of therapy should be tested, hoping for a positive response to one of them.

In probation and parole classification is directed at caseload management "as a means of identifying the level of perceived risk posed by the offender, as a guide for allocation of officer time, and as a measurement of workload carried by officers, both individually and collectively" (Nelson et al., 1978: 19). Some agencies place new cases in the highest supervision category, others classify in terms of the seriousness of the offense and danger posed to the community, and a few use the level of services required by the case. Nelson and colleagues suggest (pp. 19–20):

Suggested strategy. Case classification should be perceived as the initial phase of case management planning. Specific objectives to be achieved by the offender and the agency should be identified. Ideally, such planning should involve the investigating officer, the officer responsible for case supervision, the first line supervisor, any specialist involved in the case assessment, and the offender.

Case classification should determine (1) control requirements (restrictions on movement, residence, associations; frequency of contact with the probation or parole officer; reporting requirements); (2) treatment needs (employment, training, education, residence, and financial needs; counseling and guidance addressing specific problems such as drug or alcohol abuse; treatment of any other psychological or emotional abnormalities); and (3) the administrative categorization of the case as to the extent and nature of staff allocation of time; possible assignment to specialized caseload or treatment program; and specification of the degree of perceived risk posed by the offender. Identification of strategies and resources to meet needs is essential.

Classification is an ongoing process. It should provide for periodic review (probably quarterly) of actions initiated and completed by the offender and the agency. Reviews are a time for reclassification or change of plan as indicated by changing circumstances or reassessments of needs for control or treatment. Achievement of defined objectives should trigger a reduction in controls and restraints, as well as in staff time invested, and look toward the earliest possible release from supervision consistent with public safety.

The development of specific, objective norms or guidelines for categorization of risk and intensity of supervision will permit more consistent handling of cases and provide a more rational basis for determining staff time requirements. The development and consistent use of a logical classification process provides a basis for rational management of probation or parole caseloads and is a prerequisite for the determination of the numbers and kinds of staff and other resources needed.

The classification of offenders permits the setting up of specialized caseloads (e.g., for drug addicts or retarded offenders), discussed in Part Four.*

SUPERVISION CLASSIFICATION IN UTAH†

The classification system categorizes individual cases according to the amount of supervision or structure considered to be necessary to provide appropriate accountability and treatment. In classifying cases, both the protection of society and the resolution of the individual offender's problems and ultimate rehabilitation are considered. Four classification categories have been developed. The classification categories are maximum, medium, minimum, and administrative. Corresponding standards of supervision have also been

---

*For a classification system that is based on the result of the Minnesota Multiphasic Personality Inventory (MMPI), a psychological test, see Megargee and Bohn (1979).

†Utah Adult Probation and Parole Manual of Policies and Procedures.

established for each classification category. The classification system and standards of supervision are to be applied uniformly to both felony and misdemeanor probation/parole cases. The classification system relies heavily on the professional judgment and experience of individual probation and parole officers and their respective supervisors; however, additional objectivity has been added by the addition of the History Risk Assessment document which has been in use since July 1, 1979. District supervisors are given the responsibility to assure the uniform application of the classification system through the monthly agent case review.

Ten main criteria are to be considered in classifying cases. The ten main criteria are:

1. Prior record
2. Employment record
3. History of violence
4. Prior diagnosed or known psychological problems
5. Immediate treatment needs
6. Attitude
7. Family situation
8. Financial obligations
9. Peer relations
10. Goals and objectives

To help understand the classification process, the ten criteria are defined below in terms of a maximum supervision case.

1. Prior Record
   a. Three or more arrests for alcohol or drug offenses
   b. A prior probation or parole
   c. State Industrial School commitment
   d. Repeated arrests for same offenses

2. EMPLOYMENT RECORD
   a. Unemployed for majority of last twelve months
   b. No employment skills

3. HISTORY OF VIOLENCE
   a. Present offense for aggressive acts against person
   b. Past aggressive acts known
   c. Significant potential for violence indicated

4. PRIOR DIAGNOSED OR KNOWN PSYCHOLOGICAL PROBLEMS
   a. Suicide attempts or indication of suicidal tendencies (Severe depression)
   b. Prior commitment to State Hospital

  c. Diagnosis of mental instability
  d. Retarded or borderline retardation

5. IMMEDIATE TREATMENT NEEDS
  a. Present drug addiction
  b. Present alcohol addiction
  c. Present need for mental health treatment
  d. No place to stay and no financial resources

6. ATTITUDE
  a. Very negative with display of open hostility or anger
  b. Defensive—denies apparent problems
  c. Uncooperative—failure to report or to follow programs

7. FAMILY SITUATION
  a. Antisocial family background
  b. Recent or pending divorce or separation
  c. Lack of family support
  d. Undesirable residence

8. FINANCIAL OBLIGATIONS
  a. Large amount of restitution or fine owing
  b. Considerable personal indebtedness

9. PEER RELATIONS
  a. Associating with known offenders; i.e., drug cultures and places
      where drugs are present
  b. Loner

10. GOALS AND OBJECTIVES
  a. No immediate goals
  b. Completely unrealistic goals

The classification process commences with the preparation of a presentence report and continues throughout the supervision period. The presentence investigator is to complete the History Risk Assessment form to assist in the initial classification.

Initially, all cases should be classified in either the maximum or medium category. The medium classification includes cases where moderate problems and concerns are present but to a lesser degree than for maximum classification. Qualifications for minimum classification include low risk to society, stable employment, no outstanding problems, and the resolution of major supervision objectives including full payment of any fine or restitution ordered. The administrative classification category was developed subsequent to the Classification Report of September 30, 1977. This category includes all cases where direct supervision is not being provided by Adult Probation and Parole, even though the agency is still accountable to the court or Board of Pardons for the current status of the case. Paperwork cases constitute the majority of the administrative category, and they include cases that have been formally accepted in other states, fugitive cases where the warrant issued by the court/ Board remains active, and any other cases that are in long-term treatment programs where direct supervision is provided by another agency, and direct contact with the client is minimal.

The classification system is fluid, and the classification of an individual case should change according to the changing circumstances and needs surrounding that individual case. The classification of all cases is to be reviewed on a monthly basis and the classification recorded on the client progress summary form, which is located on the back side of the field sheet. An explanation of the standards of supervision which corresponds to the levels of classification will further assist in understanding the classification process.

The following minimum standards of supervision have been established by Adult Probation and Parole.

Standards of Supervision For Maximum Cases

1. Conduct a personal office interview with the client.
2. Make one personal field contact with the client at his residence or place of employment.
3. Verify during the month:
   a. employment and/or school
   b. treatment program
   c. restitution and/or fine
4. Make collateral contacts as needed.
5. Formulate and evaluate a supervision plan (to be documented in case history).
6. Make a minimum of one typed case history summary per month.
7. Conduct a police records check.

Standards of Supervision for Medium Cases

1. Client to report in person at probation/parole office monthly.
2. Verify objectives as needed:
   a. employment and/or school
   b. treatment program
   c. restitution or fine
3. Formulate/evaluate supervision plan.
4. Dictation in file once every two months.
5. Police records check.

Standards of Supervision for Minimum Cases

1. Client to mail report to office monthly. Personal contact with supervising officer minimum of every 90 days.

2. Dictation in file quarterly.
3. Police records check.

Standards of Supervision for Administrative Cases

1. Review each case every 90 days examining expiration dates, need for progress reports in compact cases, need for criminal record updates in fugitive cases, etc.
2. A typed dictation entry must be made every 90 days indicating current status, target termination dates, status of warrants on fugitive, etc.
3. Correspondence must be answered immediately as it arrives. Where appropriate, violation reports, stay reports, termination reports, etc., must be dictated and processed.

It should be noted that Adult Probation and Parole feels the foregoing standards of supervision are the minimum standards which should be maintained. It is further noted, however, that the present agency workload and manpower resources prohibit the minimum standards from being met collectively. Even though the minimum supervision standards cannot be met with the present staffing and workload, it is imperative that the classification system be applied uniformly across the state. All cases are to be classified according to the specific criteria outlined previously. DO NOT CLASSIFY CASES ACCORDING TO OUR PRESENT ABILITY TO MEET THE MINIMUM SUPERVISION STANDARDS.

PROBATION SUPERVISION CLASSIFICATION IN MASSACHUSETTS*

The Risk/Need Client Classification System is a caseload management system which provides for differential allocation of resources to probationers according to each client's individual needs and risk to the community. This system of caseload management also emphasizes the importance of setting specific goals with each client and then evaluting the client's achievement of these goals over the period of probation supervision.

In addition to the above factors, two additional realities should be remembered:

First, the courts make the ultimate decisions concerning probation and probationary terms. We must adhere to specific judicial decisions and orders concerning types and conditions of probationary supervision.

Secondly, human behavior is extremely difficult to predict and no system of caseload management can be expected to be perfect or infallible. Certainly, no

*Source: Cochran, Donald and Gann, Linda, *Risk/Need Client Classification Guidelines, Report #2.* Boston: Office of the Commission of Probation, 1980.

probation officer or office can expect to achieve absolute success with every client.

A client whose case has been comprehensively screened and determined to be low-risk may, in fact, commit a subsequent crime in the community. On the other hand, the most aggressive surveillance and active monitoring of a high-risk probationer cannot insure against recidivism. With these exceptions admitted, the position can be made that a differential case management system, such as the Massachusetts Risk/Need Classification System, will provide a comprehensive method of efficiently and effectively employing probation supervision services and resources.

The total risk assessment score is determined by the sum of points assigned for the eight screening criteria found on the *Assessment of Client Risk Form* (RN-3B 7/80). *High scoring* individuals are identified as *low risk* probation clients, and, conversely, *low scoring* individuals are considered *high risks* in the community. Risk assessment scores range from zero to thirty.

The initial assessment of risk is completed by the probation officer within 30 days of the court's placing the client under probation supervision. The client is assigned to the level of supervision that is indicated by the Risk Assessment Scale Score. However, if the individual circumstances warrant the assignment to a supervision level other than which is indicated by the Risk Assessment Scale Score, the probation officer can, after obtaining supervisory approval, make the appropriate adjustment (subjective override).

Cut off Scores

Risk Assessment	Supervision Level
14 and below	Maximum
15-23	Moderate
24 and above	Minimum

In general, *maximum* supervision clients either have a relatively high potential for continued unlawful behavior or have demonstrated substantial need for services. *Moderate* supervision clients have relatively lower probabilities of continued criminal activity but still require ongoing agency involvement. *Minimum* supervision clients manifest relatively few problems and are very likely to successfully complete the period of probation supervision without being convicted of a new crime. The minimum number of contacts required for each supervision level follow:

Maximum At least one face-to-face contact every 14 days by a probation officer; verification of special conditions of probation, employment, and residence; home visits, collateral contacts as appropriate; staffing at request of probation officer or supervisor.

Moderate At least one face-to-face contact every 30 days; verification of special conditions of probation, employment and residence; home visits and collateral contacts as appropriate.

Minimum Some contact with the client, which could include written reports, telephone, letters, or face-to-face, shall occur at least once every 60 days.

Although there is some overlap, the four styles of probation supervision which are encouraged in the use of the Risk/Need Client Classification System can be expressed in the following diagram:

III	II
EMOTIONAL NEEDS COUNSELING	CONCRETE NEEDS COUNSELING
IV SELF-HELP	I SURVEILLANCE

I. Surveillance

While usually associated with police work in the sense of watching someone, the term "surveillance" can also have a helpful intention. Surveillance is not intended to serve the single purpose of catching a client in the act of committing a crime or violating conditions of probation. Rather, it can be used as a form of continuous support and structure for a client who is not able to deal with issues which in the past have resulted in dysfunctional and generally destructive behavior. When surveillance is properly used, the client is continually sensitized to the possible results of a course of action that has made him/her vulnerable in the past.

II. Concrete Needs Counseling

When a client shows a high level of enthusiasm and motivation toward dealing with problem areas in his/her life, sometimes in the spirit of good intentions, we forget to analyze the present situation and the client's ability to meet his/her needs in specific problem areas. The absence of concrete needs counseling is suggested as a major contributing factor to recidivism rates. This type of counseling includes some of the following areas: employment, education, financial, medical, housing, etc. High Task, as well as High Relationship, behavior on the part of the supervising probation officer seems to have the best potential for success.

III. Emotional Needs Counseling

Most probation officers are not trained psychologists or social workers and should not attempt to provide in-depth psychological counseling without the aid of qualified professionals. However, in most cases there is a need for human warmth and understanding, and this can be provided by the probation officer.

The services that a probation office and its personnel provide depend upon the needs of the clientele they serve. In this type of Style III supervision, we are referring to a person who has demonstrated past ability to handle his/her own needs in various problem areas such as employment, education, financial management, marital/family relationships etc., but who is not presently willing (motivated) to deal with the problems. The initial role of the probation officer is to motivate the client toward using his/her ability in the problem area(s).

It is quite obvious that in both the concrete needs counseling and the emotional needs counseling areas that one probation office would have a difficult time attempting to provide all the services needed by the clients. In fact, it would be unrealistic and inefficient for a probation office to provide services for all the needs of the clients, especially since there are, in many instances, community resources available to the probation department. Local communities usually have many programs that can be utilized by the probation department. These include: alcohol programs, psychiatric treatment, employment agencies, community volunteers, counseling (family, group, marital, etc.), health care clinics and many more such services.

IV. Self-Help

If there is no problem in any specific need area in a client's life, do not create one. If a client has the motivation and ability to function in a law-abiding manner, he/she is entitled to opportunities to use his/her skills and knowledge. A good "rule of thumb" for probation officers is "don't ever do anything for people that they can do for themselves."

In summary, in order to be as effective as possible in the role of a probation case manager, the probation officer must learn the fine line in supervising clients between *not enough help* and *too much help*.

ITEMS FOR STUDY

1. There are several schemes for classifying offenders.
2. In prison, classification is usually for security purposes.
3. In probation and parole, classification is a case management tool.

chapter 14

Treatment Theory

Some modes of treatment are more easily applied to probation/parole (hereafter p/p) practice than others. Some require more training than most p/p officers have received, and their use may require an expenditure of time that is not realistic in most p/p agencies. In practice, p/p officers use a variety of treatment techniques, tailoring them to different clients. They often use techniques without understanding the theoretical base or even recognizing it as part of a particular mode of treatment— "flying by the seat of your pants" is characteristic of p/p.

There are three basic theoretical models for treatment in p/p:

1. Social casework
2. Reality therapy
3. Behavior/learning theory

To better understand these methods, it is necessary to review a method of treatment that is not used extensively, if at all, in p/p. The methods of treatment listed above can be delineated according to the degree to which they accept, use, or reject psycho-analytic theory and methods.

PSYCHOANALYSIS AND PSYCHOANALYTIC THEORY

Psychoanalysis is a method of treatment based on a body of theory fathered by Sigmund Freud. Over the years, both theory and method have undergone change, although Freud's basic contribution, his exposition of the importance of unconscious phenomena in human behavior, remains.

Psychoanalytic theory divides unconscious mental phenomena into two groups:

1. *Preconscious:* thoughts and memories that can easily be called into conscious awareness.
2. *Unconscious:* repressed feelings and experiences that can be made conscious only with a great deal of difficulty.

The unconscious feelings and experiences that are normally repressed relate to the stages of psychosexual development through which each person passes on the way to adulthood (psychosexual maturity). In brief, they appear as follows:

1. *Oral:* birth to 1½ years; the mouth, lips, and tongue are the predominant sexual organs of the infant. The infant's desires and gratifications are mainly oral: sucking, biting. The infant actually enters the world a "criminal": unsocialized and devoid of self-control.
2. *Anal:* 1½ and 3 years; the anus becomes the most important site of sexual gratification. Pleasure is closely connected to the retention and expulsion of feces, as well as the bodily processes involved and the feces themselves. During this stage, the only partially socialized child acts out rather destructive urges: breaking toys or even injuring living organisms, such as insects or small animals.
3. *Phallic:* 3 to 5 years; the main sexual interest begins to be assumed by the genitals, and in normal persons is maintained by them thereafter. During this period of life the child experiences *Oedipus* (in boys) and *Electra* (in girls) *wishes* in the form of fantasies of incest with the parent of the opposite sex.
4. *Latent:* 5 years to adolescence; there is a lessening of interest in sexual organs during this period and an expanded relationship with playmates of the same sex and age.
5. *Adolescence–adulthood:* 13 years to death; there is a reawakening of genital interest and awareness, and the incestuous wish is now expressed in terms of mature (adult) sexuality.

These normal stages of psychosexual development are unconscious and serve as a source of anxiety and guilt, the basis for psychoneurosis and psychosis. The stages overlap, and transition from one to the other is gradual, the time spans being approximate. In certain abnormal cases, the infantile sexual interests become the chief source of adult sexual gratification.

Each stage is left behind, but never completely abandoned. Some amount of psychic energy *(cathexis)* remains attached to earlier objects of psychosexual development. When the strength of the cathexis is particularly strong, it is expressed as a *fixation.* For example, instead of a boy transferring his affections to another woman in the adolescent–adult stage, he may remain fixated on his mother (or a girl on her father). When a person reverts to a previous mode of gratificiation, it is referred to as *regression.* This type of behavior can be seen in young children who revert to thumb-sucking or have elimination "accidents" when a sibling is born.

When a person is passing through the stages of psychosexual development, concomitantly, the mind undergoes the development of three psychic phenomena:

1. *Id.* This mass of powerful drives seeks discharge or gratification. Comprised of wishes, urges, and psychic tensions, it seeks pleasure and avoids pain. The id is the driving force of the personality, and from birth until about seven months of age, it is the total psychic apparatus.
2. *Ego.* Through contact with the reality around them and the influence of training, infants modify their expressions of id drives. This ego development permits them to obtain maximum gratification with a minimum of difficulty in the form of restrictions that their environment places on them. For example, an id drive (desire) to kill a sibling rival is controlled by the ego.
3. *Superego.* The superego is often viewed as a "conscience-type" mechanism, a counterforce to the id. It exercises a critizing power, a sense of morality. The superego is tied to the incestuous feelings of the phallic stage, at which time the development of controls becomes an internal matter and no longer exclusively dependent on external forces (parents, for example).

The id drives impel a person to activity leading to a cessation of the tension or excitement caused by the drives. The person seeks discharge or gratification. For example, the hunger drive will result in activity that eventually satisfies (gratification) the person experiencing hunger. These drives are divided into two categories, but elements of each appear whenever either drive is activated. August Aichhorn states that as a result of disturbances in one's psychosexual development (1963: 4):

> the child remains asocial or else behaves as if he had become social without having made an actual adjustment to the demands of society. This means that he has not repudiated completely his instinctual wishes but has suppressed them so that they lurk in the background awaiting an opportunity to break through to satisfaction.

The drives are exhibited through one of two processes:

1. *Primary process:* that which tends toward immediate gratification of the id impulses.
2. *Secondary process:* the tendency to shift from the original object or method of discharge, when something blocks it or it is inaccessible, to another object or method. For example, a desire to play with feces arising out of an anal cathexis, will be transferred to playing with mud as a result of toilet training. This transfer is called *displacement,* and it is one of the many *defense mechanisms* that the human mind employs to adapt to its environment. Other defense mechanisms include:
   a. *Repression:* activity of the ego that prevents unwanted id impulses, memories, emotions, desires, or wish-fulfilling fantasies, from entering conscious thought. Repression of charged material (e.g., incestuous fantasies) requires the expenditure of psychic energy and sets up a permanent opposition between

the id and the ego. The delicate balance (equilibrium) between the charged material and its opposing expenditure of energy can shift at any time, usually as a result of some stress. When repression is inadequate in dealing with charged material, psychoneurotic symptoms develop.

b. *Reaction formation:* a mechanism whereby an individual gives up some form of socially unacceptable behavior in favor of behavior that is socially acceptable. This more acceptable behavior usually takes the form of being opposite to the real desire (drive). For example, a child who desires to kill a sibling will become very loving and devoted. In adult behavior, a sadistic impulse toward animals can result in a person becoming a veterinarian.

c. *Projection:* a person attributes his/her own wish or impulse to some other person. This is pathological in cases of paranoia.

d. *Sublimation:* a drive that cannot be experienced in its primary form, such as a desire to play with feces, is accommodated by modeling clay or, perhaps, becoming a proctologist.

There is a delicate balance maintained by unconscious forces as a person experiences the various sociocultural and biological aspects of existence. When the balance is upset, the psyche passes from the normal to the psychoneurotic and/or the psychotic (mental illness). It is basic to psychoanalytic theory that there is a "very thin line" between the normal and the neurotic, and between the neurotic and the psychotic. In fact, there is only a difference of degree between the normal and the abnormal. The degree to which there is a malfunctioning in the psychic apparatus is the degree to which a person is abnormal or "sick."

Gerhard Falk points out that "the psychoanalytic theory of crime causation does not make the usual distinction between behavior as such and criminal action"; the distinction is a legal one (1966: 1). Antisocial behavior is seen as a neurotic manifestation whose origin can be traced back to early stages of development. "There is no fundamental difference between the neurotic criminal and all those socially harmless representatives of the group of neurotic characters; the difference lies merely in the external fact that the neurotic lawbreaker chooses a form of acting out his impulses which is socially harmful" (Alexander and Staub, 1956: 106).

Much of the psychoanalytic theory of crime causation is concerned with the superego, essentially an internalized parent (Aichhorn, 1963: 221):

> the superego takes its form and content from identifications which result from the child's effort to emulate the parent. It is evolved not only because the parent loves the child, but also because the child fears the parent's demands.

It is this psychic mechanism that keeps primitive (oral and anal) id impulses from being acted upon. Persons with a poorly developed superego cannot exercise adequate control over impulses and suffer little or no guilt as a result of engaging in harmful behavior. At the other extreme are persons whose superego (parental "voice") is destructive. This overwhelming superego cannot adequately distinguish between *thinking* ''bad'' and *doing* ''bad.'' Unresolved conflicts of earlier development and id impulses that are normally repressed or dealt with through other secondary processes (e.g., reaction formation, sublimation) create a severe sense of guilt. This guilt is experienced (unconsciously) as a compulsive need to be punished. To alleviate (unconscious) guilt the actor commits acts for which punishment is virtually certain. The delinquents of this type are the victims of their own morality (Aichhorn, 1963: 232). Persons employed in criminal justice often see cases in which the crime committed was so poorly planned and executed that it would appear that the perpetrator *wished* to be caught. Between these two extremes are various neurotic disorders and ego problems that cause an individual to come into conflict with the criminal law.

Superego function is viewed as the result of an actor's relationship to parents (or parental figures) during early developmental years. Parental deprivation through absence, lack of affection, and/or inconsistent discipline stifles the proper development of superego (the ''internal parent''). Parental influence is thus weakened by deprivation in childhood, and in adulthood the actor is unable to adequately control aggressive or hostile urges. Overly rigid and/or punitive parents (or parental figures) create a superego (internalized parent) that is similarly rigid and punitive.

It is obviously important for a p/p officer to be able to distinguish between those offenders with inadequate superegos from those with punitive ones. With the latter, deterring criminal behavior through the application of threats may actually have a reverse effect. With the former, the p/p officer may need to act in a parental role in place of a poorly developed superego.

Psychic disorders are treated by psychoanalysis or one of its various offshoots such as psychotherapy. Freud stated that psychoanalysis ''aims at inducing the patient to give up the repressions belonging to his early life and to replace them by reactions of a sort that would correspond better to a psychically mature condition.'' To do this, a psychoanalyst attempts to get the patient ''to recollect certain experiences and the emotions called up by them which he has at the moment forgotten'' (Reiff, 1963: 274). To the psychoanalyst, present symptoms are tied to repressed material of early life. The symptoms will disappear when the repressed material is exposed under psychoanalytic treatment.

To enable the patient to ''relive'' the past, the analyst uses dream interpretation and ''free association,'' whereby a patient gives up ideas as they come to mind. In addition, psychoanalysis takes advantage of the phenomenon of *transference*. This is the development of an emotional attitude, positive or negative, by the patient toward the therapist. It is a reflection or imitation of emotional attitudes that were experienced in relationships that had an impact on psychosexual development. Thus, the therapist may be viewed as a ''father figure'' or a ''mother figure'' by the patient. Through the use of transference the therapist recreates the emotions tied to very early psychic development, unlocking repressed material and ''freeing'' the patient from his/her burden. As Freud noted, transference ''is particularly calculated to favor the reproduction of these (early) emotional conditions'' (Reiff, 1963: 274).

Psychoanalysis is not used in p/p because it requires highly trained (and thus expensive) practitioners; treatment takes many years; and it needs a level of verbal ability in patients beyond that of most persons on p/p. Instead, psychoanalytic theory is applied in p/p through social casework.

SOCIAL CASEWORK

Social casework is one of the three basic specialties of social work, the others being group work and community organization. There have been many definitions of social casework. Swithun Bowers offers the following (Kasius, 1950: 127):

> Social casework is an art in which knowledge of the science of human relations and skill in relationship are used to mobilize capacities in the individual and resources in the community appropriate for better adjustment between the client and all or any part of his total environment.

Social work has its roots in charity work and the supplying of concrete services to persons in need. Mary Richmond, whose colleagues included many physicians, presented the practice of social casework as including (nonpsychoanalytical) psychological and sociological aspects of a person's behavior. She also set the groundwork for what is sometimes referred to as the *medical model* of treatment which deals with nonphysiological problems through the method of *study, diagnosis, and treatment*.

Following World War I, Freudian thought "impacted" on social casework. Caseworkers began examining a client's feelings and attitudes in order to understand and "cope with some of the unreasonable forces that held him in their grip" (Perlman, 1971: 76). Casework was thus expanded to include work with psychological as well as social or environmental stress.

While social casework borrowed much of its theory from psychoanalysis, it avoided the psychoanalytical goal of trying to effect personality changes. Instead it worked to help clients maintain constructive reality-based relationships, solve problems, and achieve adequate and satisfying independent social functioning within the client's existing personality structure (Torgerson, 1962: 41). To do this, social caseworkers use encouragement and moral support, persuasion and suggestion, training and advice, comfort and reassurance, together with reeducation and some sort of guidance (Kasius, 1950: 25).

The importance of social casework in p/p practice goes beyond theory and into the skills and training that schools of social work provide. These include "an extension and refinement of information on how to interview, how to obtain facts about the client's background, how to identify and distinguish surface from underlying problems, what community resources exist, and how to refer" (Wilensky and Lebeaux, 1958: 288–89). Wilensky and Lebeaux note that such practice is pragmatic, based on rule-of-thumb experience rather than on theory.

There are three basic operations practiced in social casework methodology (Perlman, 1957: 61):

1. *Study:* fact-finding.
2. *Diagnosis:* thinking about and organizing facts into a meaningful goal-oriented explanation.
3. *Treatment:* implementation of conclusions as to the what and how of action upon the problem.

Although we shall review these three operations separately, it should be noted that "study–diagnosis–treatment" have "a close mutual relationship and form one theme." Ostrower also notes that although for teaching purposes these steps are referred to separately, they "are not actually performed in sequence, but are interwoven and in reality comprise a unity" (1962: 86).

Study

During the initial phase the worker must establish a relationship with his/her client. To be able to do this, the worker must be what Hamilton calls "a person of genuine warmth" (1967: 28). Using face-to-face interviews the worker conveys acceptance and understanding. Friedlander notes that "caseworkers communicate their respect for and acceptance of the client as a person whose decisions about his own living situations are almost always his own to make" (1958: 22). Workers know that the way they communicate will have an effect on clients' perception of them and the worker–client relationship. Therefore, workers must be cognizant of the way they greet clients, their tone of voice, facial expressions, posture, and the way they express theselves verbally. In p/p practice, workers who exude authority, who are curt, and who emphasize the enforcement aspect of their position will encounter difficulties in establishing a sound casework relationship.

Workers engage clients in the helping process. They make certain judgments about a client's motivation, how much he/she wants to change, and how willing he/she is to contribute to bringing about change. Workers recognize that a client brings attitudes and preconceptions about being on probation or parole. The probation/parole client is fearful, or at least realistically on guard, since he/she recognizes the power of the p/p worker.

An anxious client will be resistant to a worker's efforts, and in the nonvoluntary p/p setting, a worker can easily raise a client's anxiety level, thus increasing resistance. P/p clients often have negative impressions of all authority figures. This is usually based on experiences with parents, school officials, police, courts, training schools, or prisons. In addition, a client may have a low self-image, a severe superego, or a chronically high anxiety level. The result will be resistance.

There are ways of lessening resistance. Workers can discuss clients' feelings about being on p/p, allowing them to ventilate some of their feelings and anxiety. This will also enable workers to clear up any misconceptions that clients have about p/p supervision.

The client's motivation can also be influenced by *transference*. He may view the worker as a friendly parent, or authoritative and demanding mother or father. The worker can be influenced by *countertransference*, since he may view the client as a childlike figure, or when there is a great age difference between worker and client, the former may view the latter as a father or older brother.

The worker prepares a psychosocial study of his client. In non-probation/parole agencies workers often stress the importance of early childhood development and experiences with a view toward applying psychoanalytic explanations to the client's behavior (Friedlander, 1958: 134). This is not the usual practice in p/p settings, where it is more appropriate to analyze "the unique constellation of social, psychological, and biological determinants of the client's current stressful situation" (p. 47). In p/p practice, the main focus is on the present or immediate past.

The p/p worker seeks information that will provide an indication of the client's view of his present situation. He concerns himself with his client's plans for improving his situation and weighs the sincerity and intensity of the latter's commitment to change. He reviews the client's relationship with his family and evaluates the impact of his current situation. While engaged in his study, the worker must also be aware of the cultural, racial, and ethnic factors that influence his client.

In p/p, material from the unconscious is not sought. However, with clients who are mentally ill, material that in the better functioning person is normally repressed may be brought into the fore. In such situations, the worker must direct his efforts toward keeping the client in touch with reality, and he usually avoids exploring the normally repressed material.

Diagnosis

A diagnosis is a "summation of the symptoms of some underlying causation" (Friedlander, 1958: 146). It determines the nature of the client's difficulty and provides a realistic assessment for individualized treatment. Some of the questions that a diagnosis seeks to answer are (pp. 84–85):

1. What are the client's social-role problems?
2. What are his dominant and alternate modes of adaptation?
3. What are the etiological factors that can be traced to his present situation?
4. What are his ego strengths and weaknesses?

The diagnosis focuses particular attention on ego functioning. The client's capacity to deal consciously with difficult inner forces is dependent on his ego functioning, a facet of personality that develops its strength through interaction with other persons (Frieldlander, 1958: 134–35). Ego adequacy will have a direct impact on the client's efforts to deal with his difficulties.

Perlman suggests that the diagnosis in casework consists of (1957: 168–69):

1. The nature of the problem and the goals sought by the client, in their relationship to
2. The nature of the person who bears the problem, his social and psychological situation and functioning, and who needs help with his problem, in relation to
3. The nature and purpose of the agency and the kind of help it can offer and/or make available.

For a diagnosis to be complete, psychological testing and/or a psychiatric evaluation is necessary. The results of a clinical examination will indicate if the client is in need of any special treatment—for example, if he is psychotic.

Perlman, in discussing the etiology of the client's malfunctioning calls this a "history of his development as a problem-encountering, problem-solving human being," and she notes that this can provide the worker with an understanding of the client's present difficulties and the likely extent of his ability to cope with them (1957: 176).

Friedlander notes that "in an on-going relationship, diagnoses are continually reformulated, as the caseworker and the client engage in appropriate corrective action or treatment" (1958: 22).

Treatment

It is a basic concept in social work that the worker has no right to impose his goals upon the client. The client has a right to *self-determination*. Obviously, the authority inherent in the p/p worker limits self-determination. How is this reconciled when social casework is the mode of treatment in p/p?

Hardman notes that a review of some of the literature on the subject reveals that in treatment, authority is considered:

1. Impossible;
2. Possible only in mild cases of delinquency;
3. Both detrimental and beneficial; or
4. Essential but not necessarily harmful.

Hardman states that "authority conflict is a major causative factor in delinquency," a proposition that is widely accepted in correctional treatment (1960: 250). Therefore, assisting the offender in coming to grips with the reality of authority is a basic goal in p/p treatment. The client's relationship with a p/p worker is often the only positive experience he has ever had in dealing with an authority figure.

However, social caseworkers in other than correctional settings must also deal with the reality of their authority. They require clients to keep appointments, provide personal information, and pay fees, usually under the threat, implied or expressed, of denying the client the service for which he is asking. Workers in child welfare agencies may even be required to remove children from their parents or guardians in neglect or child-abuse cases. In addition, because of the impact of an agency setting, or the phenomena of transference, the social caseworker is always an authority figure.

The concept and the use of authority and the limits placed on self-determination by reality are not alien to the practice of social casework.

However, we should consider the admonition of Smith and Berlin, who state that "no matter how evident the need for counseling . . . appears to the probation and/or the parole officer, it cannot be forced upon the offender unless it is directly related to his crime" (1974: 3). For example, a client who has a history of drug usage that has resulted in the need to steal could be required to accept counseling because it is "directly related to his crime." However, I question the usefulness of "counseling" that has to be "forced upon the offender." I would recommend instead that no form of treatment be forced upon any offender. This will preserve the client's right not to be treated, while allowing the worker to better use his treatment time and skills with clients who wish help.

Ross and Shireman note that the illusion "that all, or almost all, offenders need and will respond to rehabilitative efforts if such efforts are sufficiently massive and persistent" has led us "to assign most offenders to programs of active intervention in their lives. The result is the choking of programs with large numbers of individuals who do not need, do not want, and cannot use the sort of relationship-and-communication-based treatment that is the basis for most probation or parole services" (1972: 24).

The plan for treatment, based on the diagnosis, will hopefully use procedures that will move the client toward the goal of enhancing his ability to function within the realities placed upon him by society in general, and his present probation/parole status in particular. There are three basic techniques involved.

Changing the Environment

This may involve obtaining needed resources if these are available from the agency, or locating other agencies that can provide them. In using this technique the worker may assume a *mediator* or *advocate* role when the client is unable to secure a service which he needs and to which he is entitled. In p/p practice this is a common role for the worker. The technique is used by the juvenile worker when he is seeking placement for a youngster in a foster home, group home, or residential treatment center. The aftercare worker who is trying to place a juvenile back into public school after a stay at a juvenile institution is often a *mediator–advocate*. The p/p worker is often required to intervene on behalf of clients who require financial assistance from the welfare department. P/p workers may help a client to secure a civil service position or a necessary license/certificate to enter a particular trade or profession.

The p/p worker may help his client by talking to an employer or school official, at the same time helping the client to modify his behavior relative to problems encountered at work or school. Many p/p clients have had few positive work or school experiences, and their difficulty with authority extends to employers and teachers. By using role playing, reflection, and suggestion the worker tries to modify the client's behavior, at least to the degree required for continued schooling or employment.

The worker, while being of direct assistance when necessary, should promote independence on the part of his client. The worker realizes that he is not continually available, and treatment is rarely indefinite. *The worker should not do anything for his client that the client is capable of doing for himself.*

Ego Support

The use of this technique entails attempts by the worker to sustain his client through expressions of interest, sympathy, and confidence. The worker, through the use of his relationship with his client, promotes or discourages behavior according to whether or not the behavior is consistent with the goals of treatment. He encourages the client to ventilate, and he deals with any anxiety that may inhibit functioning.

The worker imparts a feeling of confidence in his client's ability to deal with problems. He makes suggestions about the client's contemplated actions. He indicates approval or suggests alternatives relative to steps that the client has already taken. He may, at the very least, provide a willing and sympathetic ear to a troubled or lonely client. It is not unusual for the p/p worker to be the only person that an offender has available to whom he can relate and talk. When the relationship is a good one, the client cannot help but view his worker as a friend.

The worker is also supportive of the client's family, parents, or spouse. In p/p practice, home visits are a usual part of the worker's responsibilities. During the home visit, the worker has an opportunity to observe the client's environment directly. This adds another dimension to the worker's knowledge of the client.

The knowledge that a client lives in substandard housing or in a high-delinquency area is easy for a worker to incorporate into his working methodology. But the concept is an intellectual one. A home visit will provide the smell of urine in the hall, the roaches, the broken fixtures and bathroom facilities; it will enable the worker to experience the presence of drug addicts huddling in a hallway waiting for their "connection." The worker will be able to see, hear, and smell the environment in which a client is forced to live. He will be able to understand the hostility and frustration that fills the life of many p/p clients almost from the time they are born.

By working directly with parents or a spouse, in addition to working with the client, the worker broadens his delivery of help to his client. The worker can make referrals for the client's children when special aid is necessary—indeed, he can intervene on behalf of his client in the role of *mediator–advocate* to get services for any family member. He can assist with marital problems. Marital discord is an acute problem in many parole cases where a client has been incarcerated for many years. The worker may try to deal with the problem directly, or he may provide a referral to a specialized agency for the client and spouse. It is not unusual for a distraught wife to call the p/p worker to complain about her husband. Sometimes she is merely seeking some way of ventilating her feelings, while at other times the situation may be more serious—for example, she may have been beaten.

When a client is living with parents, the worker strives to involve them in the rehabilitation effort. This is often difficult. The client may come from a large family where he is the perennial "black sheep." He may come from a family that has other members of the unit on probation, in prison, or on parole. This may dissipate the family's energy and resources, and directly affect their ability to help the client.

Clarification

Florence Hollis states that clarification is sometimes called counseling because it usually accompanies other forms of treatment in casework practice. Clarification includes providing information that will help a client to see what steps he should take in various situations. The worker, for example, may help the client weigh the issues and alternatives to provide a better picture on which to base a decision. Hollis notes that the client "may also be helped to become more aware of his own feelings, desires and attitudes" (Kasius, 1950: 418–19).

The client is encouraged to explain what is bothering him. If the problem is external, this may be relatively easy. However, if the difficulty is internally caused, it may go deep and provoke anxiety. This will cause resistance and the worker will require great skill to secure enough information about the problem to be able to be of assistance. In response to the information, the worker may provide a direct interpretation to the client; more often he will ask questions and make suggestions designed to help the client to think out his problem more clearly and to deal with it in a realistic manner.

REALITY THERAPY

Reality therapy was developed as a mode of treatment by William Glasser, a psychiatrist. It is probably the easiest of the three modes of treatment to describe, and its simplicity is one of its advantages in practice. Glasser's book, *Reality Therapy* (originally published in 1965), contains only 166 pages. Glasser describes reality therapy as a method "that leads all patients toward reality, toward grappling successfully with the tangible and intangible aspects of the real world . . ." (1975: 6).

Although Glasser accepts the developmental theories of psychoanalysis, he rejects it as a useful method of treatment. "It is wishful thinking to believe that a man will give up a phobia once he understands either its origin or the current representation of its origin in the transference relationship" (p. 53). Glasser believes that conventional treatment "depends far too much on the ability of the patient to change his attitude and ultimately his behavior through gaining insight into his unconscious conflicts and inadequacies" (p. 51).

In a more recent work (1976), Glasser reiterates some of his previous positions and elaborates on others. Various mental problems, Glasser argues, are merely symptomatic illnesses that have no presently known medical cause. They act as companions for the lonely people who *choose* them. Glasser states that in cases of so-called mental illness, the behaviors or symptoms are actually chosen by the person from his lifetime of experiences residing in the subconscious. Alluding to the fact that reality therapy does not always work, Glasser states that the fault is with the therapist who is unable to become involved in a meaningful way with the client.

Glasser expresses a great deal of support for the work of probation and parole officers, although he cautions persons in corrections, as well as other fields, against the use of punishment (1976: 95):

> For many delinquents punishment serves as a source of involvement. They receive attention through delinquent behavior, if only that of the police, court, probation counselor, and prison. . . . A failing person rationalizes the punishment as a reason for the anger that caused him to be hostile.

Instead of punishment. Glasser recommends that praise and positive motivations be applied through the medium of reality therapy.

Schmideberg, another reality-oriented psychiatrist, states that "dwelling on the past encourages the patient to forget his present problems, which is a relief at times, but often—undesirably—the patient feels that after having produced so many interesting memories he is now entitled to rest on his laurels and make no effort to change his attitude or plans for the future" (1975: 29). This diverts attention from the client's current problem, which is a reality that should be dealt with directly. Glasser states that conventional treatment does not deal with whether a client's behavior is right or wrong, in terms of morality or law, but "Rather, it contends that once the patient is able to resolve his conflicts and get over his mental illness, he will be able to behave correctly" (1975: 56). Glasser maintains that societal realities require direct intervention with a client, with the therapist not accepting "wrong" behavior. In his latest work, however, Glasser warns the reality therapist to be *nonjudgmental* (1980: 51).

The reality therapist denies the claims of psychoanalysis that cure depends on the recovery of traumatic early memories that have been repressed. Schmideberg states that the ability of psychoanalysis to cure persons has never been substantiated clinically (1975: 28). In place of conventional treatment, the reality therapist proposes first substituting mental health labels (neurotic, personality disorder, psychotic) with the term *irresponsible*. A "healthy" person is called *responsible,* and the task of the therapist is to help an irresponsible person to become responsible.

"Reality therapy is based upon the theory that all of us are born with at least two built-in psychological needs: (1) the need to belong and be loved and (2) the need for gaining self-worth and recognition" (Glasser, 1980: 48). According to Glasser, people with serious behavior problems lack the proper involvement with someone—and lacking the involvement, they are unable to satisfy their needs. Therefore, to help, the worker must enable the client to gain involvement, first with the worker and then with others. Whereas the traditional therapist maintains a "professional" objectivity or distance, the reality therapist strives for strong feelings between worker and client. This type of relationship is necessary for the worker to be able to have an impact on his client's behavior. The worker, while always accepting of his client, firmly rejects irresponsible behavior. He then teaches his client better ways of behaving.

To accomplish this "reeducating," the worker must know about the client's reality, the way he lives, his environment, his aspirations, his total reality. Reality is always influenced by the client's culture, ethnic and racial group, economic class, and intelligence. The worker must be willing to listen openmindedly and learn about his client (Schmideberg, 1975: 24). While doing this he develops a relationship with his client, a relationship that can effect an influence leading to responsible behavior.

Like behavior modification, reality therapy is symptom-oriented. The probation/ parole client is in treatment because he has caused society to take action as a result of his behavior. If the worker can remove the symptoms and make the client responsible, he will satisfy society and relieve the client of anxiety caused by a fear of being incarcerated. Schmideberg states that for a delinquent symptom to disappear it is usually necessary for the person to (p. 24):

1. Face it fully with all its implications and consequences.
2. Decide to stop it and consider the factors that precipitate it.
3. Make a definite effort to stop it.

She maintains that a general and nondirective method is not likely to change symptoms that the client may find quite satisfying (e.g., drugs to the addict, forced sex to the rapist, or money and excitement to the robber).

Rachin outlines 14 steps that the reality therapist follows to attain responsible behavior in his client (1974: 51–53):

1. *Personalizes*. The reality therapist becomes emotionally involved. He is a warm, tough, interested, and sensitive human being who genuinely gives a damn—and demonstrates it.

2. *Reveals self*. He has frailties as well as strengths and does not need to project an image of omniscience or omnipotence. If he is asked personal questions, he sees nothing wrong with responding.

3. *Concentrates on the "here and now."* He is concerned only with behavior that can be tried and tested on a reality basis. He is interested only with the problems of the present, and he does not allow a client to waste time and avoid confronting reality by dwelling on the past. He does not permit a person the luxury of blaming irresponsible behavior on past difficulties.

4. *Emphasizes behavior*. The reality therapist is not interested in uncovering underlying motivations or drives; rather, he concentrates on helping the person act in a manner that will help him meet his needs responsibly.

5. *Rarely asks why*. He is concerned with helping a client understand what he is doing, what he has accomplished, what he is learning from his behavior, and whether he could do better than he is doing now. Asking a person the reasons for his actions implies that they make a difference. To the reality therapist irresponsible behavior is just that—he is not interested in explanations for self-defeating behavior. He conveys to the client that more responsible behavior will be expected.

6. *Helps the person evaluate his behavior.* He is persistent in guiding the client to explore his actions for signs of irresponsible, unrealistic behavior. He does not permit the client to deny the importance of difficult things he would like to do. He repeatedly asks the person what his current behavior is accomplishing and whether it is meeting his needs.

7. *Helps him develop a better plan for future behavior.* By questioning *what* the person is doing now and *what* he can do differently, he conveys his belief in the client's ability to behave responsibly. If the client cannot develop his own plan for future action, the reality therapist will help him develop one. Once the plan is worked out, a contract is drawn up and signed by the person and the reality therapist. It is a minimum plan for behaving differently in matters where the person admits he has acted irresponsibly. If the contract is broken, a new one is designed and agreed upon. If a contract is honored, a new one with tasks more closely attuned to the person's ability is designed.

8. *Rejects excuses.* He does not encourage searching for reasons to justify irresponsible behavior, thus avoiding the implication that the client has acceptable reasons for violating his agreement. Excuses are not accepted—only an honest scrutinizing examination of his behavior.

9. *Offers no tears of sympathy.* Sympathy can indicate that the worker lacks confidence in the client's ability to act responsibly. Sad tales, past and present, are avoided. Sympathizing with a person's misery and self-pity will not lead to more responsible behavior. The worker must convey to his client that he cares enough about him that, if need be, he will try to force him to act more responsibly.

10. *Praises and approves responsible behavior.* The worker makes appropriate indications of recognition for positive accomplishments. However, he does not become unduly excited about the client's success in handling problems that he previously avoided or handled poorly.

11. *Believes people are capable of changing their behavior.* The worker's positive expectations enhance the client's chances of adopting a more productive life-style, regardless of what has occurred in the past. The worker is encouraging and optimistic.

12. *Tries to work in groups.* The use of a peer group allows for more influence or pressure on the members. It enables the members to express themselves before people with similar problems. It enables the member to test out "reality" in a controlled environment.

13. *Does not give up.* The worker rejects the idea that anyone is unable to learn how to live a more productive and responsible life. Historical information contained in long case records is not allowed to interfere with the worker's involvement with his client, and his belief that all persons can begin again.

14. *Does not label people.* Avoids the diagnostic rituals, and does not classify people as sick, disturbed, or emotionally disabled—they are either responsible or irresponsible.

Reality therapy was developed by Glasser while he was a psychiatrist at the Ventura School, an institution for the treatment of older adolescent girls who had been unsuccessful on probation. Because the technique evolved within the field of corrections and the realities of dealing with delinquent behavior, it has been widely accepted and applied to p/p treatment. It flows easily alongside the p/p officer's need to hold the offender accountable for his/her behavior. Some maintain that the value stress in reality therapy coincides with the paternalistic and perhaps authoritarian attitudes of some p/p officers. Although Glasser does not deal with theory, RT is practice-oriented, the theoretical underpinnings of RT are quite close to those in behavior/learning theory, often referred to simply as *behavior modification*.

BEHAVIOR MODIFICATION

If we view the various modes of treatment as if they were on a continuum represented by a straight horizontal line, with total acceptance of psychoanalytic theory/treatment on the extreme left, and total rejection on the extreme right, reality therapy would tend toward the right of center, while social casework would tend toward the left of center. Behavior modification would be firmly on the right of our imaginary line.

Behavior therapy, which emanated from the science laboratory and experimental psychology, rejects psychoanalytic theory as an unscientific basis for an even more unscientific mode of treatment. (For a review of research supporting psychoanalytic theory, see Silverman, 1976). Ian Stevenson, a psychiatrist, is extremely critical of the paucity of evidence indicating that the therapeutic procedures that are based on psychoanalytic theory are effective (Wolpe et al., 1964: 7).

Behavior therapists, on the other hand, take pride in displaying and subjecting to scientific analysis their methods and results. Indeed, the use of behavior modification requires the maintenance of extensive objective treatment data, including outcomes, in quantifiable terms (American Psychiatric Association, 1974: 3). A *Dictionary of Psychology* defines behaviorism as an approach to psychology that emphasizes the importance of an objective study of actual responses.

Behavior modification proceeds on the theory that all forms of behavior are the result of learning responses to certain stimuli. Disturbed behavior, for example, is a matter of learning responses that are inappropriate (London, 1964: 83). The behaviorist contends, and has been able to prove, that animal behavior, human and otherwise, can be modified through the proper application of behavior therapy. Indeed, such techniques as *conditioned reflex therapy* are "based completely on the work of Pavlov and Bechterev" (Wolpe et al., 1964: 21), who demonstrated that such observable and measurable activity as the flow of a dog's saliva could be controlled by the use of laboratory conditioning. (Pavlov's dogs were conditioned to salivate at the sound of a bell.) When behavior modification moved out of the laboratory, its use was "confined to specific problems such as children's fears and bedwetting, and alcoholism" (Wolpe et al., 1964: 170).

There is considerable opposition to behaviorism in theory and practice. To many conventional therapists the theory lessened the dignity of a human being, reducing him to the level of an animal, with the techniques used reminiscent of animal training. Ogden Lindsley, for example, humorously reminisces about his early days with behaviorism, stating "that if the bottom fell out of the whole thing, I would drop out of graduate school and try to get a job with Ringling Brothers' circus training gorillas to dance and play the piano" (Hilts, 1974: 7).

As in psychoanalytic theory, learning theory does not distinguish between behavior as such and criminal behavior; both are seen as based on the same principles of learning.* The basic learning principle is *operant conditioning*. A pioneer in behavior modification, B. F. Skinner, observed that when some aspect of (animal or human) behavior is followed by a certain type of consequence—a reward—it is more likely to occur again. The reward is called a *positive reinforcer*. When punishment is used to decrease the likelihood that some aspect of behavior will be repeated, it is called a *negative reinforcer*. These items form the basis for operant conditioning, whereby patterns of behavior are *shaped* incrementally by reinforcement (Skinner, 1972). Antisocial behavior is merely the result of learning directly from others (e.g., peers) or the failure to learn how to discriminate between competing norms, lawful and unlawful, due to inappropriate reinforcement. When conforming behavior is not adequately reinforced, or perhaps negatively reinforced, an actor can be more easily influenced by competing, albeit antisocial, sources of positive reinforcement. "Behavior modification, then, involves altering the nature of the controlling conditions, rather than imposing control where none existed before" (Stolz, et al., 1975: 1037). To be effective for learning, however, reinforcement must follow rather closely the behavior that is to be influenced. When these principles are used in treatment, therefore, timing is crucial. The need for timely reinforcement also makes operant conditioning difficult to apply in probation and parole practice. Albert Bandura points out, however, that in humans "Outcomes resulting from actions need not necessarily occur instantly" (1974: 862). This is because humans, as opposed to lower animals, "can cognitively bridge delays between behavior and subsequent reinforcers without impairing the efficacy of incentive operations" (Ibid.). Bandura warns (Ibid.: 863): "To ignore the influential role of covert self-reinforcement in the regulation of behavior is to disavow a uniquely human capacity of man." Of course, self-reinforcement can operate in a manner that enhances antisocial behavior. Reinforcement can take many tangible or symbolic forms. In reality therapy, praise and encouragement are dispensed by the therapist, while in other settings privileges are dispensed through *tokens*.

Token Economies

Operant conditioning has been used extensively in prisons (and other "total institutions") where reinforcing variables can be controlled to a degree not possible elsewhere.** In these settings it is often referred to a *token economy*. In Draper Prison

*In expounding the behaviorist position on crime, C. Ray Jeffrey states (1971: 177): "There are no criminals, only environmental circumstances which result in criminal behavior. Given the proper environmental structure, anyone will be a criminal or a noncriminal."

**Thomas G. Stampfl, a noted behaviorist, states (1970: 105):

One obvious disadvantage related to TE [token economy] is that rather close control over environmental contingencies is required. The status of the S [subject] whose behavior is to be modified is that of a "captive." In the absence of environmental control, it is not possible to introduce the critical contingencies. If control is present initially, but is then lost for whatever reason, the removal of the in Alabama inmates were given punch cards with numbers every morning. As they moved through various prison activities during the day, points were earned and punched out on the cards by correction officers trained in behavior modification. Points were earned for a variety of "good" behavior, bed making, vocational and educational performance, and so on. The points were convertible into access to certain privileges, such as the television room, cigarettes, movies, and snacks. Such programs can reduce the need for standard forms of coercion.

A widely heralded token economy was used by Harold Cohen at the National Training School for Boys (NTS) in Washington, D.C. (Cohen and Filipczak, 1971). The project involved 41 adjudicated juvenile delinquents whose crimes ranged from auto theft to homicide. A point system was tied to educational work and academic achievement. The points that were earned allowed a boy to purchase refreshments, clothing, and even items selected from a mail-order catalog. Cohen reports that by establishing this incentive plan, the program enabled youngsters to increase their academic growth "two to four times the average for American public school students."

Cohen notes that the conventional method used in the public school system and correctional institutions is to assign students on the basis of their IQ score and reading level. Those who score low are assumed to be basically imcompetent to perform in such areas as algebra and physics. They are assigned to tasks considered appropriate to their level of ability, and these usually do not require reading and other academic skills. Before Cohen arrived at the NTS, this was the method used there.

Cohen began by considering every inmate a potential student capable of upgrading. His goal was to prepare them to return to public school or to pass the high school equivalency test. "The environment was planned to include choices and perquisites normally available to the average wage-earning American but not available to these youths in a prison. The students earned points for academic performance and paid for their rooms, clothing, amusement and gifts," with them. Even showers had to be rented with points. Points could not be gained in any other way except "work." They could not be loaned, given away, or stolen.

Another aspect of the system was that the students "were able to earn some powerful nonmonetary rewards. Respect, approval by one's peers . . ." and so on. Families were permitted to visit, but all transactions within the project were made with points, and visitors were not permitted to purchase items for residents.

The principal objective of the program was the development of appropriate

---

contingencies allows the altered behavior to revert in the direction of its original baseline rate. In an effort to maintain behavior when the subject has lost his status as a captive, operant conditioners have attempted to gradually alter manipulated contingencies in respect to the behavior being modified so that the changed behavior itself would tend to result in natural (intrinsic)reinforcement.

Stampfl points out that the main difficulty with the latter solution is that delinquents/criminals "tend to be highly resistant to the usual types of natural or intrinsic reinforcement that appear to function so effectively for other 'normal' populations" (p. 105).

academic behavior. No assumptions were made by the program originators relative to the resident's adjustment when he returned to the community. However, a follow-up on recidivision indicated that during the first year the recidivist rate was two-thirds less than the norm, although by the third year the rate was near the norm. Cohen reports that the program evidently delayed a return to delinquent activity, but did not necessarily prevent it. He states that to do this would require additional services outside the institutional setting.

Other Systems

Operant conditioning can also use punishment, *negative reinforcement*. When punishment is used, it is called *aversion therapy*. This involves the avoidance of punishment in a controlled situation in which the therapist specifies an unpleasant event that will occur if the subject performs an undesirable behavior. One report stated that "the most effective way to eliminate inappropriate behavior appears to be to punish it while at the same time reinforcing the desired behavior" (American Psychiatric Association, 1974: 25). This method of treatment is obviously controversial, and many behaviorists disapprove of the use of punishment—negative reinforcement, both on ethical grounds and also because its effects do not last as long as results conditioned by positive reinforcement.

There have been some "horror" stories about the use of behavior modification and aversion therapy, which were popularized in the Stanley Kubrick movie *A Clockwork Orange*. In real life, California prisoners were injected with Anectine (succinyl-choline), a muscle relaxant that causes brief paralysis but leaves the patient conscious. The prisoners were unable to move or breathe voluntarily, a sensation that simulates the onset of death. At the same time the therapist would tell the subject that he must change his behavior. Some observers state this program was not an example of aversive conditioning, but rather merely punishment.

Criticism

The latter point is part of the behavior-modification controversy. Much of what is done in the name of "learning" is dependent on one's definition of the situation. As a "learning tool," behaviorism is amoral and politically neutral—like a gun—and thus easily lends itself to misuse. Some critics maintain that behavior modification is simply a tool for keeping persons with legitimate grievances from expressing or acting on them—behavior modification, as noted, has been successful in maintaining prison discipline and order. Where legitimate dissent ends and disorder begins is often a matter of obvious subjectivity. Unlike other forms of treatment, behavior modification does not need the acquiescence of its subjects in order to be effective. In fact, it may at times be more successful when used without the knowledge of those who are being subjected to it. Since behavior modification serves to modify *undesirable* behavior or attitudes, who is to determine what is undesirable? What one observer considers *learning,* another views as *brainwashing.* This was made quite vivid during the Korean war, when a number of American servicemen, prisoners of war, were subjected (unknowingly) to behavior modification. The success of the practice with some American prisoners was not viewed as "learning" by officials in the United States, who coined the term *brainwashing* to describe the behavior modification methods used by the Chinese and North Koreans. Stephanie Stolz and her colleagues (1975: 1040) point out: "Frequently, the goal of effective behavior modification in penal institutions is the preservation of the institution's authoritarian control." That is, "making the prisoners less troublesome and easier to handle, thus adjusting the inmates to the needs of the institution." They state (Ibid.): "A major problem in using behavior modification in prisons is that positive programs begun with the best of intentions may become subverted to punitive ones by the oppressive prison atmosphere."

The use of positive reinforcers has been criticized as being a form of "bribery," and tokens have been viewed as being "artificial" and of limited utility. Daniel O'Leary and his colleagues argue (O'Leary, et al., 1972: 2; citation deleted):

A tracing of the word bribery from the sixteenth century to the present clearly denotes immorality through its historical associations with stealing and corruption—especially of public officials. This primary definition is clearly not applicable to tangible reinforcers when they are used in intervention programs for establishing behaviors such as self-care in hospitalized patients or speaking and reading in children. That is, unless, one considers self-help, reading, or speaking as corrupt, one cannot regard the use of concrete reinforcers for their establishment as bribery.

Therapists who are psychoanalytically oriented have been critical of behavior modification over the issue of *symptom substitution.* These therapists do not question the ability of behaviorists to remove or diminish certain undesirable behavior. However, according to traditional psychoanalytic theory, this symptom reduction will merely lead to new symptoms that will replace the old ones with each new emotional difficulty experienced by the subject (Friedlander, 1947: 199). Aichhorn argues that (1963: 39):

the disappearance of a symptom does not indicate a cure. When a psychic process is denied expression and the psychic energies determining it remain undischarged, a new path of discharge will be found along the line of least resistance, and a new form of delinquency will result.

Psychic disturbances are thus conceived of as producing a lightning-like force which if manipulated in a way that denies discharge (i.e., by behavior modification), will merely strike harmfully in another direction. The American Psychiatric Association Task Force stated that this is not necessarily so. Furthermore, they argue that reduction of unwanted behavior provides an opportunity to teach a person more desirable behavior (1974: 53).

Behavior modification analyzes symptoms in terms of their observable behavior components. The therapist keeps a record of "frequency counts" on a particular behavior. For example, a parent will be asked to record the number of outbursts exhibited by a child within a given period of time. The therapist then makes a functional analysis designed to determine the circumstances under which the undesirable behavior seems to occur, and the elements within the environment that may be supporting the behavior. In this case, the parent is told to ignore the child's outbursts, no matter what the intensity, while providing rewards (reinforcement) for more positive behavior. These rewards can be praise and attention, or sweets and toys.

Positive reinforcement, the timely application of rewards, is more easily accomplished in the institutional setting, where the environment can be controlled, than in the community where most probation/parole treatment occurs. All of these reasons may account for the paucity of articles on the use of behavior modification in p/p in professional journals. However, Gaylord Thorne and his colleagues reported on the successful use of behavior modification, *operant conditioning,* in work with young juveniles on probation (1967: 21–27).

Behavior Modification in Probation/Parole

The probation officers first gained the cooperation of the child's parents—not an easy task. The officers then explained the behavioral techniques to be used and taught the parents how to apply them. Behavior was monitored by the parents, and charts were used to record frequency counts. Positive reinforcers were given for desired behavior, such as attendance at school, scholastic work, and satisfactory behavior, and were withheld when the child misbehaved. The rewards were specific and related directly to particular positive behavior. For example, a girl on probation was given telephone privileges and permitted weekend dates, contingent on her attendance at school all day. In this case the attendance officer would give a note to the child at the end of each day indicating her attendance. When the child gave her mother the note she earned the privilege of receiving and making calls that day. If she received four notes, she earned a weekend date, and five notes earned two weekend dates.

In another case, rewards included both tangible and intangible items. For example, for studying 30 minutes a day, the youngster was both praised and given permission to ride his bicycle. The authors (Thorne et al., 1967) call the praise a *backup reward.* Money, access to TV, and other "rewards" were used as reinforcers for specific behavior on a specified and scheduled basis. The authors point out that uncooperative parents can defeat any type of productive change. This form of behavior modification is often referred to as *behavioral contracting:* "an agreement in which the performance of predetermined responsibilities or duties results in receipt of privileges or rewards" (O'Leary and Wilson, 1975: 480). It has been used predominantly (if not exclusively) with children, since they can be subjected to greater environmental controls.

Polakow and Docktor report that "experimental literature on behavioral approaches to probation work with adults is almost nonexistent" (1974: 63–69). They report the use of *contingency management* in working with adult drug offenders on probation. Although contingency management is supposedly a behaviorist approach, it actually comes closer to reality therapy than behavior modification. This is because it lacks the crucial element of timeliness—the reinforcement does not closely follow the desired action. In the cases cited by Polakow and Docktor, the probation officers used reduction in probation time as a reinforcer.

Actually, most p/p agencies use some form of contingency management, without labeling it as such. For example, an offender who is employed will be placed on a reduced reporting schedule (e.g., once monthly), while an unemployed offender will be required to report in person once a week. In addition, discharge from probation and parole is often conditioned on satisfactory behavior under supervision, and this is explained to offenders at the beginning of their probation or parole.

SOCIAL GROUP WORK

Treatment of clients in groups is used in social work, reality therapy, and behavior modification. The use of a group has certain advantages over conventional one-to-one methods. Northern notes that "one of the advantages of the use of groups in social work is that stimulation toward improvement arises from a network of interpersonal influences in which all members participate" (1969: 52). The basic theory underlying the use of the group is that the impact provided by peer interaction is more powerful than worker–client reactions within the one-to-one situation.

In probation/parole, groups are comprised of members who share a common status, in this case legally determined. Groups in p/p may also be organized on the basis of age, or around a common problem such as drug addiction. The group is a "mutual aid society" in which members are given an opportunity to share experiences and assist each other with problems in a safe, controlled environment. The group helps to confirm for each member the fact that others share similar problems, thus reduing the sense of isolation.

The group can reduce the anxiety of having to report alone to a p/p officer; it tends to offset the more direct authority of the one-to-one situation; and it tends to lower the impact of sociocultural differences between client and worker.

The summary and analysis that follows is based on my experience with a group of young offenders in a parole setting. The method used reflects an approach suggested by William Schwartz (1966), who stresses several key concepts in working with groups: the *contract* is made verbally between the client group and the worker and it provides the framework for the tasks that the group will work on; the *contract* is mutually agreed upon and it is based on the common ground and needs of the group members; *work* is the means by which the group comes to grips with mutual needs and problems, and it is a part of the worker's role to *demand* that the group *work* as mutually agreed upon in the *contract*.

In 1971, the New York State Department of Correctional Services formed a specialized parole supervision unit called the Young Offender Bureau. The YOB supervised offenders released to the New York City Area Office who were under 21 years of age at the time of their parole. A most significant feature of the YOB was an expectation that each parole officer in the unit would utilize group methods in the supervision process. No particular method of group work was specified since an attempt was being made to see what kind, if any, of group techniques would be useful in the parole setting. Thus, each parole officer was free to use whatever method he/she wished, within the requirements of sound parole supervision. Caseload size was kept at about 32 to enable each p.o. in the YOB to devote more attention to each case, both individually and on a group basis.

I decided to see if a voluntary approach to forming a group would be successful. Consideration in the selection process included a parolee's reporting schedule. He could not be reporting on a monthly basis to be selected, since traditionally this is a reduced reporting schedule and is considered a "reward" for good performance on parole. The group would meet once per week, and to ask a person reporting on a monthly basis to report on a weekly basis could be considered as punitive. A parolee who worked or attended school in the evening would also not be available for the group, which would meet at night. In addition, parolees who were believed to be in violation of parole were omitted during the group formation stage.

Each parolee who was considered for the group was informed individually about the general purpose and meeting schedule of the group. Specifically, it would meet once per week for one hour to discuss topics or problems raised by group members. Attendance and participation would be voluntary, although those who did not attend were expected to report on an individual basis. The initial reaction was good, and 10 parolees volunteered out of the 12 who were asked. However, after five sessions, attendance began to fall off to a point where we no longer constituted a workable group.

Upon reflection, it appeared that most of the parolees who volunteered did so out of fear that refusal to volunteer would somehow result in some form of punishment. When they began to realize that the group was indeed voluntary, they stopped attending. I believed that a parole group could work and be beneficial to its partici-pants if only they would attend the sessions consistently enough to gain something from them. A second group was organized. This time it was decided to make the group as normal a part of the parole process as possible. Attendance was made mandatory. This was readily understood by the members, so there was no need to test out the voluntary aspect as had the first group. Each parolee was required to attend 10 sessions. After the 10 sessions, the continuance of the group would be a decision made by the group members, and no member would be required to attend any further sessions if he chose not to.

Initially, 10 parolees were selected for the group. One was arrested by the police after attending two sessions; one was arrested as a parole violator by me before the sessions began, and one was arrested as a parole violator after attending two sessions (no special consideration was given for participation in the group). Of the remaining seven members, one was a persistent attendance problem, with a rate of 30 percent, and his individual reporting was almost as bad. The other six had an attendance rate of 80 percent. Four members were added to the group after the first five sessions and they showed an attendance rate of 90 percent. At the end of the 10 sessions, only two members stated that they did not want to continue with further group sessions, and they were excused. Of the two, one was the parolee with a 30 percent attendance rate, and the other explained that traveling difficulties made it impossible for him to leave work and arrive at the sessions on time. The rest of the group requested that the sessions be continued.

When the group sessions began, the members started calling upon late arrivers to explain their tardiness. Those who missed sessions were also called upon to explain why by the group members. They were a "demanding jury," quick to point out what they believed to be falsehoods in any explanation. I told the members that each session was being limited to exactly one hour, explaining that this was being done because of the tendency in all types of groups to leave important matters until the end, often wasting time at the beginning. The purpose of the group was stated in terms of mutual concerns. I pointed out that the group members had much in common; their parole status, age, ethnicity (all were black or Puerto Rican; the author's area of supervision was the South Bronx), and difficulties with school or employment. It was suggested that in the group setting each member could help the other because of a similar background and common problems.

During the first session, the discussion turned to the rules of parole. I explained that although I was now a participant in the group, I was still a parole officer with all the obligations that that engendered. It was made clear that the rules of parole were still to be observed by all group participants. The opening sessions were filled with testing of roles, and conversation tended to dwell on the problem of employment, which, although a real problem among the group, was also a "safe" topic. Discussions were lively from the beginning, and as the sessions progressed, personal problems were discussed openly and candidly. These included problems with parents, drugs, police, and the attitude of the community toward parolees. Support was freely given by the group to those who needed it, but those who tended to boast were restored firmly but gently to their proper perspective by the group. With at least one parolee, who had an extensive history of drug usage, the group was successful in getting him to stop the use of drugs, and this parolee remained drug-free and gainfully employed months after the sessions ended.

Leaders quickly emerged in the group, and they often competed for leadership by attempting to outdo each other in confronting and supporting other members. When conversation moved into *nonwork* areas—baseball or boxing, for example—most often group members, rather than myself, would *demand* a return to *work* on areas of importance. Group members described their experiences on parole, and compared feelings about their parole status. A common recognition that others seemed to be experiencing the same feelings was something that all members received from the group experience.

During one session, Robert, a former gang member with a serious organic speech defect, who was not a member of the group, came into the session. However, he sat through the beginning of the session in silence and looked quite sullen. The other group members did not refer to Robert, so I asked what was bothering him. He began telling the group of the murder of his best friend, Dennis, whose parole officer I had been. (Dennis was killed by some adults when he shouted at them for almost running him over while he was crossing the street—he was shot several times after a furious street fight.) Another member described what he had heard about the incident. The other group members listened intently to both boys and expressed their support for Robert's feelings over the loss of his best friend. I confronted the group with the fact that they had seemingly ignored Robert, despite the fact that he seemed troubled. Members became defensive and said that they recognized that Robert had something on his mind, but felt he did not want to talk about it. Why, then, would he come to the session, I asked. They responded that it was better to let Robert bring up the matter himself.

In other sessions, the group dwelled on the question of drugs, with the non-drug users defending the use of Methadone for helping addicts, and those with drug histories calling Methadone a "cop-out" to the problem. During one session, a non-drug-using parolee asked for help in dealing with his 17-year-old sister, who had been using heroin. Members shared similar problems they had with older and younger brothers or friends. The discussion, and expressions of support for members' efforts with this problem, provided some excellent approaches and insights into dealing with their immediate concerns.

When a new member joined the group, the older members would describe the workings of the group. In particular, two things were stressed: first, that one can say whatever he wants in the group; and second, that whatever is said is confidential. The members understood that this confidentiality did not extend to me; I took notes during the sessions and had explained that these notes were reviewed by my supervisor. Confidentiality was for group members, who, according to their own *contract,* were not to discuss what happened in the group outside the group. The sessions that followed the first 10 sessions were voluntary. They included a review of one of my group recordings, a copy of which was given to each member. It proved to be a lively session, with members agreeing or challenging my observations and interpretations. This exercise enabled the group to gain some insight into how they are viewed by others, either myself or members of the group. The group expressed a great deal of pride in their ability to work together.

The use of the group approach provides an atmosphere where problems can be worked upon by others who share similar problems and who are sympathetic. It reduces the tensions created by the conventional one-to-one relationship between p.o. and parolee, and it allows for changes in behavior and attitudes that are stronger and more meaningful.

SOCIOLOGICAL THEORY

Psychological theory attempts to identify causes of criminal behavior within the individual actor; sociological theory approaches crime from a social context and can add dimension to understanding individual offenders. We will briefly review those sociological theories that are most relevant for p/p practice.*

*For an in-depth look at these theories, the reader is referred to the citations; discussions can also be found in a number of criminology texts, such as that by Fox (1976).

Anomie

The concept of anomie was developed by Emile Durkheim (1951) to explain variations in suicide rates. As reformulated by Robert Merton (1938), crime is viewed as a normal response to a social system that stresses the goal of economic success while severely limiting the means for securing the goal. This creates an *anomic* situation that can elicit a variety of responses; the two most important for p/p practice are *innovation* and *retreatism*.

Innovation is simply the adaptation of illegal means to achieve a level of success not otherwise available. *Retreatism* amounts to a repudiation of the goal of economic success, a scaling down of aspirations that can be achieved by partaking in a deviant subculture (e.g., drug addicts or alcoholics). Thus, in the first response "the means justify the ends," whereas in the second the ends are sufficiently reduced as to make achievement possible (e.g., getting "high").

What does the theory of anomie offer to the p/p officer and the very real problems of his practice? One consideration has to do with aspirations. Offenders often have quite unrealistic goals; their aspirations surpass their ability. In such cases, the role of the officer is to help the client to make a realistic assessment of the situation, and then to assist him with achieving goals that are reality-based. Each client should be encouraged and assisted to achieve to the limits of his ability. The officer has a responsibility to see to it that his client's goals are not blocked by such barriers as discrimination. In such instances he must make use of the various agencies that are responsible for enforcing equal opportunity laws.

Differential Association

Edwin Sutherland (1883–1950) is a giant among American criminologists. His most widely known theories concern "white-collar crime" and differential association. Because of its applicability to the client population on p/p, we shall review only differential association in this book.

Differential association "conceives of criminality as participation in a cultural tradition and as the result of association with representatives of that culture" (Sutherland, in Schuessler, 1973: 5). The basis for this theory is a set of beliefs that:

1. Criminal behavior is learned.
2. Criminal behavior is learned in interaction with other persons in a process with other persons.
3. The learning of criminal behavior occurs primarily within intimate personal groups.
4. The learning of criminal behavior includes techniques, motives, and attitudes.

Sutherland states that crime results when there is "an excess of definitions favorable to violation of law over definitions unfavorable to violation of law" (Schuessler, 1973: 8–9).

Crime results from the strength or intensity of criminal associations and is the result of an accumulative learning process. A pictorial portrayal of differential association can easily be conceived of in terms of a balanced scale that starts out level. On each side is accumulated the varying weights of criminal and noncriminal associations. At some theoretical point criminal activity will result if there is an excess of criminal associations over noncriminal associations.

What import does this theory have for p/p practice? As noted earlier in the discussions of p/p regulations, they invariably contain prohibitions against certain associations. A person on p/p is usually cautioned against associating with others similarly situated. This can easily be seen as a practical attempt to respond to the theory of differential association. In addition, the p/p officer can provide exposure to a noncriminal association; an exposure and influence that conceivably can help to balance our theoretical scale. The officer can assist his client with securing other noncriminal associations through charitable, community, church, fraternal, and other such organizations.

Delinquency and Opportunity

Richard Cloward and Lloyd Ohlin "attempt to integrate these two streams of thought as they apply to the problem of delinquency" (Cloward and Ohlin, 1960: x). They unite the theories of anomie and differential association in a discussion and analysis of delinquent gangs and subcultures. In focusing on the different types of criminal activities that result from anomie and differential association, they distinguish several categories:

1. Rackets—organized crime subculture
2. Fighting gang subculture
3. Retreatist drug-oriented subculture

Each of these types of subcultures arises out of a different set of social circumstances or *opportunity*. Crime is viewed not as an individual endeavor, but as part of a collective adaptation or manifestation within a given set of social circumstances. Cloward and Ohlin recognize that in some instances, not only are legitimate means of achieving success blocked, but certain illegitimate ones as well. This phenomenon is discussed by Nicholas Gage in a book appropriately entitled *The Mafia Is Not an Equal Opportunity Employer:* "no door is more firmly locked to blacks than the one that leads to the halls of power in organized crime" (1971: 113).

When access to legitimate and important illegitimate means of attaining goals is not readily available, urban ghetto youngsters may resort to less utilitarian forms of deviant behavior, such as gang fighting activities or drug addiction.

The application of this hybrid theory to p/p practice is similar to the two strains on which it is based. However, it also provides an insight into adolescent gang behavior, which appears to be on the rise in many urban areas. In addition, it offers an explanation of why many p/p clients have a history of drug addiction.

Subcultures

Albert Cohen (1955) focuses on a delinquent subculture that is negativistic and malicious, as opposed to the utilitarian *(innovative)* variation found by Merton (1938) and Cloward and Ohlin (1960). This actor steals and engages in antisocial behavior "for the hell of it"—a *flouting* of middle-class mores. This actor is a problem for the p/p officer because he/she eschews items of personal behavior that are essential for success: ambition, skills for achievement, control of physical aggression, cultivation of manners.

Walter Miller (1959) views subcultural norms not as a reaction to the middle class, but as a manifestation of lower-class culture. The focal concerns of lower-class culture include "toughness": physical prowess and daring; "smartness": ability to dupe or con; "excitement": taking risks, seeking danger. Miller points to a lower-class discrepancy over "autonomy": an overt hostility toward external controls, coupled with behavior that seeks out restrictive environments (e.g., armed forces, prisons). Thus, the p/p officer will find clients resentful of controls, yet acting in such a manner as to ensure recommitment after a period of relative freedom.

Neutralization and Drift

In contrast to Albert Cohen, Gresham Sykes and David Matza (1957) suggest that participants in delinquent subcultures are essentially committed to middle-class conformity. They are able to engage in antisocial acts, in spite of this commitment, through the use of *neutralization:* justifications for deviance that are held as valid by the actor, but not by the legal system or society at large. These include: a *denial of responsibility*—"I had to do it"—wherein there is a profound alienation from self; a *denial of the victim*—"he had it coming"—whereby injury to others is held to be justifiable, punishment; an *appeal to higher loyalties*—"I did it to help a buddy"—redefining the situation so that it expresses positive values. These statements, or variants of them, are often encountered by p/p officers. Sykes and Matza caution against dismissing them as merely postact rationalizations since they indicate a genuine commitment to societal norms, a basis for rehabilitation.

Matza (1964) argues that the delinquent youngster is not fully committed to antisocial activities, but *drifts* between criminal and conventional action. The delinquent subculture is not totally alienated from society, and most participants leave it for conventional (adult) life-styles. Indeed, adolescence is characterized (in "normal" youngsters) by acts that are at least unconventional, if not antisocial or criminal. Thus, it is important to avoid overreacting to youthful misconduct, lest we begin a complex process "of response and counter-response beginning with an initial act of rule violation and developing into elaborated delinquent self-conceptions and a full-fledged delinquent career" (Schur, 1973: 120). This statement from Edwin Schur expresses a concern with *labeling*.

Labeling

The labeling perspective emphasizes the impact of societal reaction to deviance rather than the individual characteristics of the offense or the offender. Thus, Howard Becker (1963) argues that society actually creates deviance by the making of rules or laws and then by applying these laws to the violators and labeling them as delinquents or criminals. Schur explains (1973: 119):

A societal reactions perspective, then, is more concerned with what is made of an act socially than with the factors that may have led particular individuals into the behavior in the first place. While these precipitating factors obviously have some importance, the labeling analysts believe they have been overemphasized. Many of the reaction processes that shape deviance situations remain crucial, they argue, *whatever* the precipitating factors in specific cases may be. In particular, the labeling approach stresses that the self-concepts and long-term behavior of rule-violators are vitally influenced by the interaction between them and agents of social control.

The p/p officer is constantly faced with the dynamics of labeling, as his/her clients encounter difficulty in returning to school, securing employment, obtaining housing, making friends, because of the stigma (label) of *delinquent/criminal*.

The label results in a negative self-image whereby the offender's view of himself is that of an inferior and unworthy person. In such a condition, the offender may seek the companionship of others similarly labeled; he may engage in further antisocial activities in an effort at striking back at the society that has labeled him.

The criminal label creates certain expectations that may result in what Merton refers to as the "self-fulfilling prophecy" (1957: 421–36). The public, for example, does not express much surprise when an offender is arrested for another crime. Indeed, it is usually the first question raised when a person has been arrested: "Has he been arrested before?" There is a saying among the "sages" that call the street their home: "If you have the *name*, might as well play the *game*." This fatalistic mode of thinking and acting presents a challenge to every probation/parole officer in the practice of his profession.

The labeling perspective is also concerned with the phenomenon of *secondary deviation*, a concept developed by Edwin Lemert (1951). Perhaps the best example of this concept concerns narcotic addiction. The use of heroin is a *primary deviance*. However, the societal reaction to heroin—it is unlawful to possess—creates *secondary deviance* by forcing the addict to violate the law in order to use heroin, and of course to support his expensive habit. In England, where the use of heroin is not unlawful and is under medical control, an addict may be a deviant, but not necessarily a criminal.

Critical Theory

This view considers the conventional criminal as *victim* of a stratified society into which he/she is born poor and powerless. Within this approach criminal acts are sometimes romanticized as "rebellion," and criminals as some type of "primitive rebel,'' although most conventional crime is committed by the underclass against the underclass. Critical theory sensitizes the p/p officer to some of the basic inequities in our society, certainly as they are reflected in criminal justice. Thus, our prisons are filled with the underclass, while the affluent commit antisocial acts with relative impunity, are pardoned, or otherwise dealt with leniently.* Although it is beyond the role of the p/p officer, as such, to deal with system inequities, he/she does have an advocate role, which will be dealt with later in this book.

ITEMS FOR STUDY

1. Psychoanalytic theory, a basis for social casework, stresses unconscious mental processes.
2. During early development stages the unsocialized infant/child is "criminal."
3. Associated with the stages of psychosexual development are the id, ego, and superego.
4. Psychoanalytic theory and behavior/learning theory do not distinguish between criminal and noncriminal behavior.
5. The superego is viewed as a central factor in understanding individual criminality.
6. In p/p, psychoanalytic theory is applied in modified form through social casework.
7. Reality therapy has found widespread acceptance in p/p.
8. Behavior modification developed out of experimental psychology and is the most controversial technique used in corrections.
9. The group work approach has certain advantages over the traditional one-to-one approach in p/p.
10. An understanding of certain sociological theories can add dimension to p/p practice: anomie, differential association, delinquency and opportunity, subcultures, neutralization and drift, labeling, primary and secondary deviation, critical theory.

---

*H. Jeffrey Reiman (1979) writes that *The Rich Get Richer and the Poor Get Prison:* American criminal justice is determined by economic bias in which crimes unique to the wealthy are ignored or treated lightly, while crimes of the poor—crimes of poverty—lead to imprisonment.

chapter 15

Supervision

The supervision process in both probation and parole is similar, if not identical. In fact, probation and parole are handled by the same agency in some areas. However, parolees by definition have been imprisoned, and imprisonment generally reflects the severity of the offense and the criminal history of the offender. Therefore, parolees are generally considered a greater danger to the community than are probationers. The Maryland Division of Parole and Probation provides an example*:

Table displays the types of offenses for which clients were placed under the supervision of the division state-wide. An examination of state-wide totals reveals that 65% (3,994 cases) of the parolees and 40% (15,535 cases) of the probationers are under supervision for the major offenses of criminal homicide, forcible rape, robbery, aggravated assault, burglary or larceny. In addition, the great majority of offenders convicted for criminal homicide, forcible rape, or robbery are under parole supervision; and, the majority of those offenders convicted for aggravated assault, burglary, larceny and other offenses are under probation supervision.

Parolees may differ from probationers as a result of their prison experiences. Elliot Studt reports that based on her research there are certain highlights of the reintegration process that stand out in most parole cases. She notes that the changeover from prison life to community living requires a major readjustment. In prison the offenders' lives are rigidly controlled; they are told when to sleep, when to eat, when to work, and when to have recreation. When they are released to the community they must adjust to

Source: Annual Report of the Maryland Division of Parole and Probation, 1979.

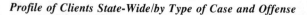

Profile of Clients State-Wide/by Type of Case and Offense

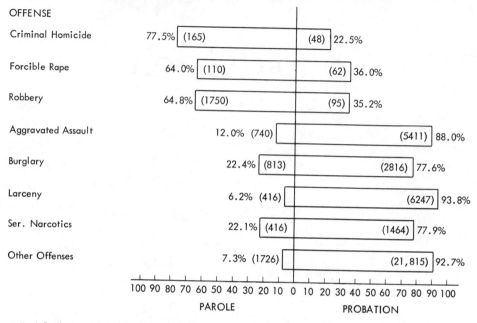

OFFENSE

Criminal Homicide	77.5% (165)	(48) 22.5%
Forcible Rape	64.0% (110)	(62) 36.0%
Robbery	64.8% (1750)	(95) 35.2%
Aggravated Assault	12.0% (740)	(5411) 88.0%
Burglary	22.4% (813)	(2816) 77.6%
Larceny	6.2% (416)	(6247) 93.8%
Ser. Narcotics	22.1% (416)	(1464) 77.9%
Other Offenses	7.3% (1726)	(21,815) 92.7%

100 90 80 70 60 50 40 30 20 10 0 10 20 30 40 50 60 70 80 90 100

PAROLE   PROBATION

( ) Indicates total clients.

Source: Division of P & P—Intake Discharge and Current Population by Sex, Race Offense and Age Report.

managing their own lives (Studt, in Law Enforcement Assistance Administration, 1973: 43). This is compounded in some cases by police harassment, especially in smaller communities. Social agencies often do not recognize parolees' needs and somehow believe that they should be receiving assistance from the parole agency. Unfortunately, most parole (and probation) agencies are extremely limited in their ability to deliver tangible services. This fact, coupled with the usual lack of employable skills, often makes parolees a burden on their families, worsening what may be an already difficult family situation (Sutherland and Cressey, 1966: 492). (Milton Burdman, Deputy Director of the California Department of Corrections, believes that the reintegration of probationers presents similar problems. He notes that there may be a long period of pretrial confinement in addition to the disabling effects of arrest and prosecution.)

Parolees have told the author that even so minor an experience as taking a bus ride can be traumatic to a newly released offender. Several stated that they were not aware of the fare and the need for exact change. They had the feeling that everyone on the bus, especially the driver, recognized that they had just been released from prison. Being in prison also isolated them from normal social contacts with members of the opposite sex. Several male parolees expressed their reactions to the new dress styles to which they were exposed for the first time after release from prison, especially "mini-skirts." They were very self-conscious, and they often felt that because of the way they looked at women everyone would realize that they had been in prison.

Studt points out that the parolee must "unlearn" prison habits and acquire new patterns of behavior if readjustment is to be accomplished quickly. Parolees are often subjected to social rejection because of their status, and they usually lack the necessary connections and economic resources that are effective in dealing with crisis situations (Law Enforcement Assistance Administration, 1973: 43–45).

CASELOAD ASSIGNMENT

The client first comes to the p/p office as the result of being placed on probation in lieu of imprisonment, or after being released from imprisonment. In either event, who will be his/her p/p officer is determined by the method of case assignment practiced by the particular agency. Eric Carlson and Evalyn Parks distinguish five assignment models. The first three of these are in general use throughout the United States (1979: 62–63):

The first model is called the *conventional model*. This model is entirely independent of any consideration of the differences and similarities among probationers, and probationers are randomly assigned to available probation officers. Because of the random distribution of the probationer population among caseloads, each probation officer handles a caseload that is a miniature reproduction of the entire probationer population, including, of course, the wide variations in personal characteristics. With the conventional caseload model, then, the probation officer must be able to supervise any type of probationer who happens to be assigned to the caseload.

Closely related to the conventional model is the *numbers game model*. This model may also ignore differences and similarities among probationer characteristics. The object of this model is to numerically balance all of the caseloads within the department. This balancing may be accomplished with or without taking the personal characteristics of the individual probationers into account. The numbers game model may be approached in two ways. First, the number of probationers to be supervised can simply be divided by the number of probation officers available to the department. Thus, if the department has 10 probation officers and 800 probationers, every officer will handle a caseload of 80. Second, the department can select an "ideal size" for each caseload and divide the number of probationers by this "ideal size," yielding the number of necessary probation officers. Under this method, if a department has 800 probationers and has selected 50 as its "ideal size" caseload, it must provide 16 probation officers. In addition to use with the conventional model of assignment, the numbers game model may also be used in modified form with the other assignment models discussed below.

The third assignment model is called the *conventional model with geographic considerations.* This model differs in one respect from the conventional model described above: the caseload is restricted to residents in one type of geographic area (i.e., urban, suburban, or rural). Given the travel time involved in supervising an entirely rural caseload, the size of a rural caseload is generally smaller than those of suburban or urban caseloads. The caseloads, however, remain undifferentiated on the basis of the personal characteristics of the probationers, except to the extent that the characteristics of urban, suburban, and rural probationers may vary.

The fourth and fifth models distinguished by Carlson and Parks are *specialized caseloads*. The *single-factor model* groups offenders according to a salient characteristic (e.g., drug abuse, age, mental retardation). The *vertical model* uses a multivariate classification scheme for grouping offenders. The outcome of the scheme, using success prediction tables, are caseloads of offenders having generally the same (predicted) chance of success or failure. "This model is referred to as the 'vertical' because it divides the offender characteristic curve into vertical slices in order to create caseloads" (p. 64). The variety of specialized caseloads, their advantages and disadvantages, are discussed in Part Four.

THE INITIAL INTERVIEW

The first meeting with the p/p officer is a time of apprehension and anxiety. Jose Arcaya states that the officer "represents a power that can, and does, limit his freedom." The offender is in the office involuntarily in a situation "where two individuals are joined by legal force in a counseling . . . relationship." The offender encounters the p/p officer for the first time with a mixture of fear, wariness, and defiance (1973: 58–59).

The "sizing up" process works both ways. The p/p officer is meeting a stranger he/she knows only through the information in the case record and/or the presentence report. While the record says much about the offender's background, it may not reflect his/her current attitude toward p/p supervision. How will the offender deal with his current problems? Will he follow p/p regulations? Will he abscond from supervision if pressured or frustrated? Will the officer be responsible for having a warrant issued and sending the offender to prison? Will this be, instead, an easy case with a minimum of problems?

The client is asking similar questions. Will this p/p officer give me a hard time? Will he be rigid about every minor p/p rule? Is this p.o. quick to seek delinquency action? Does he have the knowledge and ability to help me secure employment, training, education, a place to live?

What role will the p/p officer assume? Harry Allen and his colleagues report that a review of the literature reveals four basic role typologies (1979: 58):

1. The *punitive/law enforcement officer*, whose primary concern is the protection of the community through control of the probationer.
2. The *welfare/therapeutic officer*, whose primary concern is the improved welfare of the probationer.
3. The *protective/synthetic officer*, who attempts to effect a blend of treatment and law enforcement.
4. The *passive/time server officer*, who has little concern for the welfare of the community or the probationer, but sees the work merely as a sinecure, requiring a minimum amount of effort.

Role 4 is meaningless since it is not particular to p/p or even criminal justice settings in general. The first three roles are deficient when discussed outside a particular agency context or model, of which there are three:

1. *Control model.* Control of the offender's activities is the primary focus. Unannounced home and employment visits and a close working relationship with law enforcement agencies are the standard practice.
2. *Social service model.* Focuses on the offenders' needs, employment, housing, and counseling that provides social and psychological support.
3. *Combined model.* Requires p/p officers to provide services while attending to control functions.

Most p/p agencies would fall somewhere between the social service and combined model, with parole agencies tending toward the combined model and probation agencies tending toward the social service model. The control model would not be found in its "pure" form. What is found in the parole field are combined model agencies tending toward the control model. Now if we return to the p/p role typologies, we can see that the punitive/law enforcement officer is more likely to be found in—indeed, would be appropriate for—the control model agency. The welfare/therapeutic officer would most likely be found in the social service model. The issue, then, is not what role the p/p officer will assume with respect to clients, but, rather, is the role compatible with the agency model? In the combined model, some use can be made of p/p officer variation (I prefer the term "style"). Supervisors can assign cases on the basis of matching the p/p officer's style with certain salient characteristics of the offender (a "primitive" classification scheme). For example, an officer with a more authoritarian style will be matched with "heavy" criminals (i.e., professionals). An officer with a "gentler" style would be appropriate for certain "situational" offenders or youthful clients.

P/p officers should integrate their control or community protection role with their service role, while maintaining the flexibility to stress one over the other in an individualized response to each case. For example, a young offender under supervision for "joyriding" in a stolen car will receive a different response than an experienced offender who is associated with organized crime. In p/p treatment officers adapt those methods that are useful to their practice, while sacrificing the rest, sometimes cynically, on the altar of reality.

During the initial interview officers explain the p/p rules, answering questions while attempting to set realistic standards for clients. (For many years I struggled with a parole regulation that prohibited single parolees from engaging in sexual relations.) Several items are usually emphasized:

1. The need to make in-person, telephone, or mail reports.
2. The need to keep the p/p officer informed of his/her residence.
3. The need to seek and maintain lawful employment.
4. The need to report any contacts with law enforcement officers.

When there is a special problem, the officer may set special conditions. An offender with a history of child molestations may be required to keep out of areas where children normally congregate, such as playgrounds. An offender with a history of alcoholism may be directed to refrain from using any intoxicating beverages. A young offender may be required to keep a curfew. Offenders with substance abuse (drugs and alcohol) problems may be required to attend treatment programs, such as Alcoholics Anonymous.

The p/p officer explains that he/she will be visiting the offender's residence periodically. Officers offer clients assistance with employment or other problems. Some clients may need financial assistance. One of the immediate problems encountered by a newly released parolee is a financial one. The amount of money that an inmate receives upon release, "gate money," is usually inadequate for even immediate housing and food needs.* A parolee may have some funds as a result of prison work, but wages are well below that received by free labor. The p/p officer may refer the client to the department of welfare or to private agencies such as the Salvation Army or a halfway house.

The initial interview in p/p practice is considered a crucial time in the supervision process. The New York State parole officer is provided with the following guidelines relative to the initial interview.

INITIAL INTERVIEW

As the name implies, this is the first major interview between the parole officer responsible for the supervision of the case and the newly released parolee. If the arrival report is taken by the parole officer who will supervise the case, it may be combined with the initial interview. It is at this time that the parole officer initiates a counseling or casework relationship with the parolee.

Since the parole officer is endeavoring to establish this relationship with individuals whose knowledge of and acceptance of parole varies to a great degree, the interview must be planned and handled with the best casework skills. There are those whose attitudes toward parole are based upon prejudices, doubt, and fears brought about by rumors. With this group, only patience and skill will overcome the hostility and resistance to a working relationship.

This is the interview upon which the planning for future supervision of the parolee will be based. Therefore, it is important that the parole officer prepare for it by studying all the pertinent information contained in the case folder. It is also important that this interview be well planned, unhurried, and without interference, if possible. It is the key to the future of the case.

The parole officer undertakes the initial interview with four major objectives in mind:

---

*Richard Berk and his colleagues (1980: 766–86) found that support payments to just-released prisoners in Georgia and Texas reduced recidivism.

1. Establish a casework relationship with the parolee.
2. Secure the parolee's participation in an analysis of his/her problems.
3. Make constructive suggestions that will give the parolee "something to do" toward beginning the overall parole program.
4. Leave the parolee with some positive assurance of what there is to look forward to as the parole period progresses.

Suggested Content of Initial Interview

Realizing that the content of the interview will vary with the needs and problems of the individual case, the following items are presented for the parole officer's general guidance:

1. *Description of the parolee.* This should include a brief physical description of the parolee, pointing out any special defects such as tics, acne, blindness, lameness, noticeable scars or other physical disability, his/her reaction to these physical conditions or defects if they are apparent to the parole officer, a brief description of his dress and habit of dress, and any unusual personal attitude or habits that are obvious to the parole officer.

2. *The parolee's attitude toward the parole officer and the interview.* Information with regard to the parolee's attitude should include, in addition to a description of attitudes, the parole officer's interpretation of the attitudes and a basis for such interpretation.

3. *Analysis of problems and initiating casework processes.* In conducting an initial interview, the parole officer is expected to secure the parolee's participation in a discussion of his/her problems. This discussion should be based upon information contained in the classification or parole investigation and in the service unit chronological recording.

Since this information is contained in these various reports, it is not necessary to repeat it in the case history. It is sufficient to point up briefly problems that are discussed, the parolee's reaction to them, what suggestions are made by the parole officer toward their immediate or eventual solution.

There should be a discussion of the parole program; both the residence and employment should be gone over carefully for the purpose of answering any questions that the parolee may have regarding the program.

During the initial interview, the parole officer directs the parolee to report promptly to his/her prospective employer. The parole officer should verify the parolee's actual employment as soon as possible.

Before concluding the interview, it is imperative that the parole officer determine whether there are questions, reservations, misconceptions concerning the parolee's relationship to the Division of Parole and the conditions of parole and to assure the parolee that all parole personnel are ready and willing to assist with any problems that may arise.

4. *Reporting instructions.* Before concluding the initial interview, the parolee should be clearly told why office reports are necessary and helpful.

He/she should also be clearly told when, where, and with what frequency he/she is to report to the parole officer. If the parolee is to report to the parole officer at a different location, the address of the location should be clearly given. It might be well to give the parolee one of the parole officer's business cards, on the back of which the parole officer might write the address of the reporting station.

The parolee is to be clearly informed that permission must be obtained in advance if, for good and sufficient reason, he/she will be unable to make a scheduled report.

ONGOING SUPERVISION

The offender is usually somewhat relieved to be out of the office after the first visit. He/she generally leaves with mixed feelings. If the officer has been warm, concerned, and helpful, positive feelings will predominate. If the officer was not sensitive to the attitude conveyed and if he/she did not evince a feeling of acceptance, negative feelings will predominate. Mangrum notes that "there is nothing necessarily incompatible between warmth and acceptance and firm enforcement of the laws of the land. We must take whatever corrective measures are necessary; but these must not permit us to demean the dignity of the individual" (1972: 48).

During the periodic visits to the client's residence, the p/p officer should try to spend enough time to be able to relate to the client and/or the client's family. The home visit provides an opportunity to meet family members and interpret the role of the p/p agency to them. The worker should leave a business card and invite inquiries for information or help. When visiting the home, it is incumbent upon the officer to try to protect the confidentiality that is inherent in each case. The officer does not advertise his/her business or draw unnecessary attention to the visit to a client's home. In many cases the client's p/p status will be known to neighbors, and the officer may be a familiar figure in the neighborhood. It is not too unusual for a client, or client's family, to escort the officer back to his/her automobile, as a gesture of concern, in high-delinquency areas.

The following excerpt from a case record shows how increased understanding of an offender caused a change in the direction of treatment. It also reveals the value of home visiting as a means of gaining new insights into an offender's situation.

QUARTERLY SUMMARY, MARCH–MAY 1975

3/9   Office report.
3/23   Failed to report.
3/30   Home visit. Mother and aunt seen.
4/6   Failed to report. Notice sent, giving 48 hours to report.

4/8   Reported.
4/13   Failed to report.
4/20   Home visit. Offender and aunt seen.
4/27   Reported.
5/1   Contact made with Community Settlement.
5/11   Reported.
5/25   Reported.

During March and April attempts were made to get the offender to look for work. Early in March, he reported that he had a temporary job as a truck driver, and thought that because of this he did not have to report. I corrected this idea and emphasized the importance of keeping his appointments. He had little to say but seemed amenable to conforming. The failure to report in April was excused because of illness.

During the home visits, the mother reported that the offender is keeping reasonable hours. She informed me that he spends most of his spare time at the Community Settlement and recently won a trophy for basketball. The aunt, a single woman who lives in the home, takes an active interest in him. She said that the offender is really very shy and needs special attention, which she tries to give him because the mother has little time to spare from the younger children. She has accompanied him to State Employment Office, where he has been trying to obtain work, but as he is unskilled, he has few opportunities. Such protectiveness seems inappropriate for a 19-year-old youth.

I called at the Community Settlement and talked with the Director, Mr. Apt. He is very much interested in the offender, but told me confidentially that he is afraid he might be getting into a neighborhood gang that is beginning to form. He has noticed that when the offender leaves the settlement, he often joins other young men, some of whom have been in trouble. The settlement has an employment service for members and will try to help the offender obtain employment. When the offender reported, I suggested that he apply at the settlement employment service. The next day, Mr. Apt telephoned. The offender had been referred to a job in a downtown warehouse. He returned to the settlement in tears. He was so frightened that he had been unable to apply. He doesn't think he could do such work, although it is simple unskilled labor. Mr. Apt thinks that the offender needs psychiatric attention, but this may be the first time the offender has tried to seek work by himself.

At the time of the last report, the offender discussed some of his fears about work. He speaks warmly of the personnel at the settlement, but somewhat resentfully of his mother and aunt, who "keep nagging" him about work.

It is planned to try to encourage this offender by building up his self-esteem, giving recognition to his success in settlement activities, and by planning visits when he is at home, dealing with him directly rather than with relatives. The possibility of psychiatric referral will be explored.

The following description of an interview with an offender in jail indicates how the probation officer approached a hostile and uncooperative offender. It is important to note that the officer guides the interview to avoid futile and repetitious rationalizations but explores to find some area in which he and the offender can work constructively together.

Peter, aged eighteen, has been on probation for two months. He was accorded youthful offender treatment following indictment for an assault during which he threatened to, but did not, use a knife. During the course of our contact, he has been on a weekly reporting schedule. I have concentrated on trying to help him get work. He has conformed in rather surly fashion, and never has volunteered to discuss any of his problems. He lives at home with his mother, a divorcee, and an older brother, who is a conforming person who did well in school, has regular employment, and generally does everything he should, thereby winning the mother's approval.

Recently, Peter was arrested for drunk and disorderly conduct. He pleaded guilty and received a 30-day jail sentence, which he is just beginning to serve. The arresting officer's report indicated that he was assaultive and that it required three policemen to get him to the station. I visited him at the jail to obtain information for a violation report to be submitted to the court for action regarding his probation status. When I explained this, Peter went into what threatened to be a long harangue against the police and everyone connected with the current offense. He was in jail, he said, only because his girlfriend's father objected to him and was trying to keep him from dating her. I stated briefly and flatly what I knew about his present situation and noted that his own conduct was the reason for his being here. I asked him to tell me something about his girl, but he cut this off by saying that she and her family had moved to get the girl away from him, and he would not be seeing her any more. I asked what he had been assigned to do in jail. He was just washing dishes and it was a bore and everyone here was a jerk. Had his family visited him? His mother had, but not his brother. I wondered how he got along with his brother. As if I had turned on a faucet, the story of his resentment toward his brother gushed out. He recalled things that had happened when he was only about six years old, and revealed that he is conscious of his jealousy over the mother's favoritism.

THE PROBATION/PAROLE OFFICER
AS TREATMENT AGENT

In Chapter 14 a variety of treatment approaches were reviewed—the implications being that the p/p officer could operationalize these approaches with his/her clients. However, requirements for p/p officer positions are usually a bachelor's degree, hardly adequate to provide the background, no less the skill, for carrying out a "treatment" role. While "graduate work in the social or behavioral sciences is encouraged," the Commission on Accreditation for Corrections* sets entry-level requirements for p/p officers at the baccalaureate level (1977: 10). Shelle Dietrich points out "that the probation officer usually has not received extensive specialized training for the function of change agent; that is, the function of being competent to facilitate another person's changing his behavior, attitude, affect, or personality style" (1979: 15). Generally, the p/p officer is not educated or trained to be a "treatment" agent: "It is an unrealistic expectation of probation officers to expect themselves to be competent in an area for which they have not received adequate training" (p. 15).

In a review of the literature purporting to advise p/p officers whose background is otherwise "deficient" how to become effective change agents, Dietrich found it simplistic and at times potentially harmful to the client (pp. 16–19). Thus, she argues, professional intrusion is often advocated into areas where the p/p officer lacks training. Cynically, she proposes (p. 17): "Why not go ahead and prescribe medications, prepare legal documents, or write an insurance plan for the probationer?" Dietrich cautions (p. 18): "And what about the probationer. Certainly his position in relation to the probation officer is a vulnerable one. Shouldn't the probationer be protected from being the involuntary patient of an unlicensed and untrained person, even if the person's intentions are the most purely humanistic?"

Two other issues are also relevant: (1) Is the therapeutic enterprise possible in a p/p setting? And (2) given a positive response to this question, is it realistic to expect the delivery of "treatment" in p/p, where caseloads usually average between 80 and 100? Dietrich argues that even if the p/p officer "were optimally skillful in such therapeutic endeavors," without the full promise of confidentiality (impossible in a p/p setting), full and open discussion, the basis for a therapeutic relationship, is not possible (p. 18). Dietrich, however, is using a rather narrow definition of "therapy," and within that definition she is correct—therapy is not possible in a p/p setting. I believe that therapy is the purposeful use of self to improve the social and psychological functioning of a client, and thus therapy is possible within the confidentiality limitations of a p/p agency. Therapy, however, is *not* possible given the lack of adequate education and training and the usual excessive caseloads encountered in p/p practice.

THE PROBATION/PAROLE OFFICER AS BROKER OR ADVOCATE

Carlson and Parks see the "brokerage" approach in p/p as almost diametrically opposed to the "treatment" approach since the p/p officer "is not concerned primarily with understanding or changing the behavior of the probationer, but rather with

*Sponsored by the American Correctional Association and funded by the Law Enforcement Assistance Administration.

assessing the concrete needs of the individual and arranging for the probationer to receive services which directly address these needs'' (1979: 120). They point out (pp. 120–21):

there is significantly less emphasis placed on the development of a close, one-to-one relationship between the probation officer and the probationer. The probation officer functions primarily as a manager or broker of resources and social services which are already available from other agencies. It is the task of the probation officer to assess the service needs of the probationer, locate the social service agency which addresses those needs as its primary function, to refer the probationer to the appropriate agency, and to follow up referrals to make sure that the probationer actually received the services. Under the brokerage approach, it can be said that the probationer officer's relationship with community service agencies is more important than his relationship with an individual probationer. The brokerage approach does share with the casework approach the importance of the probationer's participation in developing his own probation plan.

However (p. 123):

the essential tasks of the brokerage orientation to probation are the management of available community resources and the use of those services to meet the needs of probation clients. There is little emphasis on the quality of the relationship which is developed between the probation officer and the probationer; rather, more emphasis is placed upon the close working relationship between the probation officer and the staff members of community social service agencies. Counseling and guidance are considered inappropriate activities for the probation officer; no attempt is made to change the behavior of the probationer. The primary function of the probation officer is to assess the concrete needs of each probation and make appropriate referrals to existing community services. Should the needed service not be available in the community, it is the responsibility of the probation officer to encourage the development of that service.

Carlson and Parks point out that the brokerage approach is amenable to *team supervision* (p. 124) or the *Community Resources Management Team* (CRMT). The CRMT evolved out of an "integration model" as opposed to the more traditional "treatment model" (p. 161), and Frank Dell'Apa and his colleagues provide the basic assumptions of the CRMT approach (1976: 38):

1. Probation and parole services are in need of improved delivery system models.
2. Most offenders are not pathologically ill; therefore, the medical (casework) model is inappropriate.
3. Most probation and parole officers are not equipped by education and experience to provide professional casework counseling even if it is needed.
4. Existing probation/parole manpower is not likely to be expanded. Consequently, these people must come to view their roles in different and perhaps radically new terms if they are to deal with the increasing numbers of offenders under supervision.
5. Services needed by the offender to "make it" in society are available in the community social service network rather than in the criminal justice system.

6. Probation and parole staff must assume advocacy roles in negotiating appropriate community-based services for offenders. They must assume a community organization and resource development role for needed services that do not exist.

7. A team approach represents a powerful and viable alternative to the autonomous and isolated individual officer and "case" relationship.

They argue that the traditional p/p caseworker role attempts to be "all things" to everyone on the caseload, a "jack-of-all-trades," and turns out to be "master-of-none," so that the client suffers. They provide a look at the different CRMT models that have been operationalized (pp. 42–43):

Model A: The basic agency team. A team is composed of a middle manager, no fewer than two line (field) staff, a clerical staff person, and a staff specialist.

> *Function:* The combined caseload of these field staff is assigned to this team. The team has responsibility to serve all needs of the caseload. Decisions are made at team meetings and the middle manager leads the team. Tasks are determined through team consensus. The team has responsibility for a specific geographic area.
>
> *Note:* The agency can assemble as many of these teams as it desires, depending upon the manpower. The teams are components of the parent agency.

Model B: The agency—community extended team. A team is composed of a middle manager, no fewer than two line (field) staff, a trainee, one or more ex-offenders, a clerical staff person, with support from interested community social service agents from legal aid, welfare, employment security, mental health, minority group organizations, health, and education agencies. In addition, community persons such as successful ex-offenders and citizens' group leaders serve as resources to the team.

> *Function:* The caseload is composed of a fixed number of clients, usually a cross section of the target population, who have distinct needs for supervision and assistance. They may come largely from one geographical area, be designated as drug- and alcohol-related offenders, represent distinct minority groups, and fall within definite age groupings.
>
> The team is analyzed to determine the skills of each member, and the workload is the determinant of who does what. The parent agency staff serve as brokers of the services and coordinators among the attached support specialists. The team meets regularly to assess community resources and needs, as well as workload needs upon which the division of labor is based. The clients may be served by all members of the team or only one or any combination.
>
> *Note:* This team model is dependent on actual cooperation between parent staff and those from support community agencies.

Model C: The specialist resource team. A team is composed of two or more line (field) staff who are supervised by a middle manager. Support community staff may be used where possible.

> *Function:* The team has a specialized caseload; all of those clients who are distinguishable by one central concern, perhaps drug addiction, violence-prone behavior, chronic unemployment, or serious family crises. The team works only with these persons. The team also marshals all resources within the community that provide services to such clients.
>
> *Note:* This team maintains autonomy but relies on good community relations.

Model D: The total department as a community resource management team. The team may encompass the entire field agency. A task analysis is made of the agency workload. Specific assignments are made to individual staff members depending upon their capabilities. Attached community agency staff are recruited to serve as support personnel to the entire parent agency rather than to a specific team within the agency.

> *Function:* The agency sets the team into operation after a careful task analysis based on the workload needs of the agency. Some staff will function as court and liaison specialists, others will prepare presentence or preparole reports, and others will supervise those who require supervision by court order or in the judgment of the agency. In some instances, a single staff person may have the assignment for a specific need area such as employment, legal aid services, health, or education. A team will have no caseload but will serve as community resources identifiers and develop advocacy plans to link these resources to all clients.
>
> *Note:* This complex organizational model requires careful task analysis and staff skills assessment as well as effective collaboration with significant community agencies. It is a total organizational approach. Its success will depend upon continuous revision of the structure and deployment of staff resources.

Dell'Apa reports that the CRMT concept has met with stiff resistance: "This thing is so radical, so different from anything that probation and parole officers have been doing that it's threatening as hell." However, "the agencies using it will never go back to the old way" (Wilson, 1978: 49). Rob Wilson notes that evaluations of CRMT units have shown a marked increase in revocations. He views this as positive, an indication that CRMT clients are being made more accountable with the CRMT approach (p. 53). An alternative explanation is more troubling: offenders having difficulty relating to/or dealing with a concept as amorphous as a team. "*Who* is *my* p.o.?" no longer has an answer. The obverse is that the officer on a team is more detached from his/her clients—hence, invoking delinquency action is less personal, "easier." An equally formidable problem is the relationship between important persons in the client's life (e.g., spouse, parents) and their ability to relate to/or deal with a team.

Let us look at one type of situation which, despite a myriad of variations, is typical in p/p practice. Charlie Smith's wife calls the p/p office: "That s.o.b. husband of mine has been out all night drinking, and he slapped me around this morning. Unless the p.o. comes here and straightens him out, I'm calling the police and having his ass locked up." The men and women I worked with who had Charlie Smith on their caseload could respond quickly and effectively. Instead of four uniformed officers and a broken billy club—a lot of "Charlies" are resentful of police authority—the p.o. goes out to the house. Charlie breaks down and cries, explaining the reason for his behavior. In many cases that I have experienced, the p.o. is the only variable capable of maintaining Charlie in the community. I am not sure what the team response would be. Perhaps it is simply a revocation decision; this doesn't help Charlie or his wife.

The team, structured, with a rational division of labor and responsibility, can provide services more efficiently and economically than can the traditional casework approach. However, there is a price to be paid for this efficiency.

The provision of necessary services in p/p practice often requires an advocacy stance on the part of the p/p officer. Private and public agencies may view the p/p client as "undesirable" or even "undeserving." Welfare, mental health, and educational agencies may see the p/p client as threatening. This reaction can cause the client to become frustrated and to react in a manner that does indeed appear threatening—a self-fulfilling prophecy. (This can also be used by the p/p officer as a vehicle for securing vital services. My partner received a telephone call from a welfare worker who was quite annoyed that a just-released parolee was asking for assistance at 4 p.m. My partner replied: "Gee, I'm sorry he came in so late, but he was just released and needed help. If I were you, I would give him help—*do you know why he was sent away to prison?*" Without further ado, the parolee received assistance.)

THE PROBATION/PAROLE OFFICER
AS LAW ENFORCEMENT AGENT*

The p/p officer as law enforcement agent is related to the *control model* of supervision much the same way as the *treatment* or *broker–advocate* role is related to the *social service model*. For a discussion of the law enforcement role of p/p officers to be meaningful, it must be considered within the context of agency model. However, many critics of a law enforcement role for p/p officers render unequivocal statements without any discussion of model: the New York State Special Commission on Attica states: "The parole officer's supervision and surveillance functions prevent the development of any beneficial relationship with parolees" (1972: 100); the Citizen's Inquiry on Parole and Criminal Justice states that the conflict between the surveillance and treatment roles of the parole officer "precludes the development of a relationship of mutual trust" (1973: 13); Charles Newman states that surveillance is essentially a police activity that should not be handled by p/p officers (1961: 14); and John P. Conrad maintains that surveillance and investigation are not the proper roles for p/p officers but for police officers, who he contends are better trained and

---

*Under general tort law an individual who has a special relationship of custody or control with respect to another person owes a duty of care to any third person(s) or the public, who may be endangered by a lack of such care. Probation officers, as agents of the court, and parole officers, as agents of the executive, have considerable control in supervising and implementing the conditions of probationers/parolees in their charge—sufficient to place them in such a relationship with their clients. Generally, it is recognized that the duties of p/p officers in this special relationship extend to protecting the public from the criminal or antisocial behavior of persons being supervised (based on Kutcher, 1977: 35–36). John R. Ackermann points out that the duty to protect the public is a vital part of p/p agency accountability. As President of the American Probation and Parole Association, Ackermann has stressed the need for a strong law enforcement role on the part of p/p officers (personal correspondence).

equipped to handle (1975). A more productive approach is to identify the agency model and then decide if it is compatible with a law enforcement role.

An issue related to the law enforcement role of p/p officers is agency policy with respect to arrests and firearms. Thus, without any attention to agency model, the Commission on Accreditation for Corrections, in its Standard 3071, recommends against p/p officers routinely carrying firearms in the performance of their duties (1977: 14). In 1975, I surveyed 53 adult parole agencies in the United States (the 50 states, the District of Columbia, Puerto Rico, and the U.S. Division of Probation, which supervises parolees). The survey indicated that parole agencies differ greatly with respect to officers* carrying firearms and arresting violators. For example, Texas parole officers are prohibited from carrying firearms and never personally arrest parole violators, whereas Massachusetts parole officers are required to carry firearms and frequently arrest parole violators. The survey revealed that:

1. Sixteen provide firearms training for parole officers.
2. Six permit parole officers to carry firearms in special situations, such as when arresting or transporting dangerous offenders, or when the officer's life has been threatened.
3. Eight encourage or mandate their parole officers to carry firearms.
4. Only four report that parole officers never personally arrest parole violators. The others report that their officers frequently (14), occasionally (16), or infrequently (19) personally arrest parole violators.

Several years later, Paul Keve conducted a similar survey of top administrators in probation and parole in the United States and found that about 56 percent of the jurisdictions prohibited the carrying of firearms (1979: 432). Keve pointed out that within some p/p agencies, the agency model has not been reconciled with agency practice (p. 434):

The survey strongly suggests that where an agency and most of its agents see themselves in a helping, casework role, there is no internal stress and strain caused by not carrying weapons. Or where agency administrators and staff see themselves as law enforcement people and at the same time freely carry weapons, there is again no strain and stress.

But agencies clearly do suffer sharp internal morale problems when agency policy seems to require surveillance and arrest activities while at the same time the agency prohibits use of firearms.

The Sacramento (California) County Probation Department provides an example of this inconsistency. Their annual report stresses the law enforcement role of the probation officer:

---

*Title varies with the agency. Several states use "probation/parole agent"; Illinois uses "parole counselor"; Arizona uses "correctional program officer"; the federal government uses "probation officer."

Duties

An officer in field supervision is faced with a multitude of demands for varying kinds of services in every case. Energies are generally channeled by two basic principles:

1. To guard and protect public interest
2. To aid and encourage probationers to make some positive changes in their lives

Enforcement

In the first instance officers strive to achieve a maximum amount of control over the probationer's activities. Officers effect increased surveillance and contact with the probationer through scheduled and unscheduled visits at varying times and places. They require the offender's close adherence to specific conditions of probation, (i.e., timely payment of fines or restitution, drug testing, nonassociation with certain individuals, evidence of employment and earnings or efforts to secure employment, compliance with no drinking or no weapon conditions, and other conditions).

This policing aspect of the job requires a field officer to collaborate with other law enforcement jurisdictions, to coordinate and participate in arrests or search and seizure efforts, and to be prepared to identify not only the probationer and other household members but also the probationer's associates, the vehicle driven, the places frequented, habits, place of employment, and other pertinent details of life style. In addition, the officer must always be alert to evidence disclosing child abuse or neglect situations, possession of drugs, possession of weapons or stolen property, or the probationer's planning or participation in other criminal acts.

In 1979, field supervision officers participated in over 150 residence searches. Two-thirds of the searches were initiated by the field supervision officers, utilizing police back-up. The deputies' involvement in other searches was in response to requests for assistance from other law enforcement agencies, including the Sacramento County Police Department, Sacramento County Sheriff's Department, narcotics enforcement agencies, and the FBI.

In 1979, as a result of the search and seizure expeditions, drugs or paraphernalia were found in 60 cases, weapons in 27 cases, and stolen property in 15 cases. Recovered property included radios, television sets, stereo sets or components, tape decks, musical instruments, jewelry, cameras, guns, power tools, bicycles and parts, $3000 worth of State office equipment, and automobiles, including two new cars which at the time had not been missed.

Field supervision officers participated in arrests on searches in 45 cases, arrests on outstanding warrants in 35 cases, and arrests on conditional violations in 22 cases. Officers also conducted over 6,200 drug tests in 1979.

> From information developed through tips, review of crime reports, mug shots, composite drawings, remote camera shots, and knowledge of wanted fugitives, officers were able to identify and/or locate, and help capture in many instances, over 150 fugitives or crime suspects. This included 3 murder suspects, 5 rape suspects, 9 robbery suspects, 2 kidnap suspects, 4 child molesters, 2 arsonists, 20 burglary suspects, and a counterfeiter—to mention a few.

Probation officers in California are "peace officers" and thus statutorily entitled to carry firearms. Under California law (Penal Code Section 832) they are required to complete law enforcement training. However, Robert E. Keldgord, the Chief Probation Officer in Sacramento, points out (personal correspondence):

> As a matter of practice, however, officers in this Department, as well as in virtually all California probation departments, may carry firearms only when specifically authorized by the Chief Probation Officer or the Assistant Chief Probation Officer. Such permission is normally granted only in response to a direct life-threatening situation. Our officers do enforce and serve warrants frequently in conjunction with a police officer.

I experienced this morale problem referred to by Keve (1979) in two agencies, one in New York, the other in California. In New York, the Narcotic Addiction Control Commission (NACC) was established under mental hygiene statutes to incarcerate (for "treatment") persons certified as narcotic addicts. The narcotic parole officers were issued handcuffs and authorized to arrest and detain addicts under their aftercare supervision; they were not, however, permitted to carry firearms. In the center where I worked, an addict whose urinalysis indicated narcotic use refused to submit to arrest. He also turned out to be the only person in the center with a firearm, the proverbial "one-eyed man in the land of the blind." The outcome was a severely wounded worker, the easy escape of the addict, and a community with an armed and dangerous person at large.

Several years ago I was called upon by the parole agents association in California to provide "expert" testimony in support of their legal action designed to force the agency into permitting agents to carry firearms while on duty. The agency issued handcuffs and expected law enforcement activities but prohibited the routine carrying of firearms. As a result, agents either ignored their law enforcement responsibilities or carried firearms in violation of agency policy (reputedly with the informal knowledge of agency administrators). I found similar situations in other states where p/p officers became sworn deputies or constables, thus providing them with a legal basis for ignoring agency firearms policy. On the other hand, several years ago, Canadian parole officers expressed concern over being placed in the corrections department since this would apparently make them law enforcement officers and require the carrying of firearms. The Canadian parole officers I spoke with saw their agency as based on a *social service model,* and viewed law enforcement and firearms as incompatible with their role.

As a private citizen with a working knowledge of probation and parole, I have certain concerns with personal safety—that of my family, friends, and neighbors. It is from this (I believe typical layperson's) perspective that I evaluate a p/p agency. Let me provide some typifications. It is not unusual during the course of an office or home visit for the p/p officer to discover that an offender is using heroin. If the offender is unemployed, the narcotic habit is probably financed by criminal activities—the offender is a clear and present danger to himself/herself and to the community. A p/p agency whose officers cannot expeditiously arrest such an individual is not providing an adequate level of safety. P/p agencies also supervise offenders who have been involved in (1) sex offenses against children, (2) vehicular homicide as a result of intoxication, (3) burglary, and (4) armed robbery. A p/p agency whose officers have no responsibility to enforce prohibitions, through investigation and arrest, against (1) frequenting play areas, (2) drinking and driving, (3) carrying tools for forced entry, and (4) to investigate money or a life-style that cannot be supported by the offender's employment is not providing the minimum acceptable level of community safety.

Some widely cited critics of parole supervision (e.g., Andrew von Hirsch, David Fogel) show little interest in the safety of the community. Von Hirsch (with Hanrahan, 1978), for example, expresses concern only with providing parolees with procedural rights in excess of those voted by the legislature or ordered by the court. He decries lower standards of proof needed to revoke parole, as opposed to those required for conviction in a criminal court (p. 17). He concludes that postrelease programs should disavow community protection and adopt a voluntary social service model (p. 26): "The criterion of success would not be recidivism control, but the programs' ability to alleviate suffering and disorientation among ex-inmates. Programs for ex-prisoners would thus be judged as social service." They would be voluntary, and an offender who did not wish to accept the services would incur no penalty (p. 27).

The adult p/p client is a law violator who has proved to be a potential danger to the community. Many have been involved in crimes of violence, and the public and its lawmakers expect that probationers and parolees will be under the scrutiny of p/p authorities. This is why the law of most jurisdictions empowers p/p agencies with law enforcement responsibilities. However, the question is often raised as to whether the p/p officer should be the law enforcer or merely the treatment agent. Many p/p agencies employ warrant officers or use other law enforcement agencies to enforce their violation warrants. Do arrest powers and the carrying of a firearm interfere with the p/p officer's ability to form a relationship with which to provide treatment? I am of the opinion that they do not. Indeed, because of the p/p officers' relationships with their clients, in delinquency situations, they are able to effect an arrest without the tension and hostility that often accompanies arrests made by other law enforcement officers. However, whether or not the p/p officer actually makes the arrest, the client knows that the p/p officer initiated the warrant action. As noted, p/p clients are potentially dangerous, reason enough to be armed.*

On the basis of my experience, I recommend that all p/p agencies review their approach to law enforcement and reevaluate their methods with a view toward effective casework and community protection. Items that should be reviewed include:

1. Police lack of interest in enforcing warrants.
2. The attitude of probation/parole officers toward the carrying of firearms and making arrests.
3. Incidents and/or complaints arising out of enforcement of warrants by non-probation/parole officers.
4. Probation/parole officers being threatened or assaulted.
5. The inability of an agency to expeditiously arrest and detain serious probation/parole violators.
6. Probation/parole officers reluctant to make field visits.
7. Indications that probation/parole warrants are being used to extort money or force violators into becoming informants.

RECORD CONFIDENTIALITY IN PROBATION/PAROLE†

(The information contained in this section is for the purpose of exposing the reader to the complexity of issues in this area. It is not meant to serve as a legal guide to receiving or disclosing confidential information.)

There is a bewildering array of laws and regulations covering confidentiality of personal information. This refers to information that the p/p officer needs to acquire for his/her records (e.g., presentence report), or requests for the disclosure of client information from other agencies within and outside of the criminal justice system. There are seven items that most concern the p/p officer:

1. *Criminal History Records.* There are four categories:
(a) Information from the Federal Bureau of Investigation (FBI) "rap sheet" or out-of-state entries on a local or state "rap sheet," whose source is the FBI.
(b) Non-FBI entries on arrests within the state that *resulted in convictions.*

---

*This facet of parole work was dramatically revealed while I was a parole officer in New York. My colleague, 32 year old Donald Sutherland, attempted to arrest a parole violator and was shot to death. The parolee was arrested at the scene by other parole officers. After being convicted of murder the parolee escaped from prison and eluded law officers for several weeks, on one occasion after an exchange of gunfire. He was finally killed after refusing to surrender to a combined force of city and state police and parole officers.

†Source: James F. Jones, *Records Confidentiality for Adult Probation Officers—A Guideline.* Austin: Texas Adult Probation Commission, 1980.

(c) Non-conviction information; entries concerning arrests that did *not* result in a conviction (including arrests for which no disposition is indicated).

(d) Information on an arrest for which the subject is still within the criminal justice system even though s/he may not have been convicted.

In the first case (a) you can acquire FBI-furnished criminal history information. You can disclose this information to another criminal justice agency (but to no one else). In the second case (b) federal regulations place no restrictions on disclosure of non-FBI conviction information. State and local regulations may restrict disclosure. In the third case (c) non-conviction information is restricted by federal regulation. In general, non-conviction information can be disclosed to other criminal justice agencies and agencies directly involved in research, client services and rehabilitation (but not to potential employers, etc.). In case four (d) there are no restrictions on disclosure of information on the offense for which a client is under your supervision.

In some cases state law authorizes the setting aside of a guilty adjudication upon the successful completing of a term of probation. The offense may thus become a non-conviction. Under certain circumstances a person's arrest can be expunged from the record and the p/p officer will need to know (and abide by) state regulation in these cases. In New York, for example, a 1976 law makes confidential most of the records and papers concerning the arrest and prosecution of persons ultimately acquitted. The law requires that courts, with some exceptions, order the sealing of all records of arrest and prosecutions and order the return of all fingerprints and other identifying data when a criminal action has been terminated in favor of the accused. However, the Criminal Procedure Law (160.50) also provides access to the sealed records for p/p officers.

2. *Drug and Alcohol Abuse Treatment Information.* This type of information is considered highly confidential (restricted). The courts may authorize disclosure only when "good cause" is shown in a hearing in which all parties are represented. Such an order, if issued, would remove a prohibition to disclosure, but would *not compel disclosure.* Compulsion would require a subpoena and have to be justified under law. Federal regulations do not prevent communication between a drug or alcohol treatment program and a probation/parole agency.

3. *Mental Health Consultation and Treatment Records.* As with number 2 above, this information is highly confidential. It may also be under the control of physicians who may not be willing or obligated to release this type of information to anyone other than another physician. Client consent forms are advisable, if not required, although client consent does not compel disclosure.

(Probation/parole officers who permit police officers access to their records are cautioned against allowing police officers (or other law enforcement agents) to view the type of information referred to in items 2 and 3.)

4. *Medical Records* (not including mental health, alcoholism, drug abuse, or mental retardation). In general medical records can be disclosed with a consent form from the patient. However, a physician or medical facility is not required to disclose such information. P/p officers should secure client consent before disclosing medical information to prospective employers, treatment agencies, etc.

5. *Educational Records*. Federal law prohibits disclosure by the school of other than "directory information" (the type that normally appears in annuals, school directories, athletic event programs, etc.) without parent permission for those under eighteen or client's permission if over eighteen. Re-disclosure by the p/p officer requires specific consent from the client.

6. *Employment History*. There are no overall regulations governing this information. Consent forms are advisable.

7. *Military Records*. Although there is no statutory obligation to do so, the federal government usually honors a request by a p/p officer for an individual's military record with a signed consent. For information on the release of disciplinary information, the latest Uniform Code of Military Justice should be consulted.

Getting Sued

The remedy for an "inappropriate" release of confidential information is the lawsuit. Such lawsuits may be litigated by the federal government if a violation of federal law is involved. P/p officers, as public employees, enjoy "conditional immunity" (as opposed to "absolute immunity"). This covers the performance of "ministerial" and "discretionary" duties. *Ministerial duties* are those required by law to be performed in a manner devoid of judgment or discretion. The failure to perform what is required, or a negligent performance, which results in damage, leaves the officer without immunity.

Discretionary duties require the exercise of discretion and judgment in their performance. A p/p officer carrying out a discretionary duty enjoys conditional immunity from a lawsuit if s/he is acting:

(a) within the scope of his/her duties;
(b) in "good faith"; and
(c) without discrimination.

A p/p officer collecting information during a presentence investigation, obtaining information pursuant to the supervision of probationers or parolees, and enforcing the conditions of supervision is clearly within the *scope of his/her duties*. The handling of personal information about clients is an integral part of the officer's duties. *Good faith* requires honest intentions, under law, the absence of fraud, deceit, collusion or gross negligence. In sum, there should be no dishonesty or hidden motives in an exchange of information that could work to the detriment of the client or that could personally benefit the officer or any other person. In sensitive matters, it is not only important that the act be made in good faith, but there should be no likelihood that it appears to have been other than good faith involved.

(Gross negligence is difficult to define legally. It involves a *knowing* disregard for consequences. If one fails to recognize the consequences of an act, and damages occur, you may be found negligent. But, if you recognize the consequences and commit the act in spite of the known consequences you may be found *grossly* negligent.)

Without discrimination requires that the officer in acquiring or disclosing information not take into account the client's race, religion, national origin, etc.

A final consideration that is sometimes a condition to immunity is the use of *good judgment*. James Jones provides an example (1980: VI.6):

> Take the case of a client and employee. Say the piece of information was he had been caught with his hand in the till in the three previous jobs, and his present employment is working a cash register.
>
> You have two choices: to give the employer the information, or to withhold it from him. If you give it to him, two things can happen: either the employer can keep him on, or discharge him. If he keeps him on, he has assumed the risk based on a knowledge of the client's past acts. If he discharges him, it is because he does not want to take the risk.
>
> If you withhold the information, two things can happen. Either the client will leave the employer's money alone, or he will steal some of it. If he steals some of it, either the loss will be detected or it will not. If the loss is detected, either the employer will recover the money or he will not.
>
> Now you are on the spot. You are responsible for rehabilitating the client—and the job is important to his rehabilitation—but you are also responsible for protecting the public from further crime. If the client is fired, he is damaged. If money is stolen from the employer and he does not recover it, he is damaged. What do you do?
>
> As far as vulnerability to lawsuit, what you've *already* done is very important. You have thought out the consequences, in a logical and orderly way. Along the way you will have consciously or unconsciously assigned some probabilities to the "either-or" choices. And when you finally come down to a decision—whatever it is—it will be after weighing these possibilities.

Jones continues (Ibid.: VI.7-8):

> That is what good judgment is, even if one of the "bad" outcomes happens. The big danger is *not* that it comes out badly despite your thinking the matter through; the danger occurs when you *disregard* possible outcomes, particularly when you consciously disregard them.
>
> So in summary, your best protection against successful lawsuit consists of:
> 1) following rules where rules exist;
> 2) where rules *don't* exist, making every decision based on acting within the scope

of your defined duties, acting in good faith, and acting without discrimination; and

3) using good judgment, by *thinking the problem* through.

This may sound very obvious, and you probably practice these principles every day. But in the unlikely event you should ever find yourself on the stand in your own defense, being able to say that you considered each of these matters—scope of duties, good faith, nondiscrimination—and being able to demonstrate that you used an *orderly decision-making process*—will stand you in extremely good stead.

One other question—what about libel or slander?

Given the real world situation of a probation officer exchanging information about many clients, it would seem almost inevitable that sooner or later he would release or disclose an erroneous piece of client personal information. And that erroneous information could damage the client. Given the release/disclosure of wrong information coupled with damages, the probation officer is a sitting duck for a successful lawsuit, right?

(Ibid.: VI. 9):

Fortunately, this is *wrong*. At least if he has acted in good faith, in giving the information to someone with whom he shared a valid interest in the client without malice.

Let's take this a step at a time. First, comes good faith, which we have already discussed.

Second, he must have passed the information on to another person sharing a common interest in the matter. This could apply to a treatment program, a potential employer, or anyone else, involved in the probation supervision and rehabilitation process. If these two conditions are met, i.e., good faith and shared interest, the communication is privileged, which provides an absolute defense against libel or slander.

An exception occurs, however, if the subject of the statement can prove malice, the defense of privileged communication does not hold.

So again, if you have: 1) acted in good faith; 2) communicated only with those persons sharing a valid interest with you in the client; and 3) acted without malice, you have protected yourself well against a successful libel or slander suit—even if the communication turns out to be in error.

Client Consent (Ibid.: C.2)

In years past, much sensitive or potentially sensitive personal information was disclosed to insurance companies, employers, and others on the basis of "blanket consent," signed by the individual to whom the information pertained, authorizing disclosure of information by anyone for any purpose. Sometimes such a consent was incorporated in the small print of a contract, employment application, credit application, or similar document.

With the increasing concern for privacy, however, laws and regulations have become more stringent regarding the form and content of the consent, and the circumstances under which it is granted. In addition, concerned with possible civil liability, employers and others have become increasingly wary of disclosing personal information on the basis of a "blanket consent." And, in some recent major federal regulations dealing with privacy, disclosure of certain types of criminal history record information outside the criminal justice community is not allowed even *with* the subject's consent.

It is safe to assume that the trend will continue and the custodians of information will become even more reluctant to release personal information unless they are certain that 1) the client wants the specific information disclosed for a specific purpose, and 2) the information can legally be disclosed.

A COMPOSITE DAY IN THE LIFE OF A PAROLE/PROBATION OFFICER*

5:15 a.m.   The officer is awakened by a phone call. A deputy at the local Sheriff's Office advises him that they have one of his probationers in jail charged with Breaking and Entering with Intent to Commit a Felony. The officer writes down the pertinent information supplied by the deputy, which includes the report that the probationer is intoxicated. The officer then requests the deputy to place a parole/probation officer "hold" on the individual so that no bond can be made until the officer has thoroughly investigated the situation. He then closes his eyes in hopes of getting a little more sleep before his actual work day begins. He is on duty 24 hours a day, 7 days a week.

7:56 a.m.   Upon arriving in the parole/probation office, he finds two notes on his desk telling him that the individual the deputy called about had been arrested. Both of the officers who wrote the notes had a person on their caseload who had allegedly been a codefendant with this officer's case in the breaking and entering.

The officer then turns to the stack of paperwork, which includes both unfinished business from yesterday and mail received this morning. First, he sifts through the mail, pulling out the monthly reports submitted by "his" parolees and probationers. Each person under supervision is required to send in a written monthly report on a standardized form. The officer carefully reviews this report, making certain that the person still is residing at his approved address and is still employed. He also carefully checks the reported earnings and financial status, and looks to see if there are any special problems noted.

Most of the remaining correspondence and paperwork is related directly to his caseload and he dictates the appropriate

*From the Florida Parole and Probation Commission.

responses as well as recording important entries in his field book. The officer shares a secretary with two other officers. The secretary's time is limited and often the officer must file his own material.

9:15 a.m.   An integral part of every parole/probation officer's duty is that of reporting statistical information of the central office in Tallahassee. These statistics are detailed and time-consuming. Being constantly interrupted by telephone calls as well as persons coming to his office, the officer begins his statistical reports realizing it will be five days before they are due.

Without these statistical reports it would be practically impossible to monitor what progress or impact the Florida Parole and Probation Commission is having upon the parolees and probationers in Florida. The statistical data are time-consuming to compile but the work must be done!

9:31 a.m.   Florida Bureau of Law Enforcement calls to advise that a probationer is being investigated for drug trafficking.

9:48 a.m.   A parolee calls to say he has been fired because he came in late. An appointment is set for tomorrow. The officer makes a note to call the employer before the appointment.

10:05 a.m.   The wife of one of the officer's probationers calls. She reports that her husband, John, got drunk and beat her up last night. She wants the officer to do something about it but doesn't want her husband to know she called.

10:27 a.m.   The mother of a young man arrested that morning calls, informing the officer that her son did not come in all night and that she is concerned as to his whereabouts and welfare. The officer explains the circumstances surrounding her son's arrest and questions her as to why she feels he may have become involved in the armed robbery. He queries her regarding her son's drinking habits. The information is recorded in the field book and the parole/probation officer returns to filling out his statistical reports.

10:45 a.m.   The officer collects his necessary files and goes to the local felony court. He has recommended revocation of probation on a felony probationer. As the case is called, the officer stands before the court together with the probationer, the state attorney, the defendant's attorney, and members of his family.

The charges are read and a plea of not guilty entered. The parole/probation officer is then asked to explain the reasons for recommending revocation of probation. The officer points out that the probationer has failed to pay support payments to his wife as required by court, has failed to submit his monthly reports, and has absconded from supervision. The officer spent several hours compiling and filling out the appropriate revocation reports, affidavits, and warrants for this case.

After a plea by the defense attorney of *nolo contendere,* the judge agrees to allow the individual's probation to be reinstated with the understanding that he will bring his payments of support to his wife and child up to date within two weeks; that he will never again be late with his monthly report; and that he will not leave the county again without getting approval from his parole/probation officer.

11:34 a.m.   The officer leaves court and proceeds to the local elementary school, where he is checking the school records on a person who has been referred to the Parole and Probation Commission by the court for a presentence investigation. The officer is usually given between two to four weeks to complete this investigation. The presentence report includes the individual's prior arrest record and the circumstances as well as details of the offense for which the individual has been charged. School records and employment histories are checked. Community attitudes regarding the defendant and his reputation therein are ascertained and other information obtained which will provide the court with a comprehensive diagnostic report that will assist in determining the appropriate treatment methodology, whether it be probation or prison.

The presentence investigation is the most important investigation that the officer prepares, and they consume about 60 percent of his time.

Other investigations performed by the officer include post-sentence investigation, preparole, mandatory conditional release, pardon board, work release, security, and release on recognizance investigations, as well as other specialty-type investigations.

12:10 p.m.   The officer stops by John's place of employment. Being a roofer, he is out on a job site. The employer reports that John is very dependable and doubts that he has a drinking problem. The employer feels that John's wife is a troublemaker who he suspects has a boyfriend. The employer assures the officer that if he detects any problems he will call the officer.

12:33 p.m.   The officer meets with the assistant director of the local drug counseling center to have lunch at the cafeteria. The conversation mainly centers around more effective ways to refer probationers and parolees to the drug center and to receive information regarding their progress from the center.

1:31 p.m.   The officer goes to the county jail to talk with the probationer who was arrested in the early morning hours. He admits the offense and having been intoxicated. He also admits that it is not the first time he has become intoxicated and that he and his mother have not been getting along well at all over the last three months. The officer queries further and finally, in frustration, asks him one simple question, "Why did you do it?" He receives the classic answer, "I don't know, I just did it because the other guys were doing it." In the day-to-day life of parole/probation officers successes are subtle and often go unnoticed; failures are blatant and result in an individual wasting part of his life behind bars.

This individual will probably be convicted of the new offense and be sentenced to prison for five years. In addition, he may be found guilty of violation of probation and receive an additive sentence. The officer will have to go through the lengthy process of violation reports, warrants, affidavits, court hearings, and conversations with both the defense attorney and state attorney. That will take time—precious time that will detract from his rehabilitative efforts.

2:00 p.m.   The parole/probation officer attends a meeting of the local alcohol treatment center halfway house to provide input from the Florida Parole and Probation Commission on how to deal with alcoholics. He constantly seeks ways to increase his impact and expand his range of effectiveness.

Again the officer's main concern is that of more rapid referral with a minimum of red tape and more meaningful feedback with regard to the progress that an individual is making at the halfway house.

2:30 p.m.   The officer now begins to make contacts with people under his supervision. Some of these contacts are with the individual on his job site and include conversations with the employer to make certain that the individual is on the job, remains dependable on the job, and is doing well. The officer will also contact family members, especially in the home, and will talk to neighbors or other interested citizens with whom the officer associates. In most cases the officer is expected to make at least one contact in the home, with the individual, with the employer, and with other persons in the community each month.

These contacts are recorded in the officer's case field book. Naturally, those cases that the officer considers "unstable" are visited much more frequently. Because of the vast overloading of the officer, there is a serious discrepancy between the number of and quality of contacts the officer is expected to make with his clients and what he in reality is able to make.

3:46 p.m.	The officer returns to his office to dictate information on one of the eight presentence investigations he is working on. He calls the mother of the probationer who is in jail, to explain that her son has admitted guilt and that he will have to recommend revocation of probation. The mother becomes extremely emotional and pleads on behalf of the son. The officer explains as best he can that this is in the best interests of both her son and for the protection of society. "He needs closer supervision than I can provide."
4:03 p.m.	The officer talks to John's wife. He explains that without proof or testimony on an assault, no charges can be made. She tells him that it's his job to do something, but she will not admit that she talked to the officer if he took it to court.
4:30 p.m.	The officer instructs four new probationers on the conditions of probation, trying hurriedly to explain reasons for each. Two of them do not have jobs and he sets appointments to see both again tomorrow.
5:49 p.m.	The officer leaves the stack of paperwork yet to be completed on one side of his desk—the statistical reports that remain to be done and a pile of casefiles that need study—and goes home.
7:00 p.m.	After finishing supper the officer telephones four parolees with whom he was unable to make contact during the day to assure that they are still in town. Many of the contacts must be made after regular working hours.
7:30 p.m.	The officer hurries off to a meeting of volunteers who are working on a one-to-one basis with some of the people that he has under supervision. During this meeting he elaborates on some of the specific conditions of probation and discusses ways in which the volunteers can work more effectively as role models.
9:00 p.m.	The officer finally returns home to his wife and children and settles down for the evening.
11:47 p.m.	A city police detective calls from the local hospital. He advises that John's wife is in intensive care. She had a serious cut across

her face and possible internal head injuries as well as a broken wrist. Her husband was being held for Assault with Intent to Commit Murder. Arrested with John was his employer. They were both found intoxicated at a local bar. The bartender told the police officer that the two frequented the bar often. And this ends the day of a typical parole/probation officer.

ITEMS FOR STUDY

1. There are several schemes for assigning offenders to caseloads in p/p.
2. P/p officer roles should match agency model, and the style of the p/p officer should be appropriate for the needs of the case.
3. Providing ''treatment'' in p/p settings is hampered by a number of factors.
4. P/p officers can serve as ''brokers'' or ''advocates'' within a p/p model known as the Community Resources Management Team.
5. The team approach in p/p has advantages and disadvantages.
6. The law enforcement role of the p/p officer is a matter of some controversy.

chapter 16

Offender
Employment

The securing and maintaining of employment or training for employment are crucial aspects of p/p supervision. It is generally believed that there is a relationship between successful employment and avoidance of further legal difficulties. Mary Toborg and her colleagues state (1978: 2; references deleted):

> The observed relationship between criminality and unemployment has been explained in different ways. Some researchers have proposed that there is a *causal* relationship between unemployment and crime, while other analysts have argued that unemployment and recidivism are highly correlated only because each is associated with another factor (e.g., the influence of family members or a decision to ''go straight'') which induced widespread behavioral change. Whatever the explanation, unemployment and recidivism are often closely related.

The employment problem for parolees is often a great deal more difficult than for probationers. The parolee has been separated from employment and community contacts, usually for at least 18 months, often longer. The prison environment offers little help.* The Comptroller General of the United States reports that the U.S. Bureau of Prisons and state prison systems have been deficient in their approach to training and educating inmates for employment (1979: 46):

*The Iowa Division of Adult Corrections provides an example. Of 6580 cases (from July 1973 to December 1977) in the state's adult correctional institutions, 83.38% were not in any vocational training program; 40.3% received no work experience of any kind; and for those who did obtain some work experience it was mostly menial and of little rehabilitative value.

The Bureau of Prisons and State correctional agencies have not managed their education and training programs in a manner providing offenders a maximum opportunity to improve their employability. Also, correctional agencies have not fully utilized institutional maintenance assignments and work in prison industries to assist offenders in obtaining marketable job skills. Furthermore, the Bureau and State correctional agencies have not conducted comprehensive management reviews of program activities. If such reviews had been performed, many of the problems we found would have been identified and appropriate corrective action implemented.

The Comptroller is critical of efforts to enhance offender reintegration (p. 65):

The Bureau and State correctional agencies have not placed sufficient emphasis on programs to assist offenders in making a successful transition to the community. The absence of these services detracts from the offenders' chances of reintegrating into the community and wastes valuable resources. Also, the Bureau needs to improve the administration of its gratuity program to ensure that sufficient funds are available and that gratuities are equitably distributed based upon need.

Toborg and her colleagues are also critical of institutional efforts with respect to postrelease employment (1978: 9, reference deleted):

At present prison staff sometimes act as if their primary responsibility is to maintain order within the institution, not to prepare inmates for establishing law-abiding lifestyles after release. The incentive structure perceived by corrections officials often reflects such priorities: officials receive much adverse publicity if order is not maintained in the prisons but none if few efforts are made to rehabilitate inmates or equip them to return to the community. Thus, prison staff may see little reason to cooperate with programs which help releasees adjust to post-prison life. As a result of the difficulties experienced with corrections staff, many employment services programs have deemphasized their prison outreach activities and rely on other means of identifying potential clients.

Even if prison officials are uncooperative toward programs seeking to conduct outreach activities within the institution, they may nevertheless refer releasees to these programs. In addition, a releasee's parole officer may recommend the program. Since having a job is a condition of parole in many jurisdictions, parole officers will frequently refer unemployed parolees to programs which can provide assistance in obtaining work. In some cases this mechanism may be a formalized one, in which, for example, individual parole officers are matched with specific program staff who always serve that officer's parolees. More commonly, the mechanism is a less formal one in which parolees are merely referred for service.

Basically, in addition to providing economic rewards, employment also enhances the self-worth and image of the offender. When the economy is poor, when unemployment is unusually high, this has a direct effect on p/p supervision.

In assisting clients with employment officers may make direct referrals to particular employers if they have the necessary contacts, or may refer clients to other agencies, such as the state employment services, for help. Officers may also have to provide guidance and counseling concerning some of the basic aspects of securing employment. For example, officers will emphasize the need to be on time for interviews. They will help fill out applications and may use role playing to accustom clients to job-interview situations. It is often important to discuss various aspects of good grooming and what type of clothes to wear on an interview. The following checklist is an example of interview instructions that might be given a client.

CHECKLIST FOR OFFENDER EMPLOYMENT*

Greet Receptionist

1. Give your name and reason for visit. Example—"Good morning, my name is John Smith and I have a 10:00 a.m. employment interview with Mr. Jones."
2. Be punctual. Example—For a 10:00 a.m. interview, try being there by 9:30 or 9:45 a.m.
3. Be prepared to fill out an application. Example—(refer to No. 2)—By arriving at 9:30 a.m. or 9:45 a.m., you can fill out an application and go in at 10:00 a.m. to see Mr. Jones.
4. Have a copy of your social security number, names of past jobs with addresses and dates, names of references with addresses, etc., written on a card to aid you in filling out the application.
5. Be prepared to take a test for the job you are applying for if required. Example—Electronic, clerical or industrial machines, etc.
6. Have a list of questions you wish to ask prepared. Example:
   a. How old is the company?
   b. How many employees are with the company?
   c. What is the potential for promotion and growth?
   d. What are the duties that the job entails?
   e. What is the starting salary?
   f. What is the top salary potential?
   g. What are the working hours?
   h. Is there paid overtime?
   i. What benefits are offered by the company?
   j. Does the company offer tuition for night school?
   k. Does the company promote from within?

Procedure for the Interviewer

1. Walk slowly and quietly, stand right, hold your head up.
2. Greet the interviewer.

---

*From Phyllis Groom McCreary and John M. McCreary, *Job Training and Placement for Offenders and Ex-Offenders* (Washington, D.C.: Government Printing Office, 1975), pp. 79–80.

a. Shake hands firmly if interviewer offers his hand.
b. Look interviewer in the eye and say, "How do you do, Mr. Jones."
c. Stand until the interviewer asks you to be seated.
d. Wait for the interviewer to start the interview and lead it.
e. You may smoke if the interviewer states so.
f. Be prepared to answer questions. Examples:

> Why do you want to work for this company?
> Where do you see yourself in five years?
> Are you planning to further your education?
> What do you know about this company?
> Do you have any particular skills or interests that you feel qualify you for a position with this company?
> What makes you feel you are qualified for this particular job?
> Do you have any plans for marriage in the immediate future?

Now is when you present your questions.

Attitudes and Behavior During the Interview

1. Sit up straight, feet on floor, hands in lap.
2. Sit quietly (do not keep moving around or fidget).
3. Use your best manners.
   a. Be attentive and polite.
   b. Speak slowly and clearly.
   c. Look interviewer in the eye (do not wear sunglasses).
   d. Use correct English, avoid slang.
   e. Emphasize your good points.
4. Speak of yourself in a positive manner.
5. Talk about what you can do.
6. Do not apologize for your shortcomings.
7. Do not talk to an excess about your personal problems.

What an Interviewer Sees Immediately During an Interview

1. Hygiene.
   a. Bathe just before an interview.
   b. Clean and clip nails if necessary.
   c. Brush teeth.
   d. Use a good deodorant.
   e. Wear an outfit that is clean and conservative regardless of the fashion trend or style.

Interviewer Closes the Interview

1. Do not linger when he indicates it is time to stop.
2. Be sure to thank the interviewer as you leave.

Staying on the Job

1. With the great shortage of available jobs, employers can afford to be highly selective in choosing an employee.
2. Accept positions in related fields so when positions are re-opened, you will have first choice at these positions.

In Conclusion

Remember the four A's.

1. Attendance
2. Attitude
3. Appearance
4. Ability

One critical aspect of employment for ex-offenders is the question of revealing their record. I allowed my clients to decide for themselves. However, I did provide guidance by discussing the experiences of other clients relative to this issue. Many clients reported that they believed that their candor resulted in not securing employment. Others reported that some employers were interested in providing them with an opportunity to make good. Unfortunately, many employers will not hire ex-offenders.

Some offenders are required by law or policy to reveal their records when applying for certain jobs. For example, most civil service jobs require individuals having a criminal conviction to reveal this fact. Banks, hospitals, and other sensitive areas of employment may also require disclosure. Certainly, allowing an offender with a history of drug abuse to work in a hospital or similar situation would not be advisable, especially if the employer did not know the person's record.

Sol Tropp, an expert in the field of ex-offender employment, recommends that "the employer should be made aware of an offender's status only when the pattern of the offender's behavior may result in anti-social behavior," such as a drug addict working in a hospital *(Vocational Counseling,* 1965: 8). Robert Hannum, Vocational Director of the Osborne Association, states: "We do not lie about the individual's record but, because of the prejudice that employers may have, we try to postpone complete revelation until the employer has had a chance to try out the offender on the job" *(Vocational Counseling,* 1965: 8).

Client Flow Through Employment Services Program

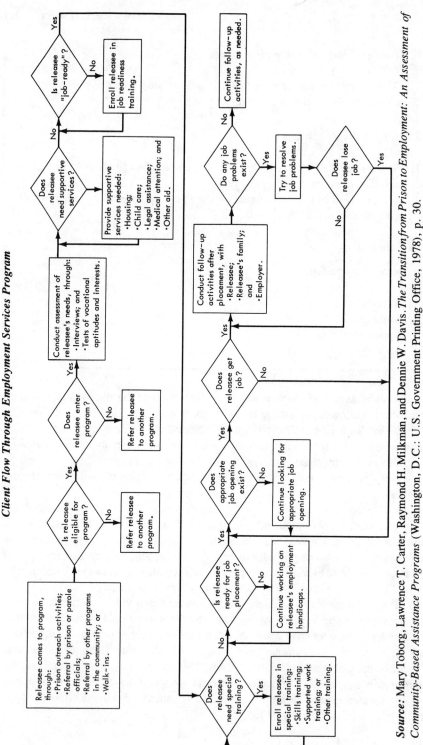

Source: Mary Toborg, Lawrence T. Carter, Raymond H. Milkman, and Dennie W. Davis. *The Transition from Prison to Employment: An Assessment of Community-Based Assistance Programs* (Washington, D.C.: U.S. Government Printing Office, 1978), p. 30.

The officer may also visit a client's place of employment to verify the employ-ment—as a New York State parole pamphlet notes: "The parole officer does not naively accept the information that a parolee provides; he goes out into the community to verify it."

THE STIGMA OF CONVICTION

John Reed and Dale Nance have stated what is all too often obvious in p/p practice: "A record of conviction produces a loss of status which has lasting consequences" (1972: 27). They note that while probation and parole are rehabilitatively thought of as more desirable than prison, "both visibly display the offender in the community under a disability—his conditions of probation of parole. In some jurisdictions, he must register as a criminal, supposedly for the protection of the community. The unintended effects of registration are to broadcast his conviction and preserve his criminal stigma" (p. 27). The authors call this a form of value conflict, whereby the protective concerns of society run counter to the rehabilitative philosophy that is espoused (p. 30).

One of the more important studies on the impact of a criminal conviction was conducted by Richard Schwartz and Jerome Skolnick (in Henshel and Silverman, 1975: 401–15). They studied the effects of a criminal record on the employment opportunities of unskilled workers. They prepared four employment folders which were the same in all respects except for the criminal record of the applicant, as follows:

1. The first folder indicated that the applicant had been convicted and sentenced for assault.
2. The second, that he had been tried for assault and acquitted.
3. The third, also tried for assault and acquitted, and with a letter from the judge certifying the finding of not guilty.
4. The fourth made no mention of any criminal record.

The study involved 100 employers who were divided into units of 25, with each group being shown one of the four folders on the mistaken belief that they were actually considering a real job applicant. The results are as follows:

1. Of the 25 employers shown the "no record" folder, 9 (36 percent) gave positive responses.
2. Of the 25 employers shown the "convict" folder, only one (4 percent) expressed interest in the applicant.
3. Of the 25 employers shown the "accused but acquitted" folder, 3 (12 percent) expressed interest in the applicant.
4. Of the 25 employers shown the "accused but acquitted" folder, which also contained the judge's letter, 6 (24 percent) expressed an interest in the applicant.

Since a significant majority of persons on probation and parole are unskilled, the ramifications of these findings are obvious.

LICENSING AND EMPLOYMENT DISABILITIES

The stigma of conviction is intensified by state laws depriving persons of certain civil rights, such as voting, holding public (or union) office, and serving on a jury, even when the offense had nothing to do with such rights. Perhaps even more serious, because of its direct effect on rehabilitative efforts, are civil disabilities that hinder an offender's efforts to gain certain types of employment. Although it is generally believed that unemployment is a factor in recidivism, most states have laws that can hinder offender employment. A study by the American Bar Association (Hunt et al., 1974) disclosed 1948 separate statutory provisions in the United States that affect the licensing of persons with conviction records. For example, 45 jurisdictions had a requirement of "good moral character," which usually translates into not having a criminal record, in order to receive a barber's license, and 24 denied the license to an applicant convicted of a felony. Other common restrictions apply to the manufacture, retailing, wholesaling, or distribution of alcoholic beverages. Occupations affected by such laws include cooks, waiters, bartenders, dishwashers, delivery persons, and all other occupations related to business establishments where alcoholic beverages are manufactured, sold, or consumed. Other commonly restricted occupations include manicurist, chauffeur, and masseur, as well as nurse, doctor, dentist, teacher, lawyer, and accountant.

A 1980 Florida case highlights this problem. A Jacksonville public school teacher had his teaching certificate permanently lifted because he was once convicted of marijuana possession. This, despite the recommendation of the Florida Attorney General, who reported that the teacher had an "outstanding record" since his conviction. The Attorney General pointed out that this type of action "makes it hard to visit prisons, as I do, and tell prisoners about being rehabilitated" *(Miami Herald,* July 16, 1980: 4-A).

In the probation and parole field it is the prevailing belief that if there is to be any bar to employment, these should be directly related to the occupation or profession. For example, a state might restrict the issuance of a pharmacy license to persons with a record of narcotic law violations. James Hunt and his colleagues state: "We expect our corrections system to correct, but we hinder that process by allowing the former offender to be subjected to continued penalties through restrictions that deny him fair consideration for a job or license even after he has supposedly paid his debt to society" (1974: 17).

In an effort to correct these restrictions and make employment easier for the ex-offender, some states have removed statutory restrictions, and a few have even enacted "fair employment" laws that benefit ex-offenders. New York, for example, has a statute that prohibits the denial of employment or license because of a conviction unless there is a *direct relationship* between the conviction and the specific employment or license, or unless it involves an "unreasonable risk" to persons or property. A direct relationship requires a showing that the nature of the criminal conduct for which the person was convicted has a direct bearing on the fitness or ability to carry out duties or responsibilities related to the employment or license. The statute requires that a public or private employer provide, upon request, a written statement setting forth the reasons for the denial. The statute provides for enforcement by the New York State Commission on Human Rights. States vary in the method and extent to which they provide relief from civil disabilities incurred by probationers and parolees. Pardon is one method, although its use is generally limited. Some states have adopted automatic restoration procedures upon satisfactory completion of parole or probation, and a large number of states have statutes designed to restore forfeited rights, although they may be subjected to restrictive interpretation in licensing and occupational area. In New York, for example, the judiciary and parole board have the power to restore certain rights through the granting of a "Relief from Disabilities."

NEW YORK STATE RELIEF FROM CIVIL DISABILITIES

Laws Governing the Issuance of Certificates of Relief from Disabilities

This certificate is issued to relieve the holder, an "eligible offender" as defined in Section 700 of the Correction Law, of all or of enumerated forfeitures, disabilities, or bars to employment automatically imposed by law by reason of his conviction of the crime or offense specified on the face of this certificate.

This certificate shall be considered a "temporary certificate" where (1) issued by a court to a holder who is under a "revocable sentence" as defined in Section 700 of the Correction Law and the court's authority to revoke such sentence has not expired, or (2) issued by the State Board of Parole and the holder is still under the supervision of the Board. Where the holder is under a revocable sentence, this certificate may be revoked by the court for violation of the conditions of such sentence and shall be revoked by the court if it revokes the sentence and commits the holder to an institution under the jurisdiction of the State Department of Correctional Services. Where the holder is subject to the supervision of the State Board of Parole, this certificate may be revoked by the Board for violation of the conditions of parole or release. Any such revocation shall be upon notice and after an opportunity to be heard. If this certificate is not so revoked, it shall become a permanent certificate upon expiration or termination of the court's authority to revoke the sentence or upon termination of the jurisdiction of the Board of Parole over the holder.

Rights of Relief from Disabilities

A. Where the certificate is issued by a court at the time sentence is pronounced, it covers forfeitures as well as disabilities. In any other case the certificate applies only to disabilities.

B. A conviction of the crime or the offense specified on the face of this certificate shall NOT cause automatic forfeiture of any license, permit, employment or franchise, including the right to register for or vote at an election, or automatic forfeiture of any other right or privilege, held by the eligible offender and *covered* by the certificate. Nor shall such conviction be deemed to be a conviction within the meaning of any provision of law that imposes, by reason of a conviction, a bar to any employment, a disability to exercise any right or a disability to apply for or to receive any license, permit or other authority or privilege, covered by the certificate. Provided, however, that no such certificate shall apply, or be construed so as to apply, to the right of such person to retain or to be eligible for public office.

C. A conviction of the crime or the offense specified on the face of this certificate shall NOT prevent any judicial, administrative, licensing or other body, board or authority from relying upon the conviction specified on the reverse side of this certificate as the basis for the exercise of its discretionary power to suspend, revoke, refuse to issue or renew any license, permit or other authority or privilege.

Under the Georgia Constitution, a person convicted of a felony or any other "crime involving moral turpitude, punishable by the laws of this State with imprisonment in the penitentiary," loses his civil and political rights, including the right to vote, the right to hold public office, and the right to serve on a jury. Using an application form available on request, a person who was convicted under Georgia law may apply to the Board for a Restoration of Civil and Political Rights. If the person was convicted under another state's law or under Federal law but is residing in Georgia and wishes to exercise civil and political rights in this State, he also may apply.

A Restoration of Civil and Political Rights carries no implication of innocence and may be granted only to a person who has completed his sentence or served four years on Georgia parole on a life sentence with a satisfactory adjustment in society (three years with exemplary adjustment) or served three years on Georgia parole on a lesser sentence with a satisfactory adjustment in society (two years with exemplary adjustment).

The Board automatically restores civil and political rights to a felony parolee or Youthful Offender Conditional Releasee upon discharge from supervision if he has no other sentence to serve or pending criminal charge against him.*

ITEMS FOR STUDY

1. Although it is generally agreed that there is a relationship between crime and unemployment, it may not be *causal*.

*Source: Georgia Board of Pardons and Paroles.

2. Prison training, education, and counseling preparatory to postrelease employment are deficient.
3. Many offenders need a great deal of counseling in rudimentary employment skills.
4. A crucial issue with respect to offender employment is the question of revealing one's criminal record.
5. Some employment positions or licenses are automatically barred to ex-offenders.

chapter 17

The Case
of
John Fenton

This is the (fictional) account of John Fenton, who was placed on probation in 1976. It illustrates an officer's use of casework skills to help an extremely dependent youth who is on probation for striking his mother with a hatchet. Although it is a probation case, the techniques used and the method of recording case contacts would be the same for a parole case.

At the time of the attack on his mother Fenton was 16 years of age, and although the assault was not fatal, it caused severe lacerations of the face and scalp. The presentence report indicates that Fenton is an out-of-wedlock child whose father died when he was an infant. Fenton's mother neglected him, and at age 8 he was removed from his mother's care by the juvenile court, and placed in a children's home.

For the·first two years his mother did not visit at the home. At age 16 he was discharged to live with her. Shortly thereafter, Fenton argued with his mother about her drinking and her boyfriend, with the resulting offense of assault. Following his arrest, Fenton was remanded to the state hospital for a psychiatric evaluation. (While in the hospital his mother died in an automobile accident.) Fenton was diagnosed as without psychosis, a "sociopathic personality." He was described as being of dull-normal intelligence.

On January 30, John Fenton was placed on probation for a term not to exceed five years, after pleading guilty to a charge of assault.

The Fenton case indicates the various steps used to help an extremely dependent client. Fenton is not, as are many offenders, "street-wise," but, on the contrary, is a young man suffering from the "social shock" of returning to the community after a life spent in institutions.

The case is written by the probation officer in the usual p/p agency chronological summary manner. It reviews some of the routine work of the p/p officer, such as assisting the offender with a residence and employment. However, in this case the officer provides more assistance than is usual in most p/p cases. Of course, Fenton requires more help than a "typical" offender. In reality, because of the considerable amount of time spent on this case by the officer, Fenton could be considered a "caseload" by himself. In most, if not all, p/p agencies a "John Fenton" would not be able to receive the service reflected in this fictionalized case.

Another routine task performed by the officer concerned his handling of Fenton's new arrest. As indicated in the case record, it is standard p/p practice to interview the client and the arresting officer, in addition to reviewing the police or court record.

As a condition of his probation, Fenton is required to go for psychiatric treatment. However, as the officer notes, Fenton is resistant to psychiatric treatment. In this case, the officer wisely decides not to coerce the offender into treatment. Unfortunately, some p/p agencies will coerce an offender into psychiatric treatment.

This case indicates a concerned officer who not only shows an interest in the tangible needs of his client, but also deals with his social needs—the client is viewed as a total person.

Office Reports: Feb. 4, 14, 19, 21, Mar. 18, 19, 26; Apr. 2, 9, 16, 23, 30

Home Visits: Feb. 4, 8, 29; Apr. 26, 29

Other Contacts: Feb. 4 (3), 5, 6, 7, 19, 25 (2), 27, 28; Mar. 28; Apr. 25

Telephone Reports: Feb. 5, 7, 9, 13, 19, 25; Mar. 7, 18, 19, 21, 22

Employment Verification: Mar. 27; Apr. 16

The probation officer had been directed to make arrangements for Fenton, who had no relatives, friends, or resources prior to his release from jail.

When Fenton obtained his possessions in two cardboard boxes from the jail, he was taken by the probation officer to the Salvation Army office, where he was given a loan of $40. He was placed in a room reserved for him several days earlier by the probation officer at the YMCA at a weekly rental of $32.50. The probation officer then accompanied him to the Department of Social Services, where at the intake unit, he applied for Public Assistance, which was granted the following day. He was also escorted by the probation officer to the Social Security Administration, where he obtained a registration card necessary for application for employment to private firms.

Fenton seemed very careful and almost childlike as he traveled about the city with the probation officer. He mentioned that everything appeared strange to him, and that it would take him a long time to adjust. He declined food, saying that he was very excited and had no appetite. The probation officer offered him suggestions as to how to look for employment and he thanked the probation officer for his assistance when they separated at 4:15 p.m. Shortly thereafter, while riding on a bus, the probation officer observed him walking in the vicinity of the YMCA, looking in every direction at buildings and people. He seemed a lost, pathetic figure.

Although Fenton made a few friends at the YMCA, he spoke several times—during both office reports and home visits—about telephoning or visiting Mr. Johnson, the director, and others at the Thomasville Home. We voiced no disapproval but suggested that he defer visiting until employment was found and he had proper clothing.

On February 9, the probationer telephoned that he had received an allowance of $35.25 from the Department of Social Services. He mentioned that he had attended the movies and had made a few friends at the YMCA. He no longer felt quite so lonesome as he had during the first few days, at which time he had difficulty sleeping. A few days later, he reported that he had received an allowance of $125.25 from the Department of Social Services for clothing. We saw the itemized account by caseworker P. Wolfe, but Fenton, before coming to our office or asking anyone for advice, had cashed the check in a cashing agency, which charged him $0.73. We pointed out that he could have saved this amount by cashing the check at any bank or department store where he purchased clothing.

When the probationer came to the office on February 19, he had a blue gabardine topcoat which he had purchased for $40.10. In addition, he had about $150 in his pockets, adding that he had saved the balance of the clothing money and some food money, as he had eaten sparingly. He mentioned happily that he had met a friend, James Westrup, whom he knew at the Williams State Hospital. Westrup, he stated, has one arm, is married, and is employed as a bookkeeper. Fenton spent the preceding Sunday with the Westrup family and had a good chicken dinner. He mentioned that it was the most enjoyable day he had experienced in recent years.

The probation officer then took Fenton to Blaston's Employment Agency and explained his situation as discretely as possible to one of the interviewers to whom the p.o. had been introduced. After filing an application, Fenton was asked to return the following day for a possible job referral. As it turned out, he was unsuccessful that day, but on February 21 he gave the agency a $25 deposit and was referred to a job as helper at the Cotton Converting Company, East River Street. The prospective employer, who had offered a salary of $92.00 per week, told Fenton that he wanted a machine operator. Fenton was rejected for the position. We suspect that the employer realized there was something amiss, as this 22-year-old man had no employment history or references.

New Arrest.   On February 24, the probation officer received a telephone call at his home from a guard at the jail relaying a message from the probationer, who requested an interview before going to Criminal Court on a new charge. The following day, Fenton was seen at the jail; he had been arrested on a larceny charge for snatching a woman's handbag, and tearfully protested his innocence. We noted, however, that despite signs of agitation, Fenton spoke in a flat, almost toneless voice, in a manner denoting apathy and resignation. He related further that he had met the woman in a bar and grill at Main Street and Monroe Avenue and that his friend had offered to take the woman home in a taxicab. Fenton went along, as he had been unable to gain entrance to the YMCA after midnight, and while waiting downstairs for Westrup, who had escorted the woman to her apartment, he had remained some 15 minutes when Westrup came toward him hurriedly and said, "Let's get out of here." As they ran a police officer commanded them to halt, fired shots, and both stopped. At that time, Fenton had $45.00 of his savings and $95.00 more in the YMCA. He had drunk no intoxicants, he claimed, and had no idea that his friend planned to commit a crime.

After reading the complaint in Criminal Court and talking with the arresting officer, Patrolman Lahey of the 2nd Precinct, the probation officer was of the opinion that Fenton had given a true account of the offense. The arresting officer acknowledged that Fenton and Westrup were both sober, but that the complainant was under the influence of intoxicants. The latter admitted she had accepted Westrup's offer to take her home, where he snatched her pocketbook. According to the arresting officer, Westrup stated upon his arrest that Fenton was not involved in the offense. In the meantime, the probation officer communicated with the Department of Social Services and the YMCA. At the latter, on February 25, the night manager was asked to vacate Fenton's room so that he would not owe more rent. The night manager promised that the probationer's effects and funds would be placed in safekeeping at the YMCA office.

The case was heard in Criminal Court on February 28 before Judge Rober, at which time Fenton was discharged while Westrup was held on a reduced charge of petit larceny. The probation officer found, on reading the court papers, that Westrup is 26 years old and resides at 1933 Eastern Drive. He had previously been arrested in Lincoln County for homicide (knife), but no disposition was recorded. Apparently, Westrup was found at that time to be psychotic and was committed to the Williams State Hospital, where he met Fenton.

After discharge in court, Fenton immediately appeared at this office and arrangements were made by the probation officer for him to revisit the Department of Social Services, reapply for assistance, and regain his former lodgings at the YMCA. The officer discussed the probationer's involvement with Westrup, causing his recent arrest, and attempted to impress upon him how important it would be in the future for him to choose his associates carefully and to confine his activities to wholesome interests.

The following day probationer reported, stating that he had obtained his same room at the YMCA and that his clothing had been returned to him. The probationer told us that he had been unable to sleep that night and had smoked a large quantity of cigarettes.

Noting that probationer appeared bewildered, the probation officer painstakingly explained to him the procedure necessary to obtain Public Assistance again. He was urged to tell his case worker what had happened and under what circumstances. At this time, Fenton was reaccepted for Public Assistance and for the first time, showed initiative by reporting that he had visited the employment agency and applied for a job. He was told to return there within a few days.

On March 20 and 22, we talked with the welfare caseworker, Mr. Carson, and his supervisor, Miss Louks. Both are interested in the probationer and plan to refer him to their employment division and possibly to a mental hygiene clinic.

An effort will be made to interest the YMCA staff further in encouraging Fenton to make wider social contacts and to partake of the supervised group activities of the YMCA.

Through the employment agency, Fenton was given a job as helper at the Downs Brass Company, 67 Wooster Street, on March 27 at a salary of $2.30 per hour for 40 hours plus overtime. The probation officer notified the Department of Social Services, which after giving Fenton $46.00, closed their case as of April 3. Upon learning this, the officer discussed it with Fenton during his office report on April 2, advising him of the amount he would receive and suggesting ways that he might budget his remaining funds so as to provide for carfares, lunches, and work clothing until his first pay. At this time he showed us his hands, which were scarred and bruised from putting threads on piping at his job. He declared that he would keep this employment until he could find something better, but that he really wants a job as a presser. While employed, he regularly showed the probation officer his paycheck stubs, indicating amounts earned, time off, and deductions. Because he was ill for four hours during the week of April 9, his gross earnings were $82.80. He mentioned that he had no complaints about the job at this time, and the probation officer gained the impression that Fenton is becoming more stable.

On his next reporting date, he asked if he could have permission to spend the weekend at Lake Nomo. He had been invited there by a friend, Jim Colin, who lives in the YMCA. He is certain that Colin, who has resided there for several years, is a decent person and it has been arranged that they will stay with Colin's grandmother.

The probation officer mentioned at this time that probationer should be receiving psychiatric treatment as indicated by the court. He said that he did not feel the need of such treatment now, but would go to a psychiatrist if the probation officer insisted. He added, with a show of apparently genuine frankness, that he would tell the probation officer first if he felt the need for such help. (The matter was later discussed with case supervisor Dawson, who said that no useful purpose would be accomplished at this time by sending Fenton to a psychiatrist if he was resistive.)

On his report the following week, the probationer mentioned that he had enjoyed the weekend at Lake Nomo at a cost of $15. In a game of chance he had won a large ham, coffee, and other items, which he gave to his friend's grandmother in exchange for her hospitality. Aside from being often tired and having little energy, Fenton made no complaints to the probation officer, but did write a letter to his former welfare caseworker, Mr. Carson, asking if he were eligible for supplementary assistance, as his gross salary was only $92.00 per week. Mr. Carson telephoned the probation officer advising of the letter, and agreed to explain his agency's policy and allowance to the probationer by return mail.

Summary: May–July

Dictated: Aug. 7

Office Reports: May 7, 14, 21, 28; June 4, 11, 18, 25; July 2, 9, 16, 18, 19, 22

Home Visits: May 22, 31; June 7, 14, 18, 21; July 24, 29

Other Contacts: July 24, 25, 29

Employment References: May 7, 21, 28; June 4, 11, 18, 21, 25; July 2, 16, 19

The probationer continued to live at the YMCA, preferring to pay a weekly rental of $32.50 for an adequate room, hot water, showers, and recreational activity, rather than seek a low-cost furnished room at a private home, where he might be unhappy. The p.o. agreed with his thinking in this regard and suggested that Fenton seek extra work, particularly as his weekly income was so small. His pay stubs verified that his salary at the Downs Brass Company was usually $92.00 per week, but on May 28, he received a 0.10 an hour raise, making his gross weekly income $96.

During each of his office reports, probationer was friendly and talkative. He frequently mentioned that his goal is to work in a dry cleaning shop, as a presser, because this is the type of work he did at Williams State Hospital. The p.o. has noticed that his hands were often cut, bruised, or blistered from his present work. Another development during the month was the probationer's report that he finds it difficult to get along with the employer's son, whom he describes as uncouth and domineering. The p.o. provided as much support to probationer as possible in this situation, pointing out the value of tolerating this difficulty, temporarily, while saving some part of his small weekly salary so that he can return to the employment agency for a better job. He indicated willingness to try both, but doubted whether he could save any sum whatever since his small income is totally consumed by rent, carfare, clothing, laundry, and food. Somehow, probationer had managed to visit friends at Lake Nomo frequently. On one occasion he mentioned that he had taken several children to the rides but that his friend's grandmother had paid the expenses.

Numerous visits have been made to the YMCA, but on these occasions even as late as 9:00 p.m., probationer has either been out or failed to answer the buzzer. The desk clerk confirmed in each instance that Fenton lives in room 607. In office visits Fenton advised that he continues to work for the same employer, his gross salary being $96. On June 18, the p.o. noted an advertisement in the *Daily Star* for a presser of pants to work for a large clothing chain. Carfare was given to the probationer to apply for this job, and he later reported that he had done so, but the job had been filled. He is making efforts to find other employment through friends met at the YMCA. He believes that he will be able to obtain a summer job shortly at Lake Nomo, but such would be of little assistance after September, when he would again have to look for regular work.

Since he reiterated that he desires employment as a presser, the p.o. arranged for him to visit a friend who has a small dry-cleaning shop. It was explained to probationer that the owner was doing the p.o. a favor and that if he found Fenton as a qualified presser, he would make a sincere effort to give him employment. Fenton visited this establishment on two Saturdays and was permitted to do some pressing and observe the owner work. When next seen, he told the p.o. that the owner had found him good on men's clothing, but inadequate on women's. He will ask the owner for further instruction. Several weeks later, the p.o. saw the owner, who stated that Fenton is a very poor presser and noted, without knowing the probationer's background, that he was a "little odd." One Saturday morning when the owner appeared in the shop rather late, Fenton was standing in front of the door and said in stern tones: "I've been here since 10 a.m. and you did not show up." The shop owner explained tactfully that he is sole owner and his own boss. Probationer mentioned during this period that he is growing more discontented with his employment at the brass company, where the work is growing heavier. He is now interested in seeking work in a large steam laundry and will apply to several toward the end of the month. He reported that he wished to resign from the brass company because he had a serious quarrel with his employer's son, who had used profane language to him. He felt like assaulting this young man, who is 22 years old, but realized the serious consequences and restrained himself.

On July 28, he notified the p.o. during an office report that he had resigned his employment at the Downs Brass Company after the employer's son had remarked that "he was going to fire him that night." At this time the probationer thought he could move to the home of his friends in Lake Nomo and find employment there. He promised to report immediately any new address or employment. However, two days later he telephoned stating that he had not moved and had not found a new job.

On July 31, he applied for Public Assistance and was accepted. He was notified by letter that he would receive $46 plus rent on the 3rd and 18th of each month. The welfare caseworker checked with Downs Brass. Fenton was regarded as a good worker and had had no trouble on the job. As the employer did not know Fenton was on probation, the p.o. refrained from contacting the employer, but obtained the necessary information through the welfare caseworker, who had similarly maintained probationer's confidence and did not disclose his probation status.

Evaluation.   During the five months Fenton was under supervision, he was cooperative and responsive. He did not want psychiatric treatment, which had been recommended by the court's psychiatric clinic as necessary. In most instances, he has shown good judgment. His one difficulty, the arrest, was the type of situation in which anyone might become innocently involved. He apparently maintained his employment under most trying physical conditions for approximately four months. Almost weekly his hands were cut, bruised, or blistered, and the net pay barely maintained his material needs. He sought work as a presser, but from a test given him by a friend of the p.o., he was not qualified at that time.

The probationer enjoys spending weekends at Lake Nomo with a YMCA friend, the latter's grandmother, and numerous children. This appears to provide him with some semblance of a family. He has wanted to move to that locale and may do so when he finds steady employment. At all times, the probationer has appeared rational and in contact with reality. Undoubtedly he is odd in some ways, but these seem to be minor deviations from the norm. We attribute some of his lacks to having spent virtually all his life in institutions. It will take time for him to learn finesse in interpersonal relationships and the ordinary demands of everyday living. His faults do not seem serious at this time. They are to be expected of one who has had little training for living in an open community.

ITEMS FOR STUDY

1. John Fenton suffers from "institutionalization."
2. The probation officer literally takes Fenton to the Welfare Department, Social Security office, and the Salvation Army, and arranges for a residence at the YMCA.
3. Fenton, because he lacks an employment history, finds it difficult to secure a job.
4. Fenton shows initiative by securing employment and by sending a letter to the Welfare Department inquiring about supplementary assistance.
5. The probation officer provides a great deal of support and offers useful advice to this almost childlike offender.
6. The probation officer refrains from contacting Fenton's employer because the latter did not know of his probation status.

chapter 18

Probation
and Parole Officers,
Paraprofessionals,
and Volunteers

The selection of probation and parole officers is by a process similar to that used to select most civil servants. Two systems are generally employed, the merit system and the appointment system. In both systems minimum qualifications are established; for probation/parole officers they are usually a bachelor's degree, and sometimes a master's degree or experience in social work or counseling.

MERIT SYSTEM

Under the merit system, applicants who meet the minimum qualifications are required to pass a written examination to be eligible. If they pass, their names are placed on a list according to the grades they received, and it is from this list that staff are selected. This system has been criticized by those who maintain that a written test cannot determine who will be a good probation/parole officer.

APPOINTMENT SYSTEM

Under the appointment system, applicants who meet the minimum requirements are hired on the basis of an evaluation by the agency. Applicants do not take a written examination, although they are usually interviewed by agency representatives. This system has been criticized because of its potential for abuse. There is a history of the appointment system being used for political purposes.

COMBINED SYSTEM

Although not necessarily a distinct system, some jurisdictions use elements of both the merit system and the appointment system. For example, applicants are first required to pass a qualifying examination, then those who pass the examination are interviewed, and the agency selects those they consider best suited for the position.

PERSONAL QUALITIES

The characteristics generally considered desirable for probation/parole officers are:

1. *Basic knowledge*. A p/p officer should have a working understanding of psychology and sociology, the criminal statutes, police operations, and the court and correctional systems.
2. *Individual characteristics*. A p/p officer needs the ability to relate to all offenders and to deal with their sometimes subtle or open hostility, to exercise authority in an appropriate manner, to work well with other staff members, and to be able to organize work properly and prepare written reports in a coherent and timely manner.
3. *The agency*. The p/p officer must be willing to accept the responsibilities engendered by working for a public agency that handles offenders, and to enforce rules and adhere to regulations.
4. *Other agencies*. The p/p officer has to be able to deal with many kinds of agencies, usually divided into law enforcement (police, district attorneys, judges, etc.) and social service (welfare, employment, educational, etc.). These agencies often have varying attitudes toward offenders that must be handled appropriately.

WOMEN PROBATION AND PAROLE OFFICERS

The 1964 Civil Rights Act, which prohibited discrimination against women (and minority groups), and the strength of the feminist movement have had an important impact on the criminal justice system. In the area of police personnel practices, police agencies are now hiring women on an equal basis with men. Women police officers are no longer only assigned to ''female duties'' but now go on uniformed street patrol.

Traditionally, probation and parole have also been a male field; approximately 90 percent of probationers and parolees are men, and prior to 1970 most probation and parole agencies did not permit officers to supervise clients of the opposite sex. This limited the number of positions available to women p/p officers. Currently, most p/p agencies routinely mix caseloads, thereby increasing the number of women who can be hired for this work.

Some agencies assign male offenders to women because they believe that women can do as effective a job as men, while others do so to better equalize the size of their caseloads. A few agencies will make an assignment on the basis of what is believed to be the needs of the particular case. Ellis Stout, probation chief in the State of Washington, notes, for example, that some agencies will have women supervise youthful male offenders who are believed to be in need of a mother surrogate. He states that some agencies do not assign "assaultive" or "aggressive" male offenders to female officers out of concern for the officer's safety. Field work assignments may be adjusted for women officers to keep them out of high-delinquency areas or from having to make night visits (1973: 68).

NONPROFESSIONALS

Probation and parole have historical roots in the work of such nonprofessionals as John Augustus and the agents of prisoner aid societies. The nonprofessional is very much a part of probation and parole practice. Indeed, the requirement of a college degree, and the use of salaried, full-time p/p officers is a relatively recent phenomenon in corrections.

Paraprofessionals

Paraprofessionals are employees who do not possess the credentials traditionally viewed as necessary for work as p/p officers in a modern p/p agency. Frequently, paraprofessionals will be further identified as being *indigenous*, which usually means that they possess a similar background—social, economic, racial, and so on—to the p/p clients serviced by the agency. They are often viewed as "an extension of the client . . . who can bridge the gap between the professional and the client" *(Overview Study,* 1974: 15). The extensive use of paraprofessionals is an outgrowth of the "war on poverty" of the 1960s. The basic motives for using paraprofessionals are *(Overview Study,* 1974: 44):

1. The desire to compensate for the shortage of skilled personnel, particularly workers trained at the graduate level.
2. The desire to increase employment opportunities for disadvantaged workers and the unemployed poor.
3. The desire to develop an efficient division of labor so that personnel with different levels of skill can be assigned appropriate duties.
4. The desire to modify organizations so that the resulting service delivery system

will be more directly related to the problem of clients and more efficient in meeting their needs.

5. The desire to provide work experience in which workers, by helping clients with problems similar to their own, improve their social functioning and become better prepared for work.

Paraprofessionals are likely to come from the same environment as the largest segment of the p/p population. Indeed, this is a basic reason for employing "indigenous" paraprofessionals in p/p; they are seen as better able to relate to persons alienated from middle-class society. In his essay "Changing Criminals," Donald Cressey argues that the reduction of alienation is a first step in rehabilitating offenders. This is effected by "positive association" with prosocial persons who are "just like me" (1955: 116–20). Carlson and Parks state (1979: 192):

It is very difficult for the professional to serve as an effective role model. The indigenous worker, conversely, has often experienced situations and problems similar to those that confront certain clients. The indigenous worker has the advantage of proximity in time and space, while typically the professional is limited to a nine to five, Monday to Friday schedule, living some distance from those served. The indigenous worker, living closer to his clients, has much greater familiarity with their environments, and has greater freedom to move about at times other than business hours. Inter-racial tensions in certain areas point out the need for non-professionals recruited from groups having an ethnic or racial affinity with certain offender populations. A communication gap resulting from social and cultural distance between middle-class professionals of any race and lower class minority group members is a growing problem in rehabilitation services.

In p/p the use of paraprofessionals has included hiring ex-offenders—this is often the basis of a paraprofessional program. The use of ex-offenders can be seen as a logical extension of Cressey's stress on correctional workers who are "just like me." Toborg and her colleagues review some of the advantages and disadvantages of using ex-offenders as counselors (1978: 13):

The usefulness of ex-offender counselors has been widely discussed in the existing literature and at employment services programs themselves. Ex-offenders are often considered to make good counselors, because they can more easily identify with the client. This may result both in greater understanding of the client's needs and in a lesser likelihood of being manipulated (or "conned") by the client. Additionally, some staff members think that certain clients may be more at ease with ex-offender counselors and that this will lead to greater honesty and openness, resulting in early identification of problems and high levels of client success.

Ex-offender counselors may pose problems, however. One problem which may occur from selecting an insufficiently mature ex-offender of the same background as the client is that the two may become stuck on the point of their fight against the "establishment," [which] becomes the scapegoat; no behavior change is demanded, and no responsibility is accepted, though the staff member may teach the participant how to beat the system.

Another problem arises when ex-offender staff think that their status as ex-offenders automatically makes them good counselors. Such staff members may resist efforts to train them in counseling techniques. In addition, ex-offenders may experience a number of role conflicts, caused by having "establishment" jobs where they deal with clients experiencing a community readjustment which the ex-offender counselors may themselves have undergone quite recently. Also, in some cases ex-offender staff may be so assertive about rejecting their criminal past that they antagonize clients, rather than creating the rapport with them which is often considered an advantage of ex-offender counselors.

Paraprofessionals receive a lower salary than professionals employed by the same agency. Some professionals in p/p agencies believe that the presence of lower-paid paraprofessionals may undermine their efforts at securing salary increases and other benefits. Some contend that the willingness of paraprofessionals to accept lower rates of pay than professionals is often the *real* reason that they are employed.

Some probation and parole officers maintain that paraprofessionals overidentify with clients, sometimes in opposition to the agency and its policies. However, others maintain the opposite—that paraprofessionals tend to overidentify with the agency (and middle-class values) and are less flexible than their professional colleagues; other observers, however, have not found either criticism to be valid.

Parole Officer Aide Program*

Probably the best known use of ex-offenders in p/p is the Ohio Parole Officer Aide Program (POA), which began in 1972. Ex-parolees who had been discharged from parole for at least six months and had been employed during that time were recruited. In addition, they could not have a long history of assaultive crimes or pending charges, and had to be free of psychopathology (as determined from parole files). The ex-offender had to demonstrate at least average intelligence and good communicative skills. They are described as the "winners" within the "offender-class."

The aides participate in a 40-hour formal instructional sequence offered to new parole officers at Ohio's Correctional Academy and must complete a six-month probationary period as required of all Ohio civil servants. They do the same work as regular parole officers, although they cannot make arrests or carry firearms. Their caseloads traditionally have had persons with more severe criminal records and multiple problems—the "loosers," who had been given up on.

A career ladder has been built into the program so that POAs can become full-fledged parole officers. Since the program began, two POAs have been promoted to other positions, one as a parole officer and the other as a correctional counselor.

---

*This section is based on Joseph E. Scott, *Ex-offenders as Parole Officers* (Lexington, Mass.: D.C. Heath, 1975); and Carol Holliday Blew, Kenneth Carlson, and Paul Chernoff, *Only Ex-offenders Need Apply: The Ohio Parole Officer Aide Program* (Washington, D.C.: U.S. Government Printing Office, 1976).

The Ohio Adult Authority reported on the outstanding features and the weakness of the POA Program*:

The most significant feature of utilizing ex-offenders as Parole Officer Aides is their obvious ability to bridge the communication gap with hard-core offenders. The 2.8 percent recidivism rate is extremely low and this reduction has resulted in savings to taxpayers in terms of costs of incarcerations. Further input from the ex-offender in developing treatment strategies has been very significant in modifying behavior. Moreover, the "reformed delinquents" have spoken to 5000 high school students regarding the fallacy of criminal careers. The students were given an opportunity to discuss their personal problems with the ex-offender—a person who has been there and tells it like it is. Further, we have demonstrated that a female ex-offender can be successful in supervising male offenders.

Two areas which are significant should be discussed. First, Aides were not employed using academic accomplishments as a criterion but were screened more on their knowledge of the criminal subculture and their ability to effectively relate this information to bring about change in the behavior of offenders they were counseling. The lack of comprehensive writing skills has created problems; however we have instituted a remedial program at the onset of training.

Second, law enforcement agencies have not fully accepted the use of ex-offenders in some areas. As a group they are opposed to the program, but individually they are receptive. In 95 percent of the law enforcement agencies throughout Ohio, the Aides are accepted and have full access to records of the police and courts. Some departments have put out broad general policies concerning ex-offenders visiting their agencies but do not adhere to the policies. It is interesting that Aides working in the same office have differential communication patterns with law enforcement agencies. It appears that policies are instituted to ban a certain Aide. It is probably more correct to say that 95 percent of our Aides have no difficulty in communicating with law enforcement and court personnel.

In a review of the evaluation literature on the POA program, Carlson and Parks conclude (1979: 230):

Overall, Ohio's Parole Officer Aide Program has been given positive, often superlative, ratings from almost everyone associated with it, including the Law Enforcement Assistance Administration. The aides have performed well in their employment and have received outstanding praise and acknowledgement for their contribution to the field of corrections.

Volunteers

Probation in the United States originated as a volunteer service, and it is in probation that the tradition was reactivated in 1959 by Keith J. Leenhouts, judge of the Royal Oak, Michigan, Municipal Court. Estimates of the number of volunteers range from 300,000 to 500,000 throughout the United States. Judge Leenhouts remains a leading

*Personal communication from Nick J. Sanborn, Regional Supervisor, Ohio Adult Authority, March 26, 1976.

figure in the volunteer movement and through his efforts a national organization, *Volunteers in Probation* (Prevention, Prosecution, Prison, Parole), or simply VIP, was formed as a division of the National Council on Crime and Delinquency. The organization publishes a newsletter, *The VIP Examiner,* which reports on the activities of volunteers in criminal justice.* VIP also established a National Criminal Justice Volunteer Resource Service Center at the University of Alabama,† where *The VIP Examiner* is published.

Carlson and Parks report four models of volunteer assignments (1979: 237):

1. The 1:1 model, where the volunteer, on a one-to-one basis, seeks to obtain the trust and confidence of the probationer and helps him to maintain his existence, clarify his role in society, and plan for the future.
2. The supervision model, where the volunteer, who works as a case aid to a probation officer, provides services to a number of probationers.
3. The professional model, where the volunteer, who is a professional or semi-professional in his field, provides special services to a number of probationers.
4. The administrative model, where the volunteer assists with project administrative functions and interacts only indirectly with probationers.

A frequently cited program is the *Volunteer Probation Counselor Program* in Lincoln, Nebraska (Ku et al., 1975). With the increase in dispositions of probation, especially for young offenders, professional probation resources are often unable to keep pace with the growing caseloads. To meet this problem, the Lincoln program assigns high-risk misdemeanants‡ between the ages of 16 and 25 to a volunteer for supervision and assistance. The youth and the volunteer are matched on the basis of mutual interests and the probationer's interpersonal needs. The volunteers are carefully screened and trained in counseling. Each volunteer works with only one probationer, and after the assignment is complete, he/she can agree to be reassigned to another offender.

Volunteers are recruited through the news media and by probation officers who appear as speakers before community and University of Nebraska groups. The screening process includes psychological testing and examines the applicant's motives for wanting to become a counselor. Training involves three sessions totaling eight hours, during which applicants are given a description of the program, a review of relevant community resources, and instruction in counseling techniques. Volunteers are sworn in by a judge at a formal ceremony at which they receive identification cards.

The program is coordinated by a member of the probation staff, and the volunteers

*VIP can be reached at 200 Washington Square Plaza, Royal Oak, Michigan 48067.
†P.O. Box 1935, University, Alabama 35486.
‡A high-risk offender was described as likely to commit additional offenses because of the presence of some or all of the following conditions: significant mental or emotional problems, antisocial attitudes, a relatively unstable family or living situation, antiauthority attitudes, and relatively limited personal assets.

also receive ongoing supervision and guidance from probation staff members. There are regular monthly seminars and the performance of each volunteer is evaluated with a view toward success in reducing recidivism. The clients are also asked for their opinion of the volunteers' availability and effectiveness. A study revealed that there has been a considerable reduction in recidivism because of the program, while there were no expenses beyond the time requirements of recruiting, training, and supervising the volunteers, about 12 percent of the total probation staff time. Chris Eskridge and Eric Carlson report that a comparison was made between the volunteer project and the regular probation program, using 44 randomly assigned high-risk probationers. This study revealed a volunteer recidivism rate of 15 percent and a regular recidivism rate of 64 percent (1979: 178).

In 1971, the Tarrant County (Fort Worth, Texas) Juvenile Probation Department began using a novel volunteer program called *Recreation and Rap*. It provides for group activities such as arts and crafts, sports, and role playing for probationers, using volunteers and professional staff. The program has the following purposes ("Recreation and Rap," 1975: 5):

1. To provide the probationer with an opportunity to experience success in activities of a creative nature and to broaden the opportunity for constructive experiences.
2. To provide youth with relationships with adults not employed by school, police, or the probation department, based on a concern and a desire to give of one's self. It is believed that the awareness that volunteers give of themselves without pay can lead to a positive experience with adults for the child in the program.
3. To afford a positive peer-group experience, in settings other than delinquent, that will fill some of the needs that precipitated the child's delinquent behavior.
4. To provide increased exposure, quantitative and qualitative, to probation officers, volunteers, and programs in an effort to bring about new experiences and change, not only in behavior but in attitudes and values.
5. To more closely involve the community in constructive relationships with delinquents.

There has been an increase in the use of volunteers in parole, with the American Bar Association, the Jaycees, and other professional and civic groups initiating volunteer programs. The ABA's National Volunteer Parole Aide Program (VPA) began in 1971; since that time over 3200 volunteer lawyers and 2500 parolees have participated in the program in more than 20 states. The VPA pairs volunteer attorneys with parolees to provide one-to-one assistance in all service areas, excluding legal help, as it was believed that the attorney-client relationship would interfere with the development of an interpersonal relationship between the parolee and the volunteer.

The volunteer attorneys help inmates to secure parole release residences and employment, and provide job counseling, tutoring, and help with personal problems. They have been particularly successful in helping to secure services for parolees from public agencies. The ABA notes that lawyers who enter parole as volunteers bring with them a knowledge of the criminal justice system, and prestige that makes their acceptance by parole agency management an easier task.

However, a study by John Berman of the VPA Program indicates that it "had no effect on arrest rates and no effect on employment rates, salaries, or job satisfaction." Berman notes that the average subject studied had been out six months before he/she became involved in the VPA Program. He states that the most critical period for parolees is generally the first month out of prison, and this could account for some of his findings (1975: 111–12).

PROJECT CREST*

The Gainesville, Florida Project CREST is a unique volunteer effort joining together the University of Florida and the Florida Youth Services Program (YSP).

CREST volunteers come from the University of Florida's Department of Counselor Education, which requires graduate students to complete three to five practica (10-week work experiences in their field of specialization). CREST is one of several programs students may choose to fulfill that requirement. During each practicum, students receive academic credit for working 20 hours a week in their chosen agency while continuing to take classes at the University. Students enrolled in the two-year graduate specialist program must also complete a one quarter internship during which they work full time in the agency of their choice. Doctoral students are required to complete a full year of internship.

A smaller number of CREST workers, known as counselor aides, come from Santa Fe Community College, also in Gainesville. These are undergraduate students who, unlike the University's graduate students, are not required to complete courses in counseling before beginning their work experience. Counselor aides begin as tutors or "big brothers or sisters," and move into counseling only after some experience and training at CREST.

Finally, there are a few volunteers from the community, usually people with previous experience working with youngsters in trouble, who serve as tutors.

Supervision of Volunteers

All new volunteers receive an intensive twelve-hour orientation and training workshop before they are paired with clients. Staff and volunteers meet together every week for at least an hour to review cases, discuss problems and exchange ideas for treatment. In addition to the full staff meeting, which is mandatory for all personnel, volunteers meet each week with their team leaders, all of whom began as CREST volunteer counselors. Team leaders know all of the clients assigned to their team members and are able to provide first-hand knowledge and much-needed encouragement for counselors. They

---

*National Institute of Justice 1980.

are also able to smooth the transition for the longer term client from one volunteer to another.

Counselors also meet weekly with each client's probation officer to discuss problems and progress. In addition, at the end of every month, counselors submit detailed reports of their work to the project director, and before each practicum they prepare a written report on each client for submission to the YSP.

The University of Florida requires practicum students to meet with professors each week, individually and in groups. Each student is required to submit seven recordings of counseling sessions to individual and group criticism. The group sessions sometimes include students working in agencies other than CREST, giving volunteers an opportunity to learn from experiences of their peers in other settings.

The Clients

Probation officers decide which youngsters to refer to CREST. They tend to refer neither the hardest nor the easiest cases to the program. They are likely to send difficult cases, youngsters who, despite their behavior, might be responsive to counseling.

CREST counseling is designed to build trust and increase the client's sense of self worth and self awareness, so that youngsters not only understand better why they do the things they do, but can better plan and control their actions.

CREST counselors attempt to develop a helping relationship with clients using a variety of counseling techniques and therapy models taught in the University's Department of Counselor Education. Individual counselors are encouraged to choose the techniques that they feel are most appropriate for each client. They may use reality therapy to help some youngsters confront the problems of the present rather than living in the past or in a fantasy world. In other cases, it may be necessary to separate irrational associations in the client's mind ("I did something bad; therefore, I am bad."). Or perhaps a client centered approach which focuses on the youngster's needs and perspectives is the basis upon which counseling proceeds. But whatever method a counselor chooses to use with a particular youngster, the basic approach of all CREST workers is non-authoritarian and oriented toward the feelings and attitudes of the clients.

In addition to individual and family counseling, CREST workers often organize small group sessions to help clients learn that their problems are not unique and to encourage them to help each other. Counselors often spend extra time with their clients, attending cultural or sports events or participating in recreational activities.

How Does Crest Work with Probation Officers?   CREST workers are taught to be part of a treatment *team* and to work closely with the responsible juvenile authorities. CREST's dual treatment concept underlies the relationship between CREST and the Youth Services Program. Probation officers provide structure and limits and can invoke sanctions. CREST counselors provide guidance and support in a non-threatening, helping environment.

In fact, YSP staff see CREST as an important supplement to probation. Before CREST came along, they had to be both probation officers and counselors, and many of them found those roles conflicting. CREST's assumption of some responsibility for counseling has reduced this tension. And CREST has also dramatically increased the amount of counseling time provided to clients. While CREST workers have no fixed schedule for counseling, they usually see their clients once or twice a week, the family once a week, and the school once every other week. Often probation officers, who may have more than fifty clients in their caseloads, are only able to see each client once a month for an hour or so.

Sometimes clients tell counselors about offenses they have committed that the probation officer doesn't know about. CREST's stated policy is to give priority to the trust between counselor and client, except where a danger to life is involved. Probation officers understand and respect this position.

Probably the most extensive use of volunteers in probation and parole is in Japan. When that country reorganized its noninstitutional treatment system after World War II, there was a debate over whether or not p/p services should be thoroughly professionalized. Because of a shortage of funds and a large potential for volunteers, a new organization combining professional and volunteer workers was formed. The 1950 Volunteer Probation Officer Law resulted in nearly 50,000 persons being nominated as Volunteer Probation Officers (VPO).

The VPO performs all the supervisory functions normally assigned to a p/p officer in the United States. The VPO is considered a public official of the national government and is entitled to the benefit of compensation if injured while performing his/her duties. The VPO receives no salary but is paid a minimal amount for expenses related to training and travel. As in the United States, the VPO program depends on a sense of mission and purpose to provide motivation for volunteer workers. In addition to the gratificiation that each VPO feels, there is a great deal of prestige and public recognition. Candidates for the VPO position are screened by an advisory committee of criminal justice specialists, and those who pass the screening are appointed by the Minister of Justice. A national federation links VPO associations throughout the country.

The actual supervision process in p/p in Japan is carried out through the collaborative efforts of the VPO and a professional probation officer. However, field work is handled by the volunteers and probation officers rarely involve themselves in field work after they have assigned a case to a volunteer. The VPOs submit regular reports to the probation officers and only when an unusual situation arises do probation officers make a field visit (Rehabilitation Bureau, 1970: 1–59).

Criticism

Some p/p agencies and staff members are critical of the use of volunteers. They may view the efforts of volunteers as interference with their prerogatives, and they may be concerned about sharing information with volunteers because of the confidential aspect of p/p practice. Some of the criticisms leveled at paraprofessionals are also used against volunteers in p/p.

Since volunteers are not paid, they need to derive some satisfaction from their work. Satisfaction results when there is a level of success, and to be successful volunteers require adequate training and supervision. Although the use of volunteers is often viewed as "free," the per client cost in Royal Oak in 1980 was estimated at about $650 annually (Knezevic, 1980: 7). Eskridge and Carlson report that an extensive review of voluntary programs "found volunteers to be at least as effective in reducing recidivism and improving probationer self-concept as the traditional system" (1979: 186). However, they question whether the improvements in offender behavior is qualitative, or merely indicative of a short-term cosmetic effect.

Eskridge and Carlson note that in some programs the regular workers see the volunteers as a threat to their jobs (p. 184). Some resented the fact that volunteers were able to play the "good guy" while they had the control and enforcement functions. Some complained of volunteers acting as advocates for the offender in opposition to the regular worker. Carlson and Parks report, however, that the lack of success of a volunteer program seems to be a function of management operations rather than the volunteer concept (1979: 242). Faulty management includes the inability to process and assign volunteers expeditiously, inadequate volunteer training, poor supervision and/or support for volunteers, and a lack of communication between volunteers and probation officers.

In the following case study, a psychosocial diagnosis provides the basis for a plan of treatment that integrates professional and volunteer help for a disturbed 17-year-old probationer.

CASE HISTORY*

Person and Offense.   M.M. was a 17-year-old male who was charged with drunkenness while engaging in a typical behavior pattern: drinking, fighting, and goofing around. The youth's problems with authority figures were long-standing; he had been referred for psychiatric treatment while in the fourth grade. The previous year he committed seven criminal offenses which involved destructive acting out or thefts.

Family.   M.M. was the oldest of seven children. The father was an alcoholic who maintained full-time employment. The mother was a kind, understanding person, overburdened with a large family and the father's drinking problem. The youth moved out of the family home because of recurring fights with his father. M.M. lived with his grandparents when arrested.

Education.   The youth did not complete tenth grade because of low grades and lack of interest. He had average intellectual ability.

---

*From Richard Ku, *The Volunteer Probation Counselor Program, Lincoln, Nebraska* (Washington, D.C.: Government Printing Office, 1975), pp. 57–62.

Employment.   The youth worked about 30 hours each week for his grand-father on a garbage route. He earned enough spending money to get by and did not worry about losing his job if he missed work.

Self and Interpersonal Relationships.   Because of the potential for serious antisocial behavior. M.M. was referred for additional psychological evalua-tion. At the time of the psychological assessment, M.M. had been on a 30-day drinking binge. The youth was pale, emaciated, distraught, and had teeth marks on his left hand. He could not recall much of what had happened to him during previous weeks, although he did acknowledge some blackouts from the exces-sive alcohol use. The youth was moderately depressed, felt hurt, rejected, lonely, and very insecure. He did appear to realize that drinking did not solve problems but only increased them.

The short-term goals were to stabilize the life situation of this individual by encouraging support from the family. He moved back into the family home, where family members made an honest effort to be supportive and sympathetic. Frequent contact with the professional staff also occurred. The basic approach was to be sensitive, warm, accepting, and concerned.

The psychological evaluation indicated that the personality structure was immature and ill suited for coping with adult responsibilities. Dependency needs were prominent, although often denied. This youth would often express his needs for independence and for handling situations on his own. He often resented people trying to tell him what to do, especially authority figures. However, unconsciously the young man greatly feared independence. Conse-quently, it was likely that gestures toward independence would be short-lived. The joys of irresponsibility and pleasure-seeking had great appeal to him. His self concept resembled an irresponsible, playful little boy who enjoyed having fun but who could not control what happened to him. He felt almost totally at the mercy of his surroundings. His self-esteem was very low. Feelings of deprivation, inferiority, loneliness, and resentment were present. Although the youth often talked big, he was very insecure and genuinely doubted his own ability to be successful. He was aloof from others, so that he was not attracted to or influenced by his friends, who were antisocial persons. He appeared to share with them an interest in drinking and expressing anger at authorities.

Resentment appeared to stem from his subconscious feeling of inferiority and the realization that he was often a failure. Much of his acting-out behavior had the quality of self-punishment. This kind of a youth could very easily give up on himself and ensure ultimate failure by breaking the law and getting himself put in prison.

Fear of his own impulses was great. Heterosexual relationships were very threatening to him and likely to produce feelings of inadequacy and inferiority. Aggressiveness, self-assertive behavior, and competing with others were likely to be inconsistently exhibited.

Dependent relationships appeared to be the only kind which would make him feel more secure. The youth appeared to get along well with older people, such as his grandparents. He also had very positive feelings toward his mother, whom he perceived as an understanding, affectionate, and caring person. Some mixed feelings about the father were present. The prediction was that he would be able to readjust to the family situation, although problems with authority and getting along with his own father were likely to recur.

The youth appeared to be very vulnerable to situational pressure. When situational stress occurred, his coping skills were likely to include drinking, running away, or fighting.

The youth appeared to have virtually no insight into himself as a person. He was remarkably insensitive to his own feelings. He was also remarkably insensitive to the needs and wishes of other persons.

Summary of In-depth Psychological Evaluation

1. The potential for more serious criminal offenses was very great.
2. Self-defeating behavior was a serious problem that could take the form of acting out which would lead to prison. Punishment through incarceration would confirm his continuing feelings of inferiority and inadequacy.
3. The youth appeared to be unable to benefit from professional treatment. He had virtually no insight into himself or the kinds of verbal skills needed to participate successfully in professional counseling. Furthermore, he was very threatened by any suggestion that he might be mentally disturbed.
4. The youth required external structure to make a stable adjustment. The exaggerated dependency needs indicated that he would feel secure with structure but that if he began to perceive the structure as authoritarian, he would resent the situation and begin to act out against the authority.
5. This was a very fragile individual whose overall adjustment was tenuous.
6. The change process was likely to be time consuming, with setbacks expected.

Relationships Needed.   Primary counseling; professional staff.

Volunteer Probation Counselor.   A 53-year-old airport executive was selected. The volunteer was a personable, likeable, self-assured individual who appeared to have good common sense. The man was a grandfatherly type of person who would not threaten M.M. in a relationship. Both M.M. and the volunteer counselor held conventional values. There was therefore little danger of a generation gap between them.

Counseling.   The youth responded well to the security of the family situation and the attention he received from the professional staff and the volunteer probation counselor. He reenrolled in high school and continued to work part time. He resolved to turn his life around and, for a while was able to devote his energy to achieving his goal. However, despite the diminishing of emotional pressure from the arrest, the familiar patterns of irresponsibility, acting out, and drinking behavior emerged.

Counseling was focused to deal with attitudes toward authority figures, especially the police. M.M. was implicated in a theft again but no legal charges were filed. The theft was retaliation against former friends, also high-risk offenders, who had stolen from him. He was tempted to get back with his old crowd of antisocial friends but did not. His attendance at school became irregular. Indeed, the only way to guarantee that he would attend school was for his mother to drive him. Despite occasional setbacks, he began to feel some rewards from his new life-style. He received praise at school for some of his accomplishments. Parents and staff praised him for breaking off with his antisocial acquaintances, who were often in jail. Gradually, the appeal of the new style became greater for him. As he became more successful, however, a new period of conflict and emotional stress occurred.

The basic problem was the long-term feeling of low self-esteem and fear of success. Because the youth perceived himself to be a failure, he greatly feared success and began to engage in self-defeating behavior. A crisis occurred when the youth was selected to be a spokesman for his school. He was to speak before educators about the special education program he was in. He panicked, became very insecure and very anxious, and began drinking. He was being pushed too far too fast. He handled the problem by running away. He left the state; his trip included more drinking, some fighting, and several scrapes which could have led to criminal charges being filed. Eventually, he ran out of money and returned home. A period of depression, emotional insecurity, feelings of guilt, and the need for support from others followed. Gradually, he was able to put himself together. Although progress continued to be steady, occasional periods of running away followed by feelings of guilt and embarrassment occurred.

Although the youth eventually began to feel comfortable with his external situation, he feared the loss of security that he had achieved on probation. He asked that his probation period be extended for another year. To be certain this would occur, he committed an additional minor traffic offense shortly before the end of probation. A tense courtroom scene occurred where he kept pleading guilty to the offense despite cries from his own attorney that he was not guilty and they could beat the ticket. The youth had strong needs to be found guilty, which he believed would guarantee additional probation for him.

Progress.   During the entire two-year period he received only one minor traffic ticket, which he deliberately caused himself. Otherwise, he was not charged with any additional offenses. Furthermore, during the second year, he usually avoided any kind of antisocial behavior.

The youth was able to complete his high school education. He maintained steady employment on a part-time basis. He was able to obtain a full-time job with a reputable firm and had good prospects for a career. He was very satisfied with the position. He paid off all debts and established an excellent credit rating for himself. Because of his excellent credit rating he was able to obtain a loan to purchase a new automobile, which he used to reward himself for his past two years of accomplishments. The youth took great pride in himself and his accomplishments. He was better able to perceive himself as a successful person.

Post-Probation.   Shortly after the probation period, he got married and tried to establish a home for himself. Unfortunately, the marriage did not go well and problems began to occur. The youth had invested much of himself, with the fantasy of a good marital life and a comfortable family situation. He was very frustrated and unable to cope with his new life and domestic strife. He also felt too embarrassed to ask for more help through probation but instead began to experience some minor problems on the job and with social relationships. He incurred two additional alcohol-related offenses, which finally forced him to his senses. He sought additional help on an informal basis. Another crisis in his life situation existed, but he could now deal directly with feelings about himself and self-esteem, which he had been unable to do before.

Because he had been able to gain some successes for himself, he was better able to look at himself objectively and see some personal weaknesses. He met with a professional staff member for informal counseling, during which time the opportunity for development of greater understanding and insight occurred. He could only tolerate so much counseling, and the change was slow.

Following the short-term professional counseling, he entered yet another period of relative stability. For two years he led a generally healthy and productive life where he was very successful with his career. He has not had additional problems with the law. The question remains as to how long the young man will be able to lead a stable and productive life. He will probably always be vulnerable to some situational stress.

ITEMS FOR STUDY

1. There are three systems used to fill p/p officer positions.
2. There are a number of qualities that are important for p/p officers to possess.
3. The role of women in p/p has, until recently, differed from that of men.
4. The use of nonprofessionals—paraprofessionals and volunteers—has advantages and disadvantages. In addition, paraprofessionals are often ex-offenders, thus offering additional advantages and disadvantages.

PART IV

SPECIAL PROGRAMS AND RESEARCH

chapter 19

Special
Programs

INTERSTATE COMPACT

In 1937, a group of states signed the Interstate Compact for the Supervision of Probationers and Parolees. By 1951, all 50 states, Puerto Rico, and the Virgin Islands were signatories of the compact. The compact provides a method for a person under supervision to leave the state of conviction and proceed to another state for employment, family, or health reasons, and at the same time guarantees that the receiving state will provide supervision of the offender. The state of original jurisdiction where the crime was committed retains authority over the offender and is kept advised of his/her whereabouts and activities.

Prior to the establishment of the compact, thousands of convicted felons were permitted to leave the state of conviction with no verified or approved plan in the receiving state. On occasion, dangerous criminals were released by states and permitted to enter other states without the knowledge of any official body of the receiving state. The compact provides a systematic method for supervision purposes for the receiving state to verify and approve a plan of residence and employment or education before a probationer or parolee is permitted to enter the state. The compact also regulates interstate travel by probationers and parolees. Each state issues a travel pass, a copy of which is sent to the Interstate Administrator, who notifies the receiving state of the impending visit.

¶The Association of Administrators of the Interstate Compact, which meets at least once per year, prepares uniform reports and procedures and attempts to reconcile any difficulties that have arisen with respect to the compact. The Council of State Governments acts as a secretariat for the Association and publishes the *Interstate Movement of Probationers and Parolees Under the Probation and Parole Compact.*

Some problems remain. One problem exists because of the differences in probation and parole administration. In all states parole is an executive function with statewide procedures; interstate activities are centralized through a compact administrator in each state. However, probation is often administered on a county basis, and it may lack statewide coordination. The local autonomy that often exists in the court system can cause difficulties in utilizing and administering the pact in probation cases.

Another problem results from different approaches to supervision in various states. One state may exercise close control and require strict enforcement of the conditions of probation or parole. Another state may be more flexible, or it may be incapable of close supervision and control because of the size of caseloads. When a "strict" state notifies a "liberal" sending state that one of its probationers or parolees is in violation, the sending state may not consider it serious, and may leave the offender in the receiving state with a request that they continue supervision. In some cases, the sending state may not wish to incur the expense of transporting a violator back to one of its state prisons. The receiving state has two options: continue to supervise an offender it considers in violation, or discontinue supervision and leave the offender with no controls at all. P/p officers faced with this dilemma generally continue supervision, since it is preferable to leaving an offender without any controls.

States sometimes allow probationers and parolees to go to a receiving state under the guise of a visit, when the offender's intentions are to stay permanently. The receiving state is then contacted by the sending state to investigate "with a view toward accepting supervision." The receiving state is faced with a *fait accompli.*

INTERSTATE COMPACT FOR THE SUPERVISION
OF PAROLEES AND PROBATIONERS

CONSENTED TO BY THE CONGRESS
OF THE UNITED STATES OF AMERICA
1934

The Uniform Enabling Act

(Contains the exact wording of the Interstate Compact for the
Supervision of Parolees and Probationers)

AN ACT PROVIDING THAT THE STATE OF . . . MAY ENTER INTO A COMPACT WITH ANY OF THE UNITED STATES FOR MUTUAL HELPFULNESS IN RELATION TO PERSONS CONVICTED OF CRIME OR OFFENSES WHO MAY BE ON PROBATION OR PAROLE

Be it enacted, etc.:

Section 1. The governor of this state is hereby authorized and directed to execute a compact on behalf of the state of——————with any of the United States legally joining therein in the form substantially as follows:

A Compact

Entered into by and among the contracting states, signatories hereto, with the consent of the Congress of the United States of America, granted by an act entitled "An act granting the consent of Congress to any two or more states to enter into agreements or compacts for cooperative effort and mutual assistance in the prevention of crime and for other purposes."

The contracting states solemnly agree:

(1) That it shall be competent for the duly constituted judicial and administrative authorities of a state party to this compact (herein called "sending state"), to permit any person convicted of an offense within such state and placed on probation or released on parole to reside in any other state party to this compact (herein called "receiving state"), while on probation or parole, if

(a) Such person is in fact a resident of or has his family residing within the receiving state and can obtain employment there:

(b) Though not a resident of the receiving state and not having his family residing there, the receiving state consents to such person being sent there.

Before granting such permission, opportunity shall be granted to the receiving state to investigate the home and prospective employment of such person.

A resident of the receiving state, within the meaning of this section, is one who has been an actual inhabitant of such state continuously for more than one year prior to his coming to the sending state and has not resided within the sending state more than six continuous months immediately preceding the commission of the offense for which he has been convicted.

(2) That each receiving state will assume the duties of visitation of and supervision over probationers or parolees of any sending state and in the exercise of those duties will be governed by the same standards that prevail for its own probationers and parolees.

(3) That duly accredited officers of a sending state may at all times enter a receiving state and there apprehend and retake any person on probation or parole. For that purpose no formalities will be required other than establishing the authority of the officer and the identity of the person to be retaken. All legal requirements to obtain extradition of fugitives from justice are hereby expressly waived on the part of states party hereto, as to such persons. The decision of the sending state to retake a person on probation or parole shall be conclusive upon and not reviewable within the receiving state, *Provided, however,* That if at the time when a state seeks to retake a probationer or parolee there should be pending against him within the receiving state any criminal charge, or he should be suspected of having committed within such state a criminal offense, he shall not be retaken without the consent of the receiving state until discharged from prosecution or from imprisonment for such offense.

(4) That the duly accredited officers of the sending state will be permitted to transport prisoners being retaken through any and all state parties to this compact, without interference.

(5) That the governor of each state may designate an officer who, acting jointly with like officers of other contracting states, if and when appointed,

shall promulgate such rules and regulations as may be deemed necessary to more effectively carry out the terms of this compact.

(6) That this compact shall become operative immediately upon its execution by any state as between it and any other state or states so executing. When executed it shall have the full force and effect of law within such state, the form of execution to be in accordance with the laws of the executing state.

(7) That this compact shall continue in force and remain binding upon each executing state until renounced by it. The duties and obligations hereunder of a renouncing state shall continue as to parolees or probationers residing therein at the time of withdrawal until retaken or finally discharged by the sending state. Renunciation of this compact shall be by the same authority which executed it, by sending six months' notice in writing of its intention to withdraw from the compact to the other state party hereto.

Section 2. If any section, sentence, subdivision or clause of this act is for any reason held invalid or to be unconstitutional, such decision shall not affect the validity of the remaining portions of this act.

Section 3. Whereas an emergency exists for the immediate taking effect of this act, the same shall become effective immediately upon its passage.

COMMUNITY ARBITRATION

In an effort to provide an alternative to arrest and formal court processing, a number of programs, similar in operation, have been developed: Dispute Settlement Programs (Conner and Surette, 1977), Neighborhood Justice Centers (McGillis and Mullen, 1977), and Community Arbitration Projects (Blew and Rosenblum, 1979). In common they provide:

1. An alternative to arrest and formal court action.
2. Mediation and/or arbitration.
3. Social service staff or referral capability.

Because it developed directly out of a probation setting and utilizes informal probation and probation workers (called Field Site Supervisors), we will look at the *Community Arbitration Project* (CAP) in Anne Arundel County, Maryland.

Community Arbitration Project*

In 1973, the administrator of juvenile intake and probation services in Anne Arundel County confronted several management problems. Dramatic increases in juvenile

*This section is taken from Carol Holliday Blew and Robert Rosenblum, *The Community Arbitration Project: Anne Arundel County, Maryland* (Washington, D.C.: U.S. Government Printing Office, 1977).

complaints had created unmanageable caseloads for intake personnel and lengthy processing delays. It had become virtually impossible to screen juvenile referrals adequately or to fashion appropriate dispositions. Attempts to provide meaningful counseling or supportive services were hampered by the frequent and often lengthy delays between complaint and intake. According to the administrator, David Larom:

> It appeared to me that any efforts we were making at intake might have little meaning to the child since we were seeing him weeks, even months after the arrest. And furthermore, the sheer volume of cases that we were seeing made it expedient to process a case as quickly as we could. Basically, I questioned whether what we were doing was of any benefit to the victim, the child, the child's family, and even the arresting officer.

Criticism from the press and the public heightened the urgency to resolve these problems. The administrator and his staff began to explore various solutions that could be implemented quickly and that would not require substantial funding. Meetings were held with other juvenile justice personnel to learn their concerns and to solicit their cooperation on any steps that might be taken. In less than a year, the Community Arbitration Program was operating and providing a rapid, innovative means of handling eligible youth.

The Arbitration Process

The Citation.   City, county, and state police officers on duty in Anne Arundel County carry an Anne Arundel County juvenile citation booklet. Originally, the citations were to be used only for CAP-eligible offenses. However, after a year of issuing citations for CAP offenses, the police requested that citations be used for all juvenile charges. Since citations are signed by both the parent and the child at the scene of the incident or at the child's home, it represented a considerable time savings over the previous process of transporting the child and the parent to the station house.

When the officer believes that a juvenile has committed an offense, he/she issues a citation similar in appearance to a parking ticket. It contains information regarding the juvenile, the time and nature of the offense, and the complainant's name. The citation notes that failure to appear may result in the filing of a petition and that counsel can be present at the hearing. Both the juvenile and a parent are requested to sign the citation and each retains a copy along with the victim. The complainant (if there is one) also receives a copy. The citation accomplishes several objectives:

1. It emphasizes to the child *and* the parents that the child has been accused of an offense.
2. The child, parent, and complainant are each notified that a hearing *will* occur at a specific time and place, and that each party will have an opportunity to be heard.
3. It states to all parties that what will be taking place is an important legal matter, carrying certain responsibilities.

At issuance, the officer dates the notice to appear seven working days hence. A copy of the citation and the police report are forwarded to the Juvenile Services Agency

(JSA), where the youth's referral offense is checked against the CAP list of eligible offenses. If the offense is on the CAP list, these documents are forwarded to the CAP office, where the case is entered on the calendar for the appropriate date.

Generally, civilian complaints comprise one-half of the complaints brought against CAP youths and the other half are issued by police officers.

The Arbitration Hearing

The arbitration hearing is conducted in a courtlike setting which was deliberately chosen by the designers of CAP for several reasons. It visually emphasizes to the child that he/she has become involved with the juvenile justice system. The more formal setting of the arbitration hearing—in contrast to traditional intake hearings in intake offices—is presumed to enable the child to quickly comprehend the importance and meaning of the procedure with which he/she is involved.

The arbitrator is provided the following information on each case:

1. Any witness statements.
2. Police report.
3. Copy of the charges.
4. Copies of any prior intake or probation files that exist on the child.

The child is requested to sit alone in front of the arbitrator during the hearing. His/her parents are seated on benches behind him. The arbitration hearing, although held in the presence of the victim (should he/she choose to attend) is legally confidential and cannot be used or admitted into evidence in any subsequent criminal or civil litigation and juvenile court adjudicatory proceedings. This is explained to the child, together with his/her right to counsel and right to refuse any arbitration decision. The child and parent are then asked to decide whether they would like to continue with arbitration. If they choose not to continue, the arbitrator can refer the case to traditional intake or to the State's Attorney's office. The arbitrator discusses with both the child and parents the "Notice and Advice of Rights for Arbitration Hearings," which explains that participation is voluntary, that the hearing and all relevant records are confidential, and that the child has a right to an attorney, which will be provided by the state if the parents cannot afford to pay. If arbitration is chosen, the arbitrator will read the police report and then request the victim to explain his/her side. Finally, the child is given an opportunity to speak.*

The arbitrator may make one of five decisions

1. Close the case for insufficient evidence.
2. Close the case with a dispositional warning.

*The CAP process does not involve arbitration insofar as the process and the results are not binding on the youth, and approximately 50 percent of the time the victim is not present. The arbitrator, who is an officer of the court, represents the state.

3. Forward the case to the State's Attorney for the filing of a petition.
4. Informally adjust the case. In this case the child has admitted to the offense. The arbitrator explains that such an offense, if committed by an adult, would result in an arrest record and criminal conviction. Furthermore, the fact that a crime is an act not merely against the particular victim, but also against society at large, is discussed. The child is then told that since he/she has done something harmful to society he/she needs to do something beneficial. The child is then assigned a specific number of hours of community work, usually between 10 and 25 hours. In addition to community service work, counseling, restitution, educational program referral, or any combination of these may be assigned to the youth as part of the informal supervision assignment. The case is then left "open," to be closed upon a successful report (within 90 days).
5. The case can be continued for further investigation, after which time one of the four alternatives listed above is chosen.

Ninety-one percent of the juveniles appear for their first arbitration appointment. Another 4.5 percent appear at a second appointment. If the youth does not appear at the second appointment, the case is forwarded to the State's Attorney for further action. These figures represent a substantial gain over the previous system, in which an estimated 20 percent did not respond to letters requesting an appointment. Moreover, CAP estimates that about 50 percent of the civilian complainants choose to come to the informal hearings. Previously, complainants were infrequently involved in the proceedings in any way. Police complainants rarely attend.

The program employs two Field Site Supervisors, whose responsibilities involve supervising and counseling assigned youth (approximately 100 youth per Field Supervisor), and visiting job sites to monitor youths' performance during the 90-day period of informal supervision. At the beginning of the program and during its first two years, the Field Site Supervisors were responsible for recruiting agencies to use as work placement sites.

Night Prosecutor's Program

A similar program for adults is the Columbus, Ohio, Night Prosecutor's Program, which handles cases involving interpersonal disputes. The program, which began in 1971, uses law students as hearing officers for cases that are referred by the police or prosecutor's office. Arrests are avoided and no record of the case is entered on any official documents, although records are kept by the program to provide background if any of the parties return. The hearings are informal, allowing each party to tell his/her side of the story without interruption. When sanctions are necessary to ensure compliance with a decision, the program uses *prosecutor's probation*, whereby a person is on probation for 60 days. If the conditions of probation are violated, the filing of a criminal affidavit is authorized (J. Palmer, 1974: 12–18).

PRETRIAL PROBATION

The President's Commission noted that prosecutors often deal with offenders who need treatment or supervision but for whom criminal sanctions would be excessive (1972: 331). Programs implementing this theory are referred to by many names, including *pretrial diversion* and *deferred prosecution*. These programs use the fact that an arrest has occurred as a means of identifying defendants in need of treatment, or, at least, not in need of criminal prosecution. They generally incorporate specific eligibility criteria, a treatment program, and the opportunity to monitor and control the decision not to prosecute. In eligible cases, the prosecutor agrees not to prosecute for periods ranging from three to 12 months, contingent upon satisfactory performance during the pretrial supervision period. At the end of a successful pretrial supervision period, the charges are dismissed. Diversion helps to remove minimal-risk cases from crowded court calendars while providing treatment to those who are in need of this service (Mullen, 1974: 5–6).

A much publicized program is the Genessee County (Michigan) Citizen's Probation Authority which began operation in 1965. The program began using volunteers with social work and other related professional backgrounds, but it has been expanded to include paid staff. Most of the CPA cases involve adults who agree to submit to supervision in return for not being prosecuted. At the end of the supervision period, charges are dropped and police records are expunged.* To qualify for the CPA program, a defendant must not have committed a crime of violence or possess an extensive criminal history (National District Attorney's Association, 1973: 26).

The Des Moines Pre-Trial Release Project is patterned after the well-known Vera Project in New York City, and it permits defendants who are not able to make bail to be released on their own recognizance under the supervision of a counselor. Each defendant is interviewed after arraignment by a program interviewer, who is a part-time court employee recruited from the Drake University Law School. If a defendant is unable to provide bond and is considered a safe risk, he/she is released on recognizance pending trial. The program is aimed at persons who, though without sufficient financial assets, have significant family and community ties to guarantee their appearance in court. The program is directed primarily at lesser offenders, although persons accused of serious crimes will be considered under more stringent procedures.

The program proceeds on the basis of the following observation: A defendant who is incarcerated while awaiting trial has the probability of obtaining probation reduced "because of his inability to obtain or maintain those positive personal and environmental circumstances that courts look to in evaluating an individual's potential for community rehabilitation" (Mullen, 1974: 17). Emanating from this is the use of pretrial supervision, which is geared to helping defendants to "cope with problems, aiding the development of a more stable behavior pattern for the defendant and thereby obtaining a more favorable disposition of his case" (p. 19). The program does not concern itself with the guilt or innocence of the defendant.

*As a practical reality, this may be difficult, if not impossible, to accomplish.

DISCHARGE ORDER: DEFERRED SENTENCE

In the District Court of the State of Iowa
in and for Polk County

Name ———————————   *Crime* ———————————

Address ——————————   *Judge* ———————————

Date of Sentence —————   *Length of Sentence* —————

STATE OF IOWA,
        Plaintiff,   *Criminal No.:*
        vs.
        Defendant

NOW, on this ——— day of ——————, 19———, it appearing to the Court that the above named defendant entered a plea of guilty to the indictment in the above entitled cause: and,

    WHEREAS the Court, after investigation, placed the defendant on Probation under the supervision of the Department of Court Services; until the ——— day of ——————, 19———, and,

    WHEREAS the said defendant has fully complied with the conditions of said probation, and has earned and received the recommendation from the Probation Officer and the County Attorney of Polk County, Iowa; and

    WHEREAS the said defendant now be permitted to withdraw the plea of guilty and that the motion to dismiss this case be sustained.

    IT IS THEREFORE ORDERED that the defendant be, and is hereby authorized to withdraw a plea of guilty; that the withdrawal of the plea of guilty is accepted by this Court; and the motion to dismiss this case with prejudice be and the same is hereby sustained.

    Dated at Des Moins, Iowa this ——— day of ——————, 19 ——.
Approved:
                                    ———————————————
                                                            Judge

———————————————   ———————————————
Probation Officer   County Attorney

The Court Resource Project

Joan Mullen provides a look at Massachusetts' pretrial diversion program:*
    The Court Resource Project (TCRP) was established in 1971 under Department of Labor funds to operate within the Massachusetts court system. The entry-level

*The remainder of this section is taken from Joan Mullen, *The Dilemma of Diversion* (Washington, D.C.: U.S. Government Printing Office, 1974).

criminal justice system in Massachusetts consists of 73 District Courts. These "neighborhood courts" have jurisdiction over all misdemeanors and most felonies. The Court Resource Project was introduced into four such courts in 1971 as a program to:

1. Deliver effective manpower and social services to some of the city's most disadvantaged people.
2. Select and train street people and ex-offenders to perform as professional counselors.
3. Break into young adult offenders' incipient cycles of crime.

Conceived as an opportunity to increase alternatives to sentencing and to provide individual attention to first and less-serious offenders, the program was introduced cautiously to the conservative judicial system. The credibility it has achieved within the system is reflected in its expansion into other District Courts in the Boston area.

TCRP's involvement with its clients begins after the arrest and arraignment of the defendant, but before trial. Following a 14-day continuance for screening, orientation and assessment purposes, candidates who accept and are acceptable to the project and the courts, begin a 90-day period of project service. Successful completion of the project leads to a recommendation for the dismissal of pending charges.

TCRP Eligibility Criteria and Participant Characteristics

Although originally developed to serve males with no more than one prior conviction, soon after operations began the program broadened its criteria to include a small number of women and a significant number of second and third offenders. Formal eligibility guidelines include the following criteria:

1. Male or female.
2. 17 to 26 years old (at the project's discretion, older cases have been accepted).
3. Resident of the project area with a verifiable address.
4. Not a drug addict.
5. Unemployed or underemployed.
6. Not charged with a felony outside of District Court jurisdiction (in a select number of cases, alleged felons under Superior Court jurisdiction have been admitted).
7. No more than one or two prior convictions.

TCRP Screening and Intake Procedures

TCRP screeners spend every morning in the courts reviewing the cards of new arrests and discussing potential candidates with the probation office, the clerks, public defenders, the district attorney, the defendants themselves, and often, the complainant or victim and arresting officer. If the defendant expresses interest in the project and all relevant parties concur, a 10-day continuance for further screening and evaluation is requested at arraignment.

Following the preliminary screening process, the defendant is assigned a counselor or "advocate" and the intake process begins. The client and the advocate meet for a preliminary interview and an evaluation of the client's needs and problems. A case conference is held, with key staff members, including the client's advocate and the court screener in attendance. They discuss possible services that can be provided and decide, on a preliminary level, whether or not the client should be accepted into the program.

The Client Orientation Director then conducts a two-day workshop for clients as a group while the acceptance decision is still pending. The director assists clients in evaluating the extent to which they are personally independent and their ability to financially ensure this independence; the director also evaluates the ability of each prospective client to respond favorably to the services of the program.

Following the orientation meetings, clients meet frequently with their advocates and career developers. Throughout the remainder of the assessment period, the purpose is to develop a plan mutually acceptable to project staff and the defendant, and adequate for presentation to the court.

Assessment techniques are used selectively according to the project staff's perceptions of the defendant's needs. For example, tests may be administered to potential candidates for vocational training programs, simple reading tests are administered, school records, hospitalization records, and other records are checked.

At the end of the continuance period, if both parties agree, a recommendation is made to the court to place the individual in the care of the project for a 90-day period.

Service Delivery in TCRP

TCRP services focus on individual counseling, career development, and group work. All clients meet with their advocates at least once a week individually, and many advocates hold additional weekly group meetings. Each client also meets with a career developer who evaluates and implements career goals with the client and advocate. In addition to direct placements, both OJT and institutional job training programs receive heavy emphasis.

The project established a small in-house educational program using volunteer tutors. Those who are referred outside the project for educational assistance generally work toward a GED at the evening public high schools.

In addition to the project's direct service capabilities, TCRP utilizes a variety of local community service agencies for supportive service assistance. A local medical center under contract with TCRP provides early physical examinations and follow-up treatment. The Massachusetts Rehabilitation Commission has a rehabilitation counselor stationed at the TCRP facility and the Welfare Department has assigned an intake supervisor to the project. The welfare worker assists the project in developing client service plans and develops work incentive programs for TCRP clients.

TCRP Termination Procedures

Clients who complete a period of successful program participation reappear in court accompanied by a screener. On a motion entered by the defendant and his/her counsel, charges will usually be dismissed.

In the event a client demonstrates marked noncooperation with the project (or is involved in a new law violation resulting in conviction), a termination letter is forwarded to the court and the client is subject to normal court procedures.

CRITICISM

There have been several unanticipated *(latent)* and generally negative consequences of pretrial intervention programs. Ann Watkins (1975a, b) found that diversion services are usually more costly than is traditional probation—diversion services are usually more concentrated, hence expensive.* This raises two additional issues:

1. Are the generous funding resources that have been enjoyed by diversion programs at the expense of improved funding for probation services?
2. Would persons being serviced by (or subjected to) pretrial diversion ordinarily be diverted from criminal justice *in any event* as the result of failure to prosecute, dismissal, or receiving a fine or suspended sentence?

The latter question raises additional issues. Is diversion adding costs to criminal justice, in addition to not really reducing volume, by actually adding cases to the system that otherwise would have been screened out? There have been indications that when such a program exists:

1. Police officers will refer persons who otherwise would have merely been reprimanded or referred to social service agencies.
2. Prosecutors will send cases that they otherwise would have declined to prosecute.

Thus, diversion has the unintended potential for widening the net of criminal justice.

Gaylin cites an unnamed judge: "Deferred prosecution is what it is called, and in effect it means no prosecution. You postpone a criminal case indefinitely, you lose your witnesses—that's the end of it" (1974: 110). From a different perspective, deferred prosecution is criticized by Balch as the "juvenilization" of the adult criminal process, with all the inherent defects on due process of the pre-*Gault* juvenile court. Balch notes that although defendants must volunteer for these programs, their alternatives may be quite limited. For innocent defendants, accepting the program means that they are admitting guilt, even if they are not doing so in the legal sense of the term (1974: 46–50).

Mullen notes that although the overwhelming majority of programs do not require an admission of guilt, there is a presumption of guilt inherent in the system. She notes

---

*This criticism may not be valid in certain jurisdictions. In Missouri, for example, the prosecutor can suspend formal criminal processing and place the defendant under the supervision of the Missouri Board of Probation and Parole. In San Bernardino County, California, the Probation Department operates a juvenile diversion program which houses probation officers in police agencies throughout the county.

that if defendants fail on pretrial supervision, they are returned for prosecution that may be more vigorous than the original prosecution without any intervention would have been. Mullen states that in attempting to circumvent basic deficiencies in the administration of criminal justice (such as crowded court calendars), "a new system with its own attractions and deficiencies has begun to mature without furnishing convincing evidence that it has seriously affected the basic problems that attend the pre-trial criminal process." She suggests that greater efforts should be made to deal with the problem of delay in disposing of court cases or moving release or diversion back to an earlier stage, perhaps "pre-arrest" (1975: 29–34).

As a result of the concern expressed over the waiver of rights attendant to these programs, some have begun to provide legal counsel before a defendant is asked to agree to diversion. Nancy Goldberg states that "to ensure that any decision by a prospective divertee is truly voluntary, counsel must become involved from the very outset" (n.d.: 500).

PROBATION SUBSIDY

Robert Smith refers to the probation subsidy as "a form of behavioral modification applied to a social institution—probation" (1971: 2–3). Indeed, the allusion is appropriate: a positive reinforcement (money) is provided for each repeated occurrence of a certain behavior (sentence of probation). Although the probation subsidy has been used, sometimes in modified form, in several states, it originated in California. There the subsidy program provides state funds to counties for not committing defendants to state institutions. The more cases not sent to prison, the greater the subsidy. Counties are reimbursed in proportion to the number of cases that are placed on probation in lieu of prison. The level of funding is determined by taking a county's commitment rate for a representative period, thereby providing a yardstick (base experience rate) for measurement. Reductions in commitments are measured against the yardstick and used to determine the level of the subsidy for the county. Thus, if on the basis of a county's population and base experience rate the state could reasonably expect the county to commit 100 persons, but in fact the county only sent 90, 10 percent reduction was realized. These 10 cases represent a savings to the state, and the county is then reimbursed a portion of the money saved. Actual reimbursement varies from county to county based on the differences between them and the amount of effort that is required for a county to make a reduction (Smith, 1971: 28).

Probation in California is operated and financed on a county basis, and prior to the 1965 subsidy law, probation standards for the 58 counties were voluntary. The probation subsidy is based on three assumptions (Smith, 1971: 5):

1. Probation is as effective, if not more effective, than most institutional forms of correctional care.
2. Probation is the least costly correctional service available.
3. Probation grants can be increased without substantially increasing the number of

crimes committed by probationers. On the basis of several studies it was concluded that probation use by county courts could be expanded safely, thus diverting a substantial number of juveniles and adults away from state correctional institutions. These studies concluded that in order to expand the use of probation, the state must offer financial incentives: "Excessive probation caseloads and rising tax rates at the county level encouraged the probation officer to dispose of probation cases by recommending commitment to the Youth Authority or Department of Corrections" (pp. 8–10).

The results of the probation subsidy in California have been subjected to scrutiny by several researchers (Hirschi and Rudisill, 1977; Kuehn, 1973; Feeney and Hirschi, 1975; Barrett and Musolf, 1977). Their findings indicate that the program significantly reduced prison commitments, a minimum of 5000 cases annually, saving California taxpayers an actual net of $10 million annually (at 1975 prices). This saving was at the expense of a slight increase in crime, as measured by arrest rates. The subsidy accounted for between 3 and 18 percent of the *total increase in arrests* in California, 1.1 to 2.1 percent of the *total increase in arrests* being for crimes of violence.

Barkdull notes that although the subsidy in California was able to reduce the percentage of convicted adult felony defendants sentenced to prison, this trend has been reversed by the passage of laws restricting the granting of probation and mandating prison commitments (1976a: 230).

"SHOCK" PROBATION/PAROLE

Ohio has statutes that provide for the early release from prison of convicted felons either on probation (within 30 to 120 days of imprisonment) or parole (within six months of imprisonment). To be eligible for shock probation the offender must be otherwise eligible for a sentence of probation and has to file a petition with the court. Those not eligible for probation may file a request with the parole board for shock parole (which excludes those convicted of such crimes as rape, armed robbery, kidnapping, major drug violations, and some burglaries). Several states have similar statutes or practices whereby an offender is sentenced to incarceration for a specific, relatively short period followed by probation supervision. In states that have abolished the indeterminate sentence and parole supervision, judges may use this option in its place. Unlike the split sentence, however, shock probation/parole is not part of the original sentence.

Allen and his colleagues reviewed the evaluation literature on shock probation and report (1979: 174, edited):

Shock probation is in part based on the notion that the criminal justice system can equitably apply a sentencing alternative which combines both punishment and leniency. In practice, however, there is evidence that shock probation may be applied in a discriminatory manner, e.g., more favorable to whites. Second, it has been found that persons who were successful on shock probation were very similar to persons given regular probation. This raises questions about whether the shock probationers might have done just as well without the short-term incarceration. Third, it was found that the variables associated with failure on shock release were also associated with failure on regular probation. Fourth, in theory, the value of shock probation lies in the "shock" impact of imprisonment for a short period which avoids the negative effects of longer-term imprisonment. Research, however, indicates that imprisonment of only thirty days, the minimum required by law, is sufficient for the negative effects of imprisonment to be felt.

In sum, the research to date has failed to clearly establish the outcome effectiveness of shock probation as compared to alternative sanctions. The research, however, has documented the difficulties of equitably applying shock to offenders, the possible negative effects of the prison sanction, and the possibility that shock may be an unnecessary sanction.

The National Advisory Commission is critical of this type of program: "This type of sentence defeats the purpose of probation, which is the earliest possible reintegration of the offender into the community. Short-term commitment subjects the probationer to the destructive effects of institutionalization, disrupts his life in the community, and stigmatizes him for having been in jail" (1975: 321).

SHOCK PROBATION IN TEXAS*

The Texas Adult Probation Commission**

The 87 departments responding to the Survey reported their courts have placed 1044 adult felons on shock probation since August 29, 1977. Of these 1044 probationers, 289 were "shock revokees"; that is, they were placed on regular probation, had their probations revoked, were incarcerated, and then recalled from incarceration and placed on shock probation. These "shock revokees" would, in all likelihood, have remained in prison had there been no shock probation. Of the remaining 755 felons, a telephone follow-up indicated that approximately 50% (378) would have been incarcerated had there been no shock probation statute. Thus the total number of felons who would have been incarcerated had there been no shock probation statute is estimated to be 667.

The cost of maintaining a prisoner in Texas Department of Corrections is estimated to be $7.50 per day. The cost to the State of supervising a probationer is estimated to be $0.65 per day. A comparison can be made between maintaining a felon in TDC for two years (730 days) with a felon who is kept in TDC for 120 days and then released on shock probation for the remainder of a two-year sentence (610 days).

---

*Source: Division of Information Services, *TAPC Shock Probation Survey*. Austin: Texas Adult Probation Commission, 1980.

**A state agency that sets and supervises probation standards for the 107 locally autonomous adult probation departments throughout Texas.

(1) Cost to maintain
667 persons in TDC
for 2 years $667 \times 730 \times \$7.50 =$ $3,651,825

(2) Cost to maintain
667 persons in TDC
for 120 days $667 \times 120 \times \$7.50 =$ $600,300

(3) Cost of probation
supervision for 667
persons for 610 days $667 \times 610 \times \$0.65 =$ $264,466

(4) Cost of shock proba-
tion for 667 shock
probationers for 2
years $864,766
                                              $- \$\ \ 864,766$

(5) Net savings from use
of shock probation
rather than incarcera-
tion for 667 cases $2,787,059

These costs estimates are not intended to arrive at exact figures; however, they are conservative, considering that many sentences are for longer than two years.

Further, these costs estimates do *not* take into consideration such *indirect* cost savings, such as: (1) taxes paid by probationers, (2) family support paid by taxpayers, and (3) restitution to victims, payment of court costs, fines, and fees, all paid by probationers.

Since shock probation has been in effect for such a short time, only a small number of shock probationers entered into the cost comparisons shown earlier. In the long run, it can readily be seen that the cost of shock probation is considerably less than that of incarceration.

Of the 87 departments responding to the survey out of the 106 queried, 75 reported having used shock probation. From these 75 departments, 1078 adults have been placed on shock probation during the time span August 29, 1977 to April 8, 1980. Of this number, 808 shock probationers are still on probation, 49 have successfully terminated their probation, and 221 had unsuccessful probations. The 221 adults considered to have had unsuccessful probations were divided as follows: 121 had their probations revoked, 66 revocations were pending, 18 probationers had absconded, and 16 probationers were considered "unsuccessful," although their probations had not actually been revoked.

Prior knowledge of subsequent shock probation by the defendant is an important issue in shock probation. The 1980 TAPC Survey showed 66% of the departments responding expressed the opinion that in order for shock probation to be really effective, a defendant should not be informed of being placed on shock probation until recalled from incarceration. In contrast, it was reported that 65% of all felony shock probationers and 68% of all misdemeanor shock probationers had prior knowledge of subsequent shock probation.

Effectiveness of shock probation was rated in various ways. Overall, 71% of the responding departments rated shock probation as effective. Of these departments, 30% gave unqualified approval; 25% thought that it should be selectively applied if it were to be effective; and 16% thought that it would be more effective if truly shock, that is, if the defendant had no prior knowledge. Twenty-two percent thought it too soon to evaluate the effectiveness of shock probation. Only 5% of responding departments thought shock probation was not very effective.

Concerning the impact of shock probation on prison population, it was estimated that approximately 64% of the shock probationers would likely have been incarcerated if shock probation had not been available.

A question not covered by the 1980 TAPC Shock Probation Survey but one of considerable interest is: "Is shock probation used as an alternative to regular probation or as an alternative to long term incarceration?" Seven departments which account for most of the shock probationers were asked this question by telephone. Based on the results of these telephone calls, our best current estimate is that about 50% of the shock probationers would not have been placed on probation had shock probation not been available to the courts; in other words, these probationers would, in all likelihood, have been incarcerated.

In addition, "shock revokees" (adults who were placed on shock probation by the courts as part of a probation revocation) would most likely have been incarcerated if there had been no shock revocation statute. Combining the "shock revokees" with the probationers mentioned above who would probably have been incarcerated, the percent of probationers who would be incarcerated if there were no shock probation statute increases from 50% to about 64%.

SPECIALIZED PROBATION/PAROLE UNITS

It has long been recognized that offenders with certain salient characteristics could benefit from specialized services. As a result, some p/p agencies have units that provide these services to particular offenders:

Alcoholic offenders
Dangerous offenders
Drug-abusing offenders
Gifted offenders

Mentally ill offenders
Retarded offenders
Young offenders

Some agencies hire specialists in these areas, whereas others send the p/p officer for special training. Quite often, "expertise" is merely developed on the job, and it includes extensive knowledge of community resources (e.g., hospitals with drug or alcohol-treatment facilities).

A characteristic of most special units is small caseloads compared to regular units in the same agency, which increases the cost of maintaining special units. An additional cost is related to the need for making field visits. In most p/p agencies offenders are assigned to a caseload according to their place of residence. Thus, a p/p officer will work in a particular geographic area, "territory," a city subsection or county(s). If specialized caseloads are utilized, several p/p officers will be entering the same territory for home visits—the p/p officer from the general unit and p/p officers from whatever specialized units are in operation. Thus, specialization may be a more efficient method for treatment and/or control, but it is administratively inefficient.

New York State parole, whose programs will be reviewed in this section, has been a leader in the development of specialized units; it has specialized caseloads for all the categories noted above. In addition, New York has a special unit of parole officers who do not supervise *any* offenders—the Bureau of Special Services.

Bureau of Special Services

The Bureau of Special Services (BSS) originated out of a recognition that parole in New York has a community protection responsibility, a responsibility that in certain select cases could not be adequately met in general supervision units. The BSS is located in offices separate from other units in order to avoid offenders becoming too familiar with members of the unit. The unit parole officers generally wear street clothes and have been mistaken for parolees. The officers are all volunteers and receive no special training beyond that required of all parole officers in the agency. The officers have conventional cars (e.g., Mustangs) equipped with two-way radios and utilize sophisticated surveillance equipment.

Cases come to the Bureau of Special Services from several sources:

1. As a result of information from other criminal justice agencies.
2. As a result of referrals from parole officers in regular or specialized units.
3. As automatic referrals from institutional parole staff based on the offender being a member of organized crime or other such salient characteristic.

Cases are screened by a unit supervisor and, if accepted for investigation, are assigned to a BSS parole officer. The work is quite tedious; the written reports are long and detailed. Much of work consists of long hours on surveilllance and "tailing" activity.

If, as a result of an investigation, a parolee is found to be in violation of parole, this information is documented and referred back to the (regular unit) parole officer and his/her supervisor for a warrant decision. In the event of criminal activity, the BSS parole officers will make a summary arrest and refer the case to the District Attorney for prosecution. During the years that the Division of Parole was part of the Department of Correctional Services, the Bureau was responsible for conducting personnel investigations of correction officer candidates; they also performed "internal affairs" (e.g., corruption) investigations of correctional (not parole) staff. The Bureau was responsible for the apprehension of escaped prisoners; their successful arrest without incident of the only inmate ever to escape from Attica (he was carrying a .357-magnum revolver) was a front-page story in many New York newspapers.

Although many BSS parole officers have been there many years, some have left to work for the Federal Bureau of Investigation, and one (John Ball) is a well-known and respected chief of police.

New York State Narcotic Treatment Bureau*

For a number of years the Division of Parole has developed specialized casework services for those parolees whose problems were of such a nature that they required special handling. Specialized caseloads have been established involving youthful offenders, mentally defective delinquents, and drug addicts under supervision by parole officers specially selected and assigned and given the opportunity to develop appropriate techniques and methods of approach.

Parole casework, by definition, involves the use of authority when the occasion demands it. One of the main areas that had to be worked out in the Narcotic Treatment Bureau was the delicate balance between traditional casework techniques and the authoritative approach as applied to addicts. For example, some professional agencies engaged in the field of addiction and treatment frowned upon the practice of arm examination to determine relapses, feeling that such a step would destroy a worker–client relationship. The bureau did not accept that concept, and arms were checked as required.

Traditionally, a parole or probation violator who reverts to the use of narcotics is the subject of delinquency action. However, when a bureau parole officer believed it to be appropriate, with approval, he/she could take the calculated risk of allowing the parolee to remain in the community. The decision had to be based on the delicate balance between community protection and an offender's sincere desire to help

*This section is based on Meyer Diskind and George Klonsky, *Recent Developments in the Treatment of Paroled Offenders Addicted to Narcotic Drugs* (Albany, N.Y.: N.Y.S. Division of Parole 1974), and my experience in the unit.

him/herself. This flexibility was the result of studies that had shown that complete and permanent abstinence was in most instances difficult to achieve immediately despite treatment. A person might relapse several times before being able to display sufficient emotional strength to abstain completely.

The criteria have changed over the years; originally, they included an upper age limit of 25; intravenous heroin use for at least six months; and persons whose main difficulties with the law revolved around drug usage. There is little difference between the casework approach used in the bureau and that utilized in the generalized caseloads. It is a matter of *degree*, not of *kind*. Bureau caseloads are limited to a maximum of 30; thus, parole officers are able to provide more extensive supervision and guidance than are workers with a much larger caseload. An initially released offender is seen by the parole officer weekly for about nine months. Frequent home visits are conducted to speak with relatives as well as with the parolee. A considerable amount of the parole officer's time is devoted to working with members of the family to get them to modify some of their attitudes so to ensure proper integration of the offender within the family unit.

The problem of the authoritative versus the traditional casework approach comes up routinely when the parole officer discovers that a parolee is using drugs. Should delinquency action be taken; should the parolee be permitted to remain in the community; or should the parolee be compelled to undergo hospitalization? Compulsory hospitalization is one of the techniques used by the bureau. Several alternatives are available. The violator can be returned to the institution, retained in the community, or placed in temporary detention or a hospital for detoxification. If the risk involved appears too great because of indications of serious criminal activities, the parolee is returned to prison. If, however, the parolee is gainfully employed and makes a satisfactory adjustment in other areas of living, no formal delinquency action is taken. If necessary, the parolee is placed in temporary detention or a hospital detoxification program.

Detecting drug usage is a difficult procedure. However, parole officers see their clients at least once a week for nine months and thereafter biweekly. They can note any changes in physical appearance, attitude, and employment patterns. The client's family is usually cooperative and often quickly reports any suspected reversion to drugs (addicts steal from whomever they can, often from family members). In most instances a parolee faced with the evidence of drug usage will admit to reverting to narcotics. Parole officers routinely subject their clients to an examination of limbs, usually arms only, in an effort to detect needle marks. Urine analysis is used on suspected cases.

The bureau works closely with several New York City hospitals that have facilities for drug addicts. Once hospitalized, parolees are not permitted to sign out against medical advice. Such action will lead to an arrest warrant being issued for parole violation. In addition, parolees discharged because of their behavior in the hospital are also subjected to parole violation, something they are warned against in advance.

Considerable activity is centered in the areas of vocational guidance and placement. Experience has shown that most drug users have little or no vocational skill or work experience. The first step in rehabilitation is the maintenance of a steady job. Idleness easily leads to readdiction and it is therefore essential that parolees be employed as quickly as possible. Parole officers utilize the resources of the New York State Employment Services, private employment agencies, and employment resources developed by each parole officer. A special liaison was established with the New York State Division of Vocational Rehabilitation, so that clients who can benefit from vocational training are referred to it for examination, training, and placement.

In cases of parolees who have been given one or more prior opportunities to remain in the community after reverting to drug usage, incarceration serves as a reminder that they have parole obligations to live up to, and failure to do so will result in arrest. The value of deterrence remains an important consideration in the treatment process of addicts in New York State Parole.

Gifted Offender Bureau*

Correctional authorities have long recognized that a small but significant percentage of the inmate population displayed creative skills, talent, and superior intelligence or possessed high, but unrealized potentials in these areas. For years these offenders were normally absorbed into regular caseloads when released to parole supervision. These caseloads were numerically too large to allow for individualization and casework efforts in the treatment process. The heavy volume of work, the need to attend to more demanding matters, and the lack of either the resources or the knowledge of the available resources absorbed so much of parole officers' time that these promising areas were permitted to lie fallow and unchallenged. Many potentially gifted offenders completed their parole but were ill equipped to become more socially productive members of society, and concomitantly they were unable to enjoy a fuller and richer existence.

These observations led to the establishment of the Gifted Offender Bureau. The original criteria was a high intelligence quotient or a demonstrated (while in the prison) interest in academic or artistic pursuits. This was expanded to include any parolee who displayed strong motivation and drive to improve or develop a latent ability or skill. The focus on academic pursuits shifted to other fields or areas, including plumbing or printing, for example. Thus, an offender who had demonstrated an interest in an educational or vocational field would be helped with the financial and other arrangements necessary to enter a college or trade school.

The Gifted Bureau parole officers function in essentially the same manner as do parole officers assigned to generalized units; the difference is in *degree*. The parole officers supervise no more than 30 cases. This allows them to explore and experiment with different methods of motivation. Since they are not beset with a host of other time-consuming problems, they are in a better position to help clients in the clients'

---

*This section is excerpted from George Klonsky, "We Must Be Doing Something Right," *American Journal of Corrections* (January/February 1969), pp. 6–10, by permission of the author.

expressed areas of interest while exploring areas of potential that the parolees themselves have never been aware of or considered.

SPECIAL UNITS IN UTAH*

Within the State Parole Office there exist several teams and specialty caseloads that are handled by specially trained and experienced agents. The use of these specialized teams results in better supervision and improved services to the offender. A primary objective of all Adult Probation and Parole supervising agents is to assist clients in obtaining and maintaining suitable employment. Adult Probation and Parole recognizes that an important factor in the success of clients is to have meaningful, productive employment. The agency provides assistance in guiding and directing a client in areas that will help him or her meet this goal.

Treatment Team

This team handles white male offenders who have been classified as amenable to progressive, rehabilitation programs. Agents of this team are specialized in employment, housing, schooling, mental health, and drug and alcohol rehabilitation programs. The goals of this team are: 1) decrease the recidivism rate of persons supervised, 2) increase the number of productive days spent by parolees under supervision, 3) extend the use of community treatment programs as an alternative to further incarceration.

Minority Team

This team specializes in the treatment of minority offenders. The minority team has special skills in coping with the needs of this group which include drug and alcohol abuse detection, program placement, and expanding opportunities for employment and housing. The goals of this team are: 1) to reduce the high recidivism rate among minorities, 2) fully utilize the community resources specifically designed to help minorities, 3) increase the number of productive days in employment or meaningful training programs and/or treatment.

High Risk Team

This team was established to provide intensive supervision to those individuals classified as high risk due to a lack of parole plan, attitude, and extensive criminal background. The goals of this team are: 1) protect the community by reducing the number of felony offenses committed by parolees by intervening in potential problem cases, i.e. halfway house placement, in-patient treatment programs and short periods of incarceration at the institution. Specialties of this

*Source: Utah Parole Officers Manual.

team include drug and alcohol abuse detection and treatment, planning treatment programs for the aggressive offender, and knowledge of the current criminal, cultural situation.

Fugitives

A parole fugitive caseload is maintained for parole cases where warrants of arrest are active. It is the agent's responsibility to actively pursue the detection and arrest of parole absconders.

CONTRACT PAROLE—MUTUAL AGREEMENT PROGRAMS

Several states are using a form of release from prison called a *mutual agreement*—contract parole. Under this system the parole board, institutional authorities, and the participating inmate agree to a three-way contract (Gettinger, 1975: 3–4):

1. Prisoners must assume responsibility for planning (with prison staff) and successfully completing an individually tailored rehabilitative program to obtain parole release at a mutually agreed upon date.
2. Parole board members must establish a firm parole date and honor it if the inmate fulfills the explicit, objective, and mutually agreed upon criteria for release.
3. Institution staff must provide the services and training resources required by prisoners and must fairly assess their performance in the program.

Different states have adapted the basic model to fit their own circumstances: for example, providing a contract parole voucher worth several hundred or even several thousand dollars to be used by the inmate to purchase educational and vocational services, largely from outside the institution, that are needed to fulfill the contract. Some states require restitution for victims to be included in an inmate's contract. Whereas some states negotiate a release date with the inmate, assuming satisfactory completion of the contractual requirements, in other states the parole board sets the date without negotiations.

Supporters of mutual agreement programs (MAP), such as the American Correctional Association, state that it forces correctional officials to review their programs and account for the availability and effectiveness of prison programs. They indicate that it is effective in holding down prison tension and for maintaining prison discipline. MAP is also viewed as a "screening device" that helps to identify "good risks" for parole. The American Correctional Association (ACA), through its Parole-Corrections Project, is a major force behind MAP. Research into MAP programming reveals that it does not have a significant impact on recidivism, nor has it provided demonstrable time savings for prison inmates—they serve just as long under contract parole as they would have under the traditional indeterminate sentence–parole release mechanism (Rosenfeld, 1975: 57).

Contract parole is clearly a "throwback" to nineteenth-century penology, when institutional behavior (and institutional officials) determined release from prison. As noted earlier, this is the system that was used by Brockway at the Elmira Reformatory. It eventually deteriorated into automatic release as a result of prison overcrowding. Critics maintain that many states are unable/unwilling to provide for meaningful services, the cost of which can be prohibitive. States that have been experimenting with the program have been receiving federal funding; without this assistance they may be reluctant to continue the plethora of training, educational, and therapeutic services that must be provided if MAP is to be meaningful. James Jacobs and Eric Steele express concern over providing enriched services to offenders: "We should not be blackmailed. That prisoners can wreak more damage on society if they are not appeased should not move us to treat them better. Their needs should be weighed against and in relation to the needs of other disadvantaged persons" (1975: 353).

Although some parole boards have accepted contract parole as a way of responding to charges of being arbitrary, the MAP concept actually meets the needs of institutional officials, and not parole release. One point is obvious: successful completion of contract terms does not mean that an offender is rehabilitated or that he/she should be released from prison.

SAMPLE CONTRACT

Mutual Agreement Program: Parole—Corrections Project
(Arizona)

Introduction

This agreement made this day between John Doe ASP 99999, the Arizona Department of Corrections, and the Arizona Parole Board defines mutual responsibilities and utilizes an individualized program to prepare John Doe for a successful community adjustment following release on parole. All parties agree as follows:

Part I   Inmate

I, John Doe, understand and agree to successfully complete with a passing grade or an evaluation of satisfactory within my reasonable capabilities the objectives outlined in this document in consideration for a specific date of parole.

I understand that, at any time, I may petition for a renegotiation of this agreement. I will to the best of my ability carry out its objectives and realize that failure to do so will cancel it.

Part II   Department of Corrections

I, <u>Ruie Green</u>, representing the Department of Corrections, agree to provide the necessary programs and services specified in PART IV below to enable John Doe to successfully complete the objectives of this agreement.

Part III   Parole Board

We, <u>Keith E. Edwards</u>, and <u>Walter G. Jacobs</u>, members of the Arizona Board of Pardons and Paroles, agree that the above named inmate will be paroled on or before July 1, 1976, CONTINGENT UPON HIS SUCCESSFUL COMPLETION of the objectives mentioned below as certified to us by the State MAP Project Coordinator but subject to minimal delay to allow administrative processing not to exceed ten working days beyond the specified date.

Inmate's Name: John Doe   *Number:* 99999

Date: November 21, 1975   *Release Date:* July 1, 1976

Part IV   Objectives

1. *Education*

2. *Skill training*   (Mr. Charles Ripley)
Will successfully complete Vocational Upholstery June 1976.

3. *Treatment*
Will participate in Alcoholics Anonymous regularly. (Mr. Ray Kimbrough)
Will meet for a minimum of 10 hours of counseling.   (Mr. N. Monohan)

4. *Discipline*   (Mr. Dale Brandfas)
Will comply with the institution rules and regulations outlined in the Inmate Rule Book and receive no referrals for serious disciplinary infractions.

5. *Work Assignment*

6. *Other*

Post-release program will include assistance in securing employment in trained area.

Part V   Interpretation Provisions

Cancellation, negotiation or renegotiation of this agreement shall take place in accordance with the terms and provisions of the approved Arizona Model. August, 1972, for Mutual Agreement Programming as amended and in effect on the date hereof. All questions, issues or disputes respecting determination of successful completion of any program or service objective shall be decided by the Board of Pardons and Paroles. Prior to his decision the Project Coordinator shall consult with both the inmate and the program staff member who made the evaluation respecting successful completion, and, in the Coordinator's discretion, he may mediate and consult jointly with the inmate and staff member respecting such question or dispute, or with any other person having material factual information regarding such question or dispute. The decision of the Project Coordinator shall be in writing and shall set forth the facts on which it is based and shall state the reasons for the decision. The Project Coordinator's decision shall be final and binding on all parties hereto except the Board of Pardons and Paroles.

IN WITNESS WHEREOF the parties undersigned have hereunto set their hands and seals this 18th day of December 1975.

(Signed)   John Doe
    Inmate

(Signed)   Keith E. Edwards
    Member—Board of Pardons and Paroles

(Signed)   Walter G. Jacobs
    Member—Board of Pardons and Paroles

(Signed)   Ruie R. Green
    Institution Representative

Approved:

(Signed)   Victor M. Reyes
Project Coordinator
Mutual Agreement Programming

WORK RELEASE

Many states have prison work-release programs, and in some instances these programs involve p/p staff. Work release allows individuals serving sentences to work in the community, returning each evening to the institution. They are still subject to institutional controls and there are usually additional regulations relative to their extrainstitutional status. Under this system inmates are able to earn a salary and pay taxes, contribute to their families' income, repay debts, and even pay toward their keep at the institution. In addition, work release increases an inmate's self-image.

Legislation authorizing work-release programs was enacted in Wisconsin in 1913, but it took more than 44 years before it spread to other states; California and North Carolina enacted work-release legislation in 1957. By 1965, twenty-four states had such legislation, and by 1975, all 50 states and the federal government had legislation authorizing some form of community work and educational release (Rosenblum and Whitcomb, 1978: 11).

States vary with respect to the criteria used in selecting inmates for work-release programs; some automatically exclude those serving a life sentence or who have detainers filed against them. In some states the court must authorize work release; in others the parole board has this responsibility. The final responsibility for selecting candidates, however, is usually under the aegis of the correctional authorities who administer the program. Most states do not have specific restrictions governing who may participate in work-release programs, but often use such general expressions as "not a high security risk," or "not likely to commit a crime of violence" (Root, 1972: 39). States vary in the number of inmates involved in work-release programs. In some states work release is combined with furlough programs, thus enabling eligible inmates to leave the institution for specific periods of time to seek employment or educational opportunities. States often set priorities for disbursing money earned by inmates through work release. Root notes that the priority order is usually (p. 41):

1. Room and board
2. Travel and incidental expenses
3. Support of dependents
4. Payments of fines and debts
5. Savings for release

Unfortunately, many correctional institutions are isolated from urban areas, where employment opportunities are usually concentrated. Responding to this deficiency, some states operate a variety of facilities for housing work-release participants in proximity to areas of employment. These facilities include minimum security prisons or work-release centers, halfway houses, or rented quarters in hotels or YMCAs.

Most states have three basic restrictions on the employment situation of participants in work release (Root, 1972: 42):

1. The offender cannot work in a skilled area that already has a surplus labor force.
2. Conditions of employment must be commensurate with nonoffenders.
3. If a union is involved, it must be consulted, and no work releasee can work while a labor dispute is in progress.

Research into the effects of work-release programs has been inconclusive. A few studies have indicated that those participating in work release tend to do better on parole. However, since the work-release group is not randomly selected, and since there were no control groups, the studies are of dubious value. Other studies using control groups report no differences in the violation rates between participants and controls.

Let us look at a work-release program designated "An Exemplary Project" by the Law Enforcement Assistance Administration.

Montgomery County (Maryland) Work Release Program*

In 1968, the State legislature passed a law authorizing the County to establish a Work Release Program through the County's Detention Center. That same year the County passed a law specifically defining the nature of and general regulations to be utilized in implementing the Work Release Program. In January 1969, the "Work Release Dorm" handling up to 16 carefully selected inmates was opened. Only minor offenders participated (i.e., nonsupport cases). The inmates worked in the community during the day and returned to detention for the remainder of the day. Since that time the program has been modified and improved. It was determined that the Detention Center was not a suitable atmosphere to operate the program, and, just as important, it was concluded that offenders had many other problems they needed to deal with besides employment. Thus, in August 1972 a separate facility was established which employed counselors, community release coordinators, etc., so a more conducive atmosphere could be created and the resources of the community could be utilized. In 1973, the program became coeducational and the very limiting restrictions on eligiblity were removed and the number of participants in the program continued to grow, from 16 to 30, then to 40. The courts began utilizing this residential treatment program as an alternative to security incarceration for selected offenders. By 1976, over 800 offenders had participated in the program. The treatment opportunities available to Center residents have increased greatly and include vocational training, social awareness training, individual and group counseling, drug therapy, alcohol therapy, academic education, etc.

The Facility

The County Pre-Release facility is a one-story brick building with a center hallway. Off the center hallway are eleven three-man rooms and one seven-man dorm (for short-term offenders), making a facility capacity of 40. Each room has its own

*This section is taken from Rosenblum and Whitcomb, 1978.

bathroom and each man has his own separate locker with keys. At least one room is set aside for female offenders. The Center has a kitchen and dining facilities. Adjacent to the main Center is the activities building, which contains one group meeting room, a large multipurpose classroom, a combination TV lounge and visiting area, and a staff office. At the front entrance of the main Center is the "front desk" for the Resident Supervisor, who provides supervision of the Center 24 hours a day, 7 days a week. A parking area is located in front of the facility for resident and staff vehicles. Also there are two large grassy areas with lawn furniture for residents visiting with their families and friends. The facility is located one block off a major thoroughfare, providing easy access to public transportation.

The Residents

PRC clients are varied. They include local residents from federal and state corrections institutions (11 percent) as well as inmates of the County Detention Center (89 percent), which houses individuals sentenced to 18 months or less. They are serving sentences for charges ranging from violent crimes and serious drug offenses to shoplifting and nonsupport. Approximately 50 percent are felons and 50 percent misdemeanants. Over 60 percent have been sentenced to six months or more and all are within six months of release or a parole hearing. The Center serves both male (88 percent) and female (12 percent) offenders. Pretrial defendants are also eligible for the program and recent legislation has opened PRC to federal probationers and state and federal parolees.

Applicants to the Pre-Release Center are carefully screened and interviewed by PRC staff and tested for psychological acceptability by a consulting psychologist. Federal Bureau of Investigation, National Crime Information Center, and local court records and other sources are checked to ensure that the PRC applicants are not legally disqualified for various reasons. The PRC screener compiles a prioritized list based on a standardized suitability rating system. As bed space becomes available, names are taken from this list using the rating score as a guide and the actual transfer to the Pre-Release Center is effected after court approval.

The Program

The Pre-Release Program has a dual commitment:

1. To the offender, who requires comprehensive treatment services to prepare for release and the responsibilities of community life.
2. To the community, which demands strict supervision of the residents' activities.

To fulfill its dual commitment, PRC offers a diversified program of services while imposing a maximum level of control. Successful integration of *treatment* and *control* is achieved through careful planning, evaluation, and systematic procedures that are evident in every facet of the program.

Treatment Services

There are four components of the treatment program:

1. *Work and educational release.* All new residents are expected to be employed within three weeks. A full-time Work Release Coordinator arranges job interviews for all unemployed residents, giving vocational and aptitude tests where appropriate.
2. *Counseling.* Every resident is assigned to a Primary Counselor, with whom he/she meets at least weekly.
3. *Community social services.* PRC residents typically participate in mental health services, drug or alcohol counseling, family counseling, pastoral counseling, or group therapy in the community.
4. *Social awareness instruction.* Social awareness classes are held on PRC premises twice a week. Seminar topics are relevant to the kinds of situations that face ex-offenders when they are released—money management, housing, family planning, etc. Seminars are designed to improve the residents' skills in problem solving, decision making, and communication.

Accountability

Control of residents' behavior is maintained in several ways:

1. Through a *contractual agreement* developed jointly by each offender and a staff member prior to arrival at the Pre-Release Center. Residents also sign a Pre-Release Agreement, a statement of program rules as outlined in the County law.
2. Through periodic, unannounced *counts and drug/alcohol testing.*
3. Through frequent *checks with employers and personnel of community service agencies* to verify the resident's continued employment and participation in those agencies' activities.
4. Through a closely supervised *furlough/release plan.*

The Pre-Release Center has adopted a triphased pre-release plan in which each successive phase affords additional privileges. Each resident's performance on the program is scored monthly on an 18-point scale which rates such activities as responsible use of money, interpersonal relations (with authority, peers, and intimates), job performance, and participation in the Center's required programs. "Graduation" from one phase to the next requires satisfactory to high scores on the monthly performance ratings.

PRC residents also have have financial responsibilities. The Center deducts 20 percent of the residents' gross earnings for room and board. An additional 10 percent is set aside for savings. Many PRC residents also make support payments to their families, and others pay restitution as required by their sentences or as part of the contractual agreement.

The consequences of violating the Center's rules and regulations or the terms of an individual's contract range from counseling to revocation from the program and return to security confinement. Written disciplinary guidelines provide a measure of the seriousness of each violation and prescribe appropriate sanctions.

MONTGOMERY COUNTY PRE-RELEASE AGREEMENT

As a voluntary participant in the Pre-Release Program, I agree to follow the program's rules as stated below:

1. I agree to industriously work at my employment, training or educational program. I will go to and from its location by the most direct route in the least amount of time. After each day's approved activities I will immediately return to the Pre-Release Center. If any situation occurs which prevents me from returning at the prescribed time, I will immediately call the Pre-Release Center for instructions. I will not be absent from the approved day's activities without approval of a Center staff member.

2. I will not act as a strike breaker, or participate in any strikes, demonstrations, or similar activities and I will report any similar situations to the Pre-Release Center staff.

3. I agree to buy the necessary materials, clothing and/or equipment essential to my employment.

4. Prior to making any move to change my employment I will inform the staff of the Pre-Release Program and obtain their approval.

5. I agree to deposit with the Work Release Superior my earnings less payroll deductions and I further agree to pay the County 20% of my income for room/board, etc. while working and at the Pre-Release Center. I also agree to pay my valid debts. Prior to borrowing money, incurring debts, opening bank or charge accounts, etc., I will obtain approval from Center staff.

6. I will arrange my own transportation to and from work. I understand that before operating a motor vehicle I must have a valid driver's license, automobile registration, and proper insurance coverage as required by Maryland law.

7. I agree not to leave the Pre-Release Center premises without prior authorization from Center staff.

8. It is, of course, understood that I will obey all laws of the State of Maryland. Should I have any contact with the police I will immediately notify a Center staff member.

9. I agree not to use, possess or introduce into the Pre-Release Center any weapons, alcoholic beverages, narcotics or drugs (unless under doctor's orders).

10. I agree to resolve the problems I confront in non-violent ways and I will not verbally or physically abuse another person.

11. I agree to submit to urinalysis or alcolyser tests when requested by Pre-Release Center staff.

12. I agree to participate in the Center's Social Awareness Program, in the group counseling program and (or) other community programs (i.e. alcohol or drug groups) dependent upon my problems, needs and goals.

13. If I earn home visitation privileges while in this program, I agree to spend my time at prearranged activities with my family or friends as approved by the Center staff, and I will conduct myself properly, obeying all laws as well as the rules of the program during my release into the community.

14. I have read the Pre-Release Center Guidebook and agree to follow the program activities and procedures of the Pre-Release Center.

I am *committed* to making those personal changes necessary for me to remain crime free. Thus, I am ready to become meaningfully *involved* in this program and the treatment opportunities made available to me. I am prepared to honestly accept responsibility for my own behavior and will demonstrate *responsibility* through my actions.

I realize that if I violate my part of this agreement I can be immediately removed from the program and placed in security confinement, and I will be subject to the penalties provided by law.

_____   _____
Resident's Signature   Date

_____   _____
Signature of Staff Member   Date

HALFWAY HOUSES

"The concept of halfway houses was introduced in 1817 by the Massachusetts Prison Commission. This group recommended the establishment of temporary homes for destitute released offenders as a measure to reduce recidivism" (Rosenblum and Whitcomb, 1978: 9).

It is intended to afford a temporary shelter in this building, if they choose to accept it, to such discharged convicts as may have conducted themselves well in prison at a cheap rate, and have a chance to occupy themselves in their trade, until some opportunity offers a placing of themselves where they can gain an honest livelihood in society. A refuge of this kind, to this destitute class, would be found perhaps humane and politic.*

According to Thalheimer (1975: 1):

The very name halfway house suggests its position in the corrections world: halfway-in, a more structured environment than probation and parole; halfway-out, a less structured

*Commonwealth of Massachusetts, Legislative Document, Senate No. 2, 1830.

environment than institutions. As halfway-in houses they represent a last stop before incarceration for probationers and parolees facing or having faced revocation; as halfway-out houses, they provide services to prereleasees and parolees leaving institutions. Halfway houses also provide a residential alternative to jail or outright release for accused offenders awaiting trial or convicted offenders awaiting sentencing.

Victor Goetting notes that "it is accepted that these facilities are based upon sound correctional theory; in order to ultimately place a person in society successfully that person should not be any further removed from that society than is necessary" (1974: 27). When used in conjunction with prison or training school release programs, the halfway house provides (Griggs and McCune, 1972: 12):

1. Assistance with obtaining employment.
2. An increased ability to utilize community resources.
3. Needed support during the difficult initial release period.

There are actually various types of halfway houses operated by public and private agencies and groups. However, they can be divided basically into those that provide bed, board, and some help with employment, and those that provide a full range of services, including treatment. The latter includes a variety of methods, from guided group interaction, to psychotherapy, to behavior modification. A halfway house may be primarily for released inmates, parolees, or for probationers as an alternative to imprisonment. Halfway houses may also be used for probationers or parolees who violate their conditions of supervision but not seriously enough to cause them to be imprisoned.

The *Talbert House* in Cincinnati was founded by Jack Brown, a professor of psychiatry at the University of Cincinnati, to aid parolees. Brown believed that an ex-offender needed the security of a homelike setting where he could get professional assistance with reintegration into the community. In addition to the professional staff employed by Talbert House, many staff members are offender ex-residents of the program. The Talbert House program involves three phases:

1. Residing under a structured environment.
2. Part-time dependence on the house and its staff for assistance.
3. Almost entire independence for the offender, with the house acting only as a crisis center in time of need.

Residents for the three Talbert Houses are selected by the program directors, who visit Ohio prisons. The basic criterion is that a person must be employable and want to change. Inmates are usually released from prison on Thursday and are taken to the police to register and to meet the parole officer. They settle in during the weekend, and on Monday begin looking for work. For those who have extreme difficulty finding employment, Talbert House has training programs available and is usually able to arrange for employment through its many community contacts. The average stay at the facility is 90 days, although some stay considerably longer. Other than parole rules, there are few restrictions on a resident's freedom to come and go; there is a midnight curfew on weekdays and a 2:30 curfew on weekends. Residents are charged for their stay at Talbert House and pay according to their means (Dodge, 1975: 197–203).

Pharos House in Portland, Maine, is also a privately initiated halfway house for offenders; however, residents must come from an area within a 25-mile radius of the facility to be eligible for the program, which usually lasts 90 days. Like Talbert House, there is a curfew and a charge for room and board. The program works closely with the resident's parole officer, who is notified of any flagrant program violations (Alper, 1974: 105–06).

The major difficulty with opening or maintaining a halfway house is community reaction. A Louis Harris poll, for example, found that while 77 percent of the representative U.S. sample favored the halfway house concept, 50 percent would not want one in their neighborhood, and only 22 percent believed that people in *their* neighborhood would favor a halfway house being located there (Bakal, 1974: 67). Some experts stress the importance of getting community support of the project before opening a halfway house; others talk of a "low profile" or even "sneaking" into the neighborhood. Among some of the strategies used in gaining community support is the formation of an advisory board made up of influential community people. Community people may be placed on the board of directors and hired as staff for the facility. Goetting notes that the local citizenry fear that unwanted criminal elements will come into the area, and he suggests two ways of dealing with such fears: first, the facility can be restricted to serve individuals who would ordinarily reside in the community; or if outside persons are to be brought in, a screening panel can be formed to alleviate some of the fear. The committee can be made up of community persons who work for the police, sheriff, courts, or parole agencies (1974: 28).

Robert Coates and Alden Miller recommend a "low profile entry into the community" when the latter is not an easily organized neighborhood. This type of area usually has a mixed racial population than tends to be transient, and is thus not easily organized to oppose halfway house projects. The authors express caution about the feasibility of moving into middle-class areas, where "in most cases in a conflict, officials, because of their desire to be reelected, will probably go with the majority or a very vocal minority of the residents" (in Bakal, 1974: 76–77). The authors also address themselves to the question of community control. They state that when a community recognizes the need for a halfway house for its own residents, they may present certain demands, such as requirements that a certain portion of staff be from the community and that community residents will have priority for entry into the program. Other demands may include representation on the board of directors and other controlling bodies. Coates and Miller state that where there is real community interest, "one probably should not resist real 'community-based corrections' by denying *shared control* over the program" (p. 81).

Massachusetts Halfway Houses, Inc. (MHHI)*

MHHI is a private non-profit corporation which began its operations in 1965 serving 31 parolees in a fifteen-bed facility. The corporation now owns seven buildings that provide residential services to more than 500 men, women, and youths who have become involved in the criminal justice system. MHHI also offers non-residential vocational and employment placement services. Most clients are from the greater Boston area.

The basic residential program lasts from 60 to 90 days and utilizes a *mutual agreement contract* to set specific goals to be achieved within that time frame. These include full-time vocational activity, money management, steps to overcome any specialized problem, e.g., substance abuse, family difficulties, and the development of a network of community resources, e.g., new peer associates, new recreational activities. The corporation also has a twenty-bed facility that provides temporary (4–6 weeks) housing for pre-release inmates, parolees, and court diversion clients. The Probation Residential Program has a twenty-bed coed program that draws its referrals from the courts; it increases the judge's sentencing options by offering an alternative to traditional incarceration. This program also provides probation officers an option for dealing with probation violators. In addition, the program provides emergency shelter for probationers.

In all of its residential programs the basic therapeutic approach is *Reality Therapy*.

The following is a composite resident profile; any similarity to an individual resident is purely coincidental.

Jason Brown arrived at 577 House on August 24th from the Suffolk County House of Correction at Deer Island. He was transferred after serving 8 months on a 2½ year sentence for breaking and entering and receiving stolen goods.

Under the Mutual Agreement Program, Mr. Brown contracted with his counselor to meet the following goals during his residency:

1. To upgrade his job and to get educational training in the field of carpentry.
2. To save at least $15 each week for furniture for his wife and four children and for Christmas expenses.
3. To establish a positive credit rating.
4. To rebuild his relationship with his family.
5. To remain drug-free.

Mr. Brown met these goals by:

1. Applying to the Massachusetts Rehabilitation Commission and receiving their acceptance for training as a carpenter.
2. Saving $200.
3. Taking out a loan of $200 to buy furniture and repaying that loan, thus establishing a good credit rating.

*Source: Various MHHI publications.

4. Spending his furloughs and program-related activity time with his family and engaging in various social activities with them. Mr. Brown and his wife received family counseling at the Division of Legal Medicine.
5. Submitting to urinalysis tests several times a week with all tests showing him to be drug-free.
6. Paying rent of $25 per week.

Program Adjustment

Mr. Brown met all his house responsibilities and was cooperative in resolving house issues. He was chosen by the residents to be on the Resident Executive Committee, helping to screen new staff members, orient new clients, and discuss residents' grievances. Mr. Brown was very involved and consistent in meeting his program responsibilities.

Employment

When he arrived at MHHI, Mr. Brown was employed by the St. Vincent de Paul Society in Boston as a furniture refinisher at $3.10 an hour. This pay rate proved inadequate to support his family. After discussing this issue with his counselor and the program director, he decided to leave this job and look for a better paying position. He began his search for a new job in October, and in 3 weeks secured a new position as a carpenter subcontractor at the Dimock Community Health Center in Roxbury.

Finances

Mr. Brown has several immediate financial needs. He borrowed $200 to buy furniture for his family, completely repaid the loan, and saved another $200 from his earnings. He maintained a very tight budget in order to support his family, pay rent, and buy food and clothes. Each week he and his counselor set financial priorities.

Community and Family Ties

Because re-establishing his relationship with his wife and four children was a major goal for Mr. Brown, he and his wife went to the Division of Legal Medicine for family counseling. The family has a number of problems but is making steady progress in resolving them. Mr. Brown has a history of drug abuse, but during the program all of his tests were drug-free.

Summary

Mr. Brown has developed more responsible ways of dealing with his problems, and has made a sincere effort to meet all of his obligations. He will have to continue working on strengthening his family relationship, his job skills, and his financial responsibilities as he re-enters the community.

ITEMS FOR STUDY

1. The Interstate Compact has obvious advantages but also poses some problems.
2. Community arbitration programs can provide an alternative to the more time-consuming and expensive procedures of criminal justice.
3. Pretrial probation or diversion offers an alternative to criminal justice processing and/or sentencing.
4. Despite some apparent success, diversion programs have been severely criticized.
5. Probation subsidy has been called a form of behavior modification applied to a social institution.
6. Shock probation/parole has been criticized for unnecessarily institutionalizing offenders.
7. Specialized units in p/p are advantageous but expensive.
8. Mutual Agreement Program/contract parole is generally favored by institutional officials, although it criticized by others.
9. Work-release programs have been used to ease offender reintegration into the community. Halfway houses can serve a similar function.
10. A major problem in developing halfway houses, as with the group home discussed in Chapter 4, is community opposition to its location.

chapter 20

Research

Although many of the special programs we have looked at contain research components or have been subjected to post hoc evaluation, their primary thrust was providing service. The programs contained in this chapter, on the other hand, were developed, primarily, with a research purpose: to test out a hypothesis or theoretical concern.

INTENSIVE SUPERVISION

Intensive supervision, usually by severely reducing caseload size, is based on the assumption that it will lead to increased contact between the p/p officer and the client or his/her significant others (e.g., spouse, parents); and that this increased contact will improve service delivery and/or control and thus reduce recidivism. Carlson and Parks point out that although intensive supervision caseloads have proved that they increase contacts, often by 50 percent or more, and the amount of time spent in contacts has also increased significantly: "The difference between spending one-half hour per month with a client and spending an hour per month with a client, is, relatively speaking, an extremely small difference considering the magnitude of the treatment and service provision task which the probation officer is trying to accomplish" (1979: 72). J. Banks and colleagues add: "Would even six or seven hours of probation contact per month have any significant impact in comparison to a total of 400 or 500 waking hours?" (1977: 24).

In an extensive review of intensive supervision projects in probation, Banks and colleagues conclude (p. 13):

> It appears that the weight of scientifically valid evidence is on the side of the hypothesis that caseload reduction alone does not significantly reduce recidivism in adult probationers. However, there is limited evidence to the contrary, and very small caseloads have proven to be effective with juveniles. Moreover, results on both sides of the question are so tainted by methodological problems that broad conclusions are not warranted.

The latter is not the case with a California project, the Special Intensive Parole Unit (SIPU), which Daniel Glaser described as "probably the most extensively controlled experiment in American correctional history" (1969: 311).

SPECIAL INTENSIVE PAROLE UNIT

From 1953 to 1964, in four phases, caseloads were varied to explore the variable of caseload size in the parole supervision process.

Phase One inmates were paroled early and placed under intensive supervision in experimental caseloads of 15 persons each. After three months they were compared to a control group of parolees who had been released at their usual time, and who were supervised in the regular 90-person caseloads. Differences in violation rates were negligible, but there was a savings in confinement costs as a result of the early releases of the experimentals.

Phase Two increased the experimental caseloads to 30 persons each and the duration of the experiment was six months. The difference between the experimental caseload and the control caseload of 90 persons was not significant in relation to violation rates.

Phase Three used experimental caseloads of 35 persons, while the control group had caseloads of 72 persons. In addition, both the experimentals and the controls were classified into various "risk" categories. Two years of study revealed that the reduced caseloads had an impact on the "lower-middle risk" category, which had distinctly fewer violations than the control group parolees in the same risk category. The smaller caseloads appeared to have no effect on "low-risk" parolees, who probably would have succeeded on parole anyway, and there was no significant effect on those parolees in the "high-risk" category (Glaser, 1969: 312).

Phase Four attempted "to explore the affects of parolee and officer types on case outcome. Caseload size was reduced to 30 and 15, and officers were matched on characteristics thought to be favorable to parole outcome. The results of the study indicated that these characteristics did not measurably affect parole outcome" (Frank, 1973: 129).

Martinson, in reviewing the results of Phase Three, found that the success of the experimental group occurred primarily in northern California, where agents were more apt to cite both the experimentals and the controls for violating parole at a higher rate than in southern California. Martinson notes that the success variable in the performance of the "lower-middle risk" experimentals appears to have been the "realistic threat of severe sanctions," not necessarily the smaller caseloads. (1974: 47). Martinson and Wilks state that "there is a slight tendency to tolerate the misbehavior of those deemed good risks" and that "considerable variation may be introduced into the tolerance rate by caseload differences" (1975: 11). P/p officers with lower caseloads have more time to spend on each case and are thus more likely to uncover p/p violations. However, they may also tend to be more tolerant of violations because they are not under the pressures that accompany large caseloads.

The New York State Division of Probation has initiated an *Intensive Supervision Program* (ISP) tied to an extensive research effort designed to measure the effect of intensive supervision on "high risk" offenders.

"High risk" probationers are identified by means of an instrument containing variables found to be predictors of probation failure. An experimental group of probationers, those with scores of 60 or above, are placed under the supervision of ISP probation officers whose caseloads do not exceed twenty-five. The ISP officers are responsible for a level of service and surveillance not available on regular caseloads. A control group of "high risk" probationers under regular supervision will provide the basis for determining the effectiveness of the ISP.*

COMMUNITY TREATMENT PROJECT

This two-part research was designed "to find out if certain kinds of juvenile offenders could be allowed to remain right in their home communities, if given rather intensive supervision and treatment within a small-sized parole caseload" (Palmer, 1974: 3). The first phase took place during 1961–1969; the Community Treatment Project (CTP) used California Youth Authority parole agents to supervise caseloads of 12 youths aged 13 to 19. Excluded from the experiment were youths who had committed such serious crimes as armed robbery, assault with a deadly weapon, or forcible rape. For purposes of research two groups were randomly selected:

1. *Experimentals:* youths placed directly into the intensive CTP program without prior institutionalization.
2. *Controls:* youths sent to an institution for several months prior to being returned home and given routine supervision within standard CYA caseloads.

The *experimentals* were classified into the following categories, based on an evaluation of personality characteristics (Palmer, 1974: 3):

    a. *Passive conformist.* This type of youth usually fears, and responds with strong compliance to, peers and adults who he thinks have the "upper hand" at the

*Source: Series of reports by the ISP Evaluation Staff of the New York State Division of Probation.

DP-70A (4/79)

New York State Division of Probation
RISK REASSESSMENT, CLASSIFICATION AND ASSIGNMENT

Name _____ Case No. _____

NYSID No. _____ Date of Birth _____

I. Risk Reassessment: Select the appropriate responses as they apply to the probationer at the time of the current offense. Enter point value in score column.

SCORE

1. Arrested within five (5) years prior to the current offense. Yes (4) _____ No (0) _____ _____

2. Nineteen or under at time of first conviction/adjudication. Yes (8) _____ No (0) _____ _____

3. Prior convictions/adjudications for robbery. Yes (16) _____ No (0) _____ _____

4. Three or more prior misdemeanor or one or more prior felony convictions/adjudications. Yes (10) _____ No (0) _____ _____

5. Incarcerated while on a prior probation or parole sentence. Yes (20) _____ No (0) _____ _____

6. Members of his family (i.e., spouse, children, parents, siblings) have a criminal record (J.D. or Adult). Yes (10) _____ No (0) _____ _____

Score the following as they best describe the probationer during the current period of ISP supervision (not less than six months).

7. Neither employed nor in school full-time. Yes (4) _____ No (0) _____ _____

8. One or more negative address changes during the period of supervision. Yes (6) _____ No (0) _____ _____

9. Living in a situation judged to be unfavorable. Yes (6) _____ No (0) _____ _____

10. Probationer currently has an attitude that is characterized by rationalization; or negativism and lack of motivation; or dependency or unwillingness to accept responsibility. Yes (14) _____ No (0) _____ _____

Reassessment Score TOTAL _____

Retain in ISP if:

1. Reassessment score is 60 or higher; or
2. A violation of probation or new arrest is pending; or
3. There has been a new conviction with a sentence to probation or a jail term of less than 90 days with a continuation of the prior probation sentence.

II. ISP Progress Index: Score the following as they best describe the probationer during the current period of ISP supervision.

SCORE

1. Employed/School None (3)_____ Part-time (1)_____ Full-time N/A (0) _____ _____

2. Compliance with probation conditions None (4)_____ Partial (2) _____ Total (0) _____ _____

3. Achievement of supervision plan objectives None (3)_____ Partial (1) _____ Total N/A (0) _____ _____

4. Resolution of primary need areas None (2)_____ Partial (1) _____ Total N/A (0) _____ _____

5. Utilization of community resources None (2)_____ Partial (1) _____ Total N/A (0) _____ _____

Progress Index TOTAL _____

Retain in ISP and go to Section III if a score of four is entered in item 2. In all other cases, go to Section III to determine if transfer is indicated.

New York State Division of Probation
RISK REASSESSMENT, CLASSIFICATION AND ASSIGNMENT

III. ISP Risk/Progress Analysis: Use following table to determine if the case is retained in or transferred
from ISP.

ORIGINAL RISK SCORE	REASSESSMENT SCORE	PROGRESS INDEX
60 to 98	60 to 98	Retain in ISP
	58 and below	6 and above — retain 5 and below — transfer
County Cutoff thru 58	60 to 98	Retain in ISP
	58 and below	7 and above — retain 6 and below — transfer
Below Cutoff (over-ride)	Above cutoff	7 and above — retain 6 and below — transfer
	Below cutoff	7 and above — retain 6 and below — transfer

ORIGINAL RISK SCORE _____   REASSESSMENT SCORE _____   PROGRESS INDEX _____

TRANSFER INDICATED: YES ____ NO ____   TRANSFER RECOMMENDED: YES ____ NO ____

REASON FOR RECOMMENDATION: _____

_____

Completed by _____ Date _____

IV. Supervisor's Review for Reclassification and Assignment/Transfer.

Case retained in ISP — Date _____

Reason for retaining case if transfer indicated _____

_____

_____

Case referred to Regular Supervision Caseload — Date _____

Supervisor _____ Date _____

360

moment, or who seem more adequate and assertive than himself. He considers himself to be lacking in social "know-how," and usually expects to be rejected by others in spite of his efforts to please them.

b. *Power oriented.* This group is actually made up of two somewhat different kinds of individuals, who, nevertheless, share several important features with one another. The first likes to think of himself as delinquent and tough. He is often more than willing to "go along" with others, or with a gang, in order to earn a certain degree of status and acceptance, and to later maintain his "reputation." The second type, or "subtype," often attempts to undermine or circumvent the efforts and directions of authority figures. Typically, he does not wish to conform to peers or adults; and not infrequently, he will attempt to assume a leading "power role" for himself.

Passive conformist and power oriented youths are usually thought of as having reached a "middle maturity" level of interpersonal development. The group which is described next is said to have reached a "higher maturity" level.

c. *Neurotic.* Here again, we find two separate personality types which share certain important characteristics with one another. The first type often attempts to deny—to himself and others—his conscious feelings of inadequacy, rejection, or self-condemnation. Not infrequently, he does this by verbally attacking *others* and/or by the use of boisterous distractions plus a variety of "games." The second type often shows various symptoms of emotional disturbance—e.g., chronic or intense depression, or psychosomatic complaints. His tensions and conscious fears usually result from conflicts produced by feelings of failure, inadequacy, or underlying guilt.

Each *experimental* was matched with a parole agent on the basis of the youth's personality or distinguishing behavior pattern in order to make the best use of the agent's particular skills and interests. The intensive supervision included ready access to the agent by the youth and extensive surveillance by the agent, extending into evening and weekend hours. There was a ready availability of such support services as group homes and cultural or recreational activities.

Palmer reports that the results of Phase I indicate that boys who participated in the CTP program did substantially better than those in the control group during the typical two- to four-year duration of their CYA supervision. Those in Category a seemed to perform somewhat better in CTP than in the traditional CYA program. Category b showed no difference, and Category c youths performed somewhat better. Experimental girls in the program performed as well as in the regular CYA program—there was no significant difference between *experimentals* and *controls.* Palmer reports that there did not appear to be any significant financial differences in expenditures for the experimental program or the conventional CYA program (pp. 3–7).

The second phase, 1969–74, was geared to correcting the deficiencies in the project relative to the 25 to 35 percent of the experimentals who were in trouble despite the intensive supervision. Phase II included the use of institutional treatment for the experimentals, who were randomly selected from males 13 to 21. (The higher age group in Phase II meant the inclusion of nonjuvenile court commitments.) The experimentals were placed into one of two treatment possibilities on the basis of an evaluation of each case:

1. Initial assignment to an intensive, CTP staffed and operated residential program—later to be followed by release to the intensive supervision program as operated in Phase I.
2. Direct release to intensive supervision, as in Phase I.

The CTP residential program consisted of a small facility for about 25 youths, who were treated by carefully selected staff. Their program was considered superior to the routine CYA treatment facility. Eligibility for the experiment was expanded to include some categories ineligible in Phase I. These youngsters constituted a separate group for research purposes.

The results of Phase II indicated that for Category a response to the CTP's residential facility has been unfavorable: for Category b the use of the residence did not significantly change the outcome of the case; and Category c youths were helped significantly by first being placed in the CTP residence. Palmer concludes that "CTP's originally stated ideal—that of changing delinquents into lifelong non-delinquents—is not being achieved in the large majority of cases. Nevertheless, the 'differential treatments' and 'differential settings' which have been utilized in this program do seem capable of *reducing* the total volume of delinquent behavior on the part of many, but by no means all, eligible males" (p. 12).

There has been considerable criticism of the CTP research—suggestions that the *experimentals* were no less delinquent than the *controls* but that the administrative treatment received affected case outcomes: they were less likely to have their parole revoked. Martinson states that the *experimentals* were actually committing more offenses than the *controls* but that they were being treated more leniently while the *controls* were being revoked for lesser violations. He concludes that the study indicated "not so much a change in the behavior of the experimental youths as a change in the behavior of the experimental *probation officers,* who knew the 'special status' of their charges and who had evidently decided to revoke probation status at a lower than normal rate" (1974: 44).

Ted Palmer (1975) responds to this criticism by pointing out that Martinson's data did not extend beyond 1967, and that subsequent data through the 1973 follow-up found that the CTP *experimentals* did indeed engage in significantly less *(unlawful)* criminal behavior than did the *controls*.

PROBATION AND PAROLE EFFECTIVENESS

An effective probation or parole system is usually conceived of in terms of recidivism,* which the *Dictionary of Criminal Justice Data Terminology* (SEARCH Group Inc., 1976) defines as "the repetition of criminal behavior; habitual criminal-

---

*For a discussion of methodological issues inherent in recidivism research see Hoffman and Stone-Meierhoefer, 1980: 53–59.

ity." However, the dictionary requires nearly a page of annotations to explain why there is simply no standard statistical definition of recidivism. For example, do we include technical violations of p/p rules? Do we include a case that was dismissed on the basis of a technicality (e.g., improper search and seizure)? Assuming a satisfactory (an agreed-upon) definition, what rate of recidivism justifies the term "effective"? In a comprehensive review of the literature on probation effectiveness, Allen and his colleagues conclude (1979: 33):

> Given the paucity of research and the caution with which recidivism data must be approached, it is nearly impossible, not to mention inappropriate, to attempt to draw any conclusions from these studies about the effectiveness of probation compared to other alternative dispositions.

In the Comptroller General's report, a probationer was considered to be a recidivist if he/she either (1) had probation revoked or (2) was convicted of an offense while still on probation or within a follow-up period. Only convictions that resulted in sentences of at least 60 days were considered (1976: 11). Using this definition, the report found "that about 55 percent of the offenders no longer on probation were unsuccessful in that they were either convicted of new offenses, had their probations revoked, or fled (absconded) from probation supervision." Of the offenders still on probation, 37 percent had been convicted of additional crimes and remained on probation. In all, about 78 percent of the offenders sampled in four representative probation systems completed probation (p. 10). Were these four representative systems "effective"? This is what the Comptroller's report concluded (p. 17):

> the estimated overall 55 percent failure rate for persons no longer on probation raises serious questions as to the probation system's ability to help offenders make a positive adjustment in the community. Furthermore, since about 45 percent of former probationers and 37 percent of current probationers had been convicted of crimes during probation, a lack of control and danger to the public are evident. We question whether society is adequately safeguarded when criminal repeaters continue to return to the community in a probationary status without adequate supervision and control.

Research into parole has suffered from the same shortcomings as that in probation: definitional, methodological, and a general paucity of data. Some recent studies that appear to be methodologically sound had differing conclusions. Mark Jay Lerner (1977) found that parole supervision in New York markedly reduced the postrelease criminal activity of a group of (conditional) releasees compared to a group of dischargees released from the same institution but not under supervision. A similar study by Howard Sachs and Charles Logan (1979) found that in Connecticut parole supervision resulted in a modest reduction in recidivism. Research by Robert Martinson (of "What Works?" fame) with Judith Wilks resulted in a plea to "save parole supervision": "The evidence seems to indicate that the abolition of parole supervision would result in substantial increases in arrest, conviction, and return to prison" (1977: 26–27). However, a rather elaborate experimental research effort in California found different results. Let us look at this most unique research study.

SUMMARY PAROLE

This research, carried out by the California Department of Corrections Research Unit (Star, 1979), involved an *experimental* group and a *control* group randomly assigned from inmates released between April 1, 1976, and December 31, 1976, with five major categories excluded from the sample—those with:

1. A major commitment for murder in the first degree.
2. A prior commitment for a sex offense.
3. A special condition of parole to attend parole outpatient clincs for psychiatric counseling.
4. A special condition of parole to abstain from drinking alcohol.
5. A special condition of parole to participate in testing for narcotic use.

Also excluded were cases released to detainers or to out-of-state supervision. By computer error, 54.6 percent of the releases during this period were accidentally omitted. Of the remaining 2198 cases, 62 percent were determined ineligible by the foregoing criteria. The final research sample (*n*) was 627: 310 *experientals* on "summary supervision" and 317 *controls* on regular supervision.

The parole agents of the *controls* were not informed of their inclusion in the research. The *experimentals* were put on "summary supervision," which is distinguished from the regular supervision of the *controls:*

1. Routine checkup contacts were waived.
2. A minimum of only two contacts were required; one at release to explain the conditions of the summary status, and another one year after release for an early discharge review.
3. Further contacts were initiated by the parole agent *only if* adverse information concerning the parolee's reinvolvement in criminal activity was received by the parole agent. When such information was received, the parole agent investigated the parolee's activities and evaluated the seriousness of the activities for possible revocation consideration.
4. Services were provided *only at* the request of the parolee.

The results of "summary supervision" were that the *experimentals* experienced an average of 7.5 contacts, whereas the *controls* experienced 14.1 contacts for the same six-month evaluation period. The distribution of contacts, however, was skewed for both supervision groups—most cases experiencing fewer contacts and a few experiencing a great many more. To "correct" for this finding, a median number of contacts for the "typical" case was used as a more satisfying statistical descriptor. Using this standard, "summary supervision" represented a 50 percent reduction in contacts compared to the *controls* (under regular supervision).

Differences between the *experiments* and *controls* were measured after six months, using the following indicators:

1. Arrests and conviction records
2. Offense type and severity
3. Dispositions
4. Custody-free time in the community

After six months; major research findings were:

1. Summary supervision "does not appear to be associated with a different arrest or conviction record than that which would exist under regular supervision in the same period of time.
2. "Summary supervision" is not associated with any more serious dispositions than exists for parolees under regular supervision.
3. "Summary supervision" cases experienced slightly fewer (not statistically significant) custody-free months than did the *controls*.

After one year, the research found that cases under "summary supervision" experienced a *lower* arrest and conviction rate than did the *control* cases under supervision, although the differences were not statistically significant (they could have resulted from random sampling).

Deborah Star, who wrote the research report, concludes (1979: 179):

> Most jurisdictions operate supervision policies where routine check-up contacts are required for almost all releases. This study has demonstrated that such narrow-ranged supervision policies may not be necessary and that resources may be safely freed in these jurisdictions by implementing such a model as summary parole for selected parolees.
>
> Finally, this study poses some important questions regarding overall parole effectiveness. This study has demonstrated with its preliminary findings that the routine contacts which have accounted for half of the parole supervision activities had no impact on the subsequent frequency and severity of criminal activity. The next question is to ask to what extent do the remaining control or service activities offered under summary supervision have an impact?

ITEMS FOR STUDY

1. "Intensive" p/p supervision is designed to increase officer–client contact. That such increased contact is beneficial has not been proven.
2. Research into p/p effectiveness is often flawed. There is a lack of generally accepted definitions for "recidivism" and "effectiveness." Research that has been methodologically sound has been contradictory.

chapter 21

Probation/Parole: Success or failure?

We appear to have reached a crossroads in criminal justice where critics agree on the problem, but diverge on the solution. Many agree, for example, that the treatment model has failed to reduce recidivism. However, each critic has his/her own alternative to rehabilitative efforts, and these alternatives often appear contradictory. Some maintain that the only guarantee against crime is incarceration, insofar as while incarcerated the offender is not free to recidivate. Others propose a drastic reduction in the use and length of imprisonment.

The cost of incarceration and the current overcrowding in most prison systems would appear to limit the viability of the increased use of imprisonment, and public opposition or political considerations would probably mitigate against any wholesale reduction in the use of imprisonment. This situation will cause probation and parole to continue to play a vital role in criminal justice.

In Chapter 20 we reviewed some of the research on probation and parole, and if we can draw any conclusion it is that the research to date cannot answer the question: Probation/parole: success or failure? The next logical question is: Will any research, given sufficient resources and time, *ever* be able to answer this question? Let us review some of the issues related to this question.

What is the *goal* of probation/parole?—success or failure can only be measured in terms of anticipated outcome. If a p/p agency is based on a *service model,* success is measured by the delivery, directly or by referral, of services (e.g., education, training, employment, counseling, etc.) and client/consumer satisfaction with the level of service. This type of agency will be affected by variables beyond its control.

For example, the unemployment rates in major American cities in 1979 ranged from 5.5 percent in Los Angeles to 14.8 percent in Detroit (for blacks and Hispanics it was 8.0 and 18.0 percent, respectively).* A p/p *service model* agency in Los Angeles will be more likely to show a greater level of success in providing employment services than will one in Detroit. Similarly, an agency located in a community with greater social services will be more likely to show a greater level of success than will one in a community without available referral resources.

If a p/p agency is based on a *control model,* success is measured according to the agency's ability to control recidivism. However, recidivism may also be related to unemployment—and to the extent that it is, the success of this type of agency will be dependent in part on the state of the economy. Recidivism is also related to other practical issues. First, we obviously cannot account for undetected criminal activity; and second, arrest and prosecution are often a measure of the law enforcement activity in a given community. Thus, different levels of law enforcement will produce different levels of "official" (i.e., statistical) recidivism, regardless of p/p agency effectiveness. Indeed, a more effective *control model* agency may enhance the law enforcement function (e.g., through close cooperation with the police) and thus help *produce* more recidivism—arrests and convictions of agency clientele. David Stanley points out that if we use recidivism as a measure: "An offender can be unemployed, ignorant, promiscuous, and drunk but still a success as far as the criminal justice system is concerned if he commits no crime" (1976: 173). Indeed, a cynic (realist?) might suggest encouraging narcotic addicts to become alcoholics instead.

Two related issues need to be considered. How are technical violations of p/p rules to be treated (statistically) with respect to agency goals? More vigorous (i.e., intensive) supervision, research indicates, *produces* more technical violations, whereas an agency that provides little or no supervision will have few (detected) technical violators, hence fewer revocations of p/p. The level of individual officer and/or agency tolerance for technical violations will also effect the revocation rate. A second issue concerns the "screening" of agency clients by judges and parole boards. A conservative judge/parole board, or perhaps one just fearful of an adverse public reaction, will release fewer offenders to probation or parole. Those who are placed on probation or parole will tend to be the "boy scouts"—low-risk offenders who will probably *produce* impressive (statistical) measurements of success for the agency. The reverse of this situation is also true.

Since neither the *social service* nor the *control model* agency need make any claim about rehabilitation, the question of postsupervision arrests and convictions need not be raised. In agencies that include rehabilitation as a (or perhaps *the*) goal, this issue will need to be considered. How long does the agency retain (statistical) responsibility for the success or failure of a client who has completed supervision: six months, a year, life? The implication is that such an agency will succeed in producing a lasting change in client behavior. An added question is how to weigh recidivism where the

*New York Times, May 25, 1980: E2.

instant offense is a great deal less serious than the original crime (e.g., a murderer is convicted of shoplifting—success or failure?).

Perhaps the most difficult (impossible?) agency to evaluate in terms of our question "success or failure?" is one based on a _combined model._ Most p/p agencies in the United States would fall into this category. In this type of agency there is usually an explicit or implicit claim relating to service, rehabilitation, and control. An agency with such broad purposes—a plethora of complicated goals—cannot _fail,_ nor can it _succeed_—it presents no clear-cut basis for measuring anticipated outcome. The claims are too broad, too many, and they are too dependent on variables beyond the control of the agency (e.g., the economy, level of law enforcement in the community, screening of offenders, availability of resources in the community, etc.) for a research effort to analyze in any relevant manner. As a result, this type of agency has been subjected to criticism on the basis of research which "microscopes" one goal and finds it wanting. The goals are literally "picked apart," leaving the agency vulnerable to those who would discredit probation and parole.

We now come full circle, returning to the very reason why probation and parole exist. As penological history in the United States indicates, probation and parole (devoid of the humanistic dynamic) exist for economic reasons. If p/p were as costly as (in terms of direct budgetary considerations) or even equal in cost to imprisonment, it would be so severely restricted as to no longer be an important issue in criminal justice. Thus, the bottom line in response to the question posed in this chapter is the degree to which p/p saves tax dollars—to this not unimportant extent, p/p is a success.*

ITEMS FOR STUDY

1. P/p success can only be relevant when measured against the goal of the agency/ service.
2. Success in meeting p/p goals will often depend on variables beyond the control of a p/p agency.

---

*Massachusetts, for example, reports that in 1979, cost per probationer was $307.22; in Texas it was less than $365; and in South Carolina it was $200 for both probationers and parolees. At the same time the cost of imprisonment ranged from about $3500 to $6000, although in some states it is considerably higher.

Bibliography

Abadinsky, Howard
  1975 "Should Parole Officers Make Arrests and Carry Firearms?" *Division of Criminal Justice Services Newsletter* (October).
  1976 "The Status Offense Dilemma: Coercion and Treatment." *Crime and Delinquency* 22 (October).
  1978 "Parole History: An Economic Perspective." *Offender Rehabilitation* 2 (Spring).
  1979 *Social Service in Criminal Justice*. Englewood Cliffs, N.J.: Prentice-Hall.

Abrahamsen, David
  1969 *Crime and the Human Mind*. Montclair, N.J.: Patterson Smith.

Adams, Stuart
  1974 "Evaluative Research in Corrections: Status and Prospects." *Federal Probation* 38 (March).

Aichhorn, August
  1963 *Wayward Youth*. New York: The Viking Press.

Alexander, Franz and Hugo Staub
  1956 *The Criminal, the Judge, and the Public*. Glencoe, Ill.: Free Press.

Allen, Harry, Eric Carlson, and Evalyn Parks
  1979 *Critical Issues in Adult Probation*. Washington, D.C.: U.S. Government Printing Office.

Allen, Harry E., Eric W. Carlson, Evalyn C. Parks, and Richard P. Seiter
  1978 *Halfway Houses*. Washington, D.C.: U.S. Government Printing Office.

Alper, Benedict S.
  1974 *Prisons Inside-Out*. Cambridge, Mass.: Ballinger.

American Bar Association
1970   *Standards Relating to Probation*. New York: American Bar Assoc.

American Friends Service Committee
1971   *Struggle For Justice*. New York: Hill & Wang.

American Psychiatric Association Task Force
1974   *Behavior Therapy in Psychiatry*. New York: Jason Aronson.

Arcaya, Jose
1973   "The Multiple Realities Inherent in Probation Counseling." *Federal Probation* 37 (December).

Augustus, John
1972   *John Augustus, First Probation Officer*. Montclair, N.J.: Patterson Smith. Original published by the National Probation Officers Association, 1939.

Bakal, Yitzhak
1974   *Closing Correctional Institutions*. Lexington, Mass.: D. C. Heath.

Balch, Robert W.
1974   "Deferred Prosecution: The Juvenilization of the Criminal Justice System." *Federal Probation* 38 (June).

Bandura, Albert
1974   "Behavior Theory and the Models of Man." *American Psychologist* 29 (December).

Banks, J., A. L. Porter, R. L. Rardin, T. R. Siler, and V. E. Unger
1977   *Phase I Evaluation of Intensive Special Probation Projects*. Washington, D.C.: U.S. Government Printing Office.

Barkdull, Walter L.
1976b   "Probation: Call It Control—And Mean It." *Federal Probation* 40 (December).

Barnes, Harry Elmer and Negley T. Teeters
1946   *New Horizons in Criminology*. Englewood Cliffs, N.J.: Prentice-Hall.

Barrett, Edward L., Jr. and Lloyd D. Musolf
1977   *An Evaluation of the California Probation Subsidy Program*, Vol. 6. Davis, Calif.: Center on Administration of Criminal Justice.

Beccaria, Cesare
1963   *On Crime and Punishments*. Indianapolis, Ind.: Bobbs-Merrill.

Beck, James L.
1975   "The Effect of Representation at Parole Hearings." *Criminology* 13 (May).

Becker, Howard
1963   *Outsiders: Studies in the Sociology of Deviance*. New York: Free Press.

Beha, James, Kenneth Carlson, and Robert H. Rosenblum
1977   *Sentencing to Community Service*. Washington, D.C.: U.S. Government Printing Office.

Beless, Donald W., William S. Pilcher, and Ellen Jo Ryan
1972   "Use of Indigenous Nonprofessionals in Probation and Parole." *Federal Probation* 36 (March).

Berk, Richard A., Kenneth J. Lenihan and Peter H. Rossi
1980   "Crime and Poverty: Some Experimental Evidence From Ex-Offenders." *American Sociological Review* 45 (October).

Berman, John
    1975   "The Volunteer in Parole Program." *Criminology* 13 (May).

Blackmore, John
    1978   "Minnesota's Community Corrections Act Takes Hold." *Corrections Magazine* 4 (March).

Blew, Carol Holliday, Kenneth Carlson, and Paul Chernoff
    1976   *Only Ex-offenders Need Apply: The Ohio Parole Officer Aide Program.* Washington, D.C.: U.S. Government Printing Office.

Blew, Carol Holliday, Daniel McGillis, and Gerald Bryant
    1977   *Project New Pride.* Washington, D.C.: U.S. Government Printing Office.

Blew, Carol Holliday and Robert Rosenblum
    1979   *The Community Arbitration Project: Anne Arundel County, Maryland.* Washington, D.C.: U.S. Government Printing Office.

Blumberg, Abraham S.
    1970   *Criminal Justice.* Chicago: Quadrangle Books.
    1971   "Criminal Justice in America," in *Crime and Justice in American Society.* Edited by Jack D. Douglas. Indianapolis, Ind.: Bobbs-Merrill.

Carlson, Eric and Evalyn Parks
    1979   *Critical Issues in Adult Probation: Issues in Probation Management.* Washington, D.C.: U.S. Government Printing Office.

Carter, Robert M.
    1966   "It is Respectfully Recommended. . ." *Federal Probation* 30 (June).
    1978   *Presentence Report Handbook.* Washington, D.C.: U.S. Government Printing Office.

Casper, Jonathan D.
    1972   *American Criminal Justice: The Defendant's Perspective.* Englewood Cliffs, N.J.: Prentice-Hall.

Chaneles, Sol
    1980   "Editorial: On Social Justice." *Journal of Offender Counseling Services, and Rehabilitation* 4 (Spring).

Chesney, Steven L.
    n.d.   "The Assessment of Restitution in the Minnesota Probation Services," in *Restitution in Criminal Justice.* Edited by Joe Hudson. St. Paul, Minn.: Minnesota Department of Corrections.

Citizen's Inquiry on Parole and Criminal Justice
    1973   *Survey Report on New York State Parole.* New York: Citizen's Inquiry.
    1975   *Prison Without Walls: Report of New York Parole.* New York: Praeger.

Clinard, Marshall, Peter C. Yeager, Jeanne Brissette, David Petrashek and Elizabeth Harries
    1979   *Illegal Corporate Behavior.* Washington, D.C.: U.S. Government Printing Office.

Cloward, Richard A. and Lloyd E. Ohlin
    1960   *Delinquency and Opportunity.* New York: Free Press.

Cochran, Donald and Linda Gann
    1980   *Risk/Need Client Classification Guidelines, Report #2.* Boston: Office of the Commissioner of Probation.

Cohen, Albert K.
  1965   *Delinquent Boys*. New York: Free Press.

Cohen, Harold L. and James Filipczak
  1971   *A New Learning Environment*. San Francisco: Jossey-Bass.

Commission on Accreditation for Corrections
  1977   *Manual of Standards for Adult Probation and Parole Field Services*. Rockville, Md.:
         American Correctional Association.

Comptroller General of the United States
  1976   *State and County Probation: Systems in Crisis*. Washington, D.C.: U.S. General
         Accounting Office.
  1977   *Probation and Parole Activities Need to Be Better Managed*. Washington, D.C.:
         U.S. General Accounting Office.
  1979   *Correctional Institutions Can Do More to Improve the Employability of Offenders*.
         Washington, D.C.: U.S. Government Printing Office.

Conner, Ross F. and Ray Surette
  1977   *The Citizen Dispute Settlement Program*. Washington, D.C.: American Bar Associ-
         ation.

Conrad, John P.
  1975   "Who Needs a Door-Bell Pusher?" Paper presented at the Annual Meeting of the
         American Society of Criminology, Toronto, November 1.

Cressey, Donald R.
  1955   "Changing Criminals: The Application of the Theory of Differential Association."
         American Journal of Sociology 61 (September).

Czajkoski, Eugene H.
  1973   "Exposing the Quasi-judicial Role of the Probation Officer." *Federal Probation* 37
         (September)

Dawson, Robert O.
  1969   *Sentencing*. Boston: Little, Brown.

Dell'Apa, Frank, W. Tom Adams, James D. Jorgensen, and Herbert R. Sigurdson
  1976   "Advocacy, Brokerage, Community: The ABC's of Probation and Parole." *Federal
         Probation* 40 (December).

Department of Correctional Services
  1970   *Corrections in New York State*. Albany, N.Y.: New York State Department of
         Correctional Services.

Dickey, Walter
  1979   "The Lawyer and the Accuracy of the Presentence Report." *Federal Probation* 43
         (June).

Dietrich, Shelle G.
  1979   "The Probation Officer as Therapist: Examination of Three Major Problem Areas."
         Federal Probation 43 (June).

Division of Information Services
  1980   *TAPC Shock Probation Survey*. Austin: Texas Adult Probation Commission.

Division of Probation
  1974   "The Selective Presentence Investigation." *Federal Probation* 38 (December).

Dodge, Calvin R.
  1975   *A Nation Without Prisons*. Lexington, Mass.: D. C. Heath.

Douglas, Jack D., ed.
1971   *Crime and Justice in America*. Indianapolis, Ind.: Bobbs-Merrill.

Durkheim, Emile
1975   *Suicide*. New York: Free Press.

Eskridge, Chris W. and Eric W. Carlson
1979   "The Use of Volunteers in Probation: A National Synthesis." *Journal of Offender Counseling Services and Rehabilitation* 4 (Winter).

Falk, Gerhard
1966   "The Psychoanalytic Theories of Crime Causation." *Criminologica* 4 (May).

Feeney, Floyd and Travis Hirschi
1975   *An Evaluation of the California Probation Subsidy Program*, Vol. 5: *Impact of Commitment Reducation on the Recidivism of Offenders*. Davis, Calif.: Center on Administration of Criminal Justice.

Female Offender Resource Center
1978   *Little Sisters and the Law*. Washington, D.C.: U.S. Government Printing Office.

Fisher, H. Richmond
1974   "Probation and Parole Revocation: The Anomaly of Divergent Procedures." *Federal Probation* 38 (September).

Florida Parole and Probation Commission
1974   *Annual Report*. Tallahassee.

Fogel, David
1975   *We Are the Living Proof: The Justice Model for Corrections*. Cincinnati, Ohio: Anderson.

Foren, Robert and Royston Bailey
1968   *Authority in Social Casework*. Oxford: Pergamon Press.

Fox, Vernon
1976   *Introduction to Criminology*. Englewood Cliffs, N.J.: Prentice-Hall.
1977   *Community-Based Corrections*. Englewood Cliffs, N.J.: Prentice-Hall.

Frank, Benjamin, ed.
1974   *Contemporary Corrections*. Reston, Va.: Reston.

Friedlander, Kate
1947   *The Psychoanalytical Approach to Juvenile Delinquency*. New York: International Universities Press.

Friedlander, Walter A., ed.
1976   *Concepts and Methods of Social Work*, 2nd ed. Englewood Cliffs, N.J.: Prentice-Hall.

Friedman, Lawrence M.
1973   *A History of American Law*. New York: Simon and Schuster.

Gage, Nicholas
1971   *The Mafia Is Not an Equal Opportunity Employer*. New York: McGraw-Hill.

Gaylin, Willard
1974   *Partial Justice: A Study of Bias in Sentencing*. New York: Alfred A. Knopf.

Gettinger, Steve
1975   "Parole Contracts: A New Way Out." *Corrections Magazine* 1 (September).

Gibbons, Don C.
1973   *Society, Crime and Criminal Careers*. Englewood Cliffs, N.J.: Prentice-Hall.

Giddens, Anthony
1976   *New Rules of Sociological Method: A Positive Critique of Interpretive Sociologies*. New York: Basic Books.

Glaser, Daniel
1969   *The Effectiveness of a Prison and Parole System*. Indianapolis, Ind.: Bobbs-Merrill.

Glasser, William
1975   *Reality Therapy*. New York: Harper & Row.
1976   *The Identity Society*. New York: Harper & Row.
1980   "Reality Therapy: An Explanation of the Steps of Reality Therapy," in *What Are You Doing? How People Are Helped Through Reality Therapy*. Edited by Naomi Glasser, New York: Harper & Row.

Glueck, Sheldon, ed.
1933   *Probation and Criminal Justice*. New York: Macmillan.

Goetting, Victor L.
1974   "Some Pragmatic Aspects of Opening a Halfway House." *Federal Probation* 38 (December).

Goffman, Erving
1961   *Asylums: Essays on the Social Situation of Mental Patients and Other Inmates*. Garden City, N.Y.: Doubleday.

Goldberg, Nancy
n.d.   "Pre-trial Diversion: Bilk or Bargain" (reprint). Chicago: World Correctional Center.

Gottfredson, Donald M., Leslie T. Wilkins, Peter B. Hoffman, and Susan M. Singer
1974   *The Utilization of Experience in Parole Decision-Making*. Washington, D.C.: U.S. Government Printing Office.

Gottfredson, Don M., Peter B. Hoffman, Maurice H. Sigler, and Leslie T. Wilkins
1975   "Making Paroling Policy Explicit." *Crime and Delinquency* 21 (January).

Gottfredson, Donald M., Colleen A. Cosgrave, Leslie T. Wilkins, Jame Wallerstein, and Carole Rauh
1978   *Classification for Parole Decision Policy*. Washington, D.C.: U.S. Government Printing Office.

Greenberg, David F.
1975   "Problems in Community Corrections." *Issues in Criminology* 10 (Spring).

Greenberg, David F. and Drew Humphries
1980   "The Cooptation of Fixed Sentencing Reform." *Crime and Delinquency* 26 (April).

Greenhouse, Linda
1979   "States Held Free to Administer Parole Systems As They Choose," *New York Times* (May 30).

Griggs, Bertram S. and Gary R. McCune
1972   "Community-Based Correctional Programs: A Survey and Analysis." *Federal Probation* 36 (June).

Hagan, John, John Hewitt, and Duane F. Alwin
1979   "Ceremonial Justice: Crime and Punishment in a Loosely Coupled System." *Social Forces* 58 (December).

Hagan, John, Ilene H. Nagel, and Celesta Alnonetti
1980   "The Differential Sentencing of White-Collar Offenders in Ten Federal District Courts." *American Sociological Review* 45 (October).

Hall, Jerome
1952   *Theft, Law and Society.* Indianapolis, Ind.: Bobbs-Merrill.

Hamilton, Gordon
1967   *Theory and Practice of Social Casework.* New York: Columbia University Press.

Hand, Richard C. and Richard G. Singer
1974   *Sentencing Computation Laws.* Washington, D.C.: American Bar Association.

Hardman, Dale G.
1960   "Constructive Use of Authority." *Crime and Delinquency* 6 (July).

Hatcher, Hayes A.
1978   *Correctional Casework and Counseling.* Englewood Cliffs, N.J.: Prentice-Hall.

Hayes, Lindsay M. and Robert Johnson
1980   "Confining Wayward Youths: Notes on the Correctional Management of Juvenile Delinquents." Unpublished paper.

Henshel, R. and R. Silverman, eds.
1975   *Perception in Criminology.* New York: Columbia University Press.

Herbers, John
1980   "Lawsuits a Growing Problem for Prison Authorities." *New York Times* (June 1).

Hibbert, Christopher
1968   *The Roots of Evil: A Social History of Crime and Punishment.* Boston: Little, Brown.

Hilts, Philip J.
1974   *Behavior Mod.* New York: Harpers Magazine Press.

Hippchen, Leonard, ed.
1975   *Correctional Classification and Treatment.* Cincinnati, Ohio: Anderson.

Hirschi, Travis and David Rudisill
1977   *An Evaluation of California Probation Subsidy Program,* Vol. 1: *Commitment Reduction and Probation Subsidy: A Summary of Available Data.* Davis, Calif.: Center on Administration of Criminal Justice.

Hoffman, Peter B. and Barbara Stone-Meierhoefer
1980   "Reporting Recidivism Rates: The Criterion and Follow-Up Issues." *Journal of Criminal Justice* 8 (No. 1).

Horowitz, Donald L.
1977   *The Courts and Social Policy.* Washington, D.C. The Brookings Institution.

Hunt, James W., James E. Bowers, and Neal Miller
1974   *Laws, Licenses and the Offender's Right to Work.* Washington, D.C.: American Bar Association.

Hurnard, Naomi D.
1969   *The King's Pardon for Homicide Before A.D. 1307.* Oxford: Oxford University Press.

Ignatieff, Michael
1978   *A Just Measure of Pain: The Penitentiary in the Industrial Revolution.* New York: Pantheon Books.

Imlay, Carl H. and Elsie L. Reid
  1975   "The Probation Officer, Sentencing and the Winds of Change." *Federal Probation* 39 (December).
Irwin, John
  1970   *The Felon.* Englewood Cliffs, N.J.: Prentice-Hall.
  1980   *Prisons in Turmoil.* Boston: Little, Brown.
Jacobs, James B. and Eric H. Steele
  1975   "Prisons: Instruments of Law Enforcement or Social Welfare." *Crime and Delinquency* 21 (October).
Jeffery, C. Ray
  1971   *Crime Prevention through Environmental Design.* Beverly Hills, Calif.: Sage.
Jones, James F.
  1980   *Records Confidentiality for Adult Probation Officers—A Guideline.* Austin: Texas Adult Probation Commission.
Kasius, Cora, ed.
  1950   *Principles and Techniques in Social Casework.* New York: Family Service Association of America.
Kassebaum, Gene, David Ward, and Danile Wilner
  1971   *Prison Treatment and Parole Survival: An Empirical Assessment.* New York: Wiley.
Keve, Paul W.
  1979   "No Farewell to Arms." *Crime and Delinquency* 25 (October).
Killinger, George and Paul F. Cromwell, eds.
  1974   *Corrections in the Community.* St. Paul, Minn.: West.
Kingsnorth, Rodney and Louis Rizzo
  1979   "Decision-Making in the Criminal Courts: Continuities and Discontinuities." *Criminology* 17 (May).
Klockars, Carl B.
  1972   "A Theory of Probation Supervision." *Journal of Criminal Law, Criminology, and Police Science* 63 (December).
Knezevic, Miki Prijic
  1980   "When a Felon Needs a Friend." *Parade Magazine* (May 18).
Knight, Michael
  1978   "Rhode Island Prison Locked in Fight for Control." *New York Times* (April 20).
Kobetz, Richard W. and Betty B. Bosarge
  1973   *Juvenile Justice Administration.* Gaithersburg, Md.: International Association of Chiefs of Police.
Krajick, Kevin
  1978a   "Profile Texas." *Corrections Magazine* 4 (March).
  1978b   "Parole: Discretion Is Out, Guidelines Are In." *Corrections Magazine* 4 (December).
  1979   "The Quality of Mercy." *Corrections Magazine* 5 (June).
  1980b   "At Stateville, the Calm is Tense." *Corrections Magazine* 6 (June).
  1980a   The Menace of the Supergangs," *Corrections Magazine* 6 (June).
Ku, Richard, Richard Moore, and Keith Griffiths
  1975   *The Volunteer Probation Counselor Program, Lincoln, Nebraska.* Washington, D.C.: U.S. Government Printing Office.

Kuehn, Lowell Lyle
    1973   "An Evaluation of the California Subsidy Program." Unpublished Ph.D. dissertation, University of Washington.

Kutcher, Judd D.
    1977   "The Legal Responsibility of Probation Officers in Supervision." *Federal Probation* 41 (March).

Larkins, Norm
    1972   "Presentence Investigation Report Disclosure in Alberta." *Federal Probation* 36 (December).

Law Enforcement Assistance Administration
    1973   *Reintegration of the Offender into the Community.* Washington, D.C.: U.S. Government Printing Office.

Lefcourt, Robert, ed.
    1971   *Law Against the People.* New York: Random House.

Lemert, Edwin M.
    1951   *Social Pathology.* New York: McGraw-Hill.
    1970   *Social Action and Legal Change: Revolution Within the Juvenile Court.* Chicago: Aldine.

Lerman, Paul
    1980   "Trends and Issues in the Deinstitutionalization of Youths in Trouble." *Crime and Delinquency* 26 (July).

Lerner, Mark Jay
    1977   "The Effectiveness of a Definite Sentence Parole Program." *Criminology* 15 (August).

Lewis, Melvin, Warren Bundy, and James L. Hague
    1978   *An Introduction to the Courts and Judicial Process.* Englewood Cliffs, N.J.: Prentice-Hall.

Lewis, W. David
    1965   *From Newgate to Dannemora.* Ithaca, N.Y.: Cornell University Press.

Lipton, Douglas, Robert Martinson, and Judith Wilks
    1975   *The Effectiveness of Correctional Treatment: A Survey of Treatment Evaluation Studies.* New York: Praeger.

Lombroso, Cesare
    1968   *Crime, Its Causes and Remedies.* Montclair, N.J.: Patterson Smith.

London, Perry
    1964   *The Modes and Morals of Psychotherapy.* New York: Holt, Rinehart and Winston.

Lou, Herbert H.
    1972   *Juvenile Courts in the United States.* New York: Arno Press. Reprint of a 1927 book.

Lubasch, Arnold H.
    1978   "Unidentified Source Held Valid in Court." *New York Times* (June 8).

Mangrum, Claude T.
    1972   "The Humanity of Probation Officers." *Federal Probation* 36 (June).

Mann, Dale
    1976   *Intervening with Convicted Serious Juvenile Offenders.* Washington, D.C.: U.S. Government Printing Office.

Martinson, Robert
  1974 "What Works?—Questions and Answers About Prison Reform." *The Public In-terest* 35 (Spring).
Martinson, Robert and Judith Wilks
  1975 "A Static–Descriptive Model of Field Supervision." *Criminology* 13 (May).
  1977 "Save Parole Supervision." *Federal Probation* 41 (September).
Matza, David
  1964 *Delinquency and Drift.* New York: Wiley.
McCleary, Richard
  1975 "How Structural Variables Constrain the Parole Officer's Use of Discretionary Powers." *Social Problems* 23 (December).
McCreary, Phyllis Groom and John M. McCreary
  1975 *Job Training and Placement for Offenders and Ex-offenders.* Washington, D.C.: U.S. Government Printing Office.
McGillis, Daniel and Joan Mullen
  1977 *Neighborhood Justice Centers: An Analysis of Potential Models.* Washington, D.C.: U.S. Government Printing Office.
McKelvey, Blake
  1972 *American Prisons: A Study in American Social History Prior to 1915.* Montclair, N.J.: Patterson Smith.
Megargee, Edwin I. and Martin J. Bohn, Jr.
  1979 *Classifying Criminal Offenders: A New System Based on the MMPI.* Beverly Hills, Calif.: Sage.
Merton, Robert K.
  1938 "Social Structure and Anomie." *American Sociological Review* 3 (October).
  1957 *Social Theory and Social Structure.* New York: Free Press.
Miller, Walter
  1958 "Lower Class Culture as a Generating Milieu of Gang Delinquency." *Journal of Social Issues* 14 (No. 3).
Mills, Robert B.
  1980 *Offender Assessment: A Casebook in Corrections.* Cincinnati, Ohio: Anderson.
Mounsey, S. C.
  1973 "Resistance to the Use of Volunteers in a Probation Setting: Some Practical Issues Discussed." *Canadian Journal of Criminology* 15 (January).
Mullen, Joan
  1975 *The Dilemma of Diversion.* Washington, D.C.: U.S. Government Printing Office.
Murray, Charles A. and Louis A. Cox, Jr.
  1979 *Beyond Probation: Juvenile Corrections and the Chronic Delinquent.* Beverly Hills, Calif.: Sage.
Nath, Sunil B., David E. Clement, and Frank Sistrunk
  1976 "Parole and Probation Caseload Size Variation: The Florida Intensive Supervision Project." *Criminal Justice Review* 1 (Fall).
National Advisory Commission on Criminal Justice Standards and Goals
  1973 *Corrections.* Washington, D.C.: U.S. Government Printing Office.
  1975 *A National Strategy to Reduce Crime.* New York: Avon.

National Council on Crime and Delinquency
1976   *Citizen Participation in a Probation Department.* Royal Oak, Mich.

National District Attorney's Association
1973   *Screening of Criminal Cases.* Chicago: NDAA Publications Department.

National Institute of Justice
1980   *Project CREST: Counseling for Juveniles on Probation.* Washington, D.C.: U.S. Government Printing Office.

Nelson, E. Kim, Howard Ohmart, and Nora Harlow
1978   *Promising Strategies in Probation and Parole.* Washington, D.C.: U.S. Government Printing Office.

Newman, Charles L.
1961   "Concepts of Treatment in Probation and Parole." *Federal Probation* 25 (March).

New York State Special Commission on Attica
1972   *Attica.* New York: Praeger.

Northern, Helen
1969   *Social Work with Groups.* New York: Columbia University Press.

Oelsner, Lesley
1977   "Court Bars Secrecy in Execution Ruling." *New York Times* (March 23).

O'Leary, K. Daniel, Rita W. Poulos, and Vernon T. Devine
1972   "Tangible Reinforcers: Bonuses or Bribes? *Journal of Consulting and Clinical Psychology* 38 (February).

O'Leary, K. Daniel and G. Terrance Wilson
1975   *Behavior Therapy: Application and Outcome.* Englewood Cliffs, N.J.: Prentice-Hall.

O'Leary, Vincent and Joan Nuffield
1973   "A National Survey of Parole Decision-Making." *Crime and Delinquency* 19 (July).

Ostrower, Roland
1962   "Study, Diagnosis, and Treatment: A Conceptual Structure." *Social Work* 7 (October).

Overview Study of Employment of Paraprofessionals
1974   Research Report No. 3. Washington, D.C.: U.S. Government Printing Office.

Palmer, John W.
1974   "Pre-arrest Diversion: Victim Confrontation." *Federal Probation* 38 (September).

Palmer, Ted
1974   "The Youth Authority's Community Treatment Project." *Federal Probation* 38 (March).
1975   "Martinson Revisited." *Journal of Research in Crime and Delinquency* 12 (July).

Parker, William
1975   *Parole.* College Park, Md.: American Correctional Association.

Perlman, Helen Harris
1957   *Social Casework: A Problem-Solving Process.* Chicago: University of Chicago Press.
1971   *Perspectives on Social Casework.* Philadelphia: Temple University Press.

Platt, Anthony M.
  1974   *The Child Savers: The Invention of Delinquency.* Chicago: University of Chicago Press.

Polakow, Robert L. and Ronald M. Docktor
  1974   "A Behavioral Modification Program for Adult Drug Offenders." *Journal of Research in Crime and Delinquency* 11 (January).

Polisky, Randy J.
  1977   "A Model for Increasing the Use of Community Supportive Services in Probation and Parole." *Federal Probation* 41 (December).

Potter, Joan
  1980   "Annual Population Survey: Growth Slows, At Least For Now," *Corrections Magazine* 6 (April).

President's Commission on Law Enforcement and Administration of Justice
  1972   *The Challenge of Crime in a Free Society.* New York: Avon.

Prison Association of New York
  1936   *The Ninety-First Annual Report.* Albany, N.Y.: J. B. Lyon.

Rachin, Richard
  1974   "Reality Therapy: Helping People Help Themselves." *Crime and Delinquency* 20 (January).

Reasons, C. E. and R. L. Kaplan
  1975   "Functions of Prisons." *Crime and Delinquency* 21 (October).

"Recreation and Rap"
  1975   *VIP Examiner* (Fall).

Reed, John P. and Dale Nance
  1972   "Society Perpetuates the Stigma of a Conviction." *Federal Probation* 36 (June).

Rehabilitation Bureau
  1970   *Non-institutional Treatment of Offenders in Japan.* Japan: Ministry of Justice.

Reichart, Irving F.
  1976   "Why Probation Fails." *Judicature* 59 (January).

Reiff, Philip, ed.
  1963   *Freud, Therapy and Techniques.* New York: Crowell-Collier.

Reiman, H. Jeffrey
  1979   *The Rich Get Richer and the Poor Get Prison.* New York: Wiley.

Robitscher, Jonas
  1980   *The Power of Psychiatry.* Boston: Houghton Mifflin.

Root, Lawrence R.
  1972   "Work Release Legislation." *Federal Probation* 36 (March).

Rosenblum, Robert and Debra Whitcomb
  1978   *Montgomery County Work Release/Pre-Release Program.* Washington, D.C.: U.S. Government Printing Office.

Rosenfeld, Ann H.
  1975   *An Evaluative Summary of Research: MAP Program Outcomes in the Initial Demonstration States.* College Park, Md.: American Correctional Association.

Ross, Bernard and Charles Shireman
    1972   *Social Work and Social Justice*. Washington, D.C.: National Association of Social
            Workers.
Ross, Irwin
    1980   "How Lawless are the Big Companies?" *Fortune* (December): 57–64.
Rousseau, Jean Jacques
    1954   *The Social Contract*. Chicago: Henry Regnery.
Ryan, Bill
    1980   "Should Delinquents Be Locked Up?" *Parade* (October): 23.
Rubin, H. Ted
    1980   "The Emerging Prosecutor Dominance of the Juvenile Court Intake Process."
            Crime and Delinquency 26 (July).
Rubin, H. Ted and Jack F. Smith
    1971   *The Future of the Juvenile Court*. College Park, Md.: American Correctional
            Association.
Rubin, Sol
    1974   "The Impact of Court Decisions in the Correctional Process." *Crime and Delin-
            quency* 20 (April).
Rutherford, Andrew and Osman Bengur
    1976   *Community-Based Alternatives to Juvenile Incarceration*. Washington, D.C.: U.S.
            Government Printing Office.
Rutherford, Andrew and Robert McDermott
    1976   *Juvenile Diversion*. Washington, D.C.: U.S. Government Printing Office.
Ryan, Bill
    1980   "Should Delinquents Be Locked Up?" *Parade* (October 12).
Sachs, Howard R. and Charles H. Logan
    1979   *Does Parole Make a Difference?* West Hartford, Conn.: University of Connecticut
            Law School.
Schafer, Stephen
    1969   *Theories in Criminology*. New York: Random House.
Schmideberg, Melitta
    1975   "Some Basic Principles of Offender Therapy: Two." *International Journal of
            Offender Therapy and Comparative Criminology* (No. 1).
Schmidt, Janet
    1977   *Demystifying Parole*. Lexington, Mass.: D. C. Heath.
Schoenfeld, C. G.
    1975   "A Psychoanalytic Theory of Juvenile Delinquency," in *Readings in Correctional
            Casework and Counseling*. Edited by Edward E. Peoples. Santa Monica, Calif.:
            Goodyear.
Schuessler, Karl, ed.
    1973   *Edwin Sutherland: On Analyzing Crime*. Chicago: University of Chicago Press.
Schultz, J. Lawrence
    1973   "The Cycle of Juvenile Court History." *Crime and Delinquency* 19 (October).
Schur, Edwin M.
    1973   *Radical Non-Intervention: Rethinking the Delinquency Problem*. Englewood Cliffs,
            N.J.: Prentice-Hall.

Schwartz, William
  1966   *Some Notes on the Use of Groups in Social Work Practice*. Address delivered to the
         Annual Workshop for Field Instructors and Faculty of the Columbia School of Social
         Work, mimeo.
Scott, Joseph E.
  1975   *Ex-offenders as Parole Officers*. Lexington, Mass.: D. C. Heath.
SEARCH Group, Inc.
  1976   *Dictionary of Criminal Justice Data Terminology*. Washington, D.C.: U.S. Gov-
         ernment Printing Office.
Sechrest, Dale
  1979   "Correctional Standards." Paper presented at the Annual Meeting of the Amer-
         ican Society of Criminology, November, Philadelphia.
Sellin, Thorsten
  1970   "The Origin of the Pennsylvania System of Prison Discipline." *The Prison Journal*
         50 (Spring–Summer).
Serrill, Michael S. and Peter Katel
  1980   "New Mexico: The Anatomy of a Riot." *Corrections Magazine* 6 (April).
Shireman, Charles H.
  1960   "How Can the Correctional School Correct?" *Crime and Delinquency* 6 (July).
Sigler, Maurice M.
  1975   "Abolish Parole?" *Federal Probation* 39 (June).
Silverman, Lloyd H.
  1976   "Psychoanalytic Theory: 'The Reports of My Death Are Greatly Exaggerated.' "
         American Psychologist 31 (September).
Simonsen, Clifford E. and Marshall S. Gordon III
  1979   *Juvenile Justice in America*. Encino, Calif.: Glencoe Press.
Skinner, B. F.
  1972   *Beyond Freedom and Dignity*. New York: Alfred A. Knopf.
Smith, Alexander B. and Louis Berlin
  1974   "Self-Determination in Welfare and Corrections: Is There a Limit?" *Federal Proba-
         tion* 38 (December).
Smith, Charles P. and Paul S. Alexander
  1980   *A National Assessment of Serious Juvenile Crime and the Juvenile Justice System:
         The Need for a Rational Response, Volume I, Summary*. Washington, D.C.: U.S.
         Government Printing Office.
Smith, Charles P., T. Edwin Black, and Fred R. Campbell
  1979   *A National Assessment of Case Disposition and Classification in the Juvenile
         Justice System: Inconsistent Labeling. Volume I, Process Description and Summary*.
         Washington, D.C.: U.S. Government Printing Office.
  1980b *A National Assessment of Case Disposition and Classification in the Juvenile
         Justice System: Inconsistent Labeling. Volume III, Results of a Survey*.
         Washington, D.C.: U.S. Government Printing Office.
Smith, Robert L.
  1971   *A Quiet Revolution*. Washington, D.C.: U.S. Government Printing Office.

Stampfl, Thomas G.
   1970   "Comment" [on token economies], in *Learning Approaches to Therapeutic Behavior Change*. Edited by Donald H. Levis. Chicago: Aldine.

Stanley, David T.
   1976   *Prisoners Among Us; The Problem of Parole*. Washington, D.C.: Brookings Institution.

Star, Deborah
   1979   *Summary Parole: A Six and Twelve Month Follow-Up Evaluation*. Sacramento: California Department of Corrections.

Stephenson, Richard M. and Frank R. Scarpitti
   1967   *The Rehabilitation of Delinquent Boys: A Final Report to the Ford Foundation*. New Brunswick, N.J.: Rutgers.

Stolz, Stephanie B., Louis A. Wienckowski, and Bertram S. Brown
   1975   "Behavior Modification: A Perspective on Critical Issues." *American Psychologist* 30 (November).

Stout, Elliot
   1973   "Should Female Officers Supervise Male Offenders." *Crime and Delinquency* 19 (January).

Sutherland, Edwin and Donald R. Cressey
   1966   *Principles of Criminology*. New York: Lippincott.

Sykes, Gresham M. and David Matza
   1957   "Techniques of Neutralization: A Theory of Delinquency." *American Sociological Review* 22 (December).

Takagi, Paul
   1975   "The Walnut Street Jail: A Penal Reform to Centralize the Powers of the State." *Federal Probation* 39 (December).

Tamaino, Louis
   1975   "The Five Faces of Probation." *Federal Probation* 39 (December).

Task Force on Corrections
   1966   *Task Force Report: Corrections*. Washington, D.C.: U.S. Government Printing Office.

Taylor, Ian, Paul Walton, and Jock Young
   1973   *The New Criminology*. New York: Harper & Row.

Thalheimer, Donald J.
   1975   *Halfway Houses*, Vol. 2. Washington, D.C.: U.S. Government Printing Office.

Thomas, Charles W.
   1976   "Are Status Offenders Really So Different?" *Crime and Delinquency* 22 (October).

Thorne, Gaylord L., Roland G. Tharp, and Ralph J. Wetzel
   1967   "Behavior Modification Techniques: New Tools for Probation Officers." *Federal Probation* 31 (June).

Toborg, Mary A., Lawrence J. Carter, Raymond H. Milkman, and Dennis W. Davis
   1978   *The Transition from Prison to Employment: An Assessment of Community-Based Programs*. Washington, D.C.: U.S. Government Printing Office.

Torgerson, Fernando G.
   1962   "Differentiating and Defining Casework and Psychotherapy." *Social Casework* 43
          (April).
Trecker, Harleigh B.
   1955   "Social Work Principles in Probation." *Federal Probation* 19 (March).
Twentieth Century Fund Task Force on Criminal Sentencing
   1976   *Fair and Certain Punishment.* New York: McGraw-Hill.
U.S. Attorney General
   1939   *Attorney General's Survey of Release Procedures: Pardon.* Washington, D.C.:
          U.S. Government Printing Office.
   1940   *Attorney General's Survey of Prisons.* Washington, D.C.: U.S. Government Print-
          ing Office.
U.S. Bureau of the Census
   1978   *State and Local Probation and Parole Systems.* Washington, D.C.: U.S. Govern-
          ment Printing Office.
Van den Haag, Ernest
   1975   *Punishing Criminals: Concerning a Very Old and Painful Question.* New York:
          Basic Books.
Vocational Counseling with the Offender
   1965   New York State Employment Services Correctional Vocational Rehabilitation Ser-
          vice. Mimeo.
von Hirsch, Andrew
   1976   *Doing Justice: The Choice of Punishments.* New York: Hill & Wang.
von Hirsch, Andrew and Kathleen J. Hanrahan
   1978   *Abolish Parole?* Washington, D.C.: U.S. Government Printing Office.
Walker, Samuel
   1980   *Popular Justice: A History of American Criminal Justice.* New York: Oxford
          University Press.
Watkins, Ann M.
   1975a *Pretrial Diversion I.* Washington, D.C.: U.S. Government Printing Office.
   1975b *Pretrial Diversion II.* Washington, D.C.: U.S. Government Printing Office.
Weeks, H. Ashley
   1958   *Youthful Offenders at Highfields.* Ann Arbor: University of Michigan Press.
Weis, Joseph G., Karleen Sakumoto, John Sederstrom, Carol Zeiss
   1980   *Jurisdiction and the Elusive Status Offender: A Comparison of Involvement in
          Delinquent Behavior and Status Offenses.* Washington, D.C.: U.S. Government
          Printing Office.
Wilbanks, William and Nicolette Parisi
   1979   "Have Legislative Sentencing Revisions Crested?" Paper presented at the Annual
          Meeting of the American Society of Criminology, November, Philadelphia.
Wilensky, Harold L. and Charles N. Lebeaux
   1958   *Industrial Society and Social Welfare.* New York: Russell Sage Foundation.
Wilkins, Leslie T., Jack M. Kress, Don M. Gottfredson, Joseph C. Calpin, and Arthur M.
   Gelman

1978   *Sentencing Guidelines: Structuring Judicial Discretion.* Washington, D.C.: U.S. Government Printing Office.

Willman, Herb C., Jr. and Ron Y.F. Chun

1973   "Homeward Bound." *Federal Probation* 37 (September).

Wilson, Rob

1977   "Release—Should Parole Boards Hold the Key?" *Corrections Magazine* 3 (September).

1978   "Probation/Parole Officers as 'Resource Brokers'." *Corrections Magazine* 4 (June).

Wolpe, Joseph, Andrew Salter, and L. H. Reyna, eds.

1964   *The Conditioning Therapies.* New York: Holt, Rinehart and Winston.

Wright, Erik Ohlin

1973   *The Politics of Punishment.* New York: Harper & Row.

Author Index

Subject Index